MORITZ BUSCH · TRAVELS

*Moritz Busch*

# TRAVELS BETWEEN THE HUDSON & THE MISSISSIPPI

## 1851-1852

TRANSLATED AND EDITED BY
Norman H. Binger

*The University Press of Kentucky*

ISBN: 978-0-8131-5160-1

Library of Congress Catalog Card Number: 74–147857

Copyright © 1971 by The University Press of Kentucky

A statewide cooperative scholarly publishing agency serving Berea College, Centre College of Kentucky, Eastern Kentucky University, Kentucky State College, Morehead State University, Murray State University, University of Kentucky, University of Louisville, and Western Kentucky University.

*Editorial and Sales Offices:* Lexington, Kentucky 40506

TO JANE

CONTENTS

PREFACE    *page ix*

INTRODUCTION    *page xi*

1  FROM GOTHAM TO PORKOPOLIS    *page 3*

2  CINCINNATI IN DIARY ENTRIES    *page 28*

3  A SHAKER TOWN AND A DUNKARD MEETING    *page 55*

4  A WEEK IN THE BLACK SWAMP    *page 92*

5  THE QUEEN OF THE WEST AGAIN    *page 125*

6  A VISIT TO THE BACKWOODSMEN OF EAST KENTUCKY    *page 150*

7  A RIVER TRIP THROUGH THE MISSISSIPPI VALLEY    *page 203*

8  A VISIT TO BELLEVILLE AND A WORD ABOUT THE GERMANS IN AMERICA    *page 238*

9  A WINTER JOURNEY FROM THE MISSISSIPPI TO THE NIAGARA AND BACK TO THE HUDSON    *page 260*

CONCLUSION    *page 272*

EDITOR'S NOTES    *page 283*

PREFACE

◊ ◊ ◊   OF ALL the many European travelers, the distinguished and the not so distinguished, who visited America during the first half of the nineteenth century and later recorded their impressions in print, none wrote more engagingly and more informatively than Moritz Busch. A well-educated German with a broad liberal arts background, a writer by profession, a conservative with liberal leanings who greatly admired the new democracy being shaped in the New World, Busch was admirably qualified by temperament and training to report on conditions as he found them. Inspired by the accounts of the many German emigrants, both voluntary and refugee, who had preceded him, Busch came with an open mind, hoping to discover what made the New World experiment seem so promising. Equipped with a good knowledge of the English language, willing to share the hardships as well as the adventurous experiences of the frontier (although occasionally deploring the excesses committed in the name of democracy), he was above all a first-rate reporter.

It is evident that from the outset Busch planned to publish his observations and impressions, for he began his diary on shipboard while crossing the Atlantic. Throughout his western journey he asked questions and gathered material on the history and customs of the young nation, frequently taking time out to write down a chapter and to sketch further plans for his book. The result is a comprehensive and well-rounded picture of life and manners in the United States in 1851–1852 and a penetrating study of the factors contributing to the evolution of the American national character.

It is surprising that the wealth of information contained in this volume has been so neglected by historians. For example, no study of the Shakers has ever referred to it, although Busch gives one of the best firsthand accounts available of a visit to a Shaker settlement. His description of a steamboat trip from Cincinnati to Saint Louis is not only entertaining but also highly informative, yet no cultural historian seems to have seen it. His account of a foot trip through the Black Swamp of northwestern Ohio when that region was still a primitive wilderness is unique, but apparently no writer of Ohio history has been aware of it. And who but Busch has left us a record of virtually the last stagecoach trip from Cleveland to Buffalo—on New Year's Eve?

No doubt the fact that Busch's account was written in German and was published primarily, if not exclusively, for German readers is the main reason for its neglect in America. Furthermore, the original edition of the two-volume work was small, it was never reprinted, and it probably was not sold in the United States; consequently only a very few copies exist in American libraries. Therefore this translation has been made to make the *Travels* available to Americans. It includes a little over half of Busch's text, chosen so as to present a continuous narrative of his journey from New York to Saint Louis and back between September 1851 and January 1852. The editor's footnotes (as distinct from Busch's own footnotes) have been kept to a minimum; their purpose is to identify allusions to German literature with which the average American reader might not be familiar, to identify more completely some of the German immigrants whom Busch mentions in his text, and to explain a number of rather obscure points of American local history and geography.

It is hoped that the reader, in accompanying Busch on his travels through these pages, will undergo the rare experience of reliving with all its flavor the life of mid-America more than a century ago and that he will appreciate the understanding and vision of the man who foresaw, in 1851, that "if flying is ever invented, it certainly will be done in the United States."

# INTRODUCTION

◊ ◊ ◊ THE WRITER

Julius Hermann Moritz Busch (starting with the publication of his first work, the *Travels*, Busch used only the forename Moritz) was born in Dresden on February 13, 1821, the son of a Saxon noncommissioned officer who had married the daughter of a Dresden schoolmaster. After studying and receiving a doctorate in theology at the University of Leipzig, Busch took part in the unsuccessful May 1849 uprising in Dresden. In the summer of 1851 he traveled to the United States, possibly with plans to emigrate, but for reasons not stated he returned to Germany in February 1852. During the years 1856–1859 he traveled extensively through the Middle East under commission for the Austrian Lloyd Steamship Line and produced a series of travel guides to Egypt, Greece, and Turkey and a handbook for travelers in Palestine. From 1857 to 1864 and again in 1865–1866 Busch was coeditor with Gustav Freytag of the popular German periodical *Die Grenzboten*. During the interim from the autumn of 1864 until February 1865 he served as press officer to the Duke of Augustenburg. Following service as the press attaché of the civil commissioner of Hannover in 1866–1867, Busch was appointed an editor in the Prussian Foreign Office in 1870. In this capacity he accompanied Bismarck during the campaign in France, serving as a member of the chancellor's personal staff until July 1871. In 1873 he was retired at his own request, becoming chief editor of the Hannover *Kurier*, a position he held until 1875. Later he was active as a freelance writer and (until

1890) as a semiofficial political writer in Leipzig and Berlin. He died in Leipzig on November 16, 1899.

The *Travels—Wanderungen zwischen Hudson und Mississippi, 1851 und 1852*—were published in two volumes by J. G. Cotta in 1854. Beginning with their publication, scarcely a year passed without the appearance of a new book or two by Busch. No bibliography of his publications has been compiled, but a glance into the annual trade lists of the nineteenth-century publishers Heinsius and Kayser indicates that it would be a lengthy one. His travel guides were quite popular, being translated into a number of languages. But his greatest popularity, especially beyond the borders of the German-language area, depended upon his association with Bismarck, especially as reported in the two books *Graf Bismarck und seine Leute* and *Tagebuchblätter*. The latter, first published in English by Macmillan of London as *Bismarck: Some Secret Pages of History*, occasioned a rather bitter controversy; the subsequently published German version, heavily censored at the insistence of Bismarck, varies considerably from the English version.

As far as can be determined, Busch made very little use of his theological training; there is mention in this text of a single engagement as guest preacher in Dayton, Ohio. Apparently he discovered early that he had a talent for writing and made it his principal career.

◊ ◊ ◊ THE HISTORICAL BACKGROUND

In all the larger towns and cities of the United States that Busch visited, he ran into old friends and acquaintances—the majority of them refugees of the German Revolution of 1848. The extent of his participation in the uprising is not recorded, but as a young man with liberal leanings he must have been at least sympathetic toward the movement.

The German Revolution was, of course, but a part of the revolutionary movement that spread throughout western Europe. After earlier outbreaks in France and Italy revolution came to Germany in March and April of 1848 and succeeded in overthrowing every single German state government and installing liberal ministries. The revolutionaries, among them many professors and students, were united in their demands for national and liberal reform. Foremost among these aims were political equality and liberty for all citizens and the union of the many German states into a national empire.

## INTRODUCTION

It should be noted that although Busch often speaks of "Germany" and refers to himself and his fellow countrymen as "Germans," Germany and Germans did not yet exist, politically speaking. Instead there were still a number of independent states in which German was spoken; unification was not to come until 1871. There was, to be sure, a national parliament of sorts, the *Bundestag*, but it represented the interests of the various independent sovereigns and not the German people. It is significant that Busch, a subject of the king of Saxony, never once identifies himself as a "Saxon."

In May 1848 a National Assembly elected by popular vote met in Frankfurt am Main; to it belonged many of the more progressive intellectuals and professionals whom Busch later encountered in America. The Assembly, however, lacking political experience and political discipline, soon lost itself in an endless debate about abstract matters and never was able to achieve any actual power. Moreover, it soon lost the interest and support of most Germans. Particularly the German middle class became apprehensive of the democratic radicalism of the working classes; the issuance of the *Communist Manifesto* by Marx and Engels did not help matters.

While the Assembly debated, the forces of counterrevolution gained strength. After Friedrich Wilhelm IV, the Prussian king, rejected the imperial crown that had been offered to him (along with a new constitution), the Assembly gradually disintegrated. Subsequent democratic uprisings in Saxony, Busch's home state, and Baden were easily put down by the Prussian troops called in for assistance. By the fall of 1849 all was peaceful once again, and this first attempt at German unification had proved a total failure.

For many of the revolutionaries, however, the consequences were grave. Having taken part in armed rebellion in a number of states, many were captured and imprisoned or executed. Some were able to flee before capture or to escape. Others were sentenced, but their sentences were suspended on condition that they leave the country. Some went into exile in Switzerland, others in France. The more radical gathered in London, where they continued to promote revolution. Many of those who were opposed to violent revolution but who sincerely believed in democracy emigrated to the United States—the hope of the future, as they saw it.

For a few of them the trip to America was a return trip, for they had visited there or had lived there previously, hastily returning to Germany when the drums of revolution were sounded. For most, however, it was a new and often painful experience, one compelled by necessity. Not that they were totally unfamiliar with conditions in the New World, for during the 1830s and 1840s a tremendous number of books and articles concerning America had been published in Germany. Not only were there guidebooks for would-be emigrants, but there also had appeared numerous exhaustive analyses of American political, social, and economic conditions; these were read with great interest, especially by the educated middle class. Of special importance was Alexis de Tocqueville's *De la démocratie en Amérique,* of which several translations into German had gained wide circulation. Indeed, much of the debate in Frankfurt centered on the problem of the extent to which the United States Constitution should be copied or adapted to German needs.

Yet most of the refugees were "green," newcomers in a new environment, and they found the struggle to adapt themselves to American conditions a most difficult one. When Busch visited the United States in 1851–1852, most had been in this country no more than a year or two. In a word, many of them were homesick, or, as Busch puts it, these exiles still "longed for the fleshpots of Egypt." Add to this the fact that many of them still hoped for success in the political struggle in the homeland, and one understands why Busch encountered such a strange mixture of resignation and hope among the Forty-eighters.

◊ ◊ ◊ THE SOURCES

Although most of this account is based upon Busch's personal experiences in America, with additional material supplied by what he terms "reliable informants," certain sections of the text obviously were copied, through translation, from previously published American books. This, of course, would now be considered plagiarism, but it was a well-known and accepted practice of European travelers to America in the early nineteenth century. And to some extent it was justifiable, for the traveler could not see everything in the time at his disposal and had to rely upon other sources if he wanted to give a complete picture. Busch was no exception to this general rule. But when one considers the extent to which many other European writers of travel accounts relied upon outside information and upon their imagination, the degree to which Busch depended upon his own observations is astonishing. Even today one can follow his travel route from the accuracy of his topographical descriptions.

It appears that Busch principally relied upon—or "plagiarized"—

INTRODUCTION

three sources for some of the material included in this selection: two books by Henry Howe, the prolific writer of histories and guidebooks, and, for background material on Cincinnati, a volume by Edward Cist, *Cincinnati in 1851*. The two Howe works, *Historical Collections of Ohio* and *Historical Collections of the Great West*, are called to the attention of the careful reader by Busch himself. In one footnote he recommends the *Ohio* volume as "a very good handbook for information." On another occasion, in his report of the trip through the Black Swamp of Ohio, he tells us that he spent one evening in a farmhouse near Findlay reading the *Ohio* book. And in still another passage, during the account of his excursion to the eastern Kentucky backwoods, he reports a salesman selling copies of the *Great West* in a barroom, a good indication of the popularity of the work.

Busch's excerpts from these works are, for the most part, cleverly inserted in his text. Since most are concerned with events and persons of the past, he cannot very well claim to have been an eye witness, so he always manages to run into an old native who does have personal knowledge. Thus the story of old Smiley and the Presbyterian preacher related in Chapter 6 is heard from the mouth of Major Sudduth, whose son-in-law is a grandson of Smiley; and the story of Simon Girty is told to Busch by a hunter whom he meets along the Maumee and whose uncle had known Girty personally. The result is a continuous narrative with a strong ring of authenticity.

To be sure, Busch frequently rephrases a borrowed expression —possibly to make its meaning clearer to his German readers, possibly to adjust it to his personal style, possibly to cover up the source of his borrowing. Thus when Howe writes about a settlement consisting of "three rows of six cabins each," Busch describes it as a "rectangle of about eighteen cabins."

The reader, however, is never aware of this borrowing. When one considers that Busch was writing primarily for German readers, none of whom would ever see his sources, the "plagiarism" is pardonable, for otherwise a great deal of valuable material concerning America would have been unavailable to them.

◊ ◊ ◊ THE STYLE

Busch was (in the words of the *Neue Deutsche Biographie*) neither a historian nor a biographer, but he had the ability to portray people and things with the accuracy of a photographic plate. He possessed that most important quality of a good journalist, acribie—that preciseness which lent to his reporting the highest degree of credibility. He often included the slightest, seemingly insignificant details, adding to the reliability of his account. In addition he was thoroughly honest in reporting his own deficiencies and mistakes: note his report of the difficulties resulting from his unfamiliarity with horseback riding (Chapter 6). To use his own phrase, the "brutal realism" of his portraits permitted no shading or retouching of the picture. Yet it is obvious that he was not unaware of the artistic principle of selection. Much could have been included that has been omitted. In consequence the narrative progresses smoothly from scene to scene, from event to event, and a vast panorama of life in these United States is unrolled before the eyes of the reader.

It is likewise obvious to anyone at all familiar with the history of German literature that Busch must have been influenced greatly by the *Reisebilder* ("travel pictures") of the early nineteenth-century German poet Heinrich Heine. These *Bilder,* published in three volumes from 1826 to 1829, produced a remarkable impression in Germany. They were widely read, particularly by those Germans with liberal sympathies who approved Heine's attacks on political and religious institutions (which led to the Prussian *Bundestag*'s ban in 1835 on the publication of any further works by Heine). Readers were strangely fascinated by the mingling of prose and poetry, humor and pathos, and often caustic reflections on the existing order of things. The style is reminiscent of that of Laurence Sterne and that of the German Romantic poet Jean Paul, but it is still uniquely Heine's own. The sentences are smooth and clearflowing, concise and graceful, yet the reader is impressed by the abundance of illustration and the flights of fancy.

All these qualities can be found in the writings of Busch. To be sure, the *Herr Doktor* often becomes lost in those long, neatly balanced periodic sentences—the bane of the translator—that were so characteristic of German scholarly style in the nineteenth century, but such are employed chiefly in his philosophical reflections upon the nature of American life. When Busch describes an event in which he actually participated or a scene which he actually viewed, his style approaches the lightness and lucidity of Heine at his best.

INTRODUCTION

◊ ◊ ◊ THE LANGUAGE

In general Busch uses standard High German, although occasionally lapsing into his native Saxon dialect, for example *Dinte* instead of the more usual *Tinte, löken* instead of the standard *lecken*. But these lapses are infrequent; in fact, they cannot properly be termed lapses, for German orthography had not yet been standardized.

Far more interesting is Busch's reproduction of the American language as he heard it used in 1851—a feature which led to Mitford Mathews's use of Busch's work as one of the sources for his *Dictionary of Americanisms*. It is evident that Busch must have been fluent in English before he set out on his journey, for nowhere in the text does he report any difficulty in carrying on conversations with native Americans. His use of published source material indicates that he also had a good reading knowledge of English. To be sure, at times he betrays a lack of familiarity with American idioms. For example, when one of his sources, Howe's *Great West*, reports the Indian fighter Wetzel as slaying a "bullock," Busch changes it to a "deer or turkey," probably having no dictionary at hand to tell him what a bullock was. Or when Howe has Mike Fink, the legendary riverboatman, say of himself, "I'm a Salt River roarer! I'm chuck full of fight!" Busch changes it to "a real howling devil from the Salt River, full up to the neck with pugnacity!" On the whole, however, he exhibits a much greater acquaintance with English than did most non-British European travelers of the period, even serving on occasion (according to his account) as interpreter for some of his less linguistically skilled countrymen.

His contributions to the history of the American language fall into two classes. Throughout the *Wanderungen* various American words and phrases are printed in Roman type, while the body of the text appears in German *Fraktur*. By this means the German reader's attention was directed to peculiarities of American English, the prospective emigrant was provided with stock phrases from which to draw to facilitate his transition to life in America, and the credibility of Busch's report was enhanced. A few of these words and phrases are defined by Busch in German, but most are not. The near-phonetic reproduction of many of them indicates that Busch frequently relied upon his ear rather than upon the printed page. These Americanisms, along with a number of words from other foreign languages, are italicized in this translation.

Even more frequent is Busch's use of English words in Germanized form, printed in *Fraktur* and adapted to German spelling and inflection: *die Codfish-Aristokratie, der Newsboy, des Barkeepers, das Lumber.* In addition Busch produces a number of loan-translations, such as *hartschalige* ("hard-shelled") *Baptisten.* To be sure, the German language has borrowed many words from English, and the borrowings were especially numerous during the first half of the nineteenth century, so it is fair to assume that the average educated German reader could be expected to understand most of these expressions. But the extent to which Busch employs such vocabulary is striking, and one wonders if perhaps he didn't go a bit too far in his attempt to achieve "brutal realism."

◊ ◊ ◊ THE TEXT

Busch's original text, published in two volumes, runs to a total of 771 pages and is divided into eighteen chapters and a conclusion. Of these, nine chapters and the conclusion have been included in the translation, and the chapters have been renumbered accordingly. The few omissions that have been made in the included chapters (indicated in the editor's notes) relate either to sections concerning historical and economic background, material not original with Busch, or to excessive and repetitious illustrative material. Hence the essentially narrative character of the account has been preserved.

Summaries of the content of the nine omitted chapters follow. The chapter numbers and titles are those of the original.

1. "A Journey across the Spanish Sea."

    The eight-week voyage across the Atlantic; conditions on an emigrant ship; the passengers and crew.

6. "Thirteen Songs and a Portrait of America's Negroes."

    A people best characterized by its poetry and religion; translations into German of thirteen Negro spirituals; visit to the African Methodist Church in Cincinnati.

10. "The Saints of the Latter-Day."

    An account critical of the dogma but sympathetic toward the experiences of the Mormons; historical sketch of Mormonism; *The Book of Mormon* summarized; eye-witness description ("from a friend's diary") of Salt Lake City in 1851; discussion of Mormon theology.

INTRODUCTION

13. "A Bird's-Eye View of New York."

    Word-picture of the city and its surroundings; statistics.

14. "Tales of Broadway."

    Broadway the focal point; Wall Street; a book auction; the American Art Union; Barnum's Museum; the Metropolitan Hotel; the New York aristocracy "above Bleeker"; visit to the home of a wealthy family.

15. "The Feet of the Peacock."

    The shadier side of life in New York; secondhand clothing and furniture stores, pawnshops; gambling dens; loafers, rowdies, and firemen; the "Tombs"; the Five Points, center of crime; restaurants of all types.

16. "A word about the Newspapers and a Look at the New York Stage."

    Venality of most journalists; visit to William Cullen Bryant; portrait of a typical newsboy; visits to various theaters; low social level of the stage.

17. "Adventures with Unclean Spirits."

    A "spiritualist" meeting; miserable existence of poor emigrants in New York; later experiences of acquaintances made on shipboard.

18. "The Sons of St. Tammany."

    A short history of the United States, with emphasis upon the evolution of the political parties; the significant role played by Tammany Hall.

◊ ◊ ◊ THE JOURNEY TO AMERICA

Departing from Bremerhaven, Germany, on July 7, 1851, on the bark *Baltimore,* Busch arrived in New York on August 31. The voyage across the Atlantic was an exceedingly monotonous one, with the ship becalmed for days at a time. Busch, who had never before been at sea, suffered from the constant alternation of expectation and disappointment and was quite annoyed that the travelers were entirely dependent upon the whims of the unpredictable wind. But once the lights of New York were sighted, all the hardships were forgotten; the annoyance, ill humor, disgust, and depression of the trip were left behind; and Busch looked forward with enthusiasm to his experiences in the New World.

MORITZ BUSCH · TRAVELS

# 1

## FROM GOTHAM TO PORKOPOLIS

◊ ◊ ◊ IT WAS my plan to remain in New York until the end of September, then go to Boston, the Yankee Athens, for a few days, and to travel from there to the western states by way of Niagara. A letter from Ohio canceled these plans and compelled me to take leave of Gotham's throng after I had scarcely recovered from the boundless joy of finally having solid land under my feet. I just had time to cast a glance down upon Broadway and the Bowery from the crow's-nest perspective of the Trinity Church steeple, to make a fleeting visit to the Battery and the charming Hoboken, and to learn in the latter place with depressing certainty that Mr. Stevens's wonder-ships[1] (described with such enthusiasm by Julius Fröbel[2]—you recall that they sailed so swiftly that their planks had to be filled artificially with air to decrease the friction of the water) had already left.

"Left? Hm, yes, probably left. For the Land of Humbug," dryly remarked the small, black-bearded man from the Hotel Constanz to whom I complained of my disappointment.

"What do you mean, 'Humbug'?" another skeptic joined in with irony. "They have gone to Nicaragua to deliver the necessary hundred thousand hundredweight of fever powder to those who have built themselves cabins there in the shade of the imagination of that same truthful reporter."

That sounded too malicious to allow much confidence in the objectivity of the mocker. Unfortunately, I later had to hear confirmation of those bitter remarks from other voices, and, to be sure, from such as had absolutely no connection with Fröbel.

To name only a few of the accusers: thus spoke Dr. Hiller in Saint Louis, who at the end of the previous year had returned from California by way of Nicaragua—he compared that country to a magnificent poisonous flower against which no one had to be more on guard than the just immigrated German; and another Californian with whom I made the return trip from New York to Hamburg carried traces of the climate of Fröbel's Paradise so clearly on his fever-worn features that it hardly was necessary for him to tell us that in Granada he had been closer to death than to life for months.

But that by the way. Everyone might draw his own conclusion from this. *Relata refero,* and if the accused would send us a convincing apology (perhaps by one of those miraculous fast-sailing ships), it would contribute to my pleasure and not to the disadvantage of the immigration office that has since been opened in New York under the name "Zitz, Kapp, and Fröbel."[3]

Whatever else of interest I experienced in the four days I spent in New York can be better interspersed in the observations I found occasion to make during my longer stay there at the conclusion of my journey. It might only be mentioned that the deception lying in wait for the newcomer upon American soil in all forms and under the most enticing names, be it as a sympathetic countryman, as an unselfish friend of humanity, as an agreeable barkeeper, or (when this is advantageous) as a political refugee, raised a rich tribute among the immigrants landed by the *Baltimore*. Often it was just the most timid fish who bit first and swallowed most deeply the bait held before them, and despite all remonstrances they blindly followed the gallows physiognomies that snuggled up to them as guides and advisers when the ship had scarcely anchored.

And why not? They were "folks from home" who could describe most accurately to the stupid peasant the situation of his village in Rhine-Hessen and in a few cases were even able to enumerate on their fingers the entire kith and kin. They warned the credulous listener—in whom, if it were feasible, they discovered a distant relative—most strongly against this or that dive and against this or that "big fellow who merely wanted to humbug him out of a couple of kreutzer from his purse." They spoke as if they had actually learned by heart the warning of the German Society[4] that had been distributed among us. How could such "goodhearted people" have evil intentions? It would mean throwing away one's opportunities if one did not believe them. "Plenty of work, a chance to travel to the West dirt cheap, accomodations at half price and not a hundred steps from the landing" had come on board with them. Would it not have been discourteous to decline the invitation of the extremely friendly uncle (encountered so unexpectedly) who wouldn't be denied the opportunity to honor the "cousin from dear old Germany" with a bottle of "genuine Rhine wine"?

"Well, isn't it so, dear cousin, old fellow? — Top, agreed, eh? — To the *Freischütz* then?" — Settled and done. For to resist such cordial eloquence was the most impossible of impossibilities, and the half-bewildered, half-deluded ones, led by the inwardly chuckling rascals, flocked to those robbers' nests in Greenwich Street. There they'd discover in the next few days that the overly agreeable relative could not even get them a job as streetsweeper, let alone the promised splendid position; that their inexpensive railroad ticket had turned into one for the canal boat costing three times as much; that they'd fallen right into the trap that one had feigned to lead them around; and that finally the "uncle," after having emptied their pockets in this manner, turned out to be not much more closely related to them than by way of Adam, and had proven this by no longer being concerned one iota about them.

I could give dozens of examples, based upon personal observation, for these allusions; I could bring out from the parlors of such thieves' dens weeping men and hand-wringing women who had lost their last cent; I could ask the Hudson with pathos how many of these despairing souls had plunged into its yellow waters during the year. However, scenes of this sort have been described often enough without changing the matter. Whatever might be done in a private way to remedy this situation has been done by the German Society, but it has been little more than a drop upon a hot rock. An effective protection would be possible—would be possible with some good intention on the part of the authorities of the city of New York. The construction of a large emigrant house such as that in Bremerhaven, the appointment of a dozen sworn agents for the mentioned purposes, the establishment of a newspaper that would watch over the latter and would be open to complaints about possible derelictions of duty—these would suffice as a beginning, according to an apparently knowledgeable friend. But how far it is from such wishes to their fulfillment, and how true in this respect is the saying of the wise man: Blessed are those who expect nothing, for they will not be disappointed!

◊ ◊ ◊ The evening of the fifth of September found me on one of the giant steamboats that wait at the docks below Courtland Street for travelers planning to use the Erie Railroad for the journey to the West. About six o'clock the lungs of our Leviathan began to groan from its two chimneys and, after two tugs had been attached, it floated out from the forest of masts of Manhattan Island into the open river, setting the waters of the majestic Hudson into motion for a great distance.

I was permitted only to suspect the scenic beauties of this region. They are supposed to equal those of the Rhine in its best sections, just as the charm of the Bay of New York is considered by experts to be no less than that of the Bay of Naples. Whether or not this is the case, the fog which rose from the river allowed us to see only the shadows of wooded hills and mountains, and soon the darkness of night swallowed up even these outlines.

After nine o'clock we landed at the small town of PIERPONT on the west shore of the Hudson. Here we left the steamer to board the railway cars waiting for us for the departure to Dunkirk on Lake Erie. I had decided upon the emigrant train because it made more frequent and longer stops and thus gave more opportunity to observe the country. If the inconveniences connected therewith at times gave me occasion to regret this decision, it was all balanced out by the fact that in this way I now and then could be helpful to a poor countryman as an interpreter. Moreover, I saw myself in a position to continue for a bit my emigration studies started on the ship and through comparisons between Germans and Irish to improve somewhat my rather weakened national pride.

When the day dawned, a fresh, resinous forest fragrance breathed upon us. Mountains with pine trees enclosed a valley that narrowed down at times to a craggy gorge and at times widened to beautiful, fertile basins. The axes of woodcutters let their cheerful voices be heard. Lone birds of prey flew up from the rocks. Here and there at the foot of hills stood an isolated, poor log cabin in the center of a clearing just begun. Girdled giant trees stared with dead, leafless tops at the civilization that had penetrated with the railroad into the long-preserved primitiveness of their homeland. White ashes flew up from still-burning areas of the forest, black smoke whirled up, and red flame licked at half-charred stumps. Zigzag fences upon which thieving squirrels hopped about enclosed scanty cornfields. Here and there grazed a herd of lean cattle or sheep. Now and then we stopped at a small village or town, the frame houses of which revealed that it had been established only recently along the sustenance-bringing railroad.

In fact, nowhere is the importance of steam to civilization as obvious as in these and similar districts of America. This western part of New York state had remained uninhabited for decades because of its relatively infertile soil, and only the canal that winds through had brought some life into the wilderness. Then the tracks that cut through the valleys of the Delaware and the Susquehanna were started, and even before they were completed, town after town sprang up on both sides of the projected line, to grow with the same rapidity as their sister settlements in more favored regions, despite the disadvantages of nature, the rocky soil and rockbound elbowroom for plow and harvest wagon.

About noon we reached NARROWSBURGH, the vicinity of which is notorious for its many rattlesnakes. The route from here to Binghamton, a friendly little town with neat white houses and churches, runs close to the Pennsylvania border and has many romantic sections. Narrow valleys crossed by ravines, rugged, dark-wooded cliffs, and the Delaware, now flowing in the shadows, now presenting its surface to the sun, will someday provide the painters of New York with material for many a good picture.

A few miles beyond BINGHAMTON the region becomes more open and fertile, and rather stately frame houses are frequently seen instead of the dismal log cabins. Indeed, a sort of luxury architecture with columns and balconies appears here and there. To be sure, it exhibits little taste, but at least comfortable circumstances and a certain striving for the beautiful. WAVERLY and HONESDALE are towns that have increased fourfold since the origin of the railroad; and the most charmingly situated Elmira is a place that already is raising well-founded claims to the title of respectability and elegance and will have changed from a *town* to a *city* before ten years have passed.

We traveled along for forty-eight hours between these scenes of most gratifying growth. Thoughts about the wretched impoverishment of entire districts in the unfortunate Hessen unexpectedly crossed my mind, and I had become more than weary of the hard seats that do not permit a moment's sleep and of

the rudeness of the conductors, who consider the emigrants about
as ship captains do, that is, as freight. Then a glance into Phelps's
*Guide*[5] showed that deliverance was near at hand. As the sun
sank on the evening of the seventh, the oak forest opened before
us into a broad clearing, and in the background, on the shores of
the mirror-smooth Lake Erie, the city of DUNKIRK, our stopping
place, with the tidy *American Hotel* recommended to me, beckoned
us.

*"Get out of the cars!"* the conductor called into the coaches
after the train had stopped, and *"Clear out, you scamps!"* he cried
in a still ruder tone to those who, not understanding the first
command, hesitated to leave their seats.

"Countrymen here? German hotel—fifty cents a day—three
warm meals—right at the landing—out, out—who's coming along to
the German hotel?" croaked one of the harpies who lie in
wait at the stopping points along the route of emigration in
order to take their portion of fat left upon the soup by their
associates in the harbor towns. A large number followed the oily
fellow to his dirty bug nest. I, however, along with a young dandy
who had suggested being my travel companion to Cincinnati,
went to the mentioned American Hotel; for a dollar a day it offered
us all "the good things of this life."

Our acquaintance had been struck up in a rather unusual
manner. On emigrant trains the conductors consider it beneath their
dignity as gentlemen to answer questions as to how long the
train will stop at this or that station, whether the inquirer speaks
English or not. Thus hardly anyone in our car risked going
to the restaurants to provide himself with that which keeps body
and soul together. A small famine was the result. I finally ended it
in Otisville for myself and for those sitting near me by springing
with bold courage—defying the danger of being left behind—
to the dining establishment and bringing back an enormous cake
(nothing more substantial could be obtained in the haste)
which was cut up for the benefit of all. A well-dressed gentleman
in the opposite corner who was entertaining his neighbors with
stories from Paris likewise received his portion, and this gift was
acknowledged by courteous words, followed later by a closer
communication. My new friend was a Dr. med. Fürster; he had
fought along [with other revolutionaries] in Frankfurt and after his
flight from there had found a position in the hospital of Doctor
Ricord[6] in Paris. Now, however, he intended to go to New Orleans,

where he hoped to carry on a medical practice in association
with a brother who had been established there for some time. He
spoke some French, was well supplied with the *nervus rerum,* and
had stayed in the Broadway Hotel in New York. His German,
to be sure, was not of the sort employed in cultured circles; his
Latin quotations, in which he dealt rather generously, contained
about as many errors as words; and his confused English,
when compared to his claim of having spent three years in India
and the Levant as the house physician of a Lord So-and-so,
would have finished him at once for a less indulgent person. But I
showed forbearance and therefore also expressed no doubts
about the *summis honoribus rite adeptis* when Doctor Fürster
during the course of his story turned into a Doctor Kohl, although
I could not entirely suppress my astonishment when he took
from his beautifully worked bag, besides various medical "cribs"
from the factory of Basse[7] in Quedlinburg, more than one
case of those instruments used at home by "surgeons" to amputate
beards.

Having already gone beyond Dunkirk with this story, I shall
now make another leap forward so that the reader won't have
to drag around a half-explained mystery. With all his more than
doubtful love of truth, Fürster-Kohl was a goodhearted fellow.
Besides, tolerance is the first rule for the observer of men and conditions, and being choosey is the worst policy, so I had nothing
against it when the ambiguous doctor joined me as a companion
for the continuation of the journey. We arrived together in Cincinnati and lived in the same hotel for several weeks. Here Dr. Kohl
soon found patients, was able to come to an understanding with the
druggists, cured (as he said) a man suffering from dropsy,
brought a syphillitic given up by the hospital as incurable (he
reported) on the road to recovery by the Ricord Method, dealt on
the side in Paris lace (of which he smuggled in thousands of
francs' worth), and was already on the waiting list for a doctor's
office about to be vacated, when he suddenly left with a party going
to Texas. A few believed that he had been called to New Orleans
by a letter, but my roommate knew better. This roommate, an
Alsatian champagne maker, claimed that he could prove that the
good young man neither was named Kohl nor was *rite adeptus* but
had been employed earlier in Strassburg as a barber, then had
served an Englishman in Wiesbaden as a valet, and, after he had
won a few thousand gulden at the casino there, had gone to

Paris. There, however, he had not been the assistant of the famous Ricord but had been a simple loafer and a bit of a gambler on the side. The discovery of this fraud and the threatened publication of his secret in the newspapers (the result of a dispute between the pseudodoctor and a person in on the secret) had driven him from there.

"It's too bad about him—*anyhow!*" said the innkeeper. "He was a good soul who wanted to live and let live."

"Well, with the 'letting live' there would have been difficulties," one of the guests threw in.

"Bah, nonsense! You ought to know the country better. *Why!* Whether I studied medicine in Cleveland for four months or not, it all comes to the same thing. I can put people under the earth *anyhow* with a diploma as well as without such a thirty-dollar piece of paper. Was a fool *by God*, that he left. *By Jove,* he wouldn't have been the only one that made his fortune in this way."

He said it, and the gentlemen in the barroom agreed and were sorry for the friend for whom malicious fate had so unexpectedly and so undeservedly closed the door to *moneymaking* before his very nose.

◊ ◊ ◊ After this necessary anticipation of matters that chronologically belong in a later chapter, I take my gracious readers back to the American Hotel in Dunkirk.

After a good dinner in which backwoods dishes such as boiled corn ears and hot biscuits as well as buckwheat cakes eaten with syrup (which, by the way, are similar to the jam-filled pancakes of Saxony) already figured, we slept the sleep of the just in nice rooms and excellent beds, making up for what we had missed the previous few nights. The fine little trumpet voices of a few lost mosquitoes sang us to sleep more than they bothered us, but the instrument by means of which the signal for arising was given and, a quarter hour later, the signal for breakfast, was a horrible torture to the ears. In fact, its sound penetrated through bone and marrow, and if I'm not wrong, it was the same sort that the keepers in our zoos use to scare up the beasts in their cages when feeding time approaches. It may be practical, for even the rigor of apparent death could not easily resist it. But from this point of view a cannon shot set off before each door would be more commendable.

## FROM GOTHAM TO PORKOPOLIS

After we had had a breakfast of beefsteak and pork chops in the dining room and had read the latest news in the New York, Cleveland, and Buffalo papers in the reading room, we went down to the barroom located in the basement to strengthen ourselves with a glass of ale for a walk through the city. Such an American taproom of the better sort presents a piquant picture with its naïve mixture of the genteel and the ordinary. Behind the bar, an elegant counter of mahogany, stood the barkeeper in shirt sleeves, his hat on his head. The walls were decorated with English steel engravings presenting scenes from *As You Like It,* and beneath a large mirror a dirty comb hung from a brass chain. Behind the bar upon a counter supported by carved columns rose a pyramid of sparkling crystal bottles with liquids of all colors. Below it lay mounds of peaches along with piles of bundled cigars, and in the corner, upon a thick-planked, black-painted oyster box, stood a glass bowl in which goldfish swam. To this mixture of objects corresponded the variety of people. Here, from a china pitcher filled with ice water, a "Son of Temperance" poured into a glass the liquid permitted him by Father Matthew.[8] There a ragged Irish day laborer, half a straw hat on his head, staggered to the bar to have the whiskey bottle handed to him from the pyramid. There a foppishly dressed young salesman tripped and wriggled in with polished boots, requesting that the barkeeper prepare him a glass of julep as quickly as possible. There the waiter, using tongs, put a piece of ice into a farmer's beer—the beer flowed from a snake-necked pump on the counter. Here, finally, close to the door, even milk drinkers were represented—in a corner of the stairs, comfortably squealing, ten little pigs were sucking on a greasy sow.

The American bee-people have no idea of the comfort and convenience of a German taproom. *Always in a hurry!* buzzes in the bars as well as in the markets and railroad stations. To get to the goal in the shortest time imaginable is the guiding principle with the glass as with the work, and I interpret the preference for distilled spirits exhibited here even by educated people as due in good part to the fact that by means of whiskey one becomes intoxicated more quickly than by means of grape or barley juice. Everyone stood. There was no sign of deliberate sipping and lip-smacking. Only the julep drinkers sat or, better, rode for a quarter hour on the chairs at hand, with chests against the chair backs, sucking the bittersweet liquid from their glasses through glass tubes or straw. All the others came, drank, and went. There was little talk, and then only about business. There were no tables for card players such as at home keep all corners occupied with spread coattails and burning pipes.

A walk through the city, concluded with a bath in the magnificently clear waters of the lake, gave us opportunity to observe the astounding propelling power inherent in the American soil—it ripens the seed of cities almost as quickly as the seed of a grain crop. Every week one of the streets on the city plat has filled up with houses. Where grass had been growing two weeks before, the imposing Loder House now was sheltering two hundred travelers. Where land had been purchased three years before at the Congressional price of $1.25 per acre, a mere building lot of a quarter acre now costs $800 and in some cases twice as much. That sounds like a miracle or, if one will, like a swindler's trick. But let's be discreet and recognize in this the mighty hand of a spirit of enterprise favored by free institutions, impaired by no bureaucratic trusteeships according to outmoded models, nowhere stumbling over the stumps of rotted trees. Yes, let's be discreet, and instead of scolding about swindlers and worshipers of Mammon (as the "green" emigration[9] of 1849 does), let's rather take off our nightcaps to the vigorous *goaheadiness* of these people. Even though they now direct their entire energies to material objects and in this endeavor produce, along with much of value, many a caricature, they do not really prove by this that once the groundwork for intellectual creation has been laid they will not sacrifice to the idea just as we do and will not carry off from it the same prizes.

An illustration of what I have just said is found in the picture of such a Yankee city itself. To be sure, in Dunkirk (as I saw it) one should not picture a town of massive European solidity. The houses were mostly of wood, often mere shacks. There was no sign of pavement or lantern illumination. In some places the stumps and roots of cleared trees still projected from the roads. But whoever has had the rapid growth of Buffalo depicted for him cannot doubt that within ten years these shacks will have become beautiful, three-story stone buildings with gas-illuminated shops, and the sandy roads along the shore, crossed by remnants of the forest primeval, will have developed into a Broadway almost as magnificent and lively as that of New York, out of which these cities on Lake Erie as far as Cleveland, indeed to Toledo, are growing like shooting stars (although shooting stars in which the power is inherent) into suns with independent life.

The vicinity of Dunkirk is still a complete wilderness. If one bore this in mind and then saw the crowd of European immigrants and American emigrants brought here in streams by the railroad, and if one counted the landing and departing steamboats and observed the travelers swarming like ants from the doors of ticket offices, then one could probably accept it as honestly intended when upon the sign of one of these businesses, from the mouth of a figure representing the older inhabitants of the town contemplating the first railroad to Dunkirk, Gloucester's words sprang forth:

> *Now is the winter of our discontent*
> *Made glorious summer by the sun of (New-) York.*

◊ ◊ ◊ An oppressive heat had prevailed throughout the day, and so, as the evening enticed cooling breezes from the lake, it was an extraordinary relief to sit upon the balcony of the hotel, away from the dust of the street, allowing the perspiration to be fanned away from the brow and the fire from the veins. With this could be combined a look at the steamboat that was to take us to Cleveland; practice in the American dialect, opportunity for which was presented by a farmer from the Wabash who sat down with us; reflections about the humanity that moved to and fro at our feet; and, incidentally, an experiment for the solution of the scientific problem of whether it really is more comfortable to sit with the feet in a horizontal position with the tip of the nose projecting and rocking with the chair. You see, the situation was favorable to the *utile* as well as to the *dulce*.

The view, if not beautiful, was at least typical. The foreground showed a half dozen stores in which no less than everything was for sale: potatoes and pants, meal and medicine, syrup and salt meat, cloth, pottery, and farm tools. Between the competitors was squeezed a bookdealer, who also sold railroad and steamboat tickets, and a barbershop. In front of the latter stood (instead of our basin) the customary red, white, and blue pole, the national emblem of the trade, and beneath it sat the proprietors of the establishment, three Negroes with well-trimmed mustaches and wooly heads shining with pomade. A noisy coppersmith's workshop, a sort of apothecary pasted all over with advertisements for wonder-salves and world-redeeming pills, and a small rickety shack that with overfull mouth called itself the "Dunkirk Hotel" completed this side of the street. A colorful confusion of various kinds of vehicles rolled past us. Two-wheeled carts loaded with flour from the West alternated with the giant wagons of the *movers* that, packed with crates and household furnishings, were moving from the counties in the East to set sail for that fertile West. Ponderous post coaches, on whose boxes one sought in vain for our uniformed coachman with his horn, deposited travelers from localities that did not yet enjoy the blessings of a railroad. Delicate buggies sped along like swift-footed gazelles. Riders with broadbrimmed panama hats, using a piece of buffalo hide instead of a saddle, galloped past as if they'd bet they could overtake Time. The background of this lively picture was formed by the beautiful green lake into which projected on the left a darkly wooded point with a white lighthouse and upon whose lightly ruffled surface light gray sailing ships and the black smoke columns of steamboats passed by rapidly.

In answer to the question as to whether the American taste which favors a horizontal position of the legs is more advantageous to the "seats" of humanity than the European propriety which favors a perpendicular position: the problem can be solved just as well by a balcony railing as by the windowsills I had seen beset by the heels of gentlemen in the New York hotels. However, I had not yet completed my investigation when suddenly down below, on the corner to our left, a voice could be heard—loud, solemn, unctuous, like the voice of a preacher in the desert.

Curious, I leaned over the railing and saw a one-horse buggy surrounded by a dozen laborers in broadbrimmed straw hats; they were soon joined by others. In the buggy stood a well-dressed young man who, with lively gestures, was speaking to the men. As yet I was able to hear only isolated words. But it obviously was a matter of unusual significance that the speaker had come to urge upon the people. His eyes sparkled, and he raised his index finger in warning fashion. At times his voice was muffled, as if in mourning for departed days and men; at times it rolled like the thunder of a court of judgment; at other times it whispered like the zephyrs in a rosebush; and at times it poured cuttingly from his mouth like the sword of Alexander the Great when it severed the Gordian knot. The man spoke from conviction—that was evident. He spoke with great enthusiasm—his entire being, from his head (which had the bearing of an imperator's) to his feet (which seemed to want to stamp out any opposition), gave indisputable evidence of this. Without doubt he had to communicate a matter of the utmost importance. But what was this matter, and who was this mysterious youth with the snow-white collar and the sparkling ring on his finger? I held my hand to my ear in order not to miss anything of this splendid recital, and then I heard the most wonderful of wonderful things. His eloquence moved mountains, his power of imagination was able to produce all the great features of geography before us, his subject seemed to require that he conjure up all the marvels of history and group them about him. He showed us the snow-capped peaks of the Alleghenies, the distant, shimmering gold country of California, the dark, giant forests of Oregon, the sunlit mirror surfaces of the Northern Lakes, rippled by the wings of the west wind. His genius sprang with bold about-face from the White House in Washington and the sacred grave of the *father of his country* to the wise toga-wearers of the Senate of the Quirites, and another mighty flight of imagination put him down in the midst of the people of Athens listening to the immortal Demosthenes' speech for the crown.

He, too, was giving his speech for the crown, namely "for the support of his fellow citizens for that which he had come to recommend to them, to urge upon them, and to impress upon them with all the power of his soul and with all the weight of the facts."

At first my doctor shook his head in disbelief for a long time, for—he had been in Paris. Gradually, however, he changed his expression, and now he too was seized by the greatness of the moment. No, this was not a case of hyperbole-sickness, from which the Yankees are said to suffer just as much as from money-sickness, travel-sickness, and from consumption! This was the language of noblest inspiration, this was the flowing over of the most genuine feeling! No one could fail to recognize that—least of all I—I who would hardly have expected to find such a flight of thought among the cicerones of German patriotic societies, let alone here among the people of driest business interests.

But again: who was the eloquent youth? What was the object, the "world-benefiting" end that he pursued? What was the "great riddle" whose solution he had undertaken? What was the nature of the "gospel, as whose apostle" he represented himself? Strange, for at least a quarter hour he had greatly excited the curiosity of the circle of straw and felt hats around his buggy, and I do not believe that a single person in the entire gathering had gotten any clearer idea of what he termed his "task" than I had, despite application of all my acumen.

Was he a Methodist preacher who had come to urge upon the

people a flight from the lap of sin to the cross of the Saviour? Had he appeared as an emissary of William Miller,[10] the "Ram's-head Prophet," to announce to the wicked world the imminent emptying of the apocalyptic vials of wrath and the early appearance of the rider upon the pale horse? Or was he perhaps one of the twelve apostles of the Mormons who had come here from the great Salt Lake in the Rocky Mountains to make a last attempt to break the defiance of the "heathens" who raged against Joseph Smith's new Jerusalem? He could conceal within himself all these roles, one as well as the other, although until now he had spoken in a rather worldly fashion and even had occasionally shown that he possessed humor.

Or was the target at which he aimed a political one? He had spoken with the zeal of Elijah about fatherland and freedom and the future crushing of all tyrants, and of the feeling of his countrymen's hostility toward all oppression. What if he had been sent by Tammany Hall to enlist recruits for a third Lopez expedition[11] among the solid people of the West or to collect money (which the patriots lacked even more) for a campaign of vengeance for "the fifty American citizens cruelly murdered by the Spanish hangmen," who had been mourned so deeply the week before in all the Democratic wards of New York? Or was he supposed to shoot, with the cannon of his eloquence, breaches into Whig prejudices for the approaching election? Finally, the slave question was again in the foreground of the newspaper world. Had he perhaps, thinking in a quiet little room, discovered the long-sought arcanum with which this fateful sore on the body of the American giant was to be cured without either awakening the anger of the slaveholders or offending the sentimentality of the abolitionists? These pictures, too, could be behind the colorfully embroidered and charmingly draped curtain woven by the speech of the mystery man.

But there was still a lot more room for guessing, for even this "Brocken had a broad summit."[12] In the America that we consider so sober prevails three times as much belief in the shadow side of nature as we imagine, and the man in the buggy could be (to mention only a few of the branches of magic fashionable here) a spirit rapper from Rochester, a soothsayer such as are recommended every day in the *New York Herald* for information *de omnibus rebus et quibusdam aliis,* a pupil of Mesmer, a physiognomist, or a phrenologist. Perhaps he had an elixir to sell, drawn from the fairy spring of eternal life, curing every illness, rejuvenating the old man, resisting death in all forms, and putting far in the shade the pill distribution of the great Morrison, of the painkiller Townsend, and of the all-helper Brandreth.[13] Had he come to us to announce that he had discovered the art of flying? Or had he discovered the *perpetuum mobile* that certainly, if ever, will be figured out by the Yankees (who already are *perpetua mobilia*)? Had he gotten the idea for a giant petard to blow the hated England into the air, and had he now gone out to organize a nationwide subscription to procure the necessary materials for this humane purpose? Or, finally, was the reason for his appearance and the theme of his sermon only the trifling matter that he had succeeded in squaring the circle?

My guessing was at an end. My curiosity had reached the peak, and the oratorical magus still spoke in mysteries. From a fervent appeal to the hearts of his listeners he passed over to the remark that the hour to appeal to their intellects would soon strike. From Kossuth,[14] the "exalted martyr of patriotism," he wheeled off with a completely beautiful pirouette of speech to present the burnt offering of his enthusiasm to the Northern Nightingale (I almost said: "to the Northern Bee"), the "incomparable Queen of Song," Jenny Lind. Now he described the splendor of the flowers of the western prairies. Now he wandered about upon the agitated waves of the Gulf Stream. Now, again, he depicted a sunrise in the Green Mountains of Vermont, his beloved home. How cleverly was woven into these highly poetic tableaux an episode in which he imparted the most remarkable suggestions about the influence of cleanliness upon the human body, and with what boldness was executed a rhodian leap from this medical theme into the middle of the battle of Buena Vista, which he had helped "Old Zack" win.

My patience was about to come to an end when the lecture took a sudden turn that promised the final clearing up of the mystical cloud and the appearance of the sun concealed behind it.

Our Demosthenes had come straight from President Fillmore, to whom he had shown "a discovery much more important than that of gunpowder"; the President had graciously accepted a sample of the same. It was a discovery that provided everything that humanity needed and longed for, and a good bit more; a discovery that properly could take its place along with the miracles and metamorphoses of mythology, although (as the speaker added with praiseworthy humility) not entirely with the blessed miracles of Biblical revelation; a discovery that "fulfilled in all its glory that lofty principle of the fathers of American independence: *a-a-awl men are equal,* since it extended its blessed results to the curly-headed infant as well as to the bald octogenarian, to the strong-minded male as well as to the delicate female sex, to the rich in marble palaces as well as to the poor occupants of log cabins."

"All, I embrace all of you with loving arms!" the man shouted with drunken fervor (he surely was not acquainted with Schiller's embrace of the millions[15]). "All, I invite all of you to participate, and no one shall say that it is being done for the sake of contemptible profit!"

With these words he bent over, opened a drawer under the backseat of the buggy, and took out various packages wrapped in white paper. He then held one up with a gesture that expressed the entire importance of the momentous occasion.

Our divinatory impulse stirred anew. The content of the little package could be a small book. Was it perhaps a new golden Bible? But it could also be an angular bottle. And who knew whether in it was captured, behind a Seal of Solomon, a portion of that force that always intends evil and yet always creates good?[16] Finally, it could also be a small chest or box; and what if in it was a "Table, set yourself!"[17] or even a miniature colt of that fine little donkey that in the happy age of the fairytale each morning for his master a purse full of ducats sh——elled out.

"With this panacea," the youth apostrophized the attentively listening circle, "I cure all the afflictions of our times, all the ailments from which humanity is suffering, from the roots up. Already its praises resound loudly in the South as well as in the West. Our senators, representatives, governors, Supreme Court justices, and generals are using it with success, and over there, across the ocean, the suspicion is beginning to dawn that in it, in this epoch-making discovery, lies the salvation of the world (to the extent that up until now it has been considered mortal). Look here!" And with this, after a glance at the ladies who had occupied all windows on both floors of the hotel, he unwrapped one of the precious packages, and a milk-white mass of the shape of a small marble slab appeared.

"Out of the purest love for my sisters and brethren," he continued, "I undertook to gather the wondrous materials from a mixture of which this magic tablet was formed, this sickness-eradicator, this unrelenting enemy of all dirt adhering to the human race, this amulet against all spirits from Pandora's box. It cost me long

years of serious study before I saw light in regard to its composition. But far be it from me to exploit this divine beam of light for my own enrichment. For months I risked my life among the red men of the western prairie wilderness and upon the cliffs of the sea-gull-covered East Coast to collect the plants that the secret science prescribes for its preparation. But the thought never occurred to me that I should be rewarded for my efforts and risks. It would seem to be simony, my friends, robbing of the temple, if I did otherwise. Therefore, step up, you men with rough beards, and you, fine fellows from the Irish Emerald Isles, step up and receive from my hand, gratis, a gift of this remedy which through its causal nexus truly benefits the entire world, a sample of my"
—now, my dear reader, what was the object that the prophet in the one-horse buggy had praised with such a glow of conviction? —"a sample of my excellent New England Soap!"

If I had ever seen one of those circulating mountains that gave birth to a mouse, this was the second, and certainly not the less interesting. "Pooh!" groaned the doctor, "that goes beyond the hatband." "*I'm rumfuzzled if this don't beat everything!*" growled even the phlegmatic farmer from the Wabash, drawing his mouth into a pleased grin. The solution of the mysterious puzzle: a bar of soap! The Demosthenes at the conclusion of his speech for the crown nothing more than the salesman of a cosmetics manufacturer! By the beard of Doctor Eisenbart,[18] that was more than would have occurred to an ordinary power of imagination. I felt completely "rumfuzzled," although a dictionary could hardly have translated the backwoods expression into German for me. Yes, "rumfuzzled"—that was the only word that would describe the degree of my dumfoundedness. "Rumfuzzled," as the audience of the Hofburg Theater[19] would feel if, instead of the *dies irae dies illa* in the church scene of *Faust,* the chorus suddenly sang: "Lottie is dead, Lottie is dead, Julie is dying." Anyway, who could have been ill disposed toward the artful rascal who had been able to keep us in suspense for three-quarters of an hour with his power of persuasion? Who would not have felt inclined to add to the number of those who applauded him and shook his hand for the speech, if not for the soap? And who would not have been eager to receive a sample of the miraculous cleansing agent, particularly since it was being given out free?

I went down to get one of the tablets as a memento. But see, again a surprise! The supply of gratis packages had been exhausted, and with their end the bighearted prophet of the soap gospel who was so averse to contemptible profit had turned into a skilled salesman who quite "smartly" disposed of great quantities of his product at the best prices and would not even accept Ohio banknotes at full value. That was perhaps the most genuine and the most entertaining Yankee humbug that old Lake Erie had seen since the day when the first paleface had been reflected in it, and our farmer from Illinois certainly was not wrong when he said that the genius in the buggy was a fellow who would amount to something.

But the muse of eloquence was not the only patroness of the facile-tongued devil of a fellow. The goddesses of music and poetry, too, were subject to and favorably disposed toward him. He had to justify with examples and proofs the previous panegyric to his now unveiled secret. He felt the need for this when the crowd gradually began to disperse, and he answered this need, after bathing his weary vocal organs with a mint julep, with a long poem full of belly-shaking jokes that he sang to the popular Negro melody "*I Come from Alabama*" in a quite sonorous voice.

Among the many astonishing deeds performed by the magic spirit contained in his soap, I mention only two of the best. In Boston a sailor had purchased a bar of the precious *New England soap*, not for himself but for his sweetheart. Fortunately, however, in the haste in which he was recalled to his ship, he had forgotten to present the gift, and so he took it along in his pocket on the journey to the South Seas, where his brig was to hunt whales. A terrible storm arose at Cape Horn. The masts broke, the sails ripped, the vessel ran into an iceberg, and the water poured roaring through the leak. The lifeboats that were put out were overturned by the heavy seas or smashed on the reefs, and anyone not a swimmer drowned in the pitiless ocean. Jack was a swimmer. Thinking about his life gave him strength, and thinking about his beloved doubled this strength—but without the soap in his breast pocket he certainly would not have escaped. However, the soap now fulfilled its destiny, that is, it "washed," while he swam, washed and washed, "until it had washed him safely ashore" (*wash* used here in a double sense). With the help of another ship he returned to Yankeeland, there to offer his Susy his hand and, at the same time, the wonderful bar of soap; it has been preserved under glass and frame to this day by the grateful couple.

The other tale was even better. It, too, was concerned with

more recent times. Namely, the singer, on a trip from Washington to the North, had met a wild man in the gloomy forests of Pennsylvania. This man had to be kept on a chain in a sort of doghouse because of his fierceness. Living in swamps before his capture, the monster had never washed and had let his nails grow to claws and his beard and hair to a perfect buffalo mane. No one had been able to curb his defiance and his taste for filth to the extent that he'd exchange these bad habits for human customs. The hunter who had captured him was about ready to let him run back to his swamp again when a fortunate accident or providence led our wonder-man to the spot. Sympathetically and charitably he offered this awful creature, that ran on all fours and ate grass like Nebuchadnezzar, a piece of his soap. When the half-man, taking this gift to be edible, had eaten it up without hesitation, the soap became the means of washing his soul white of all impurities and his impulses of all filth. Straightway this fortunate change of attitude became visible, for the man covered with mud now submitted patiently to an external application of the panacea, and "Behold!" the poem and the whole delightful performance ended with:

> The dirt was gone, the mane came off, the scarecrow, so they tell,
> Became a good example of a typical Broadway swell.*
> The richest girl in old New York to him her troth did plight,
> And he'll be married in the morn, if he doesn't die tonight.

We were afraid we'd miss the departure of our steamboat if we waited to find out whether another scene would follow the pause which now occurred, during which the singer of this soap ballad had to satisfy numerous inquiries about his product. However, the boat didn't leave until midnight, instead of departing at nine o'clock, so we heard from passengers who boarded later that our untiring humbug-maker had given another performance around ten o'clock by torchlight and had thereby disposed of his entire supply of the wonder-soap, down to the last bar.

◊ ◊ ◊ The trip across Lake Erie has become disastrous for many. The lake's green waves have attained about the same sad fame as the yellow waters of the Mississippi. Not a year passes that a half dozen steamers don't go to the bottom because of the maliciousness of the destructive storms or because of the irresponsibly

---

* *Swell,* fop, dandy. In New York the parade ground of these young gentlemen is Broadway and, indeed, the sidewalks on the west side of the street, on no account those on the opposite, "ungenteel" side.

negligent ambition of the captains who overfeed the stomachs of their leviathans with coal until they burst. This carelessness is the dark side of the above-praised *goaheadiness;* and the fact that the law doesn't intervene with punishment is the unfavorable reverse side of the otherwise quite gratifying disinclination of the people toward police regulations. Today a ship blows up with three hundred people. Tomorrow the newspaper roosters crow a concert about the disaster and its thoughtless creators. Day after tomorrow? Bah, let the dead bury their dead. Our marriages are fertile enough to replace the loss of life. A trifle! On with business! *All aboard, go ahead, boys!* And merrily the steamboat of the restless ones shoots forth from the harbor. Nothing is learned, everything forgotten—only not the propensity of the captain for overracing and overheating—and if perhaps the boiler of his boat explodes, then again it is a *lamentable accident* for the press, and again no lesson for the public and the authorities.

Friendlier stars shone for us. At noon on the ninth our *Queen City* landed its cabin and steerage passengers, along with its mountains of freight, all in good shape, near the railroad station of CLEVELAND. This city belongs to the state of Ohio and is an even better example than Dunkirk of the terrifically rapid growth of these western settlements. Where, at the beginning of the century, a dozen backwoodsmen lived a lonely existence in three log shanties resembling pigsties, subsisting on bear and turkey meat and the yield of a few acres of Indian corn, and where, in 1830, a village with 890 inhabitants stood, now a beautiful city of 22,000 souls looks down upon the lake—with giant hotels adorned with columns and proud towers, with friendly dwellings, spacious streets, a medical college, and no fewer than twenty-four churches. Furthermore, on the other side of the Cuyahoga, which here empties into Lake Erie, opposite the hills crowned by the "Forest City" of Cleveland, has been established another flourishing town, the pretty Ohio City, presently numbering some 3,000 inhabitants.

The commerce here is extraordinarily active. Cleveland is the largest grain market of the largest agricultural state of the Union. Nature has destined it for this, and the enterprising spirit of its people has developed it. Its harbor is the best on the entire lake. A canal and a railroad connect it with Pittsburgh, 130 miles* away; a second railroad connects it with Cincinnati, twice as far.

---

* When "miles" are mentioned here and later, English *miles* are to be understood, if the contrary is not expressly indicated.

And a third line, to be opened by the end of 1852, will connect it with Dunkirk and through this to the metropolis on the Hudson. In the year 1850 the city had 105 vessels on the lake, representing a tonnage of 18,462; they carried on an import and export trade running to a total value of almost $10 million. In the mentioned year 2,754 ships entered its roads; included in this number were more than 1,100 steamboats.

Here, too, we stopped for a day and stayed at the Kaiser Napoleon Hotel, a small, clean inn in the upper part of the city. From here we had an excellent view. We could, to pass the time, hold a review of the uniforms of the Grand Army, illustrations of which had been used by the innkeeper, an old soldier and enthusiastic admirer of the little corporal, to decorate the walls of the barroom; we also got a quite drinkable Bordeaux at a moderate price. Less pleasant were the innumerable bedbugs that had chosen Mr. Emmerich's house for their residence. But since they are a general plague and belong to the characteristic features of American life (like the rats and the thorn apple bushes), we had to grin and bear it. Even in the elegant Wedell House down on Main Street the passengers rebelled in vain against the pricks of these vile redskins.

We spent a part of the evening in a nearby tavern whose owner was introduced to me as a former German-Catholic priest and a fighter in Baden. Here was one of the western headquarters of that part of the German emigration that had been thrown upon the shores of America by the unfortunate outcome of the uprisings of 1849. I'll save a characterization of these gentlemen for one of the following chapters. It might only be mentioned that the barricade men to whom I spoke in Cleveland lived with the conviction that the Yankee Republic, too, needed a revolution and inevitably was going to have one—a bit of silly talk for which one would have liked to have excused them when one heard how very much they longed for the fleshpots of Egypt, although such could be found here also (but not through idle talk). The delusion of many of these people is as colossal as their conceit. Instead of being grateful to the nation that has afforded them asylum, they rail against the customs of the land like a trooper using Heinzen-like[20] strong language, and instead of adapting themselves to the organism of the forces at work here and learning something of it, or at least about it, they would like to, and they would, if their giant tongue were not located in a dwarf body, throw out the Penates from the house-altar of the Union. As matters stand, they have to content themselves with mere schoolmastering about what should be done and not done. But the fact that the moon does not hear the yelping of the curs and remains true to its nature and in its orbit, transforms their grief into anger, their zeal into rancor, delusion into madness; and, in fact, one frequently doesn't know whether or not one is dealing with people who are sound in the brain.

Anyway, Germanism is represented in Cleveland by about three thousand of its inhabitants and by one newspaper, the *Germania;* the latter, until shortly before my arrival, had been edited by the well-known Fenner v. Fenneberg[21] and was counted among the better papers of Ohio.

◊ ◊ ◊ The tenth of September saw us in an elegant railroad car speeding through forest after forest and forest again toward the heart of Ohio and its capital, COLUMBUS. Contemplation of these immeasurable forests of dark, deciduous trees stirs not only primitive but, in moments of forlornness, even primeval fantasies. A poet could see in the speeding train—whose locomotives do not whistle here, but roar—one of those gigantic, many-limbed saurians that traveled through the swamp vegetation of the antediluvium. The branches of the dead tree-colossi, which here and there rise above the lower treetops on both sides of the track, could be compared to the antlers of enormous deer anxiously awaiting the passing of the smoke-spewing monster. The regions through which we passed are flat, at most crossed by rolling hills; occasionally they are damp, now and then approaching swampland. One hardly goes three miles without seeing neat, mossy pictures of farms and small towns emerging from the forest darkness. Wherever these are farther apart, clearings, girdled trunks, woodpiles, and corduroy roads leading up to the railroad testify as to the rule of human hand. Indeed, at one of the stations in the midst of the densest forest a stagecoach stopped—as pretty, as fashionably constructed, as colorfully decorated as if it had just come from the Bowling Green in New York.

Columbus, the seat of the governor and of the legislature of Ohio, is situated on the east bank of the Scioto a rifle shot from the mouth of the Olentangy, about 130 miles from Lake Erie and 100 miles from the Ohio River.[22] Like most of the newer American towns, it has a friendly but rather characterless physiognomy.

Although neither a commercial nor a manufacturing city, Columbus has grown within the last ten years from 7,000 to 19,000 inhabitants. The Germans must be very numerous here, too, for they have four churches and a newspaper, the *Westboten,* a very respectable one according to local standards. For about twenty years there also has existed a training institution for Lutheran clergymen. The city holds a special interest because of the public buildings; they are, in part, very imposing. The Deaf and Dumb Institute of the state, with 130 pupils; the Asylum for the Blind, which trains and cares for 100 of them; and, above all, the Lunatic Asylum with its 370-foot-wide front and its 440 rooms in which over 400 of the mentally ill are housed—all give evidence, through their exteriors, of the good taste of their builders. It is said that they are furnished just as practically inside as they are managed reasonably. The capitol, upon which construction has been underway for several years without getting much beyond the foundation walls, will cover an area of 55,936 square feet and will surpass all similar architectural works within the United States, not only in size but also in beauty.

Circumstances permitted me to have a look at the interior arrangements only in the case of the state prison. This imposing structure is located close to the banks of the river, the weeping willows of which are quite appropriate to this locale of civil death. The main building is of Ohio marble, contains seven hundred cells in its elongated wings, and forms the center of one side of a six-acre rectangle enclosed by high walls. The prisoners, of whom there were between five and six hundred at the time of my visit, are divided into thirteen companies. As we entered the yard, several of the companies marched past us in military order, silently, their faces turned toward the escorting guard. It has been thought necessary to take into consideration the difference in color and the aristocracy of white skin based thereupon even in the case of criminals, for one of the companies is composed of blacks. Strict discipline is maintained, and violation of the house rules (a copy of which each person exiled here receives upon his arrival) is severely punished with the whip. Some of the prisoners work in a stone quarry two miles away and some on the construction of the capitol. The others are occupied with the manufacture of wood products and similar industrial tasks, the income from which in many years has exceeded the maintenance cost of the institution by nearly $20,000. At noon, at a signal from a bell, the various companies fall in before their places of work, moving to the dining rooms at a second signal; there they seat themselves at tables to the sound of a bell. They eat from self-made wood plates and drink from tin cans. At breakfast they receive rye coffee as a beverage; at lunch, water. A Methodist preacher holds services in the prison, and for the improvement of singing a choir has been formed from those prisoners having suitable voices and a good will for this purpose. Moreover, with the chapel is connected a Sunday school in which several respected private people from the city give instruction; during the past year ninety-five prisoners participated in this. To the inventory of this school belongs a not inconsiderable library from which books are loaned to the pupils upon request.

The administrative official who imparted these notes to me added that when a temperance preacher recently inquired of the prisoners as to how many of the crimes that had brought them here had been committed under the influence of alcohol, more than four-fifths of those present had stood up. Around a hundred stated that they had been employed in the manufacture or sale of distilled spirits, and all, rising from their seats, declared their intention of abstaining from the consumption of these stimuli to sin for the rest of their lives.

With the wish that it might be lived as it had been pledged, we left our obliging guide to return to the station. A quarter hour later we were on our way to the south. In honor of the strikingly numerous squirrels occupying the forest that we now again saw darkening above us, the following curiosity from the chronicles of Columbus may be appended.

In the *Columbus Gazette* of August 29, 1822, several farmers in the vicinity published a manifesto to their neighbors and acquaintances. In it they directed the attention of the same to the danger threatened to the corn crop by the squirrels, which were increasing in a most monstrous degree. They proposed eradicating en masse these enemies of their crops by means of a great *hunting caucus*. The crusade sermon found a response. Everyone who could shoot a rifle gathered on the appointed day at the fixed place to open the attack. The destruction of the genus *Sciurus* moved from township to township. For three days the shots of the merciless ones crackled everywhere. When at the conclusion of this Bartholomew Eve the victims were counted, it turned out that 19,660 squirrels had been dispatched—not taking into account the effectiveness of the marksmen who had not turned in the skins carried off by them.

In Germany I had heard exaggerated notions (and had had them myself) about the speed with which one travels on American railroads. In fact, one was led to believe from some reports that the transatlantic locomotives run at least twice as fast as ours. I have never found confirmation of this in the West, and in the East only on the line between Buffalo and Canandaigua. If the American trains, which cover, on the average, a half mile in a minute, surpass ours in overcoming distance, this is cancelled out on longer runs by the frequent stops—in this regard the so-called express trains are only slightly inferior to the freight trains—completely in favor of the German procedure. These numerous stations are required by the circumstances, as is self-evident. However, for the person who is in a hurry, they smack somewhat of deception, and since we took a full seven hours to cover the 110 miles between Columbus and our destination for today, one will not find it incomprehensible that we were in a rather bad humor when we arrived at the CINCINNATI station at midnight.

It is in the nature of the Yankees to give their cities, in addition to their Christian names, a sonorous title of honor, or, according to the circumstances, a piquant nickname. So now we were, as the poets expressed it, in the "Queen of the West" or, as the rogues suggested, in the "City of Pork." The pseudodoctor grumbled that he found nothing queenly about the street through which we followed our drayman to the Jefferson Hotel. But I read the designation *Porkhouse* on more than one building that we passed. So, according to my first impressions, the honorable Cincinnati will be called (at least in the next chapter) what those rogues christened it—PORKOPOLIS.

# 2

## CINCINNATI IN DIARY ENTRIES

◊ ◊ ◊ THE Jefferson Hotel had been able to impress us at night by its size, but the next morning's sun showed us that it was not the place for us.¹ Ugly beetles clambered up the walls of our bedroom on long, thin legs, and spider webs in the corners of the canopy, broken windowpanes, an unlockable door, a washstand without basin, and a barroom full of ragged, unkempt Irishmen all caused us to think of hasty flight from this locale of misunderstanding, despite the beautiful view of the Ohio afforded by our windows. At Eggers and Wilde, a well-established book and stationery business on Main Street, Charley Kopf's Farmers and Traders Tavern was recommended to us as the best German boardinghouse, and I found cause to be grateful for this advice. I used the first few days that I spent here to become familiar with the situation, as is customary, and therefore I didn't write in my notebook. These days were filled with the study of the city map and address book, with the delivery of letters of recommendation and the making of acquaintances, and with soundings and being sounded. Not until the fourteenth of September did I feel enough at home in my new quarters to be in the mood to draft outlines and sketches.

◊ ◊ ◊ SEPTEMBER 15

It's strange what a variety of destinies is represented by the bit of humanity that has been washed into our hotel by the billows of American activity. There is a young man with turned-up mustache who claims to have had a royal Prussian commission as second lieutenant, with prospects for a first lieutenancy. From the descriptions of parades and maneuvers to which he occasionally treats us, this seems certain—just as certain as the waiter's job in a seaman's tavern along the canal for which he now is a candidate. Further, there is a newspaper writer who until three months ago conducted a Protestant school; since then, although still a Lutheran, he has directed a Catholic newspaper. There is our barkeeper, born and raised in Saxony, ripened for America in Texas, crowned with laurel in the Mexican War—a good man who has preserved a German heart and a heart for Germany. Then there is a queerly hypochondriac Magyar fellow who, as captain in the army of the Sultan, saw service in Troy and Tripoli, Jerusalem and Damascus, then served as a major under the "traitor" Görgey,[2] and now has come from the city of Montezuma, where he earned his bread with a most soldierly skill, namely by flower embroidery —a Hercules at the distaff, ten times more respectable than the bragging fellows who lounge around the Shakespeare Hotel in New York waiting for Kossuth and Kossuth enthusiasm to support them.[3] Here is the swaggering, comfortably prosperous fat-belly, one of the fathers of the city, "worth" his $30,000—in 1836 he took part in the digging of the Erie Canal[4] in which his buildings are now reflected. Over there the lean, black frock coat: in his homeland across the sea he had been an honest tailor's apprentice. Here he had become a farmhand, had changed himself into a pedlar, and had crept out of this chrysalis to become a trapper. Then, through a goodly number of additional metamorphoses— during which he taught the mysteries of the ABC's in Missouri, was a steamboat fireman in Illinois, worked as a commercial clerk in Kentucky, as a sexton in Indiana, and, as a preacher in Virginia, depicted heaven and hell to visitors at camp meetings —he had become one of the most esteemed lawyers in Ohio. In a word, our boardinghouse sheltered a dozen individuals who, if they wanted to talk about their pasts, would represent a sample card of at least five dozen of the most varied occupations.

Yesterday morning I went to Saint Paul's Church. Cousin Theodore[5] absolutely would not let a Sunday pass without going to church. A pretty building, at least in the interior. Much light (as a Protestant house of worship should have), clean brown benches, delicate candelabra, beautifully colored carpeting in the aisles, everything new and neat. But, unfortunately, what miserable organ playing, what unharmonious singing, and what an incredibly unseemly scene presented by the preacher and the church council! The pastor, with a questionably flushed and suspiciously bloated countenance, rattled off a prayer from Witschel[6] and then preached a sermon, neither roughhewn nor engraved, neither cold nor warm, with neither logic in it nor grammar. It was a muddle of sudden ideas, figures of speech, and commonplaces, such as one shakes from his sleeve without much reflection, even when it is not the sleeve of a cassock. There was no trace of a leading thought, of a theme, or of any organization, and just as little of dignity and enthusiasm. And then, what a conclusion! The congregation had ordered the pastor to announce its decision that on the following Sunday the sermon would be preached not by him but by the first of the candidates for the position becoming vacant through his impending dismissal. This gave him occasion for a protest. Perhaps there would have been no objection to this if he had not thereby used the most immoderate expressions and had not, completely forgetting the place where he stood and the office that he held, inveighed against various individuals. However, this did not seem to be anything unusual (and was not—as I found out later). When he finally declared bluntly that he would not read aloud the announcement in question, a member of the church council stepped before the chancel and replied, just as abruptly, that he had to do what the congregation ordered him to do. The pastor was being paid for that, and if he refused, then he, the council member, would take care of the matter. The pastor became furious. A heated exchange of words followed. A part of those present scraped, tramped, and stamped on the floor. The word "liar" was heard. I expected a fight—a few more steps, a few more poisonous speeches, and the disputants would have had each other by the collar. Since I had no desire to be a witness to such desecration of the temple, I found my way to the door and departed, little edified by this sample of German-American church life and the prospects connected with it. Theodore, however, found nothing unusual about it and knew about a congregation in Indiana whose members had fought a real battle over the preacher, with clubs and knives, in and before the church.

    A better impression was made by the ceremony that I attended in the afternoon. It was the dedication of a newly built Protestant orphan home on Mount Auburn. Here I saw assembled a large part of the local German population. The various charitable organizations, led by marshals in sashes and ribbons, decorated with all sorts of badges and provided with banners and flags, and the schoolchildren in their best dress, with wreaths and bouquets in their hands, led by their clergymen and teachers, marched in a long line through the streets north of the canal toward the hill upon which the institution is situated. It is a pretty, three-story building with some fields and a garden and is located not far from a similar benevolent establishment, a home for widows. Two bands played national songs. The entire clergy of Cincinnati let their lights shine forth from a platform erected upon the roof of an adjoining building. Upon all faces could be seen the joy of having, for once, created something good and strong through common efforts. When, at the end of the celebration, collectors passed among the crowd to urge a last contribution to the work completed on the exterior, the plates were covered with abundant gifts. Workmen of only moderate means placed banknotes of five and ten dollars upon them, and the subsequent counting showed a sum that would not have amounted to half as much at home under similar circumstances. The speakers, however, were caricatures of eloquence, with the exception of the pastor of Saint John's Church, who spoke simply, going straight to the heart, and genuinely. Instead of keeping to the point, they thundered against the atheists, abused the Jesuits, harassed the Methodists; they gesticulated with their arms like windmill sails, usually lost the thread from pure bombast, and in general seemed to be more interested in showing off than in the actual purpose. Such spiritual ranters cannot possibly mean well with the congregations that have entrusted themselves to them; it is no wonder that people of intelligence here turn away from the church in general and that people of heart turn to Methodism from the so badly represented Protestantism. A considerable part of the deficiencies for which the American Germans are reproached can certainly be chalked up to their clergy—assuming that one can draw wider conclusions from the conditions in Cincinnati, a license I am almost inclined to take after all that I have experienced in this matter.

◊ ◊ ◊ SEPTEMBER 16

Cincinnati is not a beautiful city (unless one considers regularity to be beauty), but it has an attractive location. The day before yesterday I looked down upon its back from Mount

Auburn; this morning I looked into its face from the hills above
Covington. An artist couldn't help but select for a painting the
picture presented from the latter standpoint. When looking down
from Mount Auburn, one has before one's eyes a mere mass of gray
shingle roofs and red brick and white frame walls, cut up into
regular rectangles by streets as straight as arrows—like a chessboard upon which a couple dozen larger and smaller towers
represent the chessmen. But from the heights across the river the
city presents an excellent sight, even a magnificent one. One
stands upon the southern rim of a deep basin. Directly beneath
the viewer lie the friendly Newport (with its barracks topped by
the Stars and Stripes) and the extensive Covington—the two
towns are separated by the wooded valley from which the Licking
rushes toward the Ohio. Fifty feet lower the 1,800-foot-wide Ohio
River, furrowed by steamers and enlivened by sailboats, flatboats, and rafts, flows out of a narrow, darkly shaded valley to
disappear behind a leaf-green point of land on the left that is
already clothed in the colors of autumn because of this year's
eight-week drought. On the opposite shore, however, upon two
terraces, rises the Queen of the West. It is five miles wide
(including Fulton, adjoining it to the east) and somewhat over
a mile and a half deep in the center. A row of splendid, colorfully
painted three-decked steamboats extending almost beyond the
field of vision, most of them giving off smoke from two chimneys,
forms the base of the spacious, gently sloping public landing.
The landing is covered with all sorts of bales, goods, and barrels and
is crowded with carts, porters, sailors, merchants, and departing
and arriving travelers. It is, so to speak, the face of the city, and
at the same time the entrance to the beehive that it resembles.
White or brick-red buildings with green awnings and tall, narrow
warehouses covered to the top story with advertising signs legible at
a great distance border the three other sides of the parallelogram.
From this central point of commerce, into which pours a throng
of businessmen from Main Street and two other important streets
traveled by hundreds of omnibuses and coaches, two outspread
wings extend to the right and to the left. On the right, factories are
giving forth dense clouds of smoke, the trains of the railroad
from Xenia are roaring, and an army of carpenters in the shipyards are hammering and sawing on two new steamboats, the
skeletons of which hint at future colossal bodies. On the left
rises the gothic steeple of the First Presbyterian Church; it was

planned to set a hand pointing toward heaven upon it, but unfortunately only a golden glove has been affixed. Farther on, the dome of the gigantic Burnett House looks down upon the river as Saul upon all the children of Israel. Still farther, the Catholic cathedral raises its white, tasteless tower, while in the background of the painting the crosses of four other churches of Rome sparkle above the shadows of Mount Auburn. While the city is densely packed in the center, split only by its eight main streets and the east-west secondary streets intersected by them at right angles, toward the west it becomes more scattered, frequently interrupted by still-unused building lots, and it grows poorer and more wooden until Mill Creek (in spring a brook, now a series of puddles) sets a temporary limit to it. In the east it is blocked by Mount Adams. It would be in vain if the mount wanted to prevent the city's growth, for already an observatory and a goodly number of other buildings have been placed upon its head and back. The background of the background, finally, is closed by limestone hills, partly bare, partly covered with gardens, vineyards, and country homes, and partly still covered by the forests through which the warpaths and hunting trails of the Mingos and Miamis passed sixty years ago. When the city has totally occupied the surrounding heights (to the north it has already climbed up a considerable distance and covered them with groups of houses), it will present a complete amphitheater of the most enormous dimensions. The traveler who looks upon it in the year 1900 from the hills where I stood today will see before him a spectacle more imposing than any other that the western continent will be able to offer. I have before me a woodcut depicting Cincinnati at the beginning of this century.[7] What a difference between the little village of that period and the city of today, and what a future can be predicted from the comparison!

◊ ◊ ◊ SEPTEMBER 17

In my last entry I found Cincinnati similar to a chessboard. True! But today I should prefer to compare it to a gigantic newspaper page. Anyone at all familiar with the American and especially the western dailies will know at once what I mean. To the yard-long columns of the journals correspond the mile-long streets of the city. The former are up to three-quarters advertisements; the latter are six-eighths commercial firms. The former are crowded with woodcuts illustrating the announcements; the latter exaggeratingly exhibit the originals of the illustrations in a superabundant confusion of enormous rifles advertising the gun shop, great golden mortars advertising the physician and the apothecary, monstrous boots advertising the footwear artist, and colorfully patterned building walls that advertise the rug manufacturers. Colossal umbrellas shading half the roof do not let the person needing this article seek long. Giant plows, likewise put up as high as the building permits, greet the farmer as a customer at three thousand paces. Mammoth bottles, from which a company of soldiers could get drunk, shimmer green, red, and blue from the windows of boutiques. The city is a bazaar; the newspapers are merely maps to help in getting around.

Exorbitant braggarts, these Yankees! They all ought to be named Smart and Handy. What skillful hyperbole-smiths they are! With what facility, what lovable shamelessness, what untroubled peace of soul they know how to sell their brass as gold! How well they know our saying that "advertising is part of the trade," and how naïvely they practice it. In Germany a cat is now and then served up as a rabbit. Quite right. But here one goes further and sells mice as elephants. Also at home a quack occasionally practices his quackery, to the annoyance of the district physicians and medical councils. Good, but here they crow in entire choruses, and with voices just as much louder as America's bullfrog is strongerlunged than the tree frog of our village stories.

I was not at all surprised when in New York "the famous Doctor Roback from Sweden, the seventh son of a seventh son, professor of astrology, phrenology, and geomancy, holder of a certificate from King Charles John, etc." recommended himself in the newspapers as a fortuneteller in matters of love, journeys on land and water, speculation in stocks, merchant goods, and fixed possessions, and more. Mrs. LeNormand has become wealthy in the focal point of French intelligence through the same arts. With us, too, such nonsense is carried on, and not merely with servant girls (although in obscure streets instead of in the papers). I excuse it also (as a courtesy toward the beautiful sex) with "other countries, other customs," when Mrs. Rosenbaugh offers herself in the *Daily Times* to the Cincinnati public as a *"German Doctress"* for the curing of blindness, deafness, cancer, and other "diseases not mentionable here" and in a concluding sentence adds that she reads palms. I call it merely a versatility worthy of recognition when Otto Zirkel, the former Prussian

Hussar lieutenant in Columbus, endeavors to serve half of mankind as an obstetrician and the other half as a lawyer and notary; or when another Doctor announces to his fellow citizens that he not only is engaged "in the entire field of dentistry" but recommends himself also for the manufacture of jewelry. Finally, I also lay no weight upon it when, crossing the street, I see on a corner a poster in large type that screams into the face of the passer-by, with a beam-thick exclamation point, "Steamboat sunk!" and I hurry over to read about the disaster, the Where—How—When, only to find out from the three lines below those terrible words, to my deepest satisfaction, that—Mr. Combstock has brought back from his trip to Boston the richest selection of the newest fall fashions.

As said, these are trifles and half commonplaces. But the activities of the patent-medicine doctors surpass any European concept of what is possible. Or would anyone want to consider it anything else than a joke about the past (when Doctor Eisenbart and his clown made the lame see) if any maker of golden mountains dared to expect so much faith from us that he'd let the following advertisement march into the newspaper?

> MORE THAN A MILLION TESTIMONIALS are in the possession of the proprietor of Mac Allister's CURE-ALL SALVE, given by the most skillful and the most distinguished physicians, by the most educated attorneys, the wisest judges, by messengers of the gospel whose love of truth and divine zeal have made them bright lights on the road to truth, by inspired professors, by experienced merchants, and by men of honor from all the classes existing in humanity. Just as from day to day it irresistibly widens its sphere of action along the border of our enormous country, so the proofs of its miraculous effect are increased daily. Three million boxes of this salve have been consumed in four years and have irrefutably demonstrated that it is infallible. With right it is called a "cure-all," for there is no external nor internal disease that does not yield to it. I have used it for the past fourteen years in cases of consumption and liver complaint, and never without complete success, even when the patient had already given up on all human remedies as hopeless, etc.[8]

◊ ◊ ◊ I could pluck many another leaf from the branch of this great humbug tree that shades the entire Union and, with its twigs, even pushes through the chinks in the log cabins of the backwoods. The journals, the streets, and the markets are full of its fruits. But enough is enough, and it's time for the question: What is the moral of the activity of these patent-medicine manufacturers?

It is in the nature of the matter that it is ridiculous, and it's obvious that the educated American recognizes this. But if one recalls the saying that "he laughs best who laughs last," then there appears to be no doubt that these quacks have chosen the best part. They let the wise men scoff and meanwhile build themselves the most beautiful country houses from the pockets of the simple-minded. In public opinion their business is just as respectable as any other and three times as profitable as most. Furthermore, some of the thousands of pills and salves advertised to the world as "cure-alls" may be rather good household remedies. And finally—are the "regular" physicians so much better than the patent-medicine doctors? Say, Fürster-Kohl and his colleagues? Hardly. May Dame Hygeia please prevent the misfortune from befalling me that I have to choose between one of these diploma-carriers and one of those patent-possessors. But if such a lamentable chalice were presented to me—the teeth of Charybdis and the jaws of Scylla!—I should truly not know how to decide. So again, dear goddess, preserve me from your priests in this country! To have to make a choice between these two castes is similar to the answering of the penal question as to whether one would prefer to be hanged or drowned.

The father of all these speculations on the purse of ailing humanity was the notorious Dr. Morrison in England. He shipped off his "Hygean Pills" in packages of three boxes each, marked with the numbers 1, 2, and 3. They were to be taken in regular sequence, it being impressed upon the patient that they were three different kinds of pills. They became extraordinarily popular in America, so that for a time the doctor's principal agent sold more than a hundred dollars' worth every day. However, it was later proven that this agent's pills were manufactured in New York instead of in London and that numbers 1, 2, and 3 were of exactly the same composition. The medical faculty in London warned against Morrison and the drugs that he prescribed. He therefore brought the matter into court, but his case was rejected. This, however, did not turn the people against him. In fifteen years he had acquired a princely fortune, had built himself a palace, and was about to begin a life like that of the rich man in the gospels, when death fetched him to join those from whom he had obtained his hundreds of thousands.

The successor to, or rather the imitator of, Morrison was a Dr. Brandreth who came to New York from London about 20 years ago. He adopted the system of his worthy predecessor of having his pills taken in large quantities, and so he did an enormous business. He assigned the agency in Pennsylvania to a certain Wright but took it back when he discovered the latter falsifying the accounts. Thereupon the discharged agent and fine fellow made the discovery of a new sort of disease-eradicator, the *Indian Vegetable Pills,* and won over a number of Brandreth's traveling salesmen for their distribution. A fourth Englishman tried his luck with a pill by means of which he claimed to have attained the age of 150 years. He found few who believed him, and besides the Golden Age of Pills was half past. The great Townsend had appeared, and with him the Era of Sarsaparilla; Doctor Bull brought this precious decoction to perfection; and discovery followed upon discovery. They swarmed around this profitable speculation like ephemera around a suddenly turned on light. Most of them disappeared as they had begun. Only Townsend in his templelike salesroom in New York and a few other coryphaei of quackdom were still supporting themselves from the old fame.

Then another doctor's genius put him in mind of a third system of medical bamboozling. Its secret was this: He first let loose with a philippic against all colleagues, charged them with ignorance, accused them of avarice, fraud, and shameless trespass against their suffering brethren, and finally traveled throughout the land compassionately, with the appearance of and under the name of the "Good Samaritan," to give his advice "free of charge" to the distressed and the heavily laden. To be sure, the *"Good Samaritan"* dispensed this advice gratis, but the rascal saw to it that the object of this advice and of the entire philanthropic project, the medicine, was paid for in good hard dollars; and since the world wants to be deceived, many a fat fish was caught with this bait.

At present the patent-medicine business isn't very good. There is too much competition. A few have filled their moneybags by it, but hundreds have frittered away the small means they had hoped to turn into mountains of gold. The cost of the medicinal material is slight. But the expense of bringing the product to the customer, which can be effected only by outshouting the thousand competitors (with incessant newspaper advertising), is so high that a great deal of capital is required even for a start. And even when such is available, it still remains a gamble. Many have believed that if they blew into a dozen newspaper trumpets right at the beginning, a tremendous number of orders for their article would stream in from all four winds. And behold! after four weeks they have to cancel the concert, and one reads in the advertising sheets: "Newly Discovered Gold Mine! Wanted: Partner with one thousand dollars, for a business in which five thousand dollars profit a month can be expected."

◇ ◇ ◇ SEPTEMBER 18

The series of these songs of the American art of advertising may be concluded with this, and I sharpen my pen anew, to transfer neatly and cleanly from my memory to the more reliable paper a visit to the "Mock Auction" on Main Street. It would be too bad if such a picture faded for me, terribly bad if—holla, there the bells of the firehouse are ringing! Dreadful! Not a day has passed without a fire, and today the wild chase is going down the street for the second time already. The Dennison House is burning, one of the city's leading hotels. Should I run down there with the people? *No, Sireel* Not quite safe at such affairs. The fire companies might feel inclined to continue their recently interrupted battle with rock-throwing and pistol-shooting, and Sirach says: Do not meddle in things that do not concern you.[9]

In addition to the strange matters I mentioned on one of the preceding pages, many another unusual feature is noted in the streets of Cincinnati by the European eye. There a public crier is galloping from ward to ward, ringing his bell at the places where main streets intersect, announcing a "lost child." There a rope had been stretched from building to building; from it, high above the awnings that shade the sidewalks, flutters the ticket of Ohio's Democratic party in the form of an enormous pennant. There the street widens to a marketplace, which, however, is built over. Here they come around the corner, drumming and fifing. A colorful militia company of twenty men and ten officers, headed by a thirty-man band, marches out to drill, stepping along martially. One man has put on a bayonet; the other has not but instead has hung on a sidearm. One man has red stripes on his pantaloons; the imagination of the man next to him has found gold braid to be more becoming. The commanders abound in embroidery and pompous epaulets. There a solemn-faced policeman with badge is standing guard so that a trash pile of venerable age, covered with wornout boots, weed stalks, and rotten eggs, will not be stolen by the pigs that roll upon it occasionally. Here and there and there—not a thousand steps apart—stand smoke-blackened ruins, pasted over with printed and handwritten notices of changes of address to which the fire has forced the former occupants.

One passes a barber shop and sees how beards are removed from customers who are lying on their backs; their heads and faces are being washed at the same time. One meets fops dressed in the finest style who, because of the muddy weather, have their trousers rolled up to their knees; just as skillfully as economically they blow their noses through their fingers instead of into a handkerchief. One encounters an omnibus painted with flowers and adorned with a likeness of Zachary Taylor; out of it hop a half dozen young female boarders in bloomer costume. One steps into an elegant bank, finds an old man sweeping out the room, inquires after the manager, and discovers that he is the man with the broom. One has an errand in some other business and sees the manager, hat on head and in shirt sleeves, about to polish his own boots. With an Anglo-American acquaintance one visits a barroom, perhaps that of the Woodruff House or that of the Broadway Exchange, to enjoy a morning drink. Various roasts steam upon the table, next to them rises a small pile of plates, and beside it stands a basket with knives and forks. While drinking, one observes that the other guests busily serve themselves. One does the same and takes a considerable portion of juicy roast beef or venison (standing, naturally). Finally, as one reaches into one's pocket to pay, the friend smilingly slaps him upon the shoulders and says: "For heaven's sake, keep your money. The lunch is *gratis*, and the barkeeper will laugh at you if he notices that you're so green." One walks for a distance down Main Street across the canal, and the companion gets one to stop at the pub that General Mohr[10] has established here. One returns and goes down to the landing where, if one is lucky, one sees on top of a mountain of flour barrels a gentleman dressed in black who is endeavoring to wash a few Moors white—in other words, trying to convince a group of red-nosed loafers that whiskey is a poison and that abstinence is the crown of all virtues.

Strange world! But the many red flags that are waving everywhere from the windows—what might they mean? Should they —no, Porkopolis, to be sure, is a headquarters of the Democrats, but only a few German scamps here claim to know anything about the Red Republic.[11] The bloody banners have the peaceful purpose of announcing to the public that an auction is being held in the building: books, clothing, liquors, or—a Mock Auction.[12]

Mock Auctions? says my friend. You are astonished at their boldness? Bah, go to the prophets of the camp meetings. The stream of pious eloquence flows from their lips like pure gold, and it's brass to him who knows their hearts. Stand on Fourth Street, the promenade of our aristocratic world. Do you think that the ladies who pass by with lowered eyes are the purest virgin gold? It seems so, certainly. But I could take you to our *assignation houses* where these virgin-gold paragons of virtue have rendezvous with their lovers behind their husbands' backs, and brass, damned brass you would say, as I do. Then visit our courts, where the little thieves are hanged and the big ones released on bond. Brass is their stock in trade, and the only gold that does not merely glitter is that with which they are bribed. Sometime listen to our lawyers. Have the biographies of our politicians, for example, that of the honest Webster, related to you. Recall how our elections are decided by hired loafers' fists; how the partisan newspapers stamped the noble, brave Harrison as a liar, ruffian, and coward; how they transformed the hundreds of sheep that another presidential candidate had had driven to market into just as many chained, whipped slaves upon whose backs the name "Polk" was branded; how they did this to draw away from Polk the abolitionists, who, for their part, again plated the brass self-interest of the North with the gold of universal brotherly love. Take a look at that church there. It's a splendid structure, isn't it, for whose erection a pious mind united with a love of art of the noblest metal? Oh, don't be taken in, dear sir! It's brass, it's speculation. Through the high-priced rental of seats and praying chairs they hope to do a profitable business. Listen, finally, to how our newspaper writers sell their columns to the highest bidder and gild the worst matter with the eagles that are pressed into their hands for this purpose. Do this, man, and you will shout out with me: Brass, humbug—all America is a single enormous Mock Auction!

◊ ◊ ◊ SEPTEMBER 19

How the sunrise smiles down from Sycamore Hill upon the page that I filled with faultfinding wisdom last night! Take it easy, good L., and you, mocking pen, that wrote down what he said! Don't look only at the dark side, and don't pour out the baby with the bathwater! Certainly, the unlimited liberty which is the property of this nation drives the evil in human nature to the surface with the same power that it brings to light the beautiful and the just. Certainly, the *go-ahead* system which is found here in the pineal gland of even the most ordinary fellows also has something demonic about it. Certainly, the inclination to haggling and faultfinding that is attached to almost every half-mature national character stamps upon the countenance of America a physiognomy that has a most repellent feature for the European, and particularly for the German. Here, certainly, the hypocrisy, the *cant* of which Thackeray accuses his countrymen in such vigorous language, is even more clever when it's a matter of wrapping a wolf's body in the skin of a lamb. Certainly, the scum of the Old World, which for many years formed a good part of the immigration, has perceptibly added its poisons to the blood of the humanity residing there. Certainly, dearest L., you are correct in comparing the Yankees with the Carthaginians of history. And, finally, it is certain that nearly all the Americans with whom I have had contact until now, and especially the Germans, have given a decided impression of being parvenus.

But let us also reflect that boils and tumors are not always a symptom of corrupt juices but are often merely signs of an overfull life. Let us recall not only the *punica fides* but also the greatness of Hannibal. Let us not judge abstractly, not by what is seen here and there in the streets, in this or that city. Let's not treat everyone alike. And let's keep in mind that here, besides patent-medicine doctors, mock-auctioneers, bank swindlers, venal demagogues, and others of that tribe, the demigod Washington was born. Moreover, poisonous plants remain small; only good trees grow tall. Let us look at the past, at the history of these parvenus. Could it be possible that they, with mere humbug, could have prevailed upon the Lord of this history to bestow upon them the greatness that they possess, and to open to them the future that they already consider attained? Place upon your balance also the restless striving, the dauntless endurance in the struggle with fate, the grandeur of vision when it's a matter of plans advantageous to all, and the extraordinary noblesse in the giving of credit —all of which are indisputably characteristics of the Anglo-American. But then, friend Timon, don't overlook the fact that the rising and falling in the destiny of individuals as well as in the fortunes of parties and sects clearly shows that here we are not yet dealing with a distinctly marked character portrait of a nation but with an unfinished moral chaos from which, perhaps, a complete, sound individual will emerge only after the passing of a century. Yankeedom is not the life of a person but the rule of a principle. Nations as well as individuals have to pass through a stage in which they still have no character but merely exhibit the growth of its germ. Tom Jones on the one hand, and Macbeth on the other, can teach you how the catastrophe occurs in which the character is born. Whatever lies before this catastrophe (for which America is still waiting) can be rightly attributed neither to the latter (the nation) nor to the former (the individual). And now, good friend, you will excuse it if a stranger has undertaken to instruct the citizen in his own city. But two neutral eyes often can see more in eight days than two others suffering from partisanship can see in eight years. Therefore let nothing of the manner in which you spoke to me yesterday be printed without tempering marginal glosses—one might say that your judgment walked upon only one leg or that you had written it with your left hand (which is, to be sure, that one closest to the heart, but it still is not the right hand).

So go on, wave on, you stars in the heavens, you stars upon the flag of America! Victory to your paths, blessings to your orbits! And you, gray eagle of Niagara, fly up, unconfused by the censure of the shortsighted, untroubled by the foxes who scorn the grapes they cannot reach—fly up to the sun which radiates your future, fly up with the motto *Excelsior!*

Cincinnati has two remarkable features that I have only touched upon until now: its vineyards and its cathedral, the largest Catholic church in the United States. Today I sampled the product of the former, having until now consumed only German wine, available in the best selection at Pfau's on Main Street. In fact, I had not expected to taste such a respectable Deidesheimer here in the interior of America; one gets to drink it here at a price only slightly higher than that at home. But also the blood of the Catawba grape is not simply to be scorned, and although the boasting that terms the Ohio "the American Rhine" is, for the time being, nothing more than boasting, still old Longworth[13] deserves a "Vivat!" for his efforts to obtain justice for the local grape. Herewith a toast to him and to his German winegrowers, and another to that good Swiss who fifty years ago became the Noah of Yankeeland in the transatlantic Vevay.[14]

The cultivation of the grapevine for purposes of wine manufacture has been attempted in various parts of the Union.[15] Grape culture has been undertaken near Philadelphia, near New York, in Berks County (Pennsylvania), in Georgia, and in South and North Carolina. But upon none of these districts has the son of the pretty-eyed Semele bestown his blessings in such lavish measure as upon the West, which accordingly excels also in this regard. The North proves too cold, and in the vineyards of the South the grape rot occurs too frequently for any successful development. The Mississippi Valley, on the other hand, fulfills all conditions for a rewarding practice of the winegrower's trade. Kentucky counts vineyards of considerable size, said to be in a thriving condition, at Maysville, Lexington, and Louisville. In the state of Indiana the grape plantings of Vevay cover about forty acres, and those of Charlestown over two hundred. Illinois has made a praiseworthy start in the vicinity of Belleville; and the German settlement of Hermann in Missouri has achieved surprising success. But Ohio is ahead of all of them. It has planted with grapevines no fewer than a thousand acres of the sunny hills of its southern border, and of that number nine-tenths are located in the vicinity of Cincinnati. Half of them have advanced so far that they are bearing. The yield for 1850 was estimated at 120,000 gallons. The winedealer Pf. [Pfau], to whom I owe these figures, believed that he could assert that the harvest would be doubled within the next three years and that, with the continuing transformation of suitable land into grape plantings, it could be quadrupled before the end of the decennium. To be sure, as yet nothing has been produced that could be compared with the extent of German viticulture; but in any case, the results until now have demonstrated that the matter returns a nice profit and that from the native Catawba grape a drink can be pressed that in time, when its producers have gathered more experience about its nature, will attain fame and respect. For the present, patriotism is required to declare it better than, say, the vintages of the Elbe and the Saale.

The local "Sons of Temperance" would disapprove, and the jokers among my friends at home would find therein a welcome mouthful, if I were to assert that the now-demonstrated feasibility of wine culture is one of the signs pointing to America's calling in history. Still, I believe that this thought contains a certain amount of truth. The Noah myth with its grapevine planted, in a certain sense, beneath the arch of grace and emphasized by Holy

Scripture as the first and most important product of the post-diluvian world, and thus placed alongside the lost tree of life of Paradise, the first and most important growth of the antediluvian world, as a counterpart and substitute, so to speak—this myth has a deeper and broader meaning than our rationalists find in it. In the same way the mystic cult of Dionysius points to the fact that in the character of this conquering god more is to be sought than the patron of taverns and tipplers. Just as prussic acid was termed "death incarnate" by a clever researcher, so wine represents in the field of things that which in the field of ideas is called "life." Thus a part of the world that bears no grapes cannot, it seems to me, bear any truly great, any unique, powerful, and independent nation, one that is "blessed" in the deepest significance of the word.

Yet these are German *daydreams,* and I am in a country where, at present, only the speculations of healthy human understanding have any rights.

The cathedral to which I paid a visit this afternoon is certainly an expensive building, but it is anything but beautiful. Not the faintest notion of harmony of the individual parts or of an understanding of the simplest principles of higher architecture. The queer fellow who put up this architectural chimera on the corner of *Plum Street* was surely incapable of creating anything original. It would have been better if he had contented himself (as his colleagues who have achieved something tolerable have done) with the copying of a European cathedral *en miniature* rather than calling into life such a monstrosity, for which the notion of a dancehall was the father and the idea of a Greek temple was the mother. To be sure, I can't say this to the local people. They consider their cathedral the pride of the entire West, and, to judge by what I have seen here until now of church architecture, they may be right. But I should not have to look too far for the European who, when he caught sight of this portico, carried by Corinthian columns, upon which stands a "nightcap" steeple glued together from all sorts of styles and pierced by cemetery crosses, and to which is attached, first, a large, dreary parallelogram with salon windows and then, completing the caricature, a three-story dwelling, the archbishop's residence—by Erwin von Steinbach's[16] square! I shouldn't have to look too far for the European who, standing before this pride of the West, would shout out with me: What an unforgivable insult to good taste, what a shameful ravaging of beautiful marble!

In the interior much splendor is displayed. Various paintings on glass, an altar carved by Chiapri in Genoa of Carrara marble, and a mighty organ with 2,700 pipes, built by the German master Schwab in Cincinnati, to some extent provide consolation for the disappointment experienced in regard to the expectation aroused by the name of "cathedral." In addition, however, the cathedral possesses a real treasure. Among the numerous oil paintings hanging on the walls, along with a number of mediocre engravings, can be found the *Liberation of Saint Peter by the Angel*, painted by Murillo and presented by Bishop Fenwick, who obtained it from the collection of Cardinal Fesch—a masterpiece of the famous Spaniard. However, it is not hung properly and cannot develop its full effect.

Among the remaining public buildings there is little worthy of noting. Everywhere that there is a disposition to the beautiful, it is choked by the utilitarian, with material striving attaching a disagreeable appendix to it. Here and there a columned façade looks out into the street, half-smothered by warehouses and sign-covered stores. Now and then one encounters an Episcopal church built in abbey style that would show up quite well if it were isolated and surrounded by foliage. Only those institutions dedicated to the direct needs of daily life occasionally have well-formed cases. The Burnett House with its splendid entrance steps, its colossal portico, and its dome; the Freemason's Hall; and the Mechanics Institute—these are structures that are tasteful as well as imposing.[17]

◊ ◊ ◊ The following pages again bear the character of an excursion, although not to the degree as those do which form the beginning of this chapter. They are a mosaic of that which was omitted in the preceding diary entries and in those to follow. The larger portion of the material used is based upon personal experience, and the hearsay remainder comes from conversations with men whom I consider objective (in line with the old saying that one raven doesn't pick out the eyes of another). Names and dates have been omitted, since I do not want to accuse either persons or corporate bodies, but only conditions. Whenever these have pressed the pen of satire into my hand, I have dipped it into moderation. The whole thing is, according to content, an extract, accompanied by marginal notes, from the chronicle of a German-Protestant congregation in Cincinnati. It shall be dedicated to those who declare that church conditions in the "Model Republic," and especially the absolute freedom by which these are shaped, deserve unqualified praise and envy. Above this painting of the pious groaners may stand the motto and device *Quod Deus bene vertat!*

But first a few words of explanatory introduction.

In religious matters the Germans in North America fall into two main factions: a Right and a Left. The majority belong to the former, which includes Catholicism, recruiting chiefly from Westphalia, the Rhine Province, and Bavaria; Methodism, for whose aims Wilhelm Nast has worked and fought with untiring zeal; Lutheranism; the Reformed Church; the Dunkard Union, to be counted with the Baptists; and the pietistic Albrights. Only a small number belong to the innumerable other religious communities, but Old Germany has delivered a small contingent even to the dancing Shakers and the Mormons. It can be accepted as a well-known fact that this Right forms the majority. Opposing it at all times there has existed a large mass of the anticlerical—with whom, as the dead who bury their own dead, we shall not deal here—and of the nonbelievers, the sum total of whom I include under the rubric Left. For a long time the Left, insofar as it gave off any signs of life at all, was limited to a very modest number of members. Ludvigh's *Fackel*,[18] spreading the light of vulgar enlightenment first from New York and now from Baltimore, had to be regarded as the organ of the more active Leftists, but generally the endeavors of this party were heard of only infrequently until recent years. Then the destiny which caused the Revolution of 1848 to fail sent over, in addition to other more worthy champions of the same, several shiploads of those gentlemen who at home had regarded it as their duty (or of advantage) to push over, along with the thrones of princes, the chair of God, so that there would be room for the dancing of the mob for which they played the music. They had hardly landed before they began their music here, too, with those earshattering trumpet blasts remembered well enough from those topsy-turvy years at home. Newspapers that offered them accomodations for their guest roles, helpers who blew their horns, handymen who took care of the echo in the background, lovers of brutality who applauded and screamed *da capo*—all were found here, as everywhere under the moon. From a feeling of annoyance with the vice and incompetence of their clergy, even better people now and then let themselves be misled into lending a willing ear to the approaching "reformation" (as the musicians termed their atheistic-communistic potpourri). Soon the former dance-

CINCINNATI

and concerthall had a completely different physiognomy. The light of the *Fackel* by which it was illuminated did not burn red enough; papers were founded that remedied this deficiency with a fire as red as hell. The members of the orchestra were not organized properly and fashionably—"Free Congregations"[19] were established, first in Saint Louis, and then in Cincinnati. Deism didn't sound sufficiently shrill and crude—to the notes was added a text, the refrain of which was the edict: The dynasty of God has ceased to reign! For the new gospel that was being trumpeted into the world a John the Baptist was lacking, but he, too, was found, and, to be sure, in the writings of Thomas Paine. A crier was needed to invite the people to take part in the sensational piece, a ruffian to slap properly the mouths of those who didn't like it, a Cerberus to defy from three mouths the "Philistines of Freedom," a strong man who could blow the trombone and beat ten drums at the same time, and behold! beneath the tongue of the mighty Karl Heinzen[20] sat all these demons, and in his inkwell a dozen others just as powerful. In a word: atheism attempted to play the role of a power and, in all seriousness, declared life-and-death war upon the opposition with a flood of incendiary and abusive articles.

What was the result? Sound and wind, as with any bad music, and, in addition, disgrace and shame. Basically, the only certain result was that this fury that behaved as though it were the most sublime extract of our philosophy exposed the poor German name to ridicule before the Anglo-Americans in the most thorough and contemptible fashion.

However, these gentlemen of the great knife had neither eye nor ear for this [result], and so, despite many a loud "Shame!" this Walpurgis-Night's Dream of German-American atheism still plays on merrily today. Midgets attack strongholds most courageously, poodles stare like lions, honest loaferdom swaggers in hero's armor or martyr's garments through the astonished streets. Gnats, with incomprehensible naïveté, allow themselves to be admired as eagles and penny lamps as suns, and the paper of the newspapers endures it with touching patience when the strength of the horse is claimed for grasshoppers and trash piles are praised as the salt of the earth. So things continue to buzz and rumble, to hum and rattle, until someday the time will come when the geniuses up there will also sing the final verse of this intermezzo:

> Cloud and trailing mist o'erhead
> Are now illuminated:

> Air in leaves, and wind in reed,
> And all is dissipated.[21]

About the center, between this Left and that Right, stand a number of souls and shepherds whose creed runs to a more or less moderate rationalism. They recognize no fundamental difference between Lutheran and Calvinistic doctrine, and, since their clergy are not organized in synods like the orthodox ones, they, too, can be considered "free congregations." As far as I was able to find out under the circumstances, they are rather numerous in the West, have four churches in Cincinnati, and in the *Protestantischen Zeitblättern* published there possess an organ that upholds their opinions and interests.[22] The reader will find out in the following description how they split up and take on new forms, how they manage their affairs, and in whose spirit their preachers hold sway. This, however, should be preceded by a statement that the censure expressed therein applies in no lesser degree to many of those who emphatically call themselves orthodox.

In all sorts of respects the German Protestant population of Cincinnati is separated quite clearly into High and Low Germans, and one can scarcely believe with what smalltown narrowmindedness and with what disgusting thickheadedness the old discord is expressed here at times. When the need was felt for a common worship service according to the custom and in the language of the homeland, it was principally the High Germans who gathered in a private residence to listen to religious talks given by a merchant. Little by little the number of participants in these devotional hours grew to the point where they could think about the erection of a church and the hiring of a regular preacher. This happened while the High Germans were still in the majority, and so they looked upon themselves as the founders and owners of the church even after the Low Germans had gradually become the majority and now demanded consideration for their wishes. As a result, disputes and petty faultfinding of all sorts occurred whenever a decision had to be reached about any subject. The mutual ill will grew more bitter from day to day, and this factional hatred led to an actual fist fight in the church on the occasion of the selection of a new pastor. Finally, after the High Germans had regained the upper hand through all kinds of tricks and intrigues (they even bought members at five dollars a head), it was decided to separate. The Low Germans built their own church with the sum of money paid them for their interest by those remaining, and from now on the new congregation experienced a few years of tolerable harmony. Then the pastor died suddenly, and, in the selection of a new one, the discord broke out again. Two of the announced candidates gained strong support, one because he was an eloquent speaker, the other because he "spoke" Low German fluently. The supporters of the latter being the more numerous, they carried away the victory and, as the trophy, a pastor who, although devoted to drink in a scandalous way, still occupies the position. The minority thereupon announced its secession and purchased an old Presbyterian church in which it constituted itself as the third German-Protestant congregation. They had a lot of bad luck with their preachers. One deserted them twice for more profitable occupations. Another was unmasked after a few weeks as an orthodox [Lutheran] and when given notice changed over to Catholicism for a bit of money (as my informant believed). A third was too greedy even for local standards and, through incompetence and laziness in the performance of his duties, had caused damage and injury to the "collection plate" of the congregation; it meanwhile had gone into debt through the construction of a new house of worship. Hence when I arrived in Cincinnati the congregation was about to replace the unfit hireling with a more suitable subject.

A "subject"? This expression is all too justified in more than one respect. First, the pastor of such a congregation is not a "Servant of the Word" (as he signs himself) but a servant of those who pay his salary. Seldom is he hired for more than a one-year term, and if during this period he makes himself unpopular with any tradesman with influence, then he is not reappointed at the end of his term. In some cases the members dissatisfied with him secede and his income is accordingly diminished. "We want a preacher who on Sundays puts us into the proper frame of mind, who baptizes our children, blesses our bridal couples, and buries our dead; but we want no Pope"—this, approximately, is the basic thought of all constitutions under which these congregations are formed, and in many respects such caution is praiseworthy. However, since everything has two sides, the bad consequence of this jealousy of sovereignty established by law is that positions thus restricted and depressed in value are applied for only by persons who are subservient. Consequently, these people, with few exceptions, behave like bad servants, that is, they put their own advantage ahead of all other considerations. From this, then, results a bottomless brutalization in all these matters, which, since it does not attract attention in the generally prevailing pursuit of wealth and is checked only when it gets excessively out of hand, produces the most disgusting characters and situations. The profession of clergyman is above all a business, and again a business, and finally again a business. The congregation is a cow to be milked, the pulpit a source of money, and all thinking and planning are directed toward making the cow and the source as productive as possible. One preaches as desired. One is ready at all times to adapt to the situation—today, when the majority is pleased by a free skipping about with Christian truth, one serves with a mien of enlightenment; tomorrow, when the majority desires the correct faith and the pure doctrine, one attends with the unctuous countenance of orthodoxy. I have met men whose talk clearly indicated that they could have changed their skins nine times before the moon changed its coat three times. And how well one knows how to entice members of other congregations into one's own—through a thousand kinds of intrigues, through lies and slander of colleagues, and through flattery! And how roughly one defends oneself when the Jesuits come from one corner and the atheists from the other to chase the ravens away from the carrion!

It's true that there are also some honorable men here to whom one must take off one's hat and bow all the more deeply, since under such circumstances it is difficult to preserve one's dignity and moral feelings. But as far as my experience goes, such exceptions are rare. How the representatives of the clergy think about this is shown quite clearly by the reply that Pastor——gave to a friend in General Mohr's pub in response to the friend's criticism. "Do you believe, dear friend," smiled this stout theological Eumaeus, "that I shall remain a pastor forever? *No Siree,* as soon as I have collected the necessary sum, I shall go into the hog business."

Hog business? That's strong, stronger than you might have thought, isn't it, Mr. Ecclesiastical Councillor? Keep calm. The man had been a butcher before he turned to the preaching profession, and so his train of thought was only a bit abrupt and surprising for me. Most of his colleagues would have seen in his honesty nothing more than a small violation of decorum; for sidelines similar to just such porkopolitanian ideas, for example, speculations in buildings or merchant goods, form the background of all their endeavors.

Anyway, all this could be tolerated until a better time. But what should be said about the activities of those theological tramps who wander from place to place in the West, hunting for positions? Almost everywhere that the need for a minister gets them an office, they disappear after a short stay, leaving behind rumors that remind one of the children of Beelzebub! Listen to a few samples from the lives of these vagabonds and judge from these as to the tone prevailing among them. It should not be forgotten that the scene is limited to the Ohio Valley and that the time during which these incidents occurred was a short period of about ten months.

A congregation received an application for the pastorship from a young gentleman who displayed an excellent diploma from a German university. He was hired, preached for a few months with approval, and made himself liked by all through his adroit manner. Suddenly he was up and gone. It turned out that the pastor had been an unemployed actor, that his beautiful diploma had been printed in the editorial office of the *New York Democrat,* and that he had departed on account of several serious burglaries.

A similar example of a wolf in sheep's clothing was prosecuted by the police during my stay in Cincinnati because he had repaid a friend with whom he shared a hotel room for this favor by relieving his pocketbook of sixty dollars.

Pastor Kr. related a third nice little anecdote about one of these vagabonds. He had fooled everyone with his sentimental lies, had collected contributions everywhere, and had finally obtained a little ministry for himself. Then he had been unmasked one fine morning as the thief of a gold watch. To avoid scandal, the congregation had reimbursed the victim and had chased away the culprit with a good beating. Thereupon he had fled to the pale of the Roman-Apostolic Church, the representatives of which had been unwise enough to ordain him, so that he now reads mass quite neatly and cheerfully in a Cincinnati suburb.

A fourth edifying incident occurred during the filling of the ministry in the Walnut Street Church in Cincinnati. One of the candidates for the position knew in advance that his efforts were labor lost, and he therefore decided to play a trick upon the praiseworthy church committee. Having entered the pulpit, he announced to the congregation that he would preach a sermon on the text "Fear God and keep His commandments." He then spoke a little about the fear, then talked for a while about God, and finally began with the commandments, which he recited one by one. At the sixth,[23] the violation of which had gained him his bad reputation, he stopped for a moment and acted as though he had to think about it. He then continued: "Well, folks, why should I rattle them all off? You all know them by heart. But do you obey them? No, I'm sure of it, for I don't do so myself. Amen!"

My diary contains various other tales of the same stamp. But this should be enough, and I'll save for another occasion the drunkards, the prevaricators, and the secret sinners whose portraits form my little gallery. Instead of presenting them, the following genre picture may be used as an illustration of the relationship between preacher and congregation.

Following advertisement by the church committee, nineteen candidates had applied for the above-mentioned vacated minister's position in Cincinnati. Among them were: a shoemaker who in his test sermon gave such a realistic portrayal of Michael's struggle with the dragon that it seemed as though he must have served as a second to the archangel in this heroic feat; a physician from Hamburg who came from a city in Kentucky where he had practiced medicine and theology at the same time; a ruined bookseller from Leipzig who had fled from Chicago because of embezzlement of subscriptions to a rationalistic "confusion sheet" published by him and had then wandered down to the Ohio, half begging and half preaching; further, a native of Baden who claimed to have been a pastor in the Black Forest until 1849 and later president of the Revolutionary Assembly;[24] then an ordinary farmer who, however, despite his clumsy eloquence, or perhaps just because of it, was not without prospects; and finally a Prussian jurist who, at home, after serving a prison term because of a sweet tooth for cash (as an acquaintance put it), had run a leather business in Magdeburg.

The outgoing pastor, supported, as a member of the Odd Fellows, by a weak but active minority, was determined to resist the church committee that wished to dismiss him. He was ready for extreme measures and had threatened to expel by force any candidate who dared to enter the pulpit which belonged to him until the end of the year. On the other hand, in the opinion of the majority he had lost all rights through the insubordinate and unseemly demeanor reported in the first of the preceding diary entries. From this conflict of views a most unedifying scene developed when the first of the arriving candidates (a real theologian, by the way) began to give his test sermon.

The candidate in question had been fetched from his hotel by the church committee and had been solemnly introduced. He was already sitting before the altar, the organ had played, the congregation had sung, and the preacher had just gotten up to pray, when suddenly the folding doors flew open and the fat, red face of the deposed pastor appeared upon the threshold. Throwing back his head, he strode up the center aisle like an angry turkey, apparently with the intention of chasing the congregation's candidate away from the altar. Then two robust members of the church committee stepped into his path and politely directed him toward a seat in the nave, as though he had come to hear the visiting colleague. He declined this suggestion with angry gestures and tried to push on. Held back, he became louder and louder, and there commenced a violent parleying back and forth, in which several other members gradually joined. Threatening murmurs from various pews announced the approach of a general storm. The ladies were already making preparations to depart when the candidate, wisely enough perceiving that any shocking incident would be at least partly attributed to him (even though he was acting only in accordance with the will of the majority), took his hat, came down from the altar, went up to the furious pastor, and said to him: "Mr. Preacher, if you have come to claim the pulpit, I, for my part, will gladly give it up to you—not because I recognize your claim to it but because I should not wish to be the cause of a disturbance in the House of God." Therewith he left the place, despite the church committee's protests requesting him to remain. However, the obtrusive ex-pastor was now thrown out, accompanied by violent drumming and stamping, and the church closed. A few days later the mayor punished the ex-pastor for his impropriety with a fine of ten dollars, and from now on the candidates gave their sermons without disturbance.

In these tests of eloquence, the only ones that can be given, the custom prevails that the speaker has to preach two sermons, both on the same day. In the first he has a free choice of the text; in the second, however, after he has entered the pulpit, he is brought a basket containing slips from which he must select one at random. Various passages from the Bible are found on these slips, and the candidate, without reflection, must give a sermon about that text which chance has placed in his hands. The results of such tricks can well be imagined.

When it finally came time to make a choice among the various candidates, it turned out that almost every one of them found support, great or little. The physician, despite the bad reputation that had followed him from Louisville, had many on his side just because he was a Low German. The jurist–leather dealer, despite the fact that he walked on crutches, found much favor because of his fluent extemporaneous speech.

The ex-president of the Baden Assembly had made a point of emphasizing his position as a political refugee and, at the same time, in a pleading letter, his bad situation as the father of a family. The Archangel Michael's second, finally, had all the supporters of the deposed pastor as his patrons; he was the most miserable fellow of all, and his selection would cause a considerable number of members to leave, thus weakening the congregation and destroying it financially.

There is no space here to describe the activities of these supporters. It's enough to report that they finally decided upon a preliminary selection which would select for the final choice the three candidates whose names got the most votes. In the meeting held for this purpose the long-restrained anger broke out in bright flame. They fought: first with reasonable arguments, then with words of abuse, and finally with fists. A magnificent fight, with all the appurtenances of bloody noses, smashed pews, and ripped jackets, turned the church in which the council was being held into a battlefield. If the congregation had not been held back by the fear of threatening bankruptcy, who knows whether the end of the song would not have been a general rupture and a scattering of the individual members to all four winds!

# 3

## A SHAKER TOWN
## AND A DUNKARD MEETING

◊ ◊ ◊ NOT since the fire of the Reformation was extinguished by dogmatism has the religious spirit expressed itself in any part of the Christian world as powerfully as among the peoples of the United States—and in no place as chaotically and strangely. Compared to our conditions, the life of the Christian Church in America seems almost like a remnant of the fantastically fluid primeval world alongside the solid regularity and rational dryness of present-day nature. Beneath the crust of a rigid and obstinate orthodoxy (such as could not have behaved more stiffly and boringly in the time of Calov and Quenstedt[1]) has boiled since the arrival of the first Puritan ship on Plymouth's shores, and still boils and flows today, a volcanic wonder-fire. At times it runs through the land in the form of will-o'-the-wisps, so that rational people, confused, shake their heads about it; and at other times it flames up in intense revivals. After having overturned earlier principles of faith by supernatural strength and having ignited the minds of the masses with its fervor, it deposits as slag the constitution of a new sect. The spirit which once descended upon the disciples in flaming tongues is still dispensed here in abundance, and every year thousands do not merely celebrate but actually experience a Pentecost. In many circles speaking in tongues is as common as it was in the days of the apostles. Devils are driven out of possessed women without the exorcist having taken any lessons in the art from Dr. Justinus[2] of Weinsberg, and among these believers angels and archangels still communicate with the children of Adam on a "thou" basis. In short, the stranger observing such conditions (at times from their light side, at other times from their dark, mysterious, and grotesque side) might occasionally be in doubt for a while as to whether or not he had strayed into regions where time had slept away two entire centuries of progress and enlightenment—unless at the same time his glance fell upon the telegraph lines running through the primeval forest and upon the steamboat fleets of the country's rivers.

Or what person not directed to a study of the American sects by a special need would dream that on the banks of the Cocalico in Pennsylvania an institution such as the German Anabaptist Cloister of Ephrata could arise? And who would accept it as the truth if he were told, without further preparation, that not two miles from the capital of New York there exists a settlement of people—and otherwise quite reasonable and worthy people—who believe in all seriousness that they must worship God by dancing and subscribe to the view, just as seriously, that the second coming of Christ has already taken place in the form of a woman? And finally, what European German taken suddenly from his well-ordered Sunday service (running smoothly according to the rules) to the moaning and uproar of a prayer meeting of the Methodists or the Albrights[3] would not like to make the sign of the cross, be he Catholic or Protestant, and call out: I thank thee, God, that I am not as other men are?

It is true that such a cry was once uttered by a Pharisee, and the Pharisees are not exactly in the best repute. Despite this, the author of the following sketches, in including some of them, has no hesitation about joining that Pharisee. Indeed, he believes that many a German theologian would have permitted himself quite different expressions if he had stood beside him as often as the spectacles reported in the following were performed.

◊ ◊ ◊ The week from the twenty-first to the twenty-eighth of September was spent in railroad excursions and walking tours in southern Ohio. I visited CHILLICOTHE, the former state capital, and from there went up the Scioto to CIRCLEVILLE and the fertile Pickaway Plains. Here, some seventy years before, stood the villages of the Indians whose war parties were the terror of the entire Ohio Valley. I then turned toward the west, stopped for a day in the vicinity of the spa YELLOW SPRINGS in Greene County, saw the pretty waterfall of CLIFTON, and became acquainted with farmers and farms near SPRINGFIELD. In WEST BOSTON I had the place pointed out to me where once stood the wigwam in which Tecumseh, the celebrated chief of the Shawnees, had been born. Finally, on the evening of the twenty-seventh, without having experienced any adventure worth reporting, I reached the seat of Montgomery County, DAYTON, situated on the east bank of the Big Miami. Here I spent many pleasant and instructive days among relatives and friends.

Dayton is undoubtedly the handsomest city between the two Miamis, perhaps even the prettiest between the Ohio and the Northern Lakes. A most pleasant impression is made by the streets, straight as a line and eight carriage tracks wide, by the elegant homes, situated in green orchards, and by the charming views into the surrounding dark, leafy forest. The eye of the stranger, which here is offended by so many an architectural monstrosity, can again relax on Dayton's magnificently beautiful courthouse, next to which that of the Porkopolis Cincinnati would stand out like a goat shed beside a Greek temple.

But the "Star of the West"—as the oratorically pompous Buckeye has been pleased to christen the town—is not only a very friendly and, incidentally, very busy place, but it has the reputation of being an unusually pious city. If one can conclude from the number of churches the number of godly people, then the twenty-one houses of God of the approximately thirteen thousand inhabitants prove that there is some truth to this report. The piety, however, is of a very mixed nature. Dayton represents a rather complete sample card of the entire American sectarian life, and anyone desiring to become acquainted with the life within this confessional confusion need hardly look any further. Here he encounters white and black Methodists, Albrights, Catholics, Lutherans, and Reformed of the German and English tongues. Further, he can visit congregations of the Episcopal Church, of the Baptists, Presbyterians, Unitarians, Universalists, and Congregationalists. Finally, he finds here a meeting house of the Dunkards and even a half dozen Mormons. On market days he will also encounter a few members of the strange Shaker sect (described even more strangely by many travelers) that has one of its settlements six English miles from here.

On the way from Columbus to Cincinnati my attention had

already been especially directed toward these latter, and so I resolved to pay a visit there first of all. The third of October was selected. The colony, which has the name WATERVLIET (but is simply called the "Shaker Town" by most people), lies southeast of Dayton on a road which branches off from the main highway to Cincinnati, at the edge of the valley, the floor of which is covered in part by the just-mentioned town. It is a branch of the oldest and largest western settlement of the sect at Union Village, and it was established in the year 1812.[4]

It was a beautiful, clear afternoon when I left for the mysterious Shaker Town. A cheerful, deep blue sky extended over the endless forest which shades the entire region (except for the clearings where there are towns or cultivated fields), and the groves of oak, maple, walnut, and hickory were decked out in their most colorful fall foliage. The road, closed in by those ugly Virginia rail fences, wound over the hills. It was bordered on both sides by prosperous farms. Standing in the centers of these farms were tasteful homes, whitewashed and decorated with green shutters and surrounded by abundant cornfields and well-kept peach orchards. Herds of fat-bellied hogs in the fat of their mast grunted at the passers-by. Flocks of turkeys, picking up grain, tripped around the crudely built log sheds, from the cracks and crevices of which the blessings of the previous year's corn harvest were about to spill forth. Blue and red birds, similar in size to our doves,[5] gave forth their monotonous twittering from the twigs of gigantic tree-vines and flitted on rapid wings back into the dark depths of the forest whenever steps approached. Among these scenes of rural comfort and most peaceful prosperity—scenes for which one might only have wished somewhat more voice—I strode on vigorously, until finally an old woman, coming toward me from a side road, pointed out with the tip of her Irish tobacco pipe (from the stem of which she let little clouds of fragrant Cavendish's well up smartly under her bonnet) a group of houses at the foot of the wooded hills to my right; this was the goal of my excursion.

A few hundred more steps and I stood on the grounds of the settlement. A broad lane turning off from the main road cutting through this area led up to the buildings. In the right angle formed by the latter with the former is situated the small cemetery of the community. It is a simple, neglected grassy plot, without mounds, without crosses, and without flowers. In general it is marked as a place of burial only by a few plain stones betraying neither chisel nor style but having the appearance of having been simply picked up as they lay in a field a short distance away and put down again here. Opposite the place of the dead stands a two-story frame house painted a striking egg-yolk yellow. I found out later that it once had been the shelter of a "Family," but at this time, when the number of Shakers located here had decreased considerably, it was completely unoccupied. Continuing on, I reached the other buildings of the settlement; there might have been about a dozen. They are all built of wood, with the exception of the large residence hall of the community.

Looking back toward the east, the eye surveys a rather large area of tillable land that slopes down gradually in that direction. The excellent cultivation and the broad expanse of these fields indicate that the Shakers are not merely industrious worshipers but also capable farmers. From the west, however, the forest pushes down into the colony; here the boundaries consist of a few small houses and an extensive orchard of peach and apple trees.

No living creature, except for a herd of well-fed cattle, had been seen inside the fence until now; and except for the murmuring of Beaver Creek, which here meanders between thickets, not a sound had been heard. It was a painful silence that seemed to conceal within itself a mystery; it bestowed upon the large brick house in the center (not in itself mysterious) that gloomy character which Protestants associate with cloisters. Undecided as to whether I should enter, and how I should introduce myself, I walked back and forth. Then I suddenly noticed, a few steps from me, a man coming from the forest; his head was lowered and his hands were upon his back. He wore a straw hat with an unusually broad brim and a gray blue, strangely cut jacket. His wrinkled face was deathly pale, and when, upon approaching me, he raised his eyes, I believed that I saw in them the look of insanity. Yet I could have been deceived, the eeriness of the situation could have misled me, and so, despite my unfavorable opinion as to the mental condition of the stranger, I dared to address him, for he obviously was a Shaker. However, I had not been wrong. To my questions as to whether I could obtain entrance here and whether I could inspect the interior arrangement of the settlement, I received as answer an inarticulate babbling and growling.

To be sure, it didn't sound malicious, but it didn't have much of a human quality to it.

In this embarrassment, I had to regard almost as a rescue from distress the appearance of a friendly old man in Shaker costume who stepped forth from the door of the mentioned main building and inquired as to my wishes. I repeated for him the occasion and purpose of my visit and received a favorable reply. Anyone with an honest desire to learn about their teachings and form of worship who requested entrance into their houses was welcome at all times. However, the rules required that he announce me to the First Elder before a definite consent could be given. I now told him who I was and from where I had come and how, a few months before, I had left my homeland, five thousand miles from here, in order to familiarize myself with America and especially its religious conditions. That seemed to increase his confidence. He reflected for a moment and then asked me to follow him into the house.

The door led first into an entrance hall about thirty paces long and rather wide. Its yellow-painted floor was covered in the center by narrow mats. From its white walls, wainscoted in brown from the floor up to a man's height, several doors opened on both sides. Everything bore the stamp of extraordinary cleanliness and minute love of order, but here, too, not the slightest breath broke the deathlike silence of the place.

My guide rapped on the first door to the right. "*Come in!*" a deep bass voice called, and we entered. At a window opposite the entrance sat a man of about forty, busy with the weaving of a straw hat. Like the madman outside, he wore a gray blue jacket, which at the back, beneath the collar, was arranged in pleats like a smock; a like-colored vest; and wide, coffee brown trousers. Everything was made of that coarse woolen material that here bears the name *homespun* and is worn by the farmers of the West almost exclusively. His hair was cut short over his forehead in the shape of a half moon, while it hung down long at the back of his neck. A pair of large silver spectacles did not seem exactly appropriate to this suit, which was such as had been worn in America by country people of the East some fifty years before. He rose at my greeting, shook my hand with the customary *how do you do*, took down one of the rocking chairs hanging around on the wall from pegs, and invited me to sit down. The first words of our conversation convinced us that we were

## A SHAKER TOWN

fellow countrymen, and so, when my guide departed after a short stay, there no longer was any reason not to continue the talk in the more convenient language of our mothers.

The Shaker in whose room I found myself was indeed a German. From his dialect he seemed to be from the region of Hamburg. His familiarity with the conditions and personalities at our universities indicated that he probably had studied at one of them. The skillful manner in which he presented, with a few strokes, a summary of the beliefs and life of his sect led me to suspect a theologian. For the present he spoke about himself very cautiously, but the look and tone with which he accompanied his hints gave the impression that he had something on his mind that he was holding back from his tongue only with effort. In his presentation he emphasized with special eagerness the least striking teachings of the Shakers, asking after each statement: "Is that nonsense?" No matter how else matters stood, his faith in Anna Lee, the female messiah of the sect, was by no means beyond all doubt.

Postponing to a later occasion a short characterization of the Shaker confession, I here report only that part of our conversation having to do with the social organization of the local colony. At this time it consists of only one "Family," that is, community, while the neighboring settlement at Union Village has three of them. The Family in Watervliet contains fifty-four souls, two-thirds of them women. All of them together occupy one house in which the sexes are distributed in this manner: the females take up the rooms on the left side in both stories, while the men occupy the rooms to the right. Here they dwell in spacious, light, whitewashed rooms, wainscoted in brown like the entrance hall. These are furnished with large beds, old-fashioned chests, and homemade easy chairs and rocking chairs woven of wood strips. The management in spiritual as well as worldly matters is in the hands of four elders, two of each sex. A deacon among them takes care of communication with the outside world, as, for example, arranging for supplies, the taking in and paying out of money, the housing of visiting strangers, etc. It is the business of these elders to distribute the necessary work among the members of the Family according to strength and talent. It is also expected, on the other hand, that the conscience of each individual will drive him to fulfill his obligation according to this measure. Force is not employed. In general, anger and quarrels, insubordination and bad will are guests that seldom disturb the quiet and peace of these silent people. The local colonists engage in the manufacture of coarse woolstuff, in wheelwright's work, in the weaving of straw goods, and, above all, in agriculture and the breeding of cattle on the 600-acre farm belonging to the community. On the basis of location and soil the land is excellent, and no farmer in a wide area outdoes them in the production of fruit and cattle. Everywhere the "Shaker Sarsaparilla" is a famous article of trade. Their cattle are the fattest in the entire county. Their wheat is usually sold above the market price. Although the apples had failed this year in all other localities in Ohio, their orchard had produced as abundantly as ever, and during the past summer they had sold $250 worth of strawberries alone.

All of this—the movable as well as the unmovable property, the land as well as the produce—is the common possession of the entire community, in accordance with the guiding principle of *"one body and one bread."* In other words, the Shakers are "communists"[6] as far as their social organization is concerned. All share equally in the possession, each member's portion being neither decreased by laziness or inability to work nor increased by industry or skill. No one can ask for a separation of his share, to use and enjoy according to his judgment. Every new brother, and likewise every new sister, through the act of his or her entrance into the "Millennial Church"—an act which must be accompanied by the assignment of all personal property to the Family of which they become members—acquires all rights of the older church members and remains in the enjoyment of the same as long as he or she stays in the community. Finally, no one leaving can demand the surrender of the property handed over by him upon entrance or that earned during his stay in the colony. However, it is the custom in such rare cases that a portion of the money or property in question is given to the apostate to take with him *"as an object of charity,"* thus only as alms. Like all Shaker settlements, Watervliet has worked itself up from extreme want to high well-being. Every recent accounting has shown a considerable surplus; this is used for the improvement and beautification of the colony, for the printing of their generally very splendidly gotten-up religious books, and, above all, for welfare purposes.

Namely, around the beginning of winter there appear before the gates of the local settlement (which is a so-called *gathering order,* that is, a house of novitiate from which the proselytes gained

for the Shakers are sent on to Union Village after having
passed their period of preparation and testing) numerous flocks
of shelterless beggars and vagabonds. They apply for admission to
the church simply because they have no bread and no bed, or,
to state their intention more clearly, because they wish to share in
the good meals and warm rooms of the brethren and sisters.
The Shakers know quite well that such worldly needs, and not a
yearning for the Cross and the Bride of Christ, bring these people
to them. Nevertheless, no one who knocks is refused. Although
Brother Harmon, my reporter, complained that by far the overwhelming majority of these birds, after having been fed and clothed
throughout the winter, at the greening of the trees next spring
flew out again into the world and worldliness, without thanks and
leave, the leaders seem to find in the winning of the few souls
who remain with them from the flood of those flocking in
and who, at least in this way, renounce a useless life spent in
half-animal crudeness, sufficient compensation for the loss of the
remainder.

These and similar reports, interrupted frequently by visits
from curious brethren who wanted to see the stranger who had
come from so far, had held me up until late afternoon. Since
a promise prevented me from accepting the invitations to
stay extended urgently by all, preparations for my return home had
to be made, if I were not to be overtaken by nightfall along the
way. Brother Harmon ("Hermann" translated into English)
accompanied me and showed me the various farm buildings: the
workhouse of the sisters; the sap-green-painted office of the
Deacon, which also serves as quarters for visiting brethren; the
little white cabin in which profane strangers are housed;
the school where the friendly old man who had introduced me
instructed four boys; the carriageworks; and the meetinghouse of
the colony—a simple frame building without any decoration
or adornment, without any steeple and bell, even without any
symbol that would reveal its designation as a place of worship.
A footbridge across Beaver Creek then took us to the dyeworks and to
the shop where they prepare their clothing material. Here I was
introduced to one of the leaders of the settlement, Elder Richard
Pelham,[7] who was sitting behind his loom. I then bade farewell to
my new acquaintance, not, however, without having to repeat
most solemnly my already given promise that I would return the
following day and stay longer.

Attracted not so much by the secret that Brother Harmon

intended to reveal to me upon fulfillment of this pledge as by my
desire to see the Shakers perform their famous dervish dance,
I again walked out to Watervliet the next noon. A pleasant
American who caught up with me on the hilltop offered me, un-
solicited, a ride in his buggy. Since a race soon started between
this buggy and a following specimen of that neat type of
conveyance—one of those races in which the Yankee wants to
outrun the wind at the risk of his limbs—I stood before my
friend's door an hour earlier than I had expected.

I met him alone in his room, reading Dunlavy's *Manifesto*.\*
He got up joyously, and no sooner had he closed the door
and assured himself excessively that no dangerous eavesdropper
was hidden beneath his window, than his secret flowed from
his lips. It consisted of no more and no less than the request to
help him get away secretly from the colony in which life had become
a burden to him.

That was unexpected, if not exactly incomprehensible. He
had studied theology in Kiel, had been induced (because of
unfortunate cirumstances that he didn't go into) to come to America
in August 1849, and in October 1850 had sought refuge from
the pangs of hunger and the winter cold in the bosom of the thousand-
year church, just like the beggar-birds that he had criticized
yesterday. He now wanted to use this opportunity to escape from
the holy cage which had become a torture to him. To be sure,
he had been treated with gentleness and love. At first he had been
given only light manual labor, then the education of several
children had been entrusted to him, and finally he had been assigned
the supervision of three novices. In addition he had been
provided more abundantly than ever before with everything
pertinent to life's nourishment and necessities. He really had
nothing to complain about, except that to which he had sentenced
himself: the loss of his freedom and the compulsion of having
to feign a faith every day that he did not possess. On the other hand,
he was able to depict so touchingly the wretched state in which
he had sought asylum here, in rags and half starved; the spiritual
suffering that had torn him up inside since his arrival and

---

\* The most important of the religious writings of the sect. The others are *The Testimony of Christ's Second Appearing*, 3d ed., New Lebanon [N.Y.], 1823; *A Holy, Sacred and Divine Roll and Book from the Lord God of Heaven to the Inhabitants of Earth*, Canterbury [N.H.], 1843; and *A Summary View of the Millennial Church or United Society of Believers, Commonly Called Shakers*, 2d ed., Albany [N.Y.], 1848.

had brought him close to insanity; and, finally, the impossibility of fleeing out into the world in Shaker costume (which, besides, he would have to take away like a thief), that every heart would have had to be sympathetic, even if it were covered with a horny skin as thick as that of our horny Siegfried.

The entrance of a brother who asked us to leave the room, since the sisters were coming very shortly to check the linen supply, relieved me temporarily of the nevertheless indubitable necessity of answering this strange confession with a most possibly considerate paraphrase of the well-known *"tu l'as voulu, George Dandin"*[8] and of declining the request to be a guide in this surreptitious project.

We went to the office, where Deacon David,[9] a morose giant with large, pale blue eyes, was warming himself in a rocking chair near the stove, although it was at least fifteen degrees outside.[10] The frequently halting conversation was concerned with unimportant matters. Also there was nothing remarkable about the room: it was whitewashed like all the others, and from two brown pegboards on the walls hung wood-slat chairs and straw hats. Brother Harmon gave himself over to his troubled thoughts, and the monosyllabic David finally closed his eyelids for an Ambrosian slumber. The situation had developed to hopeless boredom when Elder Pelham entered. He was a small, thin, quick man with dark hair and fiery black eyes. With him life came into the party, and soon a brisk conversation ensued that led us in a few minutes into the Holy and the Most Holy of Shakerdom. He began by asking me not to address him with "Sir" and not to put a "Mister" before his name; in turn he would call me only "Friend Maurice." Such a show of titles was vain tawdriness to the successors to Christ and was therefore avoided by them. Starting from this custom, he then explained in detail the commandments and the belief of his sect. At times asking and answering, at times passing over more into the tone and flow of a sermon, he gave a very lucid and graphic summary of the spiritual possession of the Millennial Church, whereby attention was directed, if not to my conversion, at least to my conviction. He spoke very fluently, refuted cleverly, revealed that he was uncommonly well versed in the Scriptures, and used bold and original images. In short, it was a real pleasure to listen to him, and even the zeal bordering on fanaticism with which he spoke was not without a certain pleasing dedication.

Here I should like to give only a summary survey of the faith that Elder Pelham confessed, limiting my presentation out of consideration for the nontheological reader. However, before I do this, I should like to be permitted a few lines about the history of this strangest of all Christians sects in existence today.

The *Shakers*—or, as they call themselves, "the United Society of Believers of the Millennial Church"—did not, as Hase's church history[11] teaches, originate from the Methodists, and not in Wales; they therefore are not to be regarded as one and the same with the English *Jumpers*. Rather, they trace their origin back to the so-called Convulsionaires or, as they are called in the *Summary View of the Millennial Church*, the "French Prophets." These appeared at the end of the seventeenth century in the Dauphiné and in the Cévennes and produced a great awakening of the religious spirit accompanied by mysterious mental states in which heavenly visions were seen, people spoke in tongues, prophesied, and with convulsions and twitchings called upon God for mercy upon sinful mankind. In the year 1705 three of their most outstanding preachers, Elias Marlon, Jean Cavilier, and Durand Fage, left France for England, where they taught in London and gave witness against the Antichrist. Finding little success and frequently persecuted, they moved from there to Scotland and then to the Netherlands, where they finally disappeared.

They had also visited Lancashire, and there, in the town of Bolton, the tailor Wardley and his wife Jane, both former Quakers, had been converted. Around the year 1748 they, along with a few others, formed a small congregation which for the time being set up no profession of faith but maintained, rather, that it was about to reveal the new and living manner of perfect salvation that had been the subject of prophecy for so long. Then—it was in the year 1758—*Anna Lee* joined the congregation, and now came to be fulfilled that which for ten years had been the hope and longing of the enthusiasts. Anna had been born in 1736 in Manchester and had been married in her twentieth year to the blacksmith Stanley, for whom she bore four children. After she joined the Wardleys, she learned through inspiration that "the root of all human corruption was to be sought in the mixing of the sexes in sensual love, which consequently was to be abolished." Other revelations followed, and since Anna was stamped by fervent piety, extraordinary eloquence, and an exemplary behavior, she soon occupied an outstanding position in the sect; from

1768 on she was called the "Spiritual Mother." By 1772 the society had increased to thirty persons, despite many a bitter persecution. Then Mother Anna received from God the command to emigrate to America with her people, an order which she and her entire congregation complied with in 1774. After she had resided for some time in New York and Albany, had endured many hardships, and had separated from her husband (who wanted to force her to the fulfillment of her marital obligations), she joined the others. They had meanwhile founded the colony of Watervliet in the forest of Niskeyuna, six miles from Albany. Now, in the year 1779, a mighty revival had taken place in New Lebanon, a nearby town, and it had become clear to the people that the day of the Lord was approaching, that is, that the physical second coming of Christ was close at hand. By chance it happened that several people visited the strangers who had settled in Niskeyuna, and behold! they soon became aware that the second advent had already occurred in Anna Lee. Full of joy, they made their discovery known everywhere, and in a short time the news spread throughout the entire country. Believers were found everywhere, and although the authorities severely prosecuted the followers of the "Sister and Bride of Christ" and even imprisoned Mother Anna for several months, the number of faithful grew in a few years to several thousand. The number even continued to increase when, in July of 1784, William Lee, the most ardent apostle of the sect, and, a few weeks later, on September 8, Anna Lee herself departed this life.

Beginning with the first settlement in Watervliet, several colonies were established in the course of time. These were initially restricted to the state of New York, but soon the Shakers also founded several settlements in the New England states. It was the work of Anna's successors in the governing of the church to organize these and to fix and regulate the teachings of the departed "Mother."

But suddenly news of the great Kentucky Revival—a flaming up of the religious spirit in a manner similar to that of the Convulsionaires—came to New Lebanon, and the Shaker authorities residing there immediately sent several apostles to the scene of the events on the Ohio. These found ready listeners and believers for their sermons, and by 1808 they could proceed with the founding of a colony at Union Village near Hamilton, Ohio; in a few years it numbered around five hundred members. But here, too, they met with a persecution such as had never before afflicted these harmless people so unfortunately. It was instigated by the so-called Christians, a sect that had originated during, and as a result of, that revival in Kentucky; it had as its goal nothing less than the complete eradication of the Shakers in the West. On August 27, 1810, a mob, including five hundred militia, appeared before the Shaker village. A deputation demanded of the inhabitants that the Society either give up its principles and way of life or leave its property and the state, failing which, force would be used. The reply of the leaders of the colony was soft and mild but at the same time resolute. They observed to their opponents' spokesmen that their belief was dearer to them than their lives and that, on the other hand, they resided upon their well-earned property, from which no one could order them to leave with any semblance of right. This answer, as calm and well-founded as it was, hit the mark, particularly since the great majority of the enemy had pictured the Shakers as being quite different. So the foe withdrew without having used his weapons, and since then the children of Anna Lee have remained undisturbed.

The last important event in the history of the Shakers was a general reanimation of their belief in consequence of the bestowal of a sacred roll containing the new gospel. On the morning of May 4, 1842, the word of the Lord came to Philemon Stewart in New Lebanon and said: "Set out, you small one, and appear before the Lord on the sacred hill. And there you shall kneel down seven times and bow to the ground seven times. For the Lord has words for you to write down, and you shall seat yourself beside the sacred spring, and the words shall be revealed to you in flame." And Philemon did as he had been commanded, and when he approached the spring, he heard the rustling of a mighty wind and the roaring of distant thunder. But after he had seated himself, all became still, and an inexpressible feeling, as if a consuming fire were burning him up, filled his mortal body. And the voice spoke, and he wrote and wrote, until finally the curious opus, attested to by miracles and the appearance of angels in all Shaker colonies, was completed. It exists as the source of the most recent communication under the title *A Sacred and Divine Roll and Book*.

If we should now ask about the confession of the Shakers, we find that they are a branch of the *Chiliasts* or *Millennariasts* represented particularly strongly and variously in America. Indeed, they might perhaps be regarded as the root stock of all similar phenomena upon the western continent. But while all the others only hope for the imminent second coming of Christ and thus place the millennial kingdom of peace beginning therewith in a more or less distant future, the *parusie* [second coming of Christ], according to the Shaker catechism, has already occurred; they believe, accordingly, that they are already living in the millennium. In the year 452 (their dogmaticians say), with the establishment of papal power uniting church and state, began the kingdom of the Antichrist, which, according to Biblical prophecy, precedes the second coming of Christ. It grew and extended its dominion over the entire world. Then, after the Reformation (which, however, is considered by them as a mere crack in the unity and power of the "Great Dragon"), it gradually decreased until the prophesied "1,290 days of devastation" had run their course. During this period the divine spirit of Christ, the "Son of the eternal mother of wisdom," had returned to heaven from the church on earth, there to prepare the way for his return "in and with the Holy Bride, who is the daughter of eternal wisdom." When this time was fulfilled, in 1747, he descended upon Anna Lee in England to purify his shrine and to establish his millennial kingdom. Therefore this *parusie* was not the appearance of his personal being but the manifestation of his spirit; and it had to take place through the medium of a woman because the human race, for a complete redemption from the consequences of the fall, required not only a second Adam but also a second Eve, and because the rebirth to life in the spiritual world for the individual presupposes not merely a man but parents, just as does the procreation for earthly existence. This rebirth, or spiritual procreation, through Christ and "Mother Anna" is the only one that is to take place from now on; the physical [procreation] was the first sin—not the apple bite of Genesis. Thus whoever wishes to join the saints of the millennial kingdom or, as the technical expression puts it, "is desirous of taking his cross upon himself," must renounce all and every kind of sexual intercourse forever. Therefore the commandment of absolute abstinence in this matter is the first and most important one for the inhabitants of a Shaker colony. A second obligation is separation from the world and renunciation of its honors and offices as things that have nothing to do with the kingdom of Christ. A further commandment is a peaceable and harmless disposition toward everyone; for the Lord is a Prince of

Peace, and the bearing of arms against one's neighbor means sinning against God's justice and sacredness. Moreover, the Shaker is supposed to refrain from swearing (including the taking of oaths in court) and is generally expected to employ simple language, avoiding all unnecessary embellishment. Hence he may neither have a title nor give one to anybody. To have no personal possessions is an additional obligation. As was pointed out earlier, the Shakers consider all property as a communal possession. Since, in consequence of their virginal way of life, they have no heirs, civil legislation finds no cause to proceed against them. The last main commandment is obedience—first of all to God and then to their leaders. The church is a spiritual family. A family, however, must have a visible head, and this head (which represents the "parents Christ and Anna") is for all of Shakerdom the so-called Ministry in the mother colony of New Lebanon near Albany, while the individual branches of the church\* are directed by male and female elders. The worship service in a Shaker community is just as simple as it is strange. As citizens of the millennial kingdom, they no longer recognize the sacraments (which merely served as preparation for it), and they have neither altar nor chancel, neither liturgy nor clergy, and in the entire settlement at Watervliet I didn't see a single Bible. In place of all these things they worship God with dances, which are conceived of as a symbol of their unity, of the journey to heaven, and as a mere expression of their joy in the love and glory of the Creator; these dances are accompanied by pious songs of jubilation that are frequently improvised.

"God has created nothing in vain," said Elder Pelham in defense of this strange custom. "He has given us tongues and has endowed them with the ability to speak and to express our desires and feelings. He has in like manner given us hands and feet and has enabled them to perform their functions in the service of the body. Shall, now, these important faculties be used solely in the service of the flesh, or even of sin, and not also to the honor of God? Or should the tongue alone have the privilege of praising God, and not the entire body, with head and limbs, hands and feet, in harmonious cooperation?"

During the discussion of these and similar topics it had be-

---

\* At present the Shakers have 18 colonies or cloisters, of which 12 are in the East: 3 in New York, 4 in Massachusetts, 1 in Connecticut, 2 in New Hampshire, and 2 in Maine; and 6 in the West: 4 in Ohio and 2 in Kentucky. The total number of members of the sect is said to be about 4,100.

come evening. The bell rang for supper and the Shakers, with the exception of David, left. Soon after, I was escorted by the Deacon to the main building, to a room next to the kitchen where the evening meal was being served. There was no lack of tomatoes, and the fruit jelly was the best that I had tasted in America. It was not pleasant that I had to eat alone: the Shakers, as hospitable as they are, do not permit anyone not belonging to their sect to dine at their table. The reason for this is to be sought not so much in the fact that they regard themselves as too holy and pure to eat from the same dish as a worldling as in the fact that they consider the effect of strange glances and expressions as not of advantage to the younger sisters.

Having returned to the office, I read for a while in the handwritten songbook of David; it contained several very good songs, along with many unedifying outpourings of sickly devotion and pious moonsickness. Then the bell rang again, this time for worship.

Accompanied by the Deacon, I went through the rear door into the main building and up the stairs covered with mats. We went through a wide glass door at the right into a spacious hall that was decorated in the uniform of the entire establishment: white and dark brown. It was provided with eight windows, four to the east and four to the west, and in addition to the mentioned main entrance at the south was accessible through a little door at the north. As to furnishings: the room contained nothing but two narrow benches running along the south wall on both sides, a metal lamp hanging down from the ceiling, and a small blue rug, about four feet long and two feet wide, spread out on the floor a few steps from the glass door. David placed a chair for me in the northeast corner of the room. Present in the room, besides him and me, were only a few young girls of fifteen to eighteen— among them several bright faces and a pair of incomparable Madonna eyes. They giggled in a rather worldly fashion and cast wondering glances at the strange man. Their costume consisted of a sort of white Dutch hood, stitched in the back; blue or gray skirts with short waist; over these, stiffly starched white breastcloths, crossing over in front, covering the throat up to the chin, and hanging down three-edged more than halfway in the back; and, finally, coarse stockings and heavy shoes. This costume is nothing less than unbecoming and gives to even the most youthful figure a grandmotherly and stiff (I should like to say, wooden) appearance. These girls stood to the left of the main door (on the women's side observed throughout the entire building), while in the right (east) portion of the hall, the friendly old man with his four pupils (among them a small, curlyheaded mulatto) had joined Deacon David.

The bell outside now struck eight. Both sides of the glass door now opened, the already present Shakers at the right took off their jackets, and the others entered silently—women to the left and men to the right. After the latter had likewise taken off their jackets, they all arranged themselves, each sex on its side, three ranks deep in the east and west in front of the small rug, so that both sexes faced each other. Hereupon both columns bowed to each other, waving their hands in a peculiar way, and then a sonorous male voice began the following song (given in translation[12]); the entire congregation joined in after the first line. It was sung in rapid tempo to a pleasant sounding melody and went (as I got it later from Brother Harmon's songbook):

> My home is there,
> Where the loving ones live,
>     Where the Good One is enthroned in eternity.
> And how my soul yearns
> For that land of glory,
>     Where sickness and care no longer exist.
> Here in the heavenly land
> In snow-white robes
>     I see the host of glowing angels stand,
> And to the place of rest,
> To their dwelling,
>     I want to go, I want to go, I want to go!
>
> I'll not weep any more;
> For my Savior is near,
>     Who defends the lambs from the wolf,
> And transforms the trouble
> That now moistens my cheek
>     Into heavenly bliss.
> Where the seraph, adorned
> With golden wings, enraptured
>     Shouts Hallelujah, I shall be.
> In the charming song then
> With the lovely sound
>     I join in, I join in, I join in!
>
> Oh how sorry I'd be
> For the joys of the time!
>     The vain ones, that I'd gladly miss.

## A SHAKER TOWN

> The earth offers nothing
> To us of the life still worthwhile,
>   So let me go, let me go to the Lord!
> And since nothing in the world
> Pleases the soul any more,
>   And I find here neither consolation nor peace,
> I want to hasten at once
> To the place of the loving ones,
>   To my homeland, to my homeland.

At the end of this song they bowed to each other again and waved their hands with that gesture of submission—it looked rather comical in the case of the sisters, each of whom had a rectangular folded handkerchief hanging over the right forearm. Then the columns broke up, and two men with six women went to the middle of the hall, there to arrange themselves in two facing ranks. The remaining members of the male part of the congregation arranged themselves in pairs, faces turned toward the north, ready for the dance or, rather, for a march; the female Shakers who were not part of the chorus in the center did the same. Suddenly one of the female singers with a melodious soprano voice commenced singing the following verse:

> On, march heavenward, victorious troop!
>   La! la la! La la la!
> Let a song of praise, a song of thanks, full, happy, and clear,
> Rise from our hearts
> To God, our Creator,
> Who always has been a friend to us and a father!
>   La! la la! La la la!

And now all started up, the columns of the brethren in front, and marched to the rhythm of the song (in which the seven other singers joined after the first words) in the order in which they had arranged themselves. Elbows at their hips, forearms extended horizontally, fanning with their hands, they moved at a quickstep in a circle around the singers. The melody of the verse, which was repeated several times, bore the character of triumphant revelry; with its "La la la!" to which soon was added a "Ha la li!" and other sounds falling within the realm of the so-called talking in tongues, it had much more in common with the twittering of birds than with our chorales. At each repetition the enthusiasm of the singers seemed to increase, the pleasure of those travelers toward heaven seemed to grow in contemplation of the new Jerusalem beaming into their soul's eye from afar, and the abundance of their emotions seemed to flow more richly and mightily. The tree-tall Deacon stood out rather drolly alongside a short, goitrous brother whose Falstaff belly was scarcely half covered by the flaps of a colossal blue vest;[18] and an old Negress, who, with her thick lips and her dark brown face shining with perspiration in the white hood and like-colored neckerchief, waddled among these grandmotherly attired young girls like a ham wrapped in paper, would have had a full claim to the laughing muscles of a person not accustomed to such phenomena, even without these surroundings. Nevertheless, the strange circle dance and, even more, the odd jubilee song made a solemn rather than a comical impression, and when caricatures such as those mentioned are eliminated, one is indeed reminded of the Biblical prototypes of the Shakers: Miriam, the prophetess, and King David, who danced before the Ark of the Covenant.

The song and march might have lasted about five minutes. Then they halted, to pray silently with folded hands, until the choir broke out anew with a roaring hymn:

> O burn, burn, you sacred force,
> That every hour makes me purer!
>   Of the fervent glow,
>   The living good,
>   Of the purefying fire,
>   Of the heavenly salvation,
> Invited by the angels, I want to have my share.

While this was being sung, the columns first moved in a circle as during the previous song. Soon, however, the simple quickstep changed to a hopping in dactylic rhythm. A few of the older sisters who were too weak to stay with the dancing very long beat out the time with their feet while resting upon the bench running along the windows. When the dancers had circled around their singing brethren and sisters several times in this fashion, they faced each other again in the original order on opposite sides of the blue rug, prayed once more, and then went through the glass door to their rooms.

Such mimic dances are performed every day with the exception of Fridays, when the community celebrates in the corridor before the doors of their rooms a sort of pious conversational hour in which both sexes participate. Hence I found opportunity on the following morning to attend a similar spectacle. Now, however, they did not hop in a circle but, dividing into two large squares, marched across the room from south to north and back again. Then they about-faced and once again covered the same distance in the same manner. During a pause Elder Pelham gave a talk in which he compared the world, which looked upon the dance of the saints with unfavorable glances, to the brother of the prodigal son who also had witnessed with disfavor and annoyance the joy and festivity with which the return of the long-missing one had been celebrated.

I spent the rest of the morning copying a part of David's songbook. At eleven o'clock I went to lunch, and two hours later I went with the Deacon for the third time to watch Anna Lee's children dance. This time, after all had sung the introductory song, the other elder gave a talk of admonition. At its conclusion the aforementioned Falstaff (who apparently was a recently accepted novice) expressed his joy at being admitted to the community of saints. The content of Pelham's response, summed up in a charming verse, echoed shortly thereafter from the nightingale throat of one of the female singers, and the feet of the columns quickly began a rhythmic movement. At first a gentle, melting gliding, then, upon repetition, a wild whirling, the song went:

> O heavenly love surges, precious love flows!
> Hallelujah! La la la!
> Up! Let us bend and let us bow,
> Interweave into a dance now
> La la la! La la la!
> And let's drink happily as we sing
> Of the mildly flowing love
> That comes to us from above,
> From the Mother's inexhaustible spring.
> La la la!

More loudly and shrilly twittered the singers, and faster and faster the dance figure circled past my chair, and more transfigured became the faces of the dancers. An electric "something" from "somewhere" seemed to have been imparted to their sinews and nerves. A magnetic force lifted them on tiptoes. A pious intoxication, a devout drunkenness had taken hold of the entire community. An inextinguishable fervor burned in their eyes. An unquenchable thirst for the love of the Mother, the outflowing of which was represented by their dance, feasted on their pale countenances. "*And drink a little more—and drink, drink, drink a little more*" rejoiced the choir, with glances turned toward heaven and chests elevated, so that it was piercing and shattering. Suddenly one of the sisters, her arms hanging limply at her sides, began twirling in a wide circle for a few steps. A second followed, then a third. A brother did the same, another imitated him, and soon most of the dancers were in motion, each about his own axis. They moved on after several rotations, reeling, carried away by the song and its "la la la," to begin rotating again in a moment. This dance, jubilating along on the borderline between the sacred and the weird, didn't stop until several women had sunk down upon the bench, exhausted and panting loudly. The elders, the Deacon, matrons with gray hair, and young girls who had scarcely outgrown school—almost all had taken part in the "Play of the Planets," and even Brother Harmon, the former rationalistic clergyman, had made a few modest attempts to demonstrate his faith by an energetic twirling. Only the madman and the four boys were satisfied with a mere quick march.

An hour later I took leave of my hospitable host; Pelham's blessing wished me a speedy conversion to a recognition of that which would serve my true peace. Harmon requested permission to accompany me for a short distance.

For a long, painful quarter hour we walked silently side by side. Finally he repeated his request, and now no *Deus ex machina* relieved my embarrassment. I had to answer him, and could my answer be anything but a refusal? He seemed to have half expected that, and he therefore merely begged me to preserve a friendly memory of him and to keep his full name (which he had meanwhile confided in me) secret. I gladly promised him this and agreed, moreover, to write him if I found a solution to the complications in which he had been ensnared by fate. It was possible that in Cincinnati something could be done without compromising him.

Thereupon we separated. For a long time afterward I saw with emotion his tall figure standing upon the hill in the sunset, waving farewell to me with his broadbrimmed white felt hat. For a long time my ears still heard the Shaker song to the melody of which he had danced contrary to his feelings:

> O I will bend and limber be
> Like a limber willow tree,
> I'll bow and bend, yea twist and reel,
> My holy mother's love to feel.

For a long time I reflected upon what might happen if no prospect of liberation appeared. As often as I returned in spirit in the next few days to the silent Watervliet, the sad picture of the unhappy man appeared before my eyes. This man, still at a vigorous age, was condemned to mere vegetating upon a soil in which his spiritual being must become stunted and his vital marrow must gradually dry up.

But all illusions must end sometime, and the poetic veil was torn back harshly (as at the conclusion of a poem by Heine[14]), the veil which lay over the reason for friend Harmon's being driven to live among the dervishes of America. Three weeks later, when I related my adventure in the Shaker Town to Pastor Kr. in Cincinnati, he quickly sprang up and shouted, clapping his hands together: "What in Heaven's name! That is the selfsame——whom they have expelled from three congregations because a couple of times every month he has gotten the *delirium tremens* from the whiskey bottle!"

◊ ◊ ◊ The traveler journeying from southern Pennsylvania or Maryland to Ohio and Indiana by way of Virginia occasionally encounters along the road to his destination a farm that, through many features and peculiarities, reminds him of Germany (despite its generally American character). Before it he sees people who appear to have been transplanted here from another age. A black felt hat with a strikingly broad, completely flat brim, and a strangely cut dress coat, usually gray or dark brown, with a standup collar and only one row of buttons, similar to the attire in which grandfather took grandmother, do not go together very well. But how might the long wavy hair and the foot-long patriarchal beard flowing down from chin and cheeks harmonize with that costume and with the appearance of the Anglo-Saxon neighbor? However, if the traveler should step into the clean and comfortable homes of those strangely dressed men, he would find them and their families to be honest, straightforward, and hospitable people who live harmless lives in modest prosperity. As soon as the conversation turns to religion, the man of the house will attempt to convince him that only adult baptism is scriptural. But the American friend to whom he relates this encounter will tell him that they are called *Dunkards* and that they form a brotherhood whose membership includes a large part of the German farmers from the forests of Pennsylvania to the prairies of Iowa and Missouri.

Until recently many imaginative tales have been told about the Dunkards. Some have counted them with the Mennonites, others have confused them with their twin brothers, the Seventh Day Adventists, and even American writers have published false reports about them. Thus it may be of interest to clear up, as far as feasible, the obscurity that rests upon their history and their belief. Their name is connected with the word "dunk," that is, "to immerse"; it was given to them as a nickname by the Pennsylvanians because they perform baptism through immersion rather than through sprinkling. In the United States they probably number somewhat more than sixty thousand, although no definite information is available—they have never made a count, either through humility or because of fear of offending God with a census. The fact that their history is so difficult to trace is due partly to their indifference in such matters and partly to the circumstance that they constitute no real organized church with a central point, consisting, rather, of a number of widely scattered independent congregations and dioceses. Only in the past year has a book appeared from the pen of one of their bishops that to any extent gives an authoritative account of their confessional system.[15]

The sketch which now follows is a picture of their church life, something which I had the opportunity to study thoroughly.

About six miles from Dayton and a few hundred steps from the highway to Salem, in a clearing in the immeasurable forest, stands a long, low brick building covered with shingles. It is enclosed by the customary rail fence in a field of one American acre. Before it, beneath several trees, is situated a spring, beside which a crude bench has been constructed. It is a meetinghouse of the Dunkards; they have settled in large numbers in the vicinity, as well as in the entire area of the Mad River and the two Miamis.

It was on the seventh of October that I attended one of those meetings of the brotherhood to which people often come from many miles to hear the gospel preached and to celebrate communion along with the washing of feet. Because of the beautiful morning I decided to undertake the journey on foot. Leaving my residence in the suburb of Macpherson, I had soon passed the giant sycamores* that shade the banks of the Miami at the Covington Bridge and had then climbed up the hill to the frame shack that bears upon its front the aristocratic name "Montgomery Starch Manufactory." From here a road straight as a line leads entirely out of the valley up to the wooded heights. Great red barns be-

---

\* Sycamores are a kind of American plane tree; they grow especially frequently in moist locations.

hind elegant dwellings demonstrate the prosperity of those whose lucky star led them to build in this region. Riding herdsmen in bright blue frieze jackets and brown Buena Vista hats, members of the guild of the "divine Eumaeus"; rude carts drawn by two or three pairs of oxen; neat little buggies, from which fluttered the indispensable green veil of the local smalltown girls and farmers' daughters; bluebirds, butterflies, and hosts of grasshoppers—all enlivened the road upon which I saw, as I approached my destination, individual Dunkards in white coats upon handsome horses, with wives and children in the carriages beside them.

It might have been about nine o'clock when I arrived at the meetinghouse. In the grove outside the fence a vendor had set up his bar, and near him a large number of carriages and nags stood under the trees. They belonged to people who had come out, like me, without belonging to the brotherhood; among them the genus "Loafer" was abundantly represented, here as everywhere in Uncle Sam's land making up at least a quarter of the male youth. Inside the rail fence, however, it swarmed with the long-bearded figures and beavertail-shaped coats of the *brethren,* the number of them increasing from minute to minute. They walked back and forth on the grass hand in hand, and all new arrivals gave and received "the brotherly right hand" and the "sacred kiss." Yet it must be noted that the latter ceremony was performed only from brother to brother and from sister to sister. A line of the buggies, market carts, and saddle horses that had brought the faithful of both sexes had formed behind the building and along the fence. Through the one door of the meetinghouse that opened onto a small porch could be seen a merry kitchen fire, blazing about mighty pots and kettles and kept up by women in white hoods and neckerchiefs; from the chimney a blue column of smoke whirled up. Upon a rock next to the spring had been placed a tin cup; it was used to quench their thirst by those who disdained partaking of the nectar flowing from the whiskey barrel of the vendor.

Suddenly all headed for the entrances, and in a short time the building was so filled with Dunkards and spectators that several latecomers had to remain standing outside the door. The door was almost completely occupied by a colossal deacon with a long brown beard, the tallest and handsomest male figure I had encountered in America. The hall was a long rectangle with nine windows and three doors. Its low frame roof was carried by four crudely hewn beams, and at this moment it might have held between three and four hundred people. Neither choir nor pulpit, neither organ nor altar nor burning candles were to be seen. If the room, into which the kitchen fire gaily flickered and crackled, reminded one more of a large farmhouse than a German church, the appearance of the people suggested a gathering of the heroes of the Swabian Peasants' Rebellion[16] (although I noted only a few sinister, fanatic faces, but many that bore the stamp of most decided kindness). In the middle of the hall, around a white-covered table consisting of two sawhorses with crude planks laid upon them, sat about twenty men, most of them old, in the costume of the sect and adorned with long Noah beards. They were the preachers and the bishops. About them, on both sides of the aisle that divided the room lengthwise into two equal halves, sat tightly packed on the right (where the kitchen was located) the sisters in their white caps and aprons, and on the left, their hats upon their knees, the curlyheaded, bearded brethren. My good fortune had gained for me a seat directly opposite the preachers' table, and so I missed nothing of the entire strange ceremony.

The service began with an English song from the second part of the *Harp-playing of the Children of Zion*,[17] and this nothing less than melodious song was followed by a prayer in the German tongue, recited by one of the clergymen in a lachrymose voice. The profane fire crackled rudely enough through the open kitchen door, and the prayer was also accompanied unceremoniously by the terrible crying of an infant that had been brought along—a phenomenon not uncommon in American churches. After the preacher had said "Amen," one of the bishops read a chapter from Jeremiah, and to be sure from the English Bible. Then a few German verses were sung; these were recited to the congregation line by line by a preacher, a circumstance presumably having its basis in the fact that only a few of those present still possessed a songbook in the mother tongue. From this and the fact that more voices had taken part in the English song, one will perhaps draw no false conclusion if he deduces that the process of transformation to which all settlers that move away from Pennsylvania are subject is already three-fourths completed among the Dunkards of the West.

An old German preacher rose after the song to expand in English on the third chapter of Acts, which was read aloud by another in Luther's translation. In applying the text, he compared the lame man before the gates of the temple with the sinner who also cannot enter the kingdom of God unless he be ordered to walk in the name of Christ. Unfortunately, however, the good image was spun out in incessant repetitions into such a boring pulp that only a person accustomed to a peasant's diet could swallow it with relish. When the speaker became warm, he took off his coat and hung it on a line running above his head from pillar to pillar (from which several other garments were already suspended), and he found nothing unseemly in this. He might have spoken about a half hour in this manner when his sermon took a characteristic turn. He suddenly left the lame man standing in the temple in Jerusalem, forgot his English, and complained in the purest Pennsylvania Dutch about pains in his lungs. "I could still say much on this text, but my lungs wouldn't stand it. Oh, my lungs!" *But however*—and now the stream of his speech continued to flow for at least another quarter hour, without period or pause, its rising and falling resembling the tone in which we sing the collects. Even though this sample of Dunkard eloquence was not a model sermon, it at least seemed to please the congregation. In any case it was a better and more substantial one than that given in German on the same topic by his table neighbor; the German sermon was really nothing more than a bad translation of the English.

A very different impression was made by the next address, one given by a preacher who had come to the festival from southern Ohio. He had a long, lean figure and noble, prophetlike features. His pale face was wreathed in black hair, from his eyes glowed that characteristic fire, and in his otherwise strong voice lay that hollow tone that suggests consumption. The clever turns of the sermon given in good English could have been successfully followed even by a congregation of educated people. After he had concluded, there was further prayer, with the entire gathering falling to its knees; the clergyman who led the prayer, however, remained seated at the table with his head resting upon his right arm and his eyes closed. Then several other more or less talented preachers spoke, most of them in English, a few in German, and almost all of them disturbed by the screaming of the misbehaving Dunkard baby and by the fire that was cooking their noonday meal and therefore felt justified in putting in a word. All of them ended their remarks with the naïve statement that even if they had brought nothing to light for the good of the Brotherhood, they at least hoped that they had said nothing harmful.

It had become three o'clock and nine or ten speakers might

have appeared. The presiding bishop now checked any further outpourings by requesting those present to leave the building, since it now was time for the noon meal and the room had to be set up. There were not enough places for all to dine at the same time, so the old people and women would eat first, as soon as it could be arranged. The others, including those not belonging to the Brotherhood, would find their portions at the second serving. Finally, the animals, too, would be taken care of, and everyone could get whatever was necessary for this from the deacons. This was done, and soon Brethren and strangers were seen going from the kitchen to their horses with handkerchiefs full of oats in their hands and ears of corn under their arms.

I had meanwhile become acquainted with a Dunkard who had been my neighbor at the service, and he directed me with my questions to one of the bishops, a venerable figure in a coffee brown suit of the finest material, over which a well-cared-for beard as white as bleached flax hung down to the pit of his stomach. To my inquiry concerning their religious books, he replied that their only book was the New Testament. When I asked about the history of the *"denomination"*—by no means, "sect"!—whereby I first had to explain the concept "history" by translating it as *"rise and progress,"* he said that it began with the apostles and was the story of the invisible church of God. Another who joined the conversation claimed that their alliance stemmed from the Waldenses, and, as a result of further urging, the names of Alexander Mack[18] and the colony on Mill Creek appeared. The old bishop, in whose glances I believed I detected, perhaps wrongly, something of the self-sufficiency of the Pharisees that the alleged *electi* at times cannot entirely conceal from the *reprobatus*, finally went to lunch, and so I now conversed with the younger people.

It seemed that these were under the strange delusion that I had come for the purpose of a disputation, or even to convert them; or rather, as one of them clearly stated, I had been sent by Somebody in Germany. So, after a few questions, I found myself involved in a rather heated debate; it was carried on, to be sure, in a friendly tone. Several Anglo-Americans joined us, unrequested, to take my side and to accompany my comments and rejoinders with such awkward and embittering exclamations as: *"Now for it, young man! — Just give it him! — By Jove, he'll whip them fellows anyhow!"*

In truth, little can be said about the confession of the Dunk-

A SHAKER TOWN

ards. Whatever I learned in this debate and from other sources may be inserted here. Their faith is distinguished from orthodox Lutheranism only in externals—upon which, however, they place great weight. In other words, the formal principle of Protestantism —that the Bible alone is the guideline for the dogmatician—has been carried to extremes by them, so that it also embraces the adiaphora.[19] Everywhere it is zealously asserted that all instructions of Christ and the apostles are to be taken and obeyed literally. Acting consistently, they baptize only those accountable for their actions and perform the ceremony in this manner: the baptizer goes into a river or pond with the one to be baptized and there immerses him face down (not face up, as in the case of the Baptists) three times, in the name of the Father, the Son, and the Holy Ghost. Further, they partake of the Lord's Supper at night and as a real meal; communion, however, is celebrated in the manner of the Lutheran Church. And finally, they regard foot-washing as a sacred action instituted by Christ, to be performed in connection with the sacrament of the altar. The "kiss of love," also called "the holy kiss," spoken of several times in the Pauline letters, is likewise considered an indispensable commandment. Their mortally ill are anointed with consecrated oil. They are not permitted to bear arms, carry on lawsuits, or swear oaths; indeed, up until a few years ago they were forbidden to accept interest on loans, and even now the more pious demand no interest from needy church members. Their clergy consists of preachers, who sometimes are called *teacher*, sometimes *minister*, and of helpers or deacons, assisted by deaconesses. From the preachers they select the most capable as bishops. These are consecrated by the laying-on of hands, and upon them is imposed, by virtue of their office, the obligation to visit the individual congregations frequently; to preside at their love feasts, at the selection of preachers, and at the ordination of other bishops; and generally to conduct and oversee the affairs of the individual parishes. In districts where there is no bishop, that of the adjoining district conducts the business affairs, or the oldest preacher takes care of whatever is necessary. It is the duty of the deacons to care for the sick and the poor in the congregation, to mediate disputes, and to visit the individual families in their homes and lecture them on piety. All these clergymen are simple, uneducated people who seldom possess any other learning than a thorough knowledge of the Bible; they are chosen by the congregations from those members who distinguish themselves at their meetings by eloquence and piety. They receive no salaries but are reimbursed only for their travel expenses; however, only those who are too poor to be able to defray such costs themselves accept reimbursement. Most of them own farms and wield the plow and scythe like all other Brethren when not claimed by official duties. Many of them develop a considerable zeal in the affairs of their Master, and although many are in the poorest circumstances, they often leave farm and family for weeks to preach the gospel to members living in remote localities. At the time of the Pentecost they hold a great annual meeting, attended by the bishops and preachers as well as by members of other churches sent as delegates by their congregations. At such conferences, presided over by the five eldest bishops, resolutions of general validity are considered and any questions arising in matters of faith are decided. These are then published in the German and English languages and are sent to the teachers of the individual branch congregations, who read them aloud at a suitable opportunity.

Most of these principles of faith and organization were brought up during our discussion before the meetinghouse on the Salem Road, and I now learned that the teachings of the *Brotherhood* are found not only in the Bible, but that there also is a book about them by Mack (which a man living in the neighborhood promised to lend to me to look through), a second book by a Bishop Winchester, and a third by the head of the local parish, Peter Nead.[20]

At this moment Nead himself, along with that pale, dark-haired preacher, joined our group, and since I conceded that the "holy kiss" was indeed mentioned in the Scriptures, they immediately raised the question as to why, then, our pastors did not wish to recommend it to their congregations for observation. To be sure, I could only respond with a shrug of the shoulders. If this was unsatisfactory, and the resounding laughter of my unrequested Anglo-American seconds in support of my negative gesture still more disconcerting, I still was able to give the good souls a pleasant surprise with my remark that at home emperors and kings, and even the Pope, perform the ceremony of foot-washing at times.

The debate, during which my opponents constantly had their fingers in their pocket Bibles and were prepared at all times to stem the tide of objection with a dictum from the gospels or the epistles, was carried on mostly in English since the majority of participants could understand "only Dutch," that is, Pennsylvanian, but could not "chatter like the Germans." During the course of the discussion a certain initially present aversion to the suspected converter turned (as could be read on their kindly faces) into trust and liking for the listener who left them alone after obtaining the desired information. As a consequence, I received invitations to visit from many quarters. Indeed, a red, broad, friendly face even wanted to carry me off this very evening to his farm ten miles away, where I could find the books by Mack, Winchester, and Nead, and where I could stay as long as I wished—an invitation that had to be declined, unfortunately, since the Reformed congregation in Dayton expected to hear a sermon from me two days later.

If the Americans present as spectators had not already behaved badly enough during the debate, now, when the tables inside were ready for the second serving, they crowned their boorishness with a rush to the building. They ran toward the entrances like hunger-crazed wolves on the trail of food, they lifted and pushed each other through the windows, they pushed and shoved for the dishes in the hall, screaming for more when the served food had disappeared in an instant, and they played the ill-mannered scamps so naturally that the only thing lacking to complete this role was a schoolmaster behind them with a switch.

When this triumph of impudence was over, the stomachs of the "Bho-oys" had been filled, and the horror of the devastation —the bones, bits of meat, and breadcrumbs strewn everywhere on the floor—had been swept from the house of God (a labor performed with calmness by the Dunkards, accustomed to this and worse scenes), the praying, singing, and preaching began anew, to be continued until approaching darkness reminded them of the ceremonies planned for the night. Now insect lights in tin candlesticks were placed upon the tables. After a few songs concerning that which was to follow had been sung and the passion story according to the gospel of Saint Mark had been read aloud, two brethren who had rolled up their sleeves and had wrapped long towels about their bodies carried in a tub; in this the feet of the male members of the gathering were washed. The same was done on the sisters' side by two deaconesses. During this sacred act one of the bishops spoke about its significance. He saw represented therein not merely an obligation to humility (expressed by the bending down of the one washing) but just as much an authorization of the Brethren to purify one another spiritually, by admonition and forgiveness of sins, for the celebration of the Lord's Supper (symbolized by the presenting of the feet to be washed and by the act of cleansing). The Lord's Supper was conceived of by the speaker as a symbol of the supper of the faithful to be held upon the return of Christ at the end of the world.

The foot-washing was now followed by the Lord's Supper in the form of an ordinary evening meal; the congregation, after a table prayer, ate soup from tin bowls with tin spoons, and then meat, bread, and butter, as at noon.

To be sure, all these ceremonies were no longer disturbed and sneered at by the chattering fire and the strong-lunged baby, but, unfortunately, by far worse guests. Namely, in gratitude for the noon meal given them, the gang of loafers outside, when night fell, made a point of interrupting the love feast of the harmless Dunkards in the most refined manner. Some bawled and crowed in through the doors. Others sang outside, with all the strength of their throats, the popular song *"I come from Salem City with My Washbowl on My Knee."* Still others shot with pistols at the windows where the women sat, and others circled around the building in groups, imitating the cry of wild turkeys. In short, there was a great disturbance, as if a wild hunt or a chorus of witches traveling to the Brocken had settled down on the grass outside.[21] This was more than just boyish pranks; this was villainy, at which the patience of the lamb might have learned to bite. Nevertheless, the tone in which Bishop Nead, the presider, finally reprimanded them for the uproar scarcely sounded like anger, and even though one might not be able to admire this gentleness of character, one must at least show amazement.

In accordance with their theory of literalism, one might believe himself justified in expecting that the Dunkards would consider the communion following the supper as the partaking of the actual body and blood of Christ. But this is not so, as indicated by Peter Nead's talk at the beginning of the celebration. He interpreted communion as an occasion for the inward experiencing of the fellowship in faith and love of all Brethren. After this address, in which all members who bore any malice toward a brother or a sister were requested to stay away from the Lord's Table or to achieve instant reconciliation, the holy kiss went

from mouth to mouth. Then a bishop rose and said a prayer over
the bread that had meanwhile been brought in. It consists of
thin, unleavened cakes, so baked that they can easily be broken
into equal portions. The prayer concluded with a loud "Amen!"
spoken by the entire congregation, and now the administrator of the
sacrament broke off a long strip from the cake, turned to the
man sitting beside him on the right, and said: "Dear Brother, the
bread that we break is the fellowship of the body of Jesus
Christ." Thereupon he broke off a piece from the strip and gave it
to the person addressed, who placed it before himself. Then he
received the strip and dealt with it in the same manner as the
administrator, turning to his neighbor on the right. When the bread
had been distributed to all in this fashion, the presiding bishop
declared that the bread was now broken and that when they
now ate of it, they should seriously reflect on its significance,
"*shadowing forth the bruised and mangled body of our dear Redeemer.*" After the administration of the bread, the presider prayed
over the wine, which had been brought in in two green, pouch-shaped bottles and was drunk from tin cups. It was red wine,
and the cups went around the tables in the same manner as had
the bread, each member calling out in German or English: "Dear
brother, the wine that we drink is the fellowship of the blood
of Jesus Christ." Then the congregation sang a song concerning
the celebration.

The entire ceremony concluded with a prayer, after which
Nead invited those Brethren who had come from a distance to
a breakfast in the meetinghouse the next morning. They then
dispersed, and I set out for home, the road being illuminated by
the stars in a most desirable way. A few weeks later, however,
I accepted the invitation of Bishop Nead to visit him at his farm
(the invitation had been repeated at my departure). I found
this man, who had formerly carried on the occupation of a tanner
and had moved here from Virginia only three years before, to
be not only a childishly lovable soul but also a man better informed
in theological matters than I had expected. His book about the
faith of his sect is to me one of the most valuable souvenirs among
the mementos gathered in beautiful Ohio.

◊ ◊ ◊ To give a description of the total American sectarianism
would exceed the limits I have set for myself; and a brief survey of
the peculiarities of each individual sect would be inconsistent

with the character of this book, which is supposed to be a picture book and not a notebook, and, besides, would be half superfluous. Therefore it may be sufficient to remark that the origin of these sects can be traced back approximately to the following causes:

First of all, it is the sense of independence and the awareness of equality of rights (which has become second nature to all the people) by which the original stocks of old confessions have been split. According to the church constitution, the lower clergy are supposed to be subject to the higher and have no voice, or, at most, but one voice, in regard to what their office is. A bold spirit, or a striking question touching the interests of all, shows them that they can really claim greater rights. They ask for that which is due them, are flatly refused, join together, announce their departure from the previous association—and the new sect, deviating from the old in nothing but a more liberal constitution, takes its place among the others. A second seed of discord is found in the theory of literalism inherited by America from England. A meditative person applies himself to the study of the Scriptures, and one fine morning he finds a passage for which he dicovers an interpretation differing from that of traditional dogma. He regards his discovery as important, even because it is *his,* and ten other quotations prove to him that he has not erred. He then writes a book about it, wanders throughout the land as a preacher of the apostrophe or period that he has blown up into a gospel, quickly finds a following among the population always eager for something new, and lo! again there's one more *"denomination"* under the moon. A third, rich source of sects is the view, already present at an early date and now widespread throughout North America, that the day of the Lord, or, as it is sometimes expressed, the second coming of Christ and the millennial kingdom, is close at hand—a view in which, according to my judgment, is concealed but a hazy notion of the great future of the transatlantic world and of the transformation being readied there for a completely new era of history. This has frequently been exploited by swindlers and has, on the other hand, now and again given rise to enthusiastic self-deception; examples of this are Joe Smith, the Mormon prophet, and William Miller, the proclaimer of the day of judgment. However, the principal motive force acting in the production of new sects is that revival fervor mentioned above. It throws itself into this compartment of one person's phrenological brain box and into that compartment of another's, it here presses upon the imagination and there upon the will, and with the uneducated it often brings about unbelievably curious things.

Present-day Methodism has taken this peculiar religious epidemic, a little tamed, into its system. Like intermittent fever, the epidemic has settled down in all states of the Union, even the most healthful and most temperate, and has attained extremely astonishing results at its quarterly assemblies and camp meetings. A picture from the sphere of these achievements in the area of peculiarity may provide the conclusion to this chapter.

Take yourself with me to a forest clearing in Ohio a few miles from the city of Springfield; it is situated on one of the creeks that here flow toward the Big Miami. Picture the underbrush and smaller trees removed from this area and transformed into tentpoles and leaf-covered huts. Be informed by the people moving along the highway on horse, in carriages, and on foot that they are about to hold a camp meeting here on the land of a Methodist farmer; the faithful of the vicinity have been invited through the newspapers.

To the right, a small red brick house with green shutters peers forth from an orchard. To the left stretches a bit of prairie covered with half-withered grass, a few bushes, and here and there reeds and rushes. In the background can be seen an Indian mound overgrown with shrubs and young trees. Upon a plank platform beneath the leafy canopy of a mighty sycamore stand the chairs of the preachers who have appeared for the celebration. The area before the platform is filled with listeners in a wide circle and enclosed by a large number of vehicles of all kinds, from the crudest to the most tasteful. Here stand cabins woven of branches, there stand rows of white linen tents, before each a flickering cooking fire. Farther off, vendors are selling food, but among their wares is nothing that would fall under the heading of "alcoholic beverages." The lanes between these cabins and tents swarm with women in the ugly calico bonnets that the women of the American middle classes wear instead of our hoods, and with men in picturesque broadbrimmed hats, blue jackets, or those light red short jackets that they call *warmus* (the German *Wamms*). Here and there we also note gentlemen and ladies in stylish costume.

A pause has occurred, but now begins anew what they here call the "divine service." The pious ones flocking about the chancel raise their voices in a roaring song of praise, to a melody recalling our student songs, and they listen eagerly to one of the preachers who relates, with tear-flooded cheeks and loud moaning and groaning, the passion of the Savior for the sins of the world. This is followed by a wailing song of repentance, likewise sung to the gayest tempo. At its conclusion the souls reveling in ecstasy and paroxysms of pietism suddenly learn from the successor to the first speaker that, despite the service of Christ, they have absolutely no reason to feel safe; rather, the devil is walking around like a roaring lion and is even seeking among them for the one he will devour. This admonition has an instantaneous effect. It dumfounds and frightens, as evidenced by the exclamations of *"Ugh, most awful doom!—oh Lord!—oh don't don't!"* with which it is interrupted, now by this group, and now by that one. The women are ready for convulsions, but as yet the method has but half done its duty. A third black-coat with white scarf and furrowed brow steps up; he hopes to accomplish the rest by means of a sermon as long and crooked as a sassafras root. He is the lion of the day, the "thunderer." At first it doesn't seem so. He smiles, he whispers. His hand glides gently through the air, as if he were caressing an angel. Paradisaical phantasmagories flow from his mouth. Every word drips with honey or costly nard. Like a kitten, his talk insinuates itself delicately into all five senses, turns cautiously around all corners and angles, and beams splendidly and mightily into the gloomy depths of the Beyond.

"But," the preacher continues, and who would have believed that this "but" would be the signal for the unveiling of such a fearful oratorical battery as now begins to flash and crash? "But—" with this one syllable the conjurer of happy dreams has been transformed into a fanatical attacker, firing with the great cannon of his eloquence into the breach shot by his predecessors. In this furious way he literally knocks down even the most stubborn, so that, with few exceptions, the entire congregation—old and young, distinguished and lowly, men and women—throws itself to the ground, screaming for mercy, jerking, kicking, making faces, squealing, and crowing, until the fourth and fifth speakers pour balsam from the apothecary of Christ's five wounds into their lacerated hearts and command the "battered reeds" to stand up again.

And so it goes. Now, consoling words of comfort and *"Glory"*-shouting; later, salutary frightening and *"Mercy"*-groaning.

## A SHAKER TOWN

Bend or break, you sinful souls; you shall and you must repent—
this is the principle of this method of conversion. And if this
is applied for several days in a row and even continued into the
night, when the entire camp is lighted by candles and lamps, when
the shadows of the primeval trees fall into the tumult like
ghostly figures, and when numerous fires send up reddish clouds
of smoke, then it is not surprising that those anxious souls
dragged through fire and water, through heaven and hell, are not
only pounded to a pulp but are also goaded to the point where the
observer who has remained clearheaded asks himself whether
he is among madmen or drunkards.

On such occasions there may be sinning during the night, and
to the same degree that it occurs on our pilgrimages (our counterpart to these camp meetings), but certainly not to the extent that
one hears it reported. It may be a surprise that a sect that intentionally produces and regularly performs such spectacles of
fervor should number almost two million members in America.
That these scenes, reminding one more of the reeling dances
of the heathen Curetes and Corybantes than of a Christian
celebration, please "dear God" and promote morality might rightly
be doubted. It is certain, however, that old Wesley, who was a
spirit similar to Spener and thus a man of genuine piety, would
shake his head in disapproval at the actions of those who
have taken his name—not only here, but in regard to many things.

*4*

A WEEK IN THE BLACK SWAMP

◊ ◊ ◊ IN THE Dayton suburb of Macphersontown on the road to Covington stands, half-covered by foliage and shrubbery, a pretty little white brick house with a black, varnished shingle roof and a small balcony. A most charming shelter for a philosopher of Rousseau's requirements, it also was a welcome refuge for the wanderer, who wished, after weeks of swarming along in the anthills of the Yankee world, to rest again in comfortable isolation, to collect himself, and incidentally to dream a little of the beloved homeland on the other side of the ocean. It was my headquarters for the month of October, the workshop where the preceding chapters were sketched, and the starting point for my unsuccessful expedition (described in the following section) through the virgin forests of northwestern Ohio. The purpose of this campaign was the conquest of the Mormon settlement on Beaver Island near Detroit[1]—for my diary. The trip was occasioned by my meeting with the branch congregation of these strange saints that exists in Dayton. It consists of three women and two men and is led by the shoemaker and preacher Winthrop Graves. The failure of the undertaking was brought about finally by the bad weather and that puritanical sanctification of the Sabbath that does not permit the steamboats to travel between Toledo and Detroit on Sundays.

It was on the morning of the twelfth of October that Cousin Theodore* and I left Dayton on the morning train of the Mad

---

* Theodore, not Theodor. Here the German Rosenstrauch becomes Rosebough, often even before he receives his citizenship; Schuhmacher becomes Shoemaker;

River Railroad, and by noon we were seventy miles to the north in the friendly country town of BELLEFONTAINE. On the way a young farmer had attracted my attention by creating a small pool of tobacco juice on the floor of the car. He had fired the brown liquid at it twenty-seven times a minute, according to a careful calculation made with the aid of the second hand of my watch. It had been unusually interesting to observe how accurately he kept within the circle he was forming until he had produced a complete pond as round as the sun that looked down upon this fascinating pastime. In view of the distance from which this target practice was performed, I have no doubt that our fine young man would have been a good match for that virtuoso who, according to legend, could spit through a keyhole at ten paces. It's a disgusting habit, coating barroom floors and the sidewalks of Yankee cities with the nastiest marble, transforming the steamboats into floating spittoons, and lending to an American railroad car (when the weather permits the opening of windows) a strong resemblance to the hull of a battleship that fires a full volley at the enemy from its broadside! But: other countries, other customs, and as it says in the Negro song about the yellow weed of Virginia:

> It cures our double headache
> And helps digestion, too, Sir.
> And if you have no grits in your head,
> It'll get them for you, too, Sir.

So I'll forbear and keep in my pocket any further criticism of this shooting pleasure, as dangerous as it may be at times to clean coattails and trousers. Besides, that saliva-devastator was a good fellow in other respects—he cheerfully put us on the right road to the grave of Kenton, which is situated five English miles from Bellefontaine at the edge of a wood not far from the sources of the Mad River.

Why did we look up this lonely, unpretentious tomb? A weatherbeaten wood fence covered with moss and decay encloses a grassy mound, and on it has been placed a stone tablet which states that General Simon Kenton rests here. It also says that his fellow citizens of the West will long remember the deceased

---

and *Bauer* Klein becomes farmer Small, Kline, or Little. Why in the world shouldn't my dear American butterfly (who as a German caterpillar was named "Theodor") have the best right to call himself "Theodore," particularly since this lengthening of his name by one letter includes the ingenious intimation that he now is more important than he was at home?

as a brave soldier and an honorable man. This is all. History, however, provides a commentary to this laconic epitaph. From history we learn that the man sleeping under the mound is resting from a life as adventurous as that lived by anyone since the discovery of the New World. And we become aware that we are standing upon classical ground. We recall that we are about to walk through the area where the racial conflict of the whites with the reds, which had begun on the Hudson and the Delaware, was fought to its conclusion. In fact, the expansion power of civilization, which today flows through this region like a gentle, enriching Nile—the stranger can't tell from it that there once was a time when it blazed down from the Alleghenies into the western wilderness with the character of an annihilating lava flow and overthrew, with a demoniac pleasure in extermination, not only the virgin forest but also the races of primitive people. The entire district between the Ohio and Lake Erie was a single large battlefield, and someone who might be able to understand the language of the streams flowing toward the Muskingum and the Scioto would hear from them a story as full of mighty deeds and unspeakable suffering as any song sung to us about the praiseworthy heroes and the great labors of Germanic antiquity. Let us look around. Here is the grave of Kenton, the "Indian hunter." Its occupant could tell us how he endured the tortures of Mazeppa, how he went through the terrors of fiery death four times in one week, and how his existence up to ripe old age was a chain of risks, victories, and defeats, such as we should scarcely believe in a novel. But let us look farther. There towers an old oak tree, mutilated by ax and fire, without branches, a black pillar. We wonder whether the dryads that abandoned it saw the red warriors slip by who were led by Little Turtle into battle with the Kentucky horse sharpshooters of General Wayne? There a buzzard flies up screaming. We wonder whether he remembers the day when his father summoned him to the carrion feast on the field of Saint Clair's Defeat, when "the hands of the squaws were tired from scalping the dead and dying militiamen"? Here the murmuring creek. We wonder whether it heard the lament raised by the noble Chief Logan when his family was foully murdered by the Long-Knives? And over there, the sun behind the clouds. We wonder whether it watched as the seven cities of the Wyandots (that stood in this county) were laid to ashes by Clark's troops? And we wonder whether it was a witness as the Shawnees, at the place where the pretty Zanesfield has blossomed, tortured to death the prisoners taken by them in the victory over Crawford?

## A WEEK IN THE BLACK SWAMP

Yes, it was a time of blood and terror, this period of which the Virginian Simon Kenton is typical, and the "Fathers of the West" were a race as wild and crude as the nature in which they lived. But no one speaks about them any more, except for the books and graves, and the day is not far off when these, too, will become silent. The American is not much at home for the dead. The present uses up all his thoughts, and when he has any left over, he applies them to the future rather than to the past.

◊ ◊ ◊ A two-hour walk through the forest brought us to a railroad station; from here we traveled by the afternoon train to CAREY, situated some fifty miles farther north. Here the region gradually becomes wilder and shows more natural growth. Widely cleared, well-cultivated areas such as those seen for some distance beyond Bellefontaine become a rarity. The towns emerging now and then from the gloomy forest have an impoverished look. The houses and cabins more and more bear the stamp of being merely temporary shelters. Here and there is heard the buzzing of a portable steam sawmill. Now and then can be heard the hammering of carpenters building a little wood church for one of these frame towns taken freshly from the surrounding forest—it's the first thing the people in this country think of after the erection of a tavern. Occasionally a small prairie with tall green grass breaks the monotony of the scenery of gray trunks and yellow treetops. At times, also, a brook winds in picturesque curves through the tangle of bushes and roots. In general, however, this part of Ohio offers little that could satisfy a person seeking beautiful landscapes.

It was already dark when we arrived at Carey. Nevertheless we undertook to walk four miles farther to spend the night with a farmer on the Upper Sandusky–Tiffin road for whom we had a message from Dayton. The route to his cabin had been described to us as "unmistakable." But despite this, we were so thoroughly lost before we had covered half the distance that we were already thinking about returning to the hotel in Carey, when my companion discovered a faint glimmer of light way off. We quickly made up our minds and hurried across the prairie extending between us and the shimmering beam, toward the haven of rescue for our tired legs. The light, however, always seemed to stay just as far away from us. The fog that had arisen from the damp surface had not permitted us to notice that the prairie was crossed by veins of low thornbushes that made walking exceedingly difficult. Occasionally we were frightened by birds that fluttered up suddenly, and often a boot absolutely wanted to remain stuck in the marshy soil. Finally, however, after we had wandered for about an hour *"through bog, through bush, through briar,"*[2] the ground became drier and more passable. A small island of trees emerged before us from the plain. A dog barked, and we stood before the fence of a farm. What a happy surprise for us when the house, from whose open door a large hearth fire glowed forth, turned out, upon inquiry, to be the very one we were seeking!

We were received in most friendly fashion, dined with the family on the pork chops that from here on were completely unavoidable, talked politics a bit with our host about the gubernatorial election that had taken place today, and then (after having had to drink "a swallow for the fever") slept off our exertions of the prairie in good feather beds (which no longer are a rarity here).

Every farmer here who has to some extent worked himself up from the privations and labors of the first settlement possesses a bookshelf upon which are found, besides religious writings and various newspapers, a few historical and geographical works. Our host likewise paid homage to this praiseworthy custom (which is greatly promoted by the bookselling system) and enjoyed a quite respectable library. Among other items, he had Howe's *Historical Collections of Ohio*. The next morning, when I enlightened myself in it about the history of Wyandot County (where we now were), I made the discovery that we were quite near to the place where, in the year 1782, Colonel Crawford had been utterly defeated by the Indians. In response to my inquiry as to the site of the battlefield, I found out that we had cut across a part of it during our wanderings on the previous evening. Mr. Reed even pointed out to us on an oak tree in the grove near his house the traces of the axes with which the redskins, after the encounter, had hacked out the bullets that had gone into the trunk.

The stories connected with this locality give a good picture of the brutal ferocity with which the wars between the whites and the reds were waged by both sides, and thus I might be permitted to weave in a few here, in extract.

In the spring of 1782 various murders and robberies were committed in the settlements on the upper Ohio by hostile Indians.[3] According to rumor, the Christian Delawares in the Herrenhut colonies on the Tuscarawas—innocent people who long since had buried the tomahawk—had taken part in these attacks, or had at least assisted the malefactors; as a result, a campaign of revenge against them was decided upon. Ninety volunteers under the command of Colonel Williamson, a ruthless, bloodthirsty character, marched upon Gnadenhütten, the center of the Herrenhut Indians. Then, under the pretext of wanting to bring the inhabitants with wives and children to safety at Fort Pitt, they took the majority of the unsuspecting ones captive and now, changing faces, tied them up and locked them in two large buildings. A council of war was held at which the presiding officer presented two alternatives: the prisoners might be treated in accordance with the promises made to them, or it might be more appropriate, without further ado—to kill them. The gathering decided upon the latter course. Pleas for mercy were rudely rejected, and at a given signal, while from the circle of innocent victims hymns of praise to God and fiery prayers rose toward heaven, the gang of murderous backwoodsmen suddenly rushed among them, butchering in these slaughterhouses with pike and flintlock, with tomahawk and scalping knife, until not a sigh or groan revealed that a single soul was still alive.

The werewolf characters who had executed this disgraceful deed were still not satisfied. While not suffering a single loss themselves, they had tasted blood, and they desired more at the same price. They also wanted to annihilate those Herrenhut Indians who had been led up to the plains on the Sandusky by their brothers, the heathen redskins. So, at the end of May of that year, a second campaign to the north was organized. However, instead of attaining its goal, it ended in a terrible defeat in which those murderers of the innocents were amply repaid for their misdeeds. On the twenty-sixth of May, on the Mingo Bottoms where Steubenville now stands, 480 Virginians and West Pennsylvanians assembled. After Colonel William Crawford had been chosen as commander, the campaign was begun. The operation was commenced in all secrecy and haste, but despite this, before the army was a day's march away from the starting point, Indian scouts knew about the plan in detail and the number of attackers. Thus a considerable force was waiting to receive them when, on the sixth of June, they reached the prairie between the Tyemochte and the Sandusky. An encounter developed in which the whites at first held the upper hand, but on the next day they were completely put to flight. Their army dissolved into separate bands, of which scarcely half saw the Ohio again. Crawford (who, incidentally, was a friend of George Washington) had the misfortune of being taken prisoner during the retreat, along with Dr. Knight and several others, by a band of roving Delawares. No sooner had they been brought to an Indian village on the Tyemochte than, upon command of the chief, preparations were made to burn the colonel at the stake, while his companions (with the exception of the doctor) were beaten to death with clubs and scalped in the presence of the women and children.

"When we had arrived at the place set for the execution," relates Knight, who was a witness and escaped a similar fate through flight, "they stripped the Colonel and ordered him to sit down beside the firepile, whereupon they beat first him and then me with sticks and fists, as long as they could. Then they fastened a rope to the foot of a post about fifteen shoes high, tied Crawford's arms behind his back, and fastened the rope to his wrists. It was long enough for him to sit down on the ground or to walk around the post a couple of times. The Colonel now called to Girty, the renegade, and asked him whether they intended to burn him. When the latter replied 'Yes,' he said that he would submit with patience. The decisive moment was now at hand. Captain Pipe, a Delaware chief, made a speech to the assembled Indians—about forty men and sixty squaws and children—and a hideous and hearty roar signified their assent to what had been said. Then the savages reached for their rifles and shot powder into the naked body of Crawford, from the feet up to the neck. Then they crowded about him and, as far as I could tell, cut off his ears. At least, when the crowd scattered, I saw blood running down on both sides of his neck and over his shoulders. Finally they lit the fire; it formed a circle of ten to twelve feet diameter around the post and was built up of small hickory poles. Not satisfied with this slowly killing torture, some of the barbarians poked with burning splinters at the most sensitive parts of the sufferer. The squaws brought boards, heaped glowing coals upon them, and shook them off over his head, so that in a short time he was all afire. In this extreme torment he again called to Simon Girty and begged him to put an end to his suffering with a shot in the heart. But Girty replied, laughing derisively, that he didn't have a rifle with him, and then turned from Crawford to me to increase my deadly fear with derision and threats. Colonel Crawford now loudly implored the Almighty to have mercy upon his suffering. Then he began to mumble dully. Finally he seemed to submit in silence to his fate. All this might have lasted about two hours, when he threw himself upon his belly, exhausted, and remained lying there for a while. The Indians seemed to regard him as dead, for they rushed up to him and scalped him. Then they struck me in the face several times with his bloody scalp, saying: 'See, that's your great captain!'

An old squaw (whose external appearance corresponded in every respect to popular conceptions of the devil) now dragged up a board with coals and shook them upon the bleeding skull of the half-dead man, and once again the pitiable man got to his feet and staggered around the post. His tormenters again poked at him several times with firebrands, although at this time he no longer seemed to feel anything.

"The savage who guarded me," Knight concludes his report about this hell-tragedy, "now took me to the house of Chief Pipe, and so I was prevented from seeing the end of the Colonel's execution. On the following morning my guard untied me and painted me black. Then we left for the village of the Shawnees, which, it was said, was forty miles distant; there I was to die. We went past the spot where Crawford had been burned, and I saw his bones among the ashes of the fire. The Indian called to me that my big captain was lying there, and then he shouted the scalping cry."

We also passed over this place of disaster on our return to Carey. It is located on the east bank of the Tyemochte stream, about a mile and a half south of the log cabin where we had spent the night. On the site of the Delaware village now stands a well-established farm that Cousin Theodore almost purchased. Traces of the satanical spectacle have long since been blown away by the winds of seventy years, and upon the green sod which has sprouted up from the ashes of Crawford's funeral pyre a flock of guinea fowl walked in the morning sun, clucking cheerfully.

◊ ◊ ◊ From Carey, which we reached again in the course of the morning, we now set out in a westerly direction, planning to walk to Defiance, sixty miles away, and from there to travel by canal boat to Toledo at the mouth of the Maumee on Lake Erie. The road to FINDLAY, our next stop on this tour, presented little worth reporting. However, the farther we left the railroad behind, this leader and lever of civilization, the more clearly we became aware that we were now in the wilderness. And as we finally strode into the lonely shadow-forests of the Black Swamp, we were closed in by a nature and met people more primitive than those we might perhaps have encountered in the South and East three decades before.

Findlay is a splendid little town. The nucleus from which it evolved was one of those border forts that during the Indian Wars were moved, like chess rooks, to the north and east, until the game was won by the whites. It is situated in Hancock County on a tributary of the Auglaise, a dark, deep, slowly flowing forest stream that once, when the Shawnees still occupied this area, had the name Schopoquatesepe, that is, "the river of the tailor," but today is called Blanchard's Fork.[4] Until the beginning of this century there lived here a Frenchman named Blanchard who was a tailor. He is said to have been an educated man, but the story goes that he had fled from his fatherland because of a murder. Here he joined the natives in all things, married a squaw, and upon his death left behind seven sons, one of whom was a chief when the Shawnees emigrated to the Far West.

Another strange inhabitant of this area was a certain Jonathan Chapman, better known by his nickname, "Johnny Appleseed." He was an eccentric fellow but one of the most lovable of those reported in the book of human curiosities. Among the crude race of hunters and warriors living along the border, he followed the gentle occupation of a gardener in the desert. Without any claim to thanks and reward, he roamed through the inhospitable forest regions to plant them with apple trees. It just happened to be his inclination, as it was the inclination of others to wander through the wilderness as Indian killers. Having followed the advancing civilization from Pennsylvania to Ohio, he always stayed close to the borderline between the furthermost settlements of the whites and the hunting grounds of the redskins. Here, on the rich loam of river margins, he cleared away the underbrush and then planted his apple seeds, whereupon he left the place, to return when the young trees had sprouted. If settlers now came into the region to begin their clearings, Johnny was always ready for them with his seedlings; as a rule, he gave them away free or exchanged them for an old piece of clothing or some other trifle. For long years he continued this blessed activity, until the land was full of the fruits of his labors and he, like those hunting-mad and bloodthirsty nine-killer souls, had to seek new elbowroom for his inclination in the Far West. In the matter of faith he was a follower of Swedenborg, whose writings he distributed along with his apple trees. It thereby occasionally happened that he did not have a sufficient supply of a certain book, so he'd tear one in two and give the two halves to different persons. It was another peculiarity of his that he regarded it as a sin to kill an animal, and in this connection a few typical anecdotes are in circulation. One cold autumn night, sitting before his campfire out in the woods, he observed that the mosquitoes were flying into the flame and being burned. He stood up at once, filled with water the tin vessel that he used as hat, cooking pot, and bowl, and quenched the fire, saying: "God forbid that I, merely for the sake of my comfort, should be the cause of the death of one of my fellow creatures!" Another time, walking across the prairie, he was bitten by a rattlesnake. Some time later a friend inquired about the incident. Johnny sighed and replied, with tears in his eyes: "The poor thing! Hardly had it touched me than I, overcome by godless passion, cut off its head with my sickle. The poor, poor, innocent little animal!"

These stories were told us by a farmer in whose home, five miles from Findlay on the road to Gilboa, we spent the night.[5] He had known Johnny personally and described him as a small, deformed man with a long, dark beard and black, sparkling eyes, quick and restless in speech and gesture. His clothing was, for the most part, old, and for a time he even went around in a coffee sack, in the bottom of which he had cut holes for his arms and head. Inured to privation and hardship, he often slept in the open during the hardest time of the year, and it frequently happened that he wandered barefoot through the snow for miles. Here belongs a third anecdote about the queer little man that was told to us later on the Maumee. Once a Methodist traveling preacher was giving an address in the marketplace of a city, and during its course he shouted out: "Where is the barefoot wandering Christian who is on the march to the kingdom of heaven?" Johnny, resting on a woodpile, had been listening to him attentively; he took the question literally and so, raising his naked feet, he cried out in a loud voice: "Here, my man, here he is!"

There were many things about our host that recalled the typical backwoodsman. He still wore the *hunting shirt* of olden times, and he still engaged actively in hunting, although enfeebled by age and lame from a fall. Our rifles were a subject of his most serious inquiry, and when he learned that we were on our way to Michigan, and possibly even would make an excursion to Illinois, he seemed to regret that he would be unable to accompany us. He owned a farm with 140 acres of the most fertile soil, and from this he harvested eighty to ninety bushels of corn per acre and more than half as much wheat. A peach orchard with about a hundred trees extended beyond his farmyard. The stalls in his barn contained "enchantingly beautiful cattle" (as the doctor who spent the night with us here expressed it), and his two-story frame house was one of the handsomest and most spacious that we had seen between Carey and here. Nevertheless, it was clear from his talk that, with a good opportunity, he had a great mind to sell, to move farther west again (and indeed for the fourth time since his immigration to Ohio), and to begin once more, exchanging abundance and comfort for a meager but unrestricted log-cabin existence. At dinner we enjoyed, in addition to a selection of other delicacies of the backwoods, something quite new to me—roast squirrels, of which the oldest son had shot a half dozen. With the tea we were offered, besides sugar, some honey gathered from wild bees; there still is a large number of them in the hollow trees of the surrounding forest.

On the following morning we set out early to reach Defiance before nightfall, if possible. As far as GILBOA, the next town, we had a traveling companion, a young man whose acquaintance we had made the previous evening before the fireplace. He had tried various occupations without success and now wanted to attempt his salvation with the occupation held in lowest esteem in this country, that of schoolmaster. Although scarcely twenty years old, he had been married for twelve months and seemed—may heaven forgive me if I err!—a thorough ne'er-do-well. Anyway, we drew some benefit from his company, for as we walked along Blanchard's Fork he called our attention to a rare freak of nature. Here, at a spot we reached by clambering across a log bridging the stream, stand two maple trees; at their bases they are about fifteen steps apart, but at a height of forty feet they are so joined to each other that they form a single trunk and top. However, this side trip from the road could have turned out badly for us. Still occupied in looking at the two-in-one wonder, I suddenly heard a soft rustling close beside me, and when I looked down, the wide-open jaws of one of those little poisonous snakes that here are called "copperheads" were yawning at me. Fortunately, the cold had paralyzed the striking power of the malicious thing, so that it possessed no more than evil intentions, and I found time to put my rifle butt on its neck and hack off the hissing head with my bowie knife. These noxious animals are extraordinarily numerous wherever their chief enemies, the hogs, do not come, and even though the largest are not more than twenty inches long, it may be possible, to judge by the length of their fangs that they can wound even through boots. However, the cure which our schoolmaster claimed to have applied against their bite might be adopted with some hesitation. He asserted, namely, that the surest help was to drink, immediately after the injury, as much whiskey as one could procure and to continue with this until the swelling of the injured limb went down. The strangest thing about this was supposed to be that in such cases the spirits did not intoxicate, and Mr. Maxwell had had a friend (I no longer recall where) who on such an occasion had consumed no less than two gallons of distilled spirits. The matter was corroborated for me elsewhere by a reputable source; since it cannot be explained, however, I shall leave its correctness open for the present. It is possible that whiskey is a poison, just as possible that Hahnemann's *"similia similibus"*[6] contains a truth, and consequently that the backwoods horse remedy is unknowingly based upon the doctrines of the homeopaths and the apostles of temperance.

Following a more northwesterly course from Gilboa, we were soon made aware by the mightier growth of the trees, by the denser and more luxuriant underbrush between the trunks, and by the blacker and wetter soil that we had crossed the border of the "Black Swamp."[7] This name is given to an area of land that with a length of 120 miles and an average width of 40 miles includes no fewer than eight counties of northern Ohio. At present it is still sparsely populated, the number of its inhabitants being not much over 80,000, but in fifty years, when the forests are cleared and the lowlands drained, it will be called the "Garden of Ohio" and will support a half million people. In only a few places is it a real swamp, with reed-filled ponds and stagnant cane puddles; for the most part it is a broad expanse of fertile marsh soil and profusely covered with an enormous tree growth—various oak species, ash, poplar, hickory, cottonwood, and sugar maple are the most frequently occurring varieties. The cover of treetops, toward which the branches of this magnificent primeval forest entwine, is absolutely impenetrable for sunlight, and the forest's main features are a melancholy semidarkness and a majestic silence. Its mysterious depths may still conceal many a treasure for the botanist. With its motionless, half-denuded gray trees, it gave to us who passed through it in autumn and on calm days an impression of dread, of inhospitality, and, in the long run, of monotony. But it must be a real pleasure to roam through its exuberant greening and blossoming in the springtime, and it must be a delight to hear it rustle with that rustling with which Eden's treetops greeted the first man on the sixth day of creation.

In all probability the Black Swamp once was a bay of Lake Erie, when the lake's water stood 150 feet higher. The uniformity of its soil and its flatness, like the surface of the sea, are the reasons that its tree growth is of the same height almost everywhere, so that the forest stands out on the horizon like an immeasurable dark blue wall. It was the last refuge of the aborigines before their emigration to the lands beyond the Mississippi. On its west border they fought their last battle of despair against the white conquerors of their inheritance. While the rest of Ohio has no beasts of prey and only a few deer, here is still a rich ground for the lover of the hunt. In its hollow trees live bears, raccoons, opossums, and wildcats in great numbers. Troops of small deer sprang across our path more than once, and we heard the gobbling of wild turkeys. Eagles and hawks and a colorful variety of songbirds, some attired in the most magnificent plumage, nest in its branches. Veins of limestone from a half to a whole mile wide pass across its surface, from east to west, like the crests of waves; these are covered with black walnut, butternut, sugar maple, and red elms. Usually the settlements are situated upon these, the most healthful parts of the region, and likewise the roads generally run along them. The soil of the lowlands, however, consists first of all of a layer of decaying plant material, from a foot to a foot and a half deep and extraordinarily fertile, but emitting all sorts of fever as soon as the plow cuts into it. Below this humus a rich yellow clay goes down for several yards, strongly mixed with constituents of calcareous and siliceous earth, and beneath this rests a stratum of blue marl. The water of the swamp is strongly impregnated with sulphur and therefore has a bad taste, but it is supposed to be healthful and even to possess curative powers for skin diseases. One can deduce how productive the land is from the fact that we saw cornstalks 15 feet high, and we were shown an orchard in which the apple trees had grown to a height of 20 feet in the space of five years and their trunks had attained a circumference of 18 inches at the base.

    The road that winds through this wilderness and at times loses itself in piles of fallen leaves, at times is interrupted by muddy spots, and at times has been improved with corduroy in a manner precarious for wagons and riders, becomes lonelier and more silent the farther one proceeds westward. The fences following it almost without interruption as far as Gilboa gradually disappear completely. Now and then, off to the side in the depths of the forest, the bells of grazing cows can be heard, or the crashing of a falling branch scares up crowing birds. Here and there a couple of forked branches stuck into the ground, across which a horizontal pole has been placed and beneath which, in addition to a pile of ashes, crudely carved wooden troughs are lying around, indicate a place where maple sugar has been boiled. Occasionally an oxcart is encountered,

laboriously rolling toward its destination through the mud road and
its holes. Once in a while the wanderer, coming around a corner
of the forest or emerging from a thicket into a reed-covered prairie,
overtakes a procession of those *"movers"* who, following a roving
impulse inherent in the Yankee, are traveling to the sparsely populated regions of the Far West after selling their unmovable possessions in the East. In advance on his nag comes the father of the
family, in blue pilot cloth or crab-red warmus, leggings wrapped
around his legs, the long rifle with the beautifully inlaid butt over
his shoulder, the powder horn and the bullet pouch on his back.
Then appears the wagon, drawn by handsome small horses and
driven by a second pilot cloth jacket or, according to circumstances,
the wife; under its white canvas are stowed the children, the trunks,
and the best of the household equipment. Finally, as a rear guard,
follow a few breeding cattle, led and accompanied by other armed
riders. Thus they move slowly toward their new home, spending the
night with farmers and sometimes also camping out in the woods,
when the weather permits or necessity compels. When all roads
cease, they are guided by the evening star and the compass.

Walking along such a road was rather difficult, and it was
already growing dark when we reached MEDARY.[8] We were now in
the heart of the Black Swamp. A sad picture, this forest village of
Medary, particularly at the time of year when I saw it. Gloomy old
trees with mossy beard and grim-looking knothole eyes push out
from the forest galleries and across the fences, along with a thicket
of bushes, vines, and broad-leaved weeds that rise up from the rotting tangle at the feet of the trees to twine over them or to recon-
quer the area lost to cultivation by them. They form a steep-walled,
giant basin in which twenty to thirty poor, gray-roofed little houses
stand grouped about the center of the town, a towering steam sawmill constructed of wood. A doleful, almost depressing sight, the
impression of which, augmented by the cloudy sky, the approaching
twilight, and the prevailing dense air mixed with the vapor of decaying foliage and rotting trees, soon led us to think about corpses.
Not a soul was to be seen in the street, and if the chimneys had
not been smoking and if the gnawing of the sawteeth in the mill
could not have been heard, one might have taken the place to be
deserted—so mysterious and inhospitable, so disconsolately melancholy appeared the town in this stiff, scrubby, fallow desert.

Undecided as to whether or not we should remain here, we
were frightened on our way by the unpleasant interior of the hotel

which we finally entered. An enormous fireplace beside which a rifle was leaning, a rickety rockingchair in which an ashen-colored, sullen landlady was sitting, and a bar with a whiskey bottle and two dirty glasses—these were the complete furnishings of which this uncomfortable shack boasted. Although it was a severe test of endurance to drag along with my blistered toes for another 2½ miles over a corduroy road that had just been completed, I should rather have walked twice as far as to spend a night here. We did not regret our decision. The supper and the beds that we found at *Heischberger's Farm* at the end of that martyrs' road across those logs recompensed us abundantly, and at the same time it proved that even in the middle of the Black Swamp one could live cheerfully and comfortably.

Heischberger's is the first farm on one of those above-described ridges that runs several miles from here to the west, and it is called *the German Ridge* because for its whole length it is covered with settlements of Germans. Daniel Heischberger himself is a German; however, if I had pleasantly anticipated hearing the mother tongue spoken again, I was disappointed. Coming from Virginia, he had completely forgotten the Alsatian in which his father had still been fluent, and he knew so little about the land of his ancestors that he thought the Germans were subjects of Queen Victoria. He was a jovial fellow and famous far and wide as a daring and skillful bear hunter. His dwelling, a spacious log cabin, had been profitably set up as an inn, since it is situated at the intersection of two roads, and, in fact, no one could have desired in this region a more delicious supper than that presented by his table. After the meal, at which a wild turkey played the main role, we were regaled before the fireplace with the best hunting tales, and Heischberger showed us the skins of two bears, one of which he had slain directly behind the house and the other even on the threshold of the back door. We received an unusual surprise when, at bedtime, the host conducted us to his guestroom. The walls, timbered in good backwoods taste, were pasted over with a gallery of colorfully printed Barnum menagerie posters and illustrated advertisements for patent doctors, trick riders, election agitators, and other quacks, to such an extent that only a few feet of space were left unfilled; the gallery, it must be said, was superbly selected in regard to the richness of color. Still more pleasant was the surprise we received at the elegant, flower-embroidered bedspreads belonging to the decoration of this magnificent chamber. And I hardly dared believe my eyes when, in the morning, I saw my boots, that had not been taken care of for four days, standing at the foot of my bed splendidly polished. Heischberger himself had performed this good deed and had thus revealed that he was not as yet a thoroughly Americanized German, since a genuine son of Uncle Sam hardly shows this consideration to his own shoes.

When Heischberger found out that my companion was looking around for a bit of land suitable for settlement, he at once wanted to keep us here. Several pieces of half-cleared farmland were to be had at the slight price of $5 per acre, and one of them had so many advantages that it was difficult to restrain Cousin Theodore from buying it. Embracing an area of 124 acres, of which only a quarter was "wet soil" and nearly a third had been cleared of the smaller trees, it would have made a splendid farm. The clay present everywhere would have supplied the material for a little brick house that Heischberger promised to build for $100, complete except for the furnishings, in place of the log cabin that now stood in the center of the tract. Defiance, the closest market, was no more than ten English miles distant. The slight education of the neighbors assured a man of intelligence and knowledge an important voice in community affairs, and it was even suggested that election to the legislature might be possible in the future. If one took into account the certainty that a piece of land purchased now would have to increase at least threefold in value within ten years, without any effort on the part of the owner, merely through the approach of civilization, the intention to settle here surely could not have been criticized—if only the earthen gray, fever-wracked face of the landlady in Medary had not looked over our shoulders at the idyll which grew out of this calculation. To our inquiries as to the healthfulness of this region, Heischberger gave the customary answer: *"Only a little ague,"* but in those of its inhabitants that we were able to see, the entire *German Ridge* gave evidence that the demon whose mouldering breath we had so clearly detected in Medary also reigned here and that consequently the people suffered not merely "a little" but uncommonly much from intermittent fever.

So we then left behind our good friend Heischberger, hope of a seat in the capitol at Columbus, and the prospect of three months' fever in each of the next ten years, along with all the Romanticism connected with this, and continued our pilgrimage through swampland and forest shades until, in the course of the afternoon, we stepped out into the wide clearing intersected by the Miami Canal in which is spread out the town of Defiance, crossed by the Maumee River and the Auglaise, which flows into it here. In the tavern here we found a merry hunting party that with its booty of deer, snipe, and raccoon half filled the barroom; with them we drank away several very pleasant hours until the arrival of the packet boat.

◊ ◊ ◊ The arrangement of the packet boats on the canal between Cincinnati and Toledo is, on the whole, appropriate and convenient. Drawn by horses that are kept at a trot almost constantly, they attain the utmost in regard to the chief requirement of American transportation: speed. The price is low. The three daily meals included in the fare differ little from those provided on the steamboats. The apparatus by means of which, at nightfall, the cabin is transformed into a sleeping room (as if by the turn of a hand) is extremely practical. On the other hand, the republican theory of equality that maintains free access for even the most undesirable fellows sometimes displays itself in a manner that could convert many of its adherents to the opposite point of view. But still more unpleasant in its consequences is that greed for the "almighty dollar" that causes the captains of these vessels to take on still more passengers, even though they already have more than enough in proportion to the size of the cabin. Thus the boat that we boarded was overfilled with travelers of all sorts, and it was due only to our good fortune and to that national determination (quickly acquired) which does not shun a slight bit of insolence that we were at least allotted sleeping space on the bare deck, since all the hammocks had long since been occupied. But some consolation could be gained from the observation that things were no better for a dozen others; indeed, some were not even as well off, for they had to spend the cold, damp night upon the roof of the cabin.

I had become aware on other occasions that the Americans are completely free of "title-sickness." Nevertheless, I should not have suspected that our boat carried a cargo of such distinguished and learned people as I discovered in the morning. A colonel had slept to my right. My fat neighbor on the left, who had snored like a night watchman's horn lost in insanity, was greeted with the title "*Judge.*" During the conversation at breakfast I became acquainted with at least a half dozen majors and captains, and, in fact, I myself was honored at various times with the rank of a "*Captain,*" presumably in the same way in which a Viennese cab driver addresses each complete jacket with "Your Grace." This matter, which leads to many a delightful caricature, is due in part to the militia and in part to the Mexican War. The regiments of volunteers returning from the war poured forth over the entire country masses of officers' titles; the martial sounds of these act in a very exhilirating manner upon the ear of the stranger, particularly when compared to the peaceful occupations that their possessors now pursue. The people of the West, and especially the younger people, are filled with a surprisingly warlike spirit, and Taylor's victory, won mainly with volunteers, might prove that battles can also be won by soldiers who do not possess the normal mustache and who have not been drilled for years in the school of the guardroom and the parade.

TOLEDO, where we arrived early on the sixteenth, is a thriving commercial city of thirty-five hundred inhabitants. It is situated where the Maumee flows into a bay of Lake Erie, and it would enjoy a still more rapid growth if the flat region in which it stands did not have the reputation of being unhealthful. The town, which originated from two separate settlements that are now connected by a double row of houses, stretches along the shore for over a mile. The view of the harbor is extremely attractive. The eye surveys the river, which widens more and more into a bay, for a great distance. Wooded peninsulas reach out in picturesque forms into the surface of the stream, and a considerable number of steamers, canal boats, and sailing ships—some decorated with the starry banner and some unfolding the British flag—move about in the harbor and give evidence of the lively commerce of which Toledo is the center.

It has been mentioned above why our plan to visit Prophet Strang and his Mormons failed. An excursion over to Canada was not to be recommended because of the rainy weather, and a side trip to Indiana would not have rewarded us for the expended time; so there was nothing left for us to do but wait for the passing of the rain clouds and then return through the Maumee Valley to the south.

This valley, which is part of the Black Swamp along its entire length, is one of the most remarkable regions in Ohio history. Almost every city has originated from a border fort. The wanderer can hardly walk a couple of miles without encountering a place famous from the Indian period or from the last war with England—a battleground or an old campsite. It was here in 1794, in the "battle of Fallen Timbers," that "Mad Anthony" avenged Saint

Clair's Defeat; it was here that Harrison won his first laurels in 1812; and it was here that the hero Tecumseh made the final attempt to defend the last bit of land remaining to the red men of their boundless hunting grounds against the encroaching power of the white intruders. It was here, finally, in 1835, that the Militias of Ohio and Michigan faced each other to fight out a border dispute that came within a hairbreadth of leading to war between the two states. However, it was settled just in time by the intervention of Congress, so that it amounted to no more than the destruction of a few melon beds and the robbing of several chicken coops by the Michigan militia and a few gruff proclamations by the governor of the Buckeye State. Another tragicomedy that played in the valley was the failure of a magnificent swindle that agitated the entire Northwest of the Union some fifteen years ago. The height of the land speculation, which falls in the period from 1834 to 1837, directed public attention to this area. The extraordinary fertility of the soil and the probability—guaranteed by the rivers, canals, and lakes—that a center of commerce would develop here, attracted a large number of enterprising spirits. It was as though the people believed they had found the place where the millennial kingdom was to begin. From the mouth of the river up to the rapids the region swarmed with adventurers who planned to become rich in this easy way. Wherever any advantage could be figured out from a piece of land, it was acquired and divided into city lots which should yield, if possible, twenty times the original purchase price. Every month a new example of one of these imaginary cities was created; in it were to be seen the most splendid churches, town halls, public squares, and parks—naturally only upon the map. As a result, many people let themselves be lured to the "paradise of the Maumee," and, when the boasted qualities did not prove true, ninety-nine out of a hundred of these gullible persons saw themselves transformed into beggars and fled from the district, hopelessly in debt. All of these cities (eleven in number, if I recall correctly), instead of obeying the magic word of speculation, have remained stuck in the Black Swamp. Where they were supposed to stand, the forest again rises above the decaying cabins of those deceived and of the deceivers, and the names they bore have passed over into the storeroom from which the wits of the West draw the material for their jokes.

It was on the morning of the seventeenth, after the weather

had cleared, that we began our return trip. MAUMEE CITY, the first town we reached going up between river and canal, is connected with PERRYSBURGH, situated on the opposite shore of the Maumee, by a wood bridge resting upon stone pillars. Both towns have shipyards, carry on a considerable trade, and possess a friendly, prosperous appearance. The ridges upon which they stand rise about a hundred feet above the surface of the river and, curving inland in an attractive fashion, form an amphitheater a mile wide and about twice as long. We looked over the region from the hilltop to the left of Perrysburgh where Fort Meigs once stood. Only the earth walls and cemetery of this border fortification, famous for the heroism with which it was defended by the Americans under Harrison against the British-Indian superiority under Proctor and Tecumseh, are still visible. The view from here is most charming. There, to the left in the dark forest, the Maumee rapids rush over their rocky bed behind and between two long, narrow islands. Directly at the feet of the observer the river, which here has settled down to a mirror surface, flows through meadowland, carrying sailing ships, rafts, and small boats, until it loses itself again in a gloomy forest region beyond the hill upon which once stood the English Fort Miami. To the right of the bridge a large island and several small ones rise from the water. Beyond them, however, on the opposite shore, the white frame houses of Maumee City laugh, while to the left of this cheerful little picture a bay wreathed by trees and bushes is seen.

Various circumstances contributed to making the area around Maumee City a favorite sojourn of the Indian tribes occupying the land in ancient times, and at the beginning of the present century the region from here to Defiance was still densely filled with their wigwams, cornfields, and peach orchards. As early as 1680 the French had a trading post here. In 1794 the English erected upon this spot the above-mentioned Fort Miami, of which traces are still visible. A part of the city covers the ground where the "battle of Fallen Timbers," which had begun about an hour's distance upstream, was decided. At that point, right beside the highway that runs past Presque Isle Hill, is located a large rock marking the grave of an Indian chief. This Chief Turkeyfoot here rallied a part of the Shawnees put to flight by Wayne's troopers in that bloody encounter, and with them he resisted the enemy forces until, bleeding from a number of wounds, he fell down dead. In the rock next to which he had fallen the Indians chiseled a couple of turket feet, still clearly recognizable today; and the story goes that the early colonists of the Maumee Valley frequently found pieces of tobacco on the rock, placed there as offerings to propitiate, to a certain extent, the angry spirit of the departed hero.

From here to PROVIDENCE the right bank of the river forms a single, immense deciduous forest, while the canal on the left has called into existence a number of farms and small towns. The landscapes still retain much of the wild character of those primitive times when nature was left to itself and the demons dwelling therein played their riotous game undisturbed and untamed by the hand of the earth king. Floods have created a chain of swamps and ponds from whose greenish waters project moss-covered trees and stumps. Occasionally the river grows broader and shallower, and gray limestone terraces exposed to the waves stand out from its bed like a mighty dam. Then it flows silently and deep again through the shadows of the forest that feeds it from its thousand springs. Here and there it embraces a wooded island, the treetops of which have been painted by autumn with all its colors, from the darkest brown to the brightest red. Then again it has demonstrated the power that its anger possesses at high water by piling up a mass of uprooted trees. Often the pale, weatherbeaten countenance of a rock giant stares forth from the black humus cover with which the decaying forest has bestrewn his body; and again a wide field of reeds, above which chattering flocks of birds hover, pushes out into the middle of the river.

We were not equipped to undertake a regular hunt in these marshes, but even the margins would have yielded a quite substantial booty if we had had several more hours. As matters stood, we had to content ourselves with a duck and a half dozen snipe; we used these to pay for the trip from Providence to Napoleon on the canal boat since they could not be utilized in any other way.

In the cabin we observed a spectacle such as has to be witnessed only too frequently on the highways of America. I mean that mixture of awkwardness and timidity with which German immigrants usually make themselves ridiculous when traveling in the company of Yankees. The example that we met with here surpassed everything that had come before my eyes previously.

It was a shoemaker and his wife (if I'm not wrong) from the
vicinity of Heilbronn. They had paid for cabin space from Toledo
to Cincinnati but were far from making use of the privilege
they had thus purchased and pressed themselves timidly into the
corner of a sort of anteroom where the Negro servants stayed.
Only with effort could they be persuaded to undertake the risk of
sitting at the table with the other passengers. In vain did I
exhaust my eloquence in attempting to convince the woman that
her place was in the ladies' cabin. She stuck to her meek belief
that the beautiful divans there were too elegant for her. I finally
gave up any further efforts at persuasion, annoyed and red-faced
from the scornful whispering and giggling of the Americans who
were restrained from loud laughter only by the sex of this
obstinate bit of overhumility. When, around ten o'clock, preparations were made to transform the interior of the boat into a
sleeping room, the foolish woman still sat in the men's cabin,
causing general embarrassment.

I was glad that I didn't have to watch the last act of this
tragicomedy—probably ending with a forcible removal—for the
pilot called in at the door that we were at NAPOLEON. But for a
long time I was troubled by this disgusting picture of German
servility, and it no longer seemed strange to me when I heard
the Americans speak of *"dutchmen"* with ill-concealed scorn.

In Napoleon, after a long search in the pitch-black night, we
found comfortable lodging in the inn kept by Judge Craig.[9]
In the morning we attended a court scene in which our good judge
became so absorbed in the peeling of an apple that, at the conclusion of their philippics, he had to ask the lawyers (by whom
oratorical fire and tobacco juice were spit forth alternately) what
they had actually said. After we had continued on our way for
a few miles upstream, we changed our course and had ourselves
rowed across the Maumee to Wood County by a boy who was
fishing at a place called Girty's Point. Here the river is as wide as
the Saale where it empties into the Elbe, and very deep. The
point at which we crossed has its name from the circumstance that
here in olden times stood the wigwam in which Simon Girty,
the notorious renegade, spent the last years of his life. The
farmer whose fields now cover the spot could report nothing
about the man whose former property he now occupies except that
Girty had been a traitor to his country and a terrible monster—
the mere mention of his name (like the bogeyman) had been

enough to frighten ill-behaved children. However, a hunter whom we met a short distance from here in the woods knew Girty's story in more detail, and according to his account the life of the renegade would have been a worthy subject for a heroic poem in the tone of Byron's "Corsair."

Simon Girty was the son of an Irishman who had settled in Pennsylvania not far from the present location of Pittsburgh.[10] The old man (the average American always designates the head of a family as *"the old man"*) was a drunkard and had alienated the love of his wife through this vice. Having become indifferent to her duty, she had given her heart to another. In order to remove all obstacles with one blow, this man one day put a bullet through the head of the unpopular husband and departed with the trophy of his crime. The four sons of the lovable couple became Indian hunters, a very common occupation of the border people at that time. In the practice of the same, during Braddock's campaign, they had the misfortune of being captured by the redskins, who, however, did not lead them to the torture stake, as was customary, but received them in their midst by adoption. While the three other brothers joined the tribe of the Delawares, Simon was adopted by the Senecas. Among these he had soon acquired the reputation of a great hunter and warrior, and his former countrymen, the whites, cursed his name and regarded him as the most frightful monster on this earth. But this opinion seems to be erroneous. It is certain that Girty led the savages repeatedly in their raids against the colonists of Kentucky and Ohio, and it appears just as certain that he was guilty of many cruelties. But the reason for this was different from that generally believed. Simon Girty had become a complete Indian down to the skin. The Indians' enemies were his, and so were their customs and their concepts of duty and justice. In addition it can be proven that he saved many a prisoner from a fiery death and that the reports of various infamous deeds of his brothers—who must have been absolute devils—seem to have been entered under his account. However this may be, Girty, with all his barbarity, had many noble features. He stood by those whose business he had made his own—to the last breath. He was brave to the point of rashness. He kept his promises and once sold his only horse rather than not satisfy a creditor at the appointed time. Although he took part in all the chief battles of the fifty years' war between the Long-Knives and the redskins and was wounded several times, his ardent desire to die on the battlefield was not fulfilled by destiny. He lived to a ripe old age, suffered much from gout during the last years of his life, and finally was even afflicted with blindness. An uncle of our reporter had seen him in this condition in 1813. He had entered a tavern in the town of Malden in Canada (now Amherstburgh) and had met an old, white-haired, blind man with a deep, wide scar across his forehead. The woman of the house had asked him if he knew who the old man was, and when he replied "No," he had been given the answer that it was Simon Girty, the renegade.

The hunter to whom we owed this information was so kind as to accompany us diagonally through the forest to the so-called Napoleon Road; we were heading toward it in order to walk past Heischberger's farm up to Kalida and on from there to the canal, by means of which we planned to return home. In this way we cut across the entire breadth of the Black Swamp and saw it in its loneliest and wildest sections.

The Napoleon Road has been constructed by drawing a line south from the Maumee shore opposite the city of Napoleon and then clearing the trees from it to a distance of twenty paces. Part of the trunks have been pushed to the side; the others remain where they have fallen. There has been no thought of removing the stumps, but here and there the various creeks have been bridged and the knee-deep mudholes filled. So the road is passable for wagons only in dry weather. After a continuing rain it becomes completely bottomless; it was quite believable when a farmer at whose home we had lunch told us that during the past spring he had needed almost two full days to cover the distance of nine English miles between his farm and Napoleon with a lightly loaded wagon. The farther one penetrates into this wilderness, the poorer and farther apart the farms become. I believe that their occupants live a life like the worms in a head of cabbage. Thick and tall cornfields, richly rewarding the seeding, surround the log cabins, although the squirrels that swarm along the fences by the hundreds share the fruits of the same with the legal owner. Fat cattle graze in the forest, from whose branches the wind shakes down all kinds of nuts for them. Beautiful orchards supply the material for cakes, preserves, and other sweets; the wives of the backwoodsmen accomplish miracles in their preparation. If one wants sugar, one taps the maple trees outside. If one desires honey, enough is found in the hollow trees.

If one has an appetite for game, the rifle stands there in the corner—and within a mile of the farm deer are going to the waterhole, turkeys and doves are flying, and squirrels as fat as rabbits and with a flavor like partridge jump about in great numbers through the treetops. Frequently, too, a bear is kind enough to carry his hams into the path of the hunter. If one also takes into account that the settler enjoys unlimited freedom and that, as soon as the labors of clearing and of the far more difficult fencing are accomplished, he no longer has half as much work as a peasant in Germany, then there can hardly be any objection to such an existence from those for whose caterpillar-consciousness the goal of human existence is a well-filled stomach. One would then have to find the pale faces uncomfortable that also sit before all doors here and tell of the visits paid before and after each winter by that wicked fairy Malaria to the mortals pushing into her realm.

From the farm where we stopped at noon the road curved into the forest; from now until approaching darkness we walked through a wilderness in which nothing but the road and the surveyor's marks on the tree trunks reminded us that it had been frequented by any living beings other than deer and bear. If the road had been a test of patience until now, it became more so with each of the ten remaining miles. The quotations with which Cousin Theodore had earlier consoled himself when, balancing on the edge of a mud puddle, he had lost his equilibrium and had sunk into the morass above his boot tops, now gave way to a selection of the best German oaths when, with a similar gymnastic trick, he fell into the cool mud up to his thighs. I, too, could not restrain myself from a few blasphemies when, in order to avoid a similar undesired mudbath, I climbed across a fallen oak trunk, and crash! plunged into flying mud and slimy decay up to the chest. So we did gymnastics and stormed on, until we found our good humor again in a repeated falling into a hollow tree, from which an opossum sprang up and away. Upon one of those ridges that cross the swamp we met with the strangest sight: for a considerable distance the top of the hill was quite regularly patterned with light brown stripes, the decayed remnants of tree trunks that a windfall had knocked down. Wading through a creek, we killed a black snake over three feet long; and shortly before our arrival at Heischberger's we shot—all's well that ends well—a wild turkey that was just preparing to go to

## A WEEK IN THE BLACK SWAMP

sleep in the top of an oak tree. My companion's bullet had passed through its breast and the fall must have stunned it. Nevertheless, it tried to fly up again, and we didn't completely subdue it until I had taken away almost its entire head with a load of buckshot. Heischberger, with whose family we consumed it that same evening, estimated its weight at eighteen to twenty pounds; but he asserted, smiling, that he would never shoot at a turkey more than once.

An Irishman with whom we spent the night at Heischberger's farm claimed to have ridden here from Kalida in five hours, but we got lost and required more than three times as much time. At a creek blocking the way to walkers we got on a trail turning off to the left and followed it until it stopped at a great ashpile where maple sugar had been boiled. Then we continued to walk toward the south, reading the direction from the position of the sun and the moss on the trees until, after hours of difficult wandering about, we came upon a second creek. We followed this for a mile, and then another mile, forgetting to hold our direction toward the south, and finally found ourselves quite unexpectedly on the bank of a broad, deep forest stream flowing silently in the shade. Unfortunately, I had left my map of Ohio at Heischberger's. Nevertheless, a little reflection would have put us upon the right track even here, for it would have told us that the dark, slow river flowing toward the sinking sun could be none other than Blanchard's Fork. Our thoughts were now confused, whether by a malicious swamp demon or by mere anxiety about the approaching night—enough, we were completely at a loss as to whether we should follow the stream or head in the opposite direction. We finally decided upon the most unintelligent thing that we could do under the circumstances: we asked the buttons of my jacket for advice, and that oracle gave us the reply we deserved for our stupidity. It told us to go to the left, and thus wander upstream, the direction exactly opposite that we should take if we wanted to reach Kalida. Each quarter hour that we proceeded along the winding river, constantly looking—in vain—for a road, a bridge, or a human habitation, brought us into a wilder wilderness. A couple of times our steps startled small herds of deer. We now and then saw small turtles under piles of dry leaves. Flocks of ducks were swimming in the river, and white birds of prey darted back and forth, snapping up fish that rose in clumsy leaps from the sunset waters. And when we had worked our way down into a hollow formed by a caved-in bank, we saw a raccoon slip away from a projecting root, upon which he had been making his toilet, into a hollow sycamore.

All these things certainly were uncommonly interesting, but the necessity (growing more and more urgent) of finding a road leading to shelter soon caused us to pay no more attention to them. Our dilemma increased in the same degree as the darkness. Fog rose from the stream. The stars became visible. The twilight between the trees changed to blackness. We looked at each other. Our situation was so ticklish that we should have liked to laugh aloud from sheer desperation. It could not be more than three miles to the nearest farm. But how to find it? To go on was as little to be recommended as to turn back. In both cases we ran the risk in the darkness of getting too close to the undermined riverbank and plunging in. Theodore listened with an ear to the ground. I climbed a tree. Wasted effort! Not a sound was to be heard, not a light to be seen. We sent up a "hallo!" in unison. A second, and a third. Nothing, no reply, not even an echo. We finally had to resign ourselves, for better or worse, to camping out in the woods for the night, although this was the surest way to catch a violent fever, since we were unaccustomed to it and, besides, had eaten nothing since morning. We were just about to light a fire, when—listen! What was that? — Hurrah! It was one of those horns with which the farmwomen of the West signal their husbands working in the forest that the meal is ready.* Again. Yes, no doubt. We had heard that sound too often on our journey to mistake it now. It came from the north, and at once we gave up our firemaking and hurried, as quickly as the circumstances would permit, toward the triply welcome voice. Before us and behind us there was a hopping, rustling, and fluttering, a crowing and peeping of startled creatures. Up and down went our path, across a tangled confusion of broken branches and trunks. And again the melancholy tones swelled through the forest halls; they were louder and more distinct, a sure sign

---

* These horns are usually straight, nonspiralling tin tubes running to a conical point, without tone holes and valves, often up to six feet long. In view of the length of these instruments of such primitive construction, the higher tones are produced only by stronger or thinner puffs of air in blowing, not by holding a hand in the opening. The skill with which the women are able to entice complete melodies from them is astounding. A person not accustomed to them is seized by a strangely solemn feeling when, walking in the virgin forests of the West or sailing along its streams, he suddenly hears these sounds, evolving into a pious melody, resounding through the silent forests.

that we were on the right track. A creek checked our advance, but we got to the opposite bank by straddling a fallen tree. A hill rose before us, and—victory! When we reached its crest, a merry fire flickered toward us from a hollow not two hundred paces away. Dark figures were lying about the fire. Nearby stood a white tent, and a short distance from it a ford in the creek reflected the heartwarming flame. A couple of large bloodhounds began barking as we approached. The faces of the group turned toward us, and an inquiring *"Hulloh, boys?"* was directed toward us. At home we would have thought of Rinaldo Rinaldini,[11] or at least of a gang of poachers. But from the rifles leaning on an improvised rifle stand before the tent, from the various pieces of game hanging from the trees, from the elegant blankets that the men had wrapped around themselves as coats—from all these things we deduced that our good fortune had led us to one of those hunting parties that each year travel from Cincinnati and other cities in whose vicinity the wild game has been exterminated to the Black Swamp, to the forests of Indiana and Michigan, and even to the wilderness of Arkansas, to indulge for a few weeks the passion for hunting inherited from their ancestors.

We related our adventures and asked about the road to Kalida. It wasn't known, for we had gotten by chance to the vicinity of Gilboa. We now inquired about the nearest farm. The hunters felt that we could hardly find our way there, and they invited us to spend the night with them. This friendly offer was gratefully accepted. From their speech, our hosts were people of fine manners, and this was proved even more by the way in which they provided us with everything necessary to our comfort, even plates and glasses. A place was courteously cleared for us near the fire. With polite words, the captain of the group, a lawyer from Columbus, welcomed us to the delicious dinner of roast venison and to the subsequent wine bowl. And when half the night had been passed in cheerful conversation and finally one after the other began to nod, we were even given a buffalo skin as a blanket.

◊ ◊ ◊ The morning showed us how much we had been mistaken in believing that we were in a complete wilderness, for the nearest log cabin was scarcely two miles away. From there we got on the road to KALIDA without difficulty, and without further adventure we arrived at that town about noon. From there it is ten miles to SECTION TEN on the canal, and since we now paid closer attention to the route, it was possible for us to arrive in time to be able to continue our return trip to the south by the evening boat. This time, however, it was not granted to us to spend the night in the cabin. Not only the hammocks but also the floors were already full of sleepers, and since, moreover, an infernal sweaty heat prevailed in the room, we found ourselves compelled to pitch camp on the deck between boxes and bags.

The circumstances under which we spent this second night in the open were far more unfavorable than those during the first, but we were lucky that the weather was not cold. We were still in the Black Swamp, but we were approaching its border. The boat glided slowly in a straight line along its waveless watery path through the moonless forest landscape. The dark woods rose without interruption on both sides. Only a narrow strip of dark gray sky kept us from thinking that we were traveling through a cave; it required no very lively imagination to compare ourselves to the souls sailing down the rivers of Hades. Everything was quiet in the cabin. Not a breath of wind, only the soft lapping of the water on the keel disturbed the deep calm all around. The beam of the hanging lantern below flitted about on the water and ran like an uncertain, nimble will-o'-the-wisp through the mists and shadows on the shore. Occasionally something like a falling star became visible in the distance. It became brighter and more distinct. A bell began to tinkle and was answered by ours. Then another canal boat floated past us, with red-curtained, faintly illuminated cabin windows. Then silence and solitude again, and that half-slumber in which the embryos of the future hover above the soul and the death-dance of the past strides by on the mirror of memory. I crawled deeper into my blanket, and my eyelids became heavier.[12]

Then a rough hand pushed me, and dream suddenly gave way to reality. The pilot who had awakened me told me to hurry to leave the boat, since we were in SAINT MARYS, where I had intended to get off.

◊ ◊ ◊ Three miles west of the town of Saint Marys is located the great reservoir from which the Miami Canal is fed.[13] It had been described to us as the most extensive artificial lake in the world, and I actually believe that for once the Yankees had not exaggerated. The basin is nine miles long and between three and four miles wide. In its natural state about half of it had been a

prairie and the remainder had been covered with forest. It was
constructed by throwing up earthen walls ten to twenty feet high
in the east and west, while the south and north sides of the basin
were formed by natural chains of hills. The reservoir was begun
in 1837 and completed in 1845—after it had been subjected
to partial destruction in 1843 by an act of illegal self-help.
Namely, in that year the western earth wall had been completed.
The water flowed in at the upper end to a depth of three feet.
However, since the ground rises only gradually toward the east,
here, for a distance of several miles, it was covered by only a
few inches of water. If no countermeasures had been taken, the
local action of the sun's rays would soon have produced a swamp,
and the inhabitants of the entire county would have had to flee
from the region because of the vapors. In addition entire farms,
which at that time had not yet been paid for by the state, had been
flooded by the rising water. Under these circumstances about
150 citizens who saw themselves being damaged set to work and
cut through the western embankment, so that in a few hours the
flooded area was once again completely dry. Among those participating
in this illegal action were some of the most respected people, and
many wielded pick and shovel who on this occasion for the
first time raised blisters through hand labor. According to the law,
all could expect prison sentences, but in the entire county no
grand jury could be found before which charges could be brought.

Viewed from its east shore, the reservoir presents an unusual
picture. In the foreground can be seen, here and there, isolated
dead trees and stumps, between which the roofs and chimneys of
abandoned cabins project from the water. In the center the
flooded surface of the former meadowland extends as far as the
eye can reach, broken here and there by small islands covered
with prairie grass. On both sides, however, a forest of dead trees
with bare, jagged branches and mossy black trunks stares forth
from the shadowy waters. When we visited the place, a strong
south wind blew over the desolate scene, and the miniature ocean
rocked and foamed with such a fury that our boat saved itself
from shipwreck on the trees only with difficulty. Flocks of waterfowl
flew back and forth over the raging waves, there was a crackling
and crashing in the trees, and broken-off branches of critical size
whirled through the air; we had to hurry to get back to the safe
shore from the dangerous center of the basin.

Another point of interest in Mercer County is a colony of

colored people established several years ago in the southern
part of this district. It has prospered—a rare occurrence in such
undertakings. We did not have an opportunity to visit it, but,
by chance, on the boat we were taking to Piqua we made
the acquaintance of a black preacher who had belonged to the
settlement for a time and could therefore give us exact information
about it. According to his report the colony had originated
through the efforts of a Mr. Wattles of Connecticut. Instead of
merely spouting pretty words like the other abolitionists, he had
taken hold of the matter by the right end and, without getting
involved in the quarrel about slavery, had taken steps to improve the
*free* colored and thus emancipate them from the scorn that rests
upon them in the North with the same weight as does servitude
in the South. In the winter of 1833 he had become acquainted with
the state of the Negro population of Cincinnati and found that
(with a few exceptions) they were completely ignorant of the
conditions under which they could become good citizens. Without
delay he went to work to redress this grievance. First of all he
established a school, and the number of pupils soon rose to several
hundred. However, it soon became clear that there could be no
thought of a thorough moral elevation of these people unless they
were removed from the corrupting influences of big-city life.
Wattles therefore suggested to his charges that they purchase
Congressional land in a less populated region and move there en
masse. The Negroes agreed to this under the condition that their
teacher and benefactor head the undertaking. Wattles promised
to do this, traveled through Canada, Michigan, and Indiana looking
for a suitable site, finally found what he sought in Mercer County,
and settled upon the purchased land with about two hundred
colored people. Through his foresight and untiring activity he
saw the land of the colonists increase in five years to thirty thousand
acres and the number of people to four hundred. The noble man
traveled constantly throughout the West, establishing schools for
colored children and striving to acquire participants in his
colonization plans among the adults. Upon returning from one
of these trips, he bought himself a piece of land and set up
an industrial school for the colored. This had extraordinary success,
although the means for its support were very limited until the
year 1842. About this time, however, the executors of the will in
which the Quaker Emlen had set aside $20,000 for the training of
African and Indian boys as handworkers and farmers learned

about the institution of the philanthropic Wattles. They joined the means at their disposal to his, purchased Wattles's farm, and named him director of the [Emlen] Institute. From now on it enjoyed a doubly speedy growth. In 1846, however, Judge Leigh of Virginia purchased a part of the land belonging to the Negro colonists in order to settle upon it the freed slaves of the famous John Randolph of Roanoke. They arrived, numbering about four hundred, but were forcibly prevented from taking up residence by the white inhabitants. Since then the members of the institution as well as of the entire colony, of which Emlen Institute is the center, have been subjected to all sorts of torment and mistreatment, so that several have given up their property and left the district.

In addition to this the state of Ohio has a second Negro settlement. It is located in Shelby County and has about 350 inhabitants. The people are in good circumstances, although the colony is unfavorably situated, the region being damp and therefore subject to frequent fevers. Here, too, the emancipated slaves of Randolph were not tolerated by the whites, and so the homeless ones had to be sheltered individually in neighboring counties with families that were less prejudiced. Finally, two colonies of colored exist in Ohio in the vicinity of Georgetown, each with about 500 members. They emigrated from Virginia in 1818 and were originally the slaves of Samuel Gist; through a provision in his will he freed them and granted them homes here. Regretfully, their present situation is not a happy one; this turn of affairs, according to our reporter, is their own fault and due chiefly to their laziness.

◊ ◊ ◊ The above notes were written down on board the canal boat *Saint Louis* with which we traveled through well-cultivated regions past PIQUA and TROY down to Dayton. Also this part of the country is full of historical memories of the Indian Wars. The Miami Valley, and especially the area around Piqua, was a favorite haunt of the redskins, and long after their removal to the Black Swamp they returned here from time to time to weep at the graves of their fathers over the memories of their childhood. At the location of the last-mentioned town there were still standing at the end of the previous century the wigwams of an Indian village that is said to have numbered over four thousand inhabitants. Indeed, legend even locates here the scene of a miracle through which the place became a sort of shrine. Incidentally, the story is poetic enough to provide an appropriate conclusion to this chapter full of backwoods Romanticism. "Piqua" was the name of a tribe of the Shawnee Nation, and the meaning of the word is "the one born from the ashes." With regard to this, tradition relates the following myth: In dim antiquity the entire people of the Shawnees had gathered here to celebrate their yearly festival. They sat in a circle around a mighty fire and with devout prayers called upon the Great Spirit to bless their hunt and to increase their race. The flames had died down when suddenly a loud hissing, crackling, and puffing could be heard in the pile. Astonished, the worshipers looked up from their devotions, and, behold! from the glowing coals stepped forth the figure of a completely grown red man, who from then on lived among them and became the father of the Piqua tribe.

# 5

## THE QUEEN OF THE WEST AGAIN

◊ ◊ ◊ THE week of the twenty-first to the twenty-eighth was devoted to digesting and working up the material collected during the excursion described in the preceding chapter and to cultivating old acquaintances and making new ones. In small towns here (as elsewhere) life offers little worthy of notice. Its monotonous course is interrupted only by the noise with which an exceedingly exuberant partisanship plagues itself and by an occasional bit of humbug surpassing the usual in originality and brazenness. Incredible things are accomplished in regard to the first, and, to be sure, the Germans greatly outdo the Anglo-Americans in their proclivity to form factions. In fact, the concept of the "individual" must have been eliminated from the philosophy of these people. Their behavior, at least, comes pretty close to a practical denial of the same. Every immigrating individual, as soon as he has become acclimated to a certain extent, takes care to split himself into fractions representing the various sides of his existence; accordingly, he encloses himself in the individual receptacles into which society is divided by this strange impulse. The old guild form was abolished because it hindered trade and commerce. But the old guild spirit, in league with a passion for titles and gambling, is as evident here as anywhere. From the outset the individual in question—or rather, the "di-vidual"—is convinced that because he first saw the light of the world north of Schöppenstedt[1] he must stick with the North Germans, or because his mother delivered him south of this honorable city he must stick with the Swabians and regard all others as born rascals. Then, as soon as he hears the beating of the veins in which Schleiermacher's feeling of dependency[2] pulses—and often even without this, but merely for the sake of respectability or because of the almighty dollar—he joins one of the societies which here have taken a lease on the operations of religion. Further, if he is at all a *zoon politikon*, he enters the stable of the Whigs, the Democrats, or the Freesoilers—for this or that reason, perhaps because a cousin or chum advises it, rarely from conviction. Finally he discovers that he is still lacking one quality and that he absolutely has to split once more, and behold! a kindly fate has also taken care of this remainder of the desire for division. The "di-vidual"—or now, rather, the "hyphen"—has a choice as to whether he wants to crawl into the Masonic tapeworm articulated in thirty-three degrees, to ride his hobbyhorse in a "Grove" of the "Druids," or to join the sacrificers in a "Temple of Honor" of the "Sons of Temperance." And last, he can help make the world happy as a member of the "Ancient and Honorable Order of Odd Fellows." All these secret doll boxes of a pompous caste-feeling are crammed to suffocation. Speaking only of the last-mentioned, the *Odd Fellows:* this brotherhood\* has 190 lodges in the state of Ohio alone, and on the day before my departure for Cincinnati I saw a parade of nearly two thousand of them marching through the streets of Dayton. With its four bands, its adornment of bright-colored bandoleers and gold braid and tassels, and its pompous speeches and toasts, the procession (as the newspaper put it) "made an unforgettable impression upon every soul receptive to beauty and the sublime."

On the twenty-ninth of October I left for MIAMISBURGH from the place where Dayton, according to European ideas of propriety and necessity, should have a station. I wanted to visit the Indian grave located at Miamisburgh, said to be the largest in America.

---

\* The Odd Fellows, like the Freemasons, place the origin of their society in gray antiquity; indeed, it is supposed to have originated in A.D. 65 among the soldiers of a Roman camp and to have been recognized in the year 97 by the Emperor Titus through the presentation of a golden tablet with all sorts of symbols. In truth, however, the order was not founded until 1800, in Manchester, England. From there it was transplanted to Baltimore in 1812. Since then it has grown in America to such an extent that within the United States it currently has 31 Grand Lodges and about 2,500 Encampments with nearly 200,000 members. Its annual revenues are estimated at $1,225,000, consisting chiefly of the burial and widow support funds. The Freemasons may be just about as strong. The Druids, however, are an organization of more recent origin and count relatively few members; still they are increasing rapidly, especially among the lower-class Germans, because of active recruitment.

## THE QUEEN OF THE WEST

It is a steep, conical hill that at the base may have a circumference of four hundred paces and may be seventy to eighty feet high. The forest trees which covered it originally have given way to a peach orchard. This cone of earth, probably a monument to a battle between tribes pushing up from the south and the northern Indians, presumably contains, like smaller ones found all over Ohio, two tombs situated one above the other; they probably are filled with the bones of those slain in the encounter. Several years ago an attempt was made to penetrate from the top into the interior by means of a shaft. When, however, at a depth of two fathoms human bones were encountered and the ground gave off a hollow sound under the picks and shovels, the frightened workers hastily abandoned the commenced work, and since then nothing further has been done.[3]

On the evening of the same day I arrived back in Cininnati, safe and sound, and my following three weeks here were both pleasant and instructive. It was the pickling season, a time when the city is "Porkopolis" more than the nose likes. Despite this, the longer I remained, the more I felt inclined to award it the title of "queenly." Many a prejudice had been tempered during my absence. And now many a prejudice disappeared completely, leaving behind only the impression of something foreign. With much that had merely repelled upon first consideration the attracting pole now was also noted. Generally speaking, many a disgusting feature and many absolutely ridiculous things remained, but, guided by friends who directed my attention, I found far more to admire and to praise. In order to understand American life, a key to its inner rooms is required, here more than elsewhere, and the key is not simply brought to the tourist at his hotel. From the bird's-eye view with which these wandering birds content themselves, the national character cannot be judged, and especially not the local character, which is still evolving and still in the process of fermentation, the yeast still rising to the surface and the superficial person therefore unable to see anything but the yeast.

The following diary notes will now demonstrate whether the person who wrote them down may say of himself that he at times possessed the key. They contain mainly observations and descriptions, rarely judgments; therefore I should like most of all to have them regarded in the light of data from which the reader finally calculates his own results.[4]

*Moritz Busch · Travels*

◊ ◊ ◊ NOVEMBER 1

This morning I visited Dr. Meryweather, who holds an office in the local Mormon congregation. About noon I was summoned down to the public landing by a cannon salute with which the "Red Artillery" (a fourteen-pounder served by men in civilian dress and resting upon a red carriage) greeted Kinkel,[5] who had steamed down from Pittsburgh. In the evening I attended a lecture given by the "Refugee from Spandau" in the Turnhall, decorated with German and American flags.

The Mormon preacher—who, by the way, supports himself with a pawnbroker's business and by the selling of patent medicines—received me in a very friendly and communicative manner. He willingly lent me the sect's religious writings that he owned and gladly promised to take me along to their service tomorrow. In fact, his wife even presented me with a handsomely bound copy of the strange *Book of Mormon,* along with a picture of "Brother Joseph," the Mormons' murdered prophet. It's possible that they interpreted my openmindedness as an inclination and believed that they detected an intention of joining them behind my wish to become acquainted with their faith. Dr. Meryweather had formerly been a Methodist and his wife a Baptist. The conversion to the Church of Latter-Day Saints had been occasioned in his case by a visit to Nauvoo, the former center of Mormonism, and in the case of Mrs. Meryweather by a vision in which a mighty voice had called out to her: *"If you can bear it, you shall hear the word of the Most High."* Both seemed to be very enthusiastic members of the "newest union." No professor and no bishop, he said during our conversation, could nowadays teach the world anything other than that which has already been. But the Holy Ghost was always instilling new knowledge and fresh life in them, the Mormons. To the question of why the gospel of Joseph Smith was no longer being preached in the streets and markets as before, he replied that that was all finished. At present the main duty of the Saints was to prepare for the emigration to the new Jerusalem on Salt Lake. I inquired as to the reason for this, and I found out that before thirty years will have passed, the second coming of Christ, the extermination of the gentiles (*alias* non-Mormons), and the establishment of the heavenly kingdom upon earth will have taken place. When I left, he advised me to study the new Bible thoroughly and I would find that it contained the *"truth and nothing but the truth."* At home, however, an attempt to convince myself of this assertion didn't turn out particularly well. That there is much truth in the book is just as obvious as the fact that its author has copied entire pages word for word from the New Testament. To see nothing but the truth in it was to expect too much of an even greater believer in miracles than I.

The poet Kinkel is counted among the ornaments of the German people, and my pen is the last that should dispute his fame. The revolutionary soldier of the same name deserved our sympathy, and perhaps even more. On the other hand, the "Revolution Loan Commissioner"[6] Kinkel, traveling throughout the Union as a Kossuth *en miniature* to gather subscribers to a new edition of the miseries of 1849, and incidentally to preach—involuntarily, to be sure, but only too loudly—the dismemberment of even the Germans in exile; this shortsighted man who does not know that he is speaking to a public that is either too "gray" to be able *still* to offer him enthusiasm or too "green"* for anything *more* than enthusiasm to be expected; this strange dreamer who imagines that his cause is being honored and promoted, while the artful dodgers who pretend to be eager merely regard his shoulders as a step for their own interests; this wag with the serious countenance who wants us to believe that the London emigration[7] in conjunction with the American is *the* German people; this visionary who with the paltry sum of twenty or thirty thousand taler (it certainly won't be more[8]) wants to bribe the history of the world to change its meaning and its course—oh, man of delusion, *si tacuisses!*

◊ ◊ ◊ NOVEMBER 4

The Mormon conventicle that Meryweather and I attended on the afternoon of the day before yesterday was held in the room of a carpenter who had stopped here for the winter on his journey from Pennsylvania to Deseret. Most of the other participants in the gathering seemed to be in the same boat. Several of them were Scots; others revealed through their speech that they had learned to talk in the broad-mouthed Yorkshire accent. Among the former was a very likable and well-educated young man who presently holds a good position in one of the local banks. Despite this, he

---

* In party and newspaper jargon in America, the "Grays" are those German emigrants who have already lived here for some time and have become Americanized in customs and inclinations; the "Greens" (connected with *Greenhorn*) are those who have emigrated just recently.

will next spring follow the call of the twelve apostles to the "gathering," that is, he will leave for the holy city in the Rocky Mountains. Among the Americans present was one who had been tarred and feathered by the mob of Independence [Missouri] in the first attack on the sect [1833]. He was a spindly, droll little man with a brownish red twisted hat and an enormous high collar. Quick and restless in manner, he later told us on the way home about his sad experience in such a droll fashion that whenever I thought about him later, I was put into an unusually merry humor, particularly when I recalled that this comical thing had been introduced to me with much pathos as *"one of our martyrs."* The service was opened with a hymn of praise for Joseph Smith; I reproduce the first verse as evidence of how highly the Mormons regard their founder. It goes:

*Praise to the man that communed with Jehova!*
*Jesus annointed this prophet and seer,*
*Blessed to open the last dispensation,*
*Kings shall extol him and nations revere.*

*Hail to the prophet ascended to Heaven!*
*Traitors and tyrants now fight him in vain,*
*Mingling with Gods he can plan for his brethren—*
*Death cannot conquer the hero again.*[9]

Hereupon Meryweather said a prayer. Then they sang a second song—to the tune of "Du, du liegst mir im Herzen," something I had not expected to hear in this circle—in which the poet lets the prophet console his people from heaven. This was followed by a three-quarter-hour sermon in the purest cockney English, given by an Englishman who came straightway from the workshops of the great tailoring firm of Moses and Son. But the high point and climax of the entire ceremony was reached with an address by the martyr of Independence; during its course his fervor gradually increased to the point where the speech changed to an inarticulate mumbling and gurgling. This continued for about two minutes, with names and words being mixed in occasionally in a tone in which a dreamer speaks. It was a sample of the "speaking in tongues" in which the Saints of the Latter-Day take pride (as well as in other charismata of the age of the apostles); from its occurrence among them they derive a proof for the genuineness and truth of the new gospel brought from the hill of Cumorah.

The Kinkeliad is in full swing. The newspaper lions are roaring loudly. A sense-stupefying debating, organizing, bragging, and carousing resounds through the German taverns. Meetings of the male and female sexes resolve that Germania must become free. Already the apothecary Rehfuss has laid a hundred dollars in cash upon the portable altar of the fatherland that the agitator's secretary carries along in his trunk. All levers have been set in operation, all stopcocks have been turned on, and all registers have been drawn up. Three American literati have declared themselves for the future German republic. The mayor of Porkopolis has tacitly recognized it by a visit to Kinkel. The rumor spreads that thirteen of the participants in the torchlight procession that paraded yesterday, two thousand strong, through the amazed streets have united into a company and on the spot have chosen the necessary five officers. They also have already ordered the big drums that are to be carried before them as regulators of their steps in the conquest of Germany for the London Revolutionary Society and for the Ruge philosophy.[10] The Nurembergers hang no one unless they already have him. The Porkopolitaners act more prudently. In yesterday's celebration the disciples of the genial atheist Hassaurek[11] carried around a hanged king in full coronation robes—for the present, to be sure, only as a transparency—but one still sees the honest intentions of these fine young men. In a word: the phlegm of the local Germans has been set afire and burns like the fields of the Philistines when Samson chased in his foxes. A doubter still mumbles here and there about humbug and blarney. A raven still crows occasionally about a certain difference between "intending" and "executing." It still seems to me at times that the head of the little mouse might now be seen to which the spinning mountain could give birth. But away with these fancies and worries, brethren, for surely the day is dawning (as Hassaurek's *Hochwächter* shouts), and fate cannot intend that the barkeeper at the Turnhall lose the twelve bottles of Rhine wine he has bet me that next May I shall land in Hamburg as a citizen of the "United States of Germany." "*Fact, Sir, by God! — Clear as mud!* And if just as many devils squeezed between intention and execution as 'if' and 'but' have been set since the invention of printing—the matter will proceed all the same, in spite of everything, *irregardless*"—so says the barkeeper at the Turnhall.

◊ ◊ ◊ NOVEMBER 8

If the ten weeks that I now have been in this country have led, in general, to some modification of the prejudice with which I came over (in regard to the crass materialism of the Americans), this has taken place far more emphatically during the past few days. I have had the opportunity to become acquainted in some detail with the organization of the local school system. Early on Thursday morning I visited the Lane Seminary established by the Presbyterians, and, for the sake of comparison, I spent the afternoon at the Xavier College conducted by the Jesuits. Having become acquainted with one of the teachers through K., I yesterday attended instruction in one of the nineteen city elementary schools. We were courteously shown the sights everywhere. If, in the explanations that were eagerly given by all, hardly a sound was heard of the ideal purpose of education, that is, "being formed," yet the "training system for moneymaking"—as friend G., the wicked Christian, likes to designate the matter—is so admirably and skillfully organized that in practice it now and then makes no difference what kind of goal the head that thought up the plan had before its eyes. Of course, there is no room for the speculative sciences. The empirical sciences, on the other hand, are partly very well off, and the elementary schools must be called very good, in regard to both the instructional method and the selection of the subjects of instruction.

Public instruction in the United States is imparted in three kinds of institutions: in elementary schools, in academies, and in colleges.[12] The first are differentiated from ours chiefly by the fact that religious instruction is excluded everywhere by law. A compulsion to attend them exists as little as any other compulsion from above. The aim of the academies (sometimes also called "high schools") is to acquaint their pupils to some extent with the higher branches of knowledge, especially with mathematics and world history. A few also include the ancient languages. In the colleges, finally, the scholars receive what is here called "a thorough classical education." With this is usually connected a course in law, medicine, or theology, and if a college has classes in all these subjects, it is termed a "university." All larger cities offer additional means of instruction in the lyceums, where traveling scholars give lectures; in scientific societies, such as the local *Mechanics Institute;* and in libraries, among which the *Mercantile Libraries* occupy a most respected position.

The elementary schools of Cincinnati comprise the city, parochial, and private schools.

The first-mentioned institutions are open to the children of everyone, with no tuition being required. The funds for their support flow from two sources: first, from the city's share in the state school fund; and second, from a direct tax levied annually by the authorities according to the current needs. The state grants $200,000 per year for pedagogical purposes. Of this, Cincinnati received about $7,600 in the period 1849–1850, while on the whole about $65,000 were required, so that the city had to raise about seven-eighths of the entire amount. The administration and direction is placed in the hands of three bodies completely separate from one another. These are the Board of *Trustees*, the *Board of Examiners*, and the Teachers' Council. The trustees are chosen by the people in the annual municipal elections, and their duties relate exclusively to business matters. They have to procure the necessary monies, erect the required buildings and keep them in good repair, hire teachers and prescribe and administer rules for them, etc. The Board of Examiners has seven members and is appointed by the city council; it is their duty to examine the teachers in regard to their fitness and the progress of the pupils. No one obtains a teaching position without their certificate, and I was told that they are now proceeding in an unusually strict manner. Cincinnati had 138 public teachers in the past year. Each of the nineteen school districts has its own schoolhouse. These are all constructed according to *one* plan, and each takes care of 700 to 800 children. In each district the direct supervision of instruction is provided by a director and a directoress (*male and female principals*). In the school I visited the number of teachers was 10, but there are districts that have 15. Judging by the household furnishings of the teachers with whom I became acquainted, the salaries must be sufficient. Until 1840 it was only required of a principal that he demonstrate to the examiners adequate knowledge in reading, writing, arithmetic, geography, and English grammar. Since then, however, the requirements have been raised, so that at present the examination includes American history, natural sciences, the Ohio Constitution, the Constitution of the United States, algebra, geometry, and land surveying. Instruction is supposed to be given in all these areas. However, since many pupils do not have the time required for higher education and therefore seldom attend school longer than their twelfth year, the trustees have established a Central [High] School for those who wish to acquire more than an elementary knowledge. This teaches everything in a college curriculum. In this way the children of the poor have a sort of "free university" in which the talented and ambitious among them have tuition-free access to the higher studies, such an ancient languages, astronomy, chemistry, and political science. The district schools, however, are divided into nine grades presenting the following scale of instruction. In the lowest division the alphabet is taught by wall charts and spelling. The eighth grade occupies itself with the first of the readers prescribed by the Board of Trustees—incidentally, extremely practical ones—and learns to count. Subjects of the seventh are the second reader and an outline of geography and mental arithmetic; of the sixth, the same as in the preceding, augmented by oral defining and the rudiments of drawing; of the fifth, the third reader, blackboard arithmetic, and local geography. The fourth grade adds instruction in writing and expands the work in geography to instruction about the entire western continent. The third has the fourth reader put into its hands and is taught arithmetic, general geography, American history, elementary grammar, the rudiments of music, and line drawing. The second includes algebra along with a further development of the mentioned subjects; and the first grade has as its tasks exercises in independent themes, declamation, singing, and a survey of world history. The Bible is read in all classes from the fourth grade on, but the teacher has to abstain from any interpretation or explanation.

The report of the School Board of Cincinnati for the year 1850, from which I partly took the above, indicates 35,004 (white) children of school age, of whom 12,240 were enrolled in the city schools and 5,557 regularly attended school. If one takes into account that there is a constant influx and outgo of pupils and that, in addition, a significant number are given instruction in the parochial schools and in the private institutions, then F.'s assertion that at least 90 percent of the youthful population of the city receive elementary instruction may not be far from the truth.

Among the parochial schools, the thirteen Catholic are to be especially mentioned. In them forty-eight teachers instruct about 4,500 children. That of the Jesuits, with 600 pupils, and that connected with the convent of the nuns of Notre Dame, with 650 pupils, are the strongest. In addition the German congregations of the Protestant confession have usually established schools along with their churches. Finally, in this category also belong the Sunday schools held by clergymen of various sects for the sake of religious instruction. The number of private educational institutions in Cincinnati runs to about fifty, with approximately 2,500 pupils. Many of them also embrace the higher branches of learning and therefore add the name of "academies." Herron's Seminary for Boys, with eleven teachers and 240 pupils, is said to be the most important of these institutes.

Among the three colleges of the city devoted to general education, that named after Saint Xavier occupies the first place. It is equipped with a good library, a museum, and a complete apparatus for the study of the natural sciences. Standing under the supervision of the archbishop, it is conducted by the Jesuits. The instruction includes the disciplines of logic, ethics, mathematics, physics, chemistry, rhetoric, the ancient languages (including Hebrew), Spanish, French, German, and history of literature. A majority of the faculty members are Belgians. At present the college has fifteen teachers and 243 students. Among the latter are many from distant regions of the Union; in fact, even Havana and Mexico are represented.

There are four colleges of medicine in Cincinnati. One is devoted mainly to botany, and another specializes in the training of dentists—the number of which, by the way, is extraordinarily large in all American cities. The number of young people studying in these institutions currently amounts to four hundred. On the other hand, there is but one law school, with thirty or so students. This would be surprising, in view of the legion of lawyers listed in the city directory, if one did not know that most of them have taken their studies in the offices of older jurists. Further, Cincinnati possesses four business schools and five colleges devoted exclusively to theology. Of the latter, two belong to the Catholics, one to the Baptists, one to the Presbyterians of the old school, and one to those of the new. The last one, Lane Seminary, is situated upon Walnut Hill, about an hour north of the center of the city, and for a time was very well attended. Richly endowed, it is open to members of all confessions who come with sufficient preparation for the curriculum and a desire to train as preachers. Its buildings include a chapel and a four-story house with lecture rooms and resident rooms for eighty-four students. The curriculum embraces three years; from this, however, must be subtracted the vacation period from the middle of June until the end of September. The instruction is free. The pupils pay $10 a year for lodging, for the use of the library (which contains over ten thousand volumes), and for the use of the reading room (in which are found the best theological quarterlies and about twenty political journals); for a place at the commons table they pay only $1.25 a week. The president of the faculty (consisting of five professors) is old Beecher, famous as a pulpit speaker and notorious (G. added with his habitual irony) as one of the most hotheaded abolitionists that Yankeeland has sent to the West. He and his followers have harmed the institution just as much as they have benefited it. Through them the seminary became the center of a revolution against the slaveholding states; without the intervention of the authorities the institute probably would have been destroyed by the rabble incited from Kentucky. This fate has threatened at various times and is the reason why the number of students, amounting to over a hundred in 1835, has dropped to thirty or so.

I should have liked also to visit the Wesleyan Female College on Vine Street, a sort of girls' high school. Here about four hundred young ladies receive instruction (partly *from* ladies), not only in those subjects which we consider proper to the sphere of women's higher education but also in the ancient languages. However, the rules of the institute did not allow visiting, so I had to content myself with the mere notice that such an offspring of fashionable refinement does exist and is flourishing.*

If these observations and reports are now summarized, they give a result that contributes to high honor for the West in many respects. If the situation is not entirely satisfactory at the present, it at least justifies the best hopes for the future. The striving for the ideal has been awakened and is distinctly marked a thousandfold. Perhaps Cincinnati does not need to fear a comparison with Boston and New York in this matter as much as the gentlemen in those focal points of transatlantic intelligence imagine. If learning is still the handmaid of speculation, and if its bearers are now and then businessmen more than priests, then this is due to the circumstances. I have seen nothing of the scorn in which the Americans are supposed to hold learning, unless I recall the Pennsylvania farmers and a few lucky Germans in this city who have no respect for intelligence because they have become fat and rich without it.

◊ ◊ ◊ NOVEMBER 11

A peculiar character, this old Nicholas Longworth, about whom the conversation turned yesterday evening at H.'s! The wealthiest citizen of Cincinnati, he is at the same time the oddest of its eccentrics. Even the spring from which his enormous fortune has flowed must be termed a miraculous miracle. In 1804 Longworth came from Newark (near New York) to the Queen of the West, where he practiced as an attorney until 1820.[13] At one time during this period he had defended a fellow against a charge of horsesteal-

---

* It is not the only one in the West, as I found out later. Among others, there exists five miles northwest of Cincinnati a complete ladies' university which is even authorized to create *bachelors* (Mephisto growls spitefully, *spinsters*) *of arts* and doctors.

ing and had received as his fee a couple of old copper stills. They were stored with an innkeeper who owned a good part of the land where Cincinnati now stands. When Longworth requested that the stills be turned over to him, Mr. Williams, who wished to incorporate them in a new distillery, offered him a piece of land of thirty acres for them; it was situated close to the west end of the town, which was still small at that time. Longworth, whose sharp intelligence always was considerably ahead of public opinion, seized the opportunity with both hands. It turned out as he had foreseen. The thirty acres were soon covered with houses and streets, and the bare ground alone, which forty years ago was exchanged for two stills, is now worth at least $2 million. Longworth continued in this manner. Building site upon building site, field upon field in the neighborhood passed over into his possession, so that now he is the largest property owner in the city. How high Longworth's fortune runs may be seen from the fact that in the past year he paid taxes of about $17,000. This is the highest sum raised from any individual in the Union, with the exception of William Astor in New York, who in the same period paid $23,116.

If, however, nothing more were to be noted about this old Croesus, it would have been wiser to go along on the rabbit hunt today today than to sit here drawing him for my silhouette collection. Longworth is at the same time a psychological puzzle, a problem for those who occupy themselves with the investigation of that mysterious thing which, in King David's opinion, is located in the kidneys; according to Prevorst's clairvoyante (if I'm not mistaken), between the pit of the stomach and the navel; and in the view of the phrenologists—who here have their own saying—somewhere behind the ears. Longworth is a wit of the best sort. He is a slyboots in a thousand things other than money matters. He has been decried as a pennypincher, although when something really good has made a claim on his purse, he has proven himself as generous as if gold were a chimera. Holding tenaciously to a once accepted idea to the point of obstinacy, he shows the most extreme tolerance for the most extravagant endeavors of others. Completely free of conceit about his money, he displays all the colors of the pride of eccentricity. The commonest road to wealth is that where others pay the fare. Longworth has preferred a less traveled road. It seems that he has proceeded from this consideration: If he could open up to somebody the possibility of earning a dollar for old Nicholas and at the same time one for himself, and if he could increase such cases to the hundreds and thousands, then he would do himself as great a favor as the others. With this system hundreds have acquired house and yard and prosperity who otherwise would have had to live at rent for the rest of their lives; despite this generous managing of his property—indeed, because of it—Longworth has become a millionaire. Every lot that he has given away for practically nothing, or only for a period of time (a so-called *lease*), has tripled the value of the adjoining land because of the street built upon it. This does not take into account the gratitude he has secured for himself by such principles, the fruit of which would be an irresistible influence in all affairs—if Longworth were eager for such a reputation.

I have already mentioned a very unique service of his. It is his unceasing activity on behalf of the improvement of the local grape. Another is his endeavor to expand the cultivation of strawberries. At present about three hundred acres of the countryside are planted to them, and it is reported that in good years eight thousand bushels are brought to market, a number attained by perhaps no other place on earth. Finally, Longworth also has stepped forth in a not insignificant manner as a writer. His many contributions to the newspapers reveal a rich vein of healthy humor and bright intelligence. His satire seldom misses the bull's-eye. Puns and striking characterizations bubble up in his head as his Catawba champagne bubbles up in the glass, and even though he may discuss the most serious matters in the world with a great show of acumen and knowledge, he is at all times a sly fellow.

Longworth has his own views about the method by which the needy are to be cared for. He holds the office of a supernumerary guardian of the poor, and his rooms are filled several times a week with a crowd of unfortunates whose circumstances he investigates with extreme care and assists according to his findings. This occurs in a way that excludes any support of laziness and mendicancy. Here, too, the rogue behind the bush occasionally peeks forth. Thus an anecdote was told by H. in which a friend of his was soliciting contributions to help an undeservedly impoverished widow. Among others, he also came to Longworth. "Who is she? Does she deserve it?" he asked. — "Yes, indeed," was the answer. "The woman has the best reputation and is doing everything possible to support her five small children and to educate them properly." — "Hm, quite right," replied Longworth. "Then I won't give her a red cent. Such people make their own way through the world and find sympathetic souls everywhere. I give a lift only to idlers, drunkards, and worthless bums for whom nobody else will perform this service. If you ever meet one of this kind, look me up again, and you'll find me ready to help." — That this had been no mere subterfuge was demonstrated a few days later when emissaries of the Mormons expelled from Nauvoo came to Cincinnati to appeal to the charity of the inhabitants. They also showed up at the home of H.'s friend, and he sent them to Longworth with a short note saying that these people had a claim to his purse, since they "were no Christians." On the spot, Longworth gave them ten dollars.

Another anecdote is no less characteristic and delightful. When the parties were preparing for the election campaign of 1844, the Whigs turned to Longworth for a contribution of a hundred dollars for "campaign expenses." This, incidentally, is understood to include the founding of abusive newspapers, the distribution of election lies (the so-called ogelism,)[14] the buying of votes, the hiring of gangs of loafers to intimidate the voters at the polls, the arranging of splendid party parades, and similar nice maneuvers. "I don't know," replied Longworth, the sly one, "whether I ought to contribute a schilling. I don't like to spend something for nothing. We could lose again with Clay, as before, and then my hundred dollars would be thrown away." The petitioner, a rich banker, assured him that there was not the slightest doubt about the election of Clay as president. "Well, then," responded Longworth, "want to tell you something. You shall have what you want. But note well: you'll personally have to guarantee me that I'll get my money back in case our candidate loses." The politician, who couldn't imagine a defeat, agreed to this. But alas! it turned out differently than he had hoped. The Coon lost the battle to the Locofocos, and the banker the hundred dollars to Longworth—*multa gemens,* the narrator added.

◊ ◊ ◊ NOVEMBER 12

Everything that these Yankees take hold of grows into the colossal under their hands; I am of the firm conviction that if construction of the Babylonian tower were taken up again here, it would be completed before ten years had passed. To be sure, the project would have to bring in a reasonable profit if it were to succeed. But what if in the coming centuries, in the course of human events, the presently prevailing instinctive striving for expansion gives way to a period of deepening? Will not that same spirit, today documenting its grandeur of vision with the erection of giant factories, follow its bent for the gigantic and the colossal also in the intellectual sphere, in art and learning? Or is it in keeping with the progress of philosophy (not at all considering Christianity and its promises) to believe that the stream of history flowing from the rise to the decline will here silt up with materialism?

These and other questions thrust themselves upon me today as I was returning home from an inspection of the best establishments in the field of manufacturing, through streets where eighty years ago not the faintest notion of civilized life had dawned.[15] The first of these establishments that I visited is Clawson's bed factory. It is a five-story brick building, about seventy feet wide and two hundred feet deep—a ratio resulting from the high value of the building site, calculated according to the frontage and therefore occurring quite frequently. The cruder work is done by steam-powered machines. Eight of them saw, seven plane, six or seven drill, two carve, and sixteen turn. At present 130 workers are employed. Three million feet of wood, from the most inexpensive to the costliest sorts, are used annually, and the value of the manufactured goods runs to $250,000. Every day the factory produces between 100 and 130 bedsteads, worth $1.33 to $75 each, and all the more important hotels of the South and West as far as New Orleans purchase their needs from it. A similar gigantic business is the Johnston chair factory, in which 170 men work; year after year they ship 30,000 chairs alone to the firm of Scarritt and Mason in Saint Louis. Other large joiners' workshops, several of them belonging to Germans, produce other household furnishings, from the simplest to the most artistic.

R. led me from Johnston's warehouse to the so-called Clayton Buildings on the corner of Sycamore Street, to show me—as he expressed it, and perhaps with truth—the greatest shoe factory in the world. Here, namely, the Messrs. Filley and Chapin have nearly two hundred male employees and no fewer women and children working in eight halls comprising an area of almost 13,000 square feet. The clerk who took us around reported that the raw material transformed by these workers into boots and shoes every year amounted to about 30,000 cowhides, 20,000 sheepskins, 3,000 calfskins, 5,000 pounds of tacks, and 600 bushels of *pegs* (for fastening the soles in the stouter kinds of shoes); that the number of people living off the business amounted to around a thousand; and that the wages they earned amounted to $60,000. As extraordinary as these figures may be, and as interesting as is the sight of such a legion of constantly moving hands, the speed with which the raw materials are transformed into sellable goods is much more worth seeing. In fact, a certain Sharky working here often has produced six pairs of boots in ten hours, and only a few weeks ago he won a bet when he boasted that he could make a full dozen pairs between sunrise and sunset. It was too bad that this miracle-worker had gone home just before our visit, for I should have liked to have verified with my own eyes my companion's assurance that Sharky was ready at any time to provide the covering for a pair of feet within sixty minutes. "Impossible! Swindle!" my good Brehme at home on Ritterstrasse will growl. "But keep cool, dear master," I shall reply to him. "The matter is well substantiated." First of all, speed is not witchcraft, as is well known. Further, pegging does not require half as much time as the sewing of soles. Then it must be taken into account that the boot legs are cut out for the worker and that they have but one seam. Finally, I lived too long in Dayton in the home of busy little Sperling not to know that here even a German boot artist moves awl and hammer at least twice as quickly as a "Germany-er" (as our good R. expresses it). The "mason's tinder" that costs our workers so much time in the lighting of pipes doesn't grow on American soil, and just as little thrive here the coziness and deliberateness with which they apply themselves in Germany to every miserable repair job. "Always in haste!" is the motto of these active, restless people. Yankee Doodle and his *as nimble as a rat, sir*" constantly echo in the ears of the observer of their doings. They live fast—for most of them are already independent at twelve and married at twenty. They sing fast—for nowhere in their churches did I hear anything like our chorales. They get drunk fast—for that seems to be the object in view (as noted above), since distilled spirits are preferred everywhere to wine and beer. They love to make money fast—for that is the intention with which anyone here who has the stuff devotes himself to business. They do everything fast, so why shouldn't they work at the same rate? To be sure, the result is not always solid, but it's always clean, pretty, and modish.

Formerly, and even up to a few years ago, almost all shoes were obtained from the East. At present, in addition to the last-named firm, ten similar and not much smaller establishments exist in Cincinnati. The New England states now supply only three-eighths of the demand, and the time will soon come when the markets from which one purchased until now will be visited to sell them.

The forty-four iron foundries of the city justify even more

optimistic conclusions. Already they have taken their place alongside Pittsburgh as of almost equal importance in this branch of industry. This holds true not only for the quantity but also for the quality of the manufactured articles. To cite only one example: Last year a pair of tailor's shears from the hardware factory of Greenwood were sold in England for the price of $75. The value of the iron goods manufactured in Cincinnati amounts, on the average, to $3.5 million annually. More than 30 percent of this is due to stoves, of which during the past year 1,050 pieces were cast on a single day. Forty-five hundred men are employed in these establishments, of which one of the most extensive is owned by a German. The largest employers are Greenwood, with 350 workers, and Niles and Company, with 200. From the latter, Louisiana and even a part of Cuba order their sugar mills, while until 1846 these were supplied exclusively by Pennsylvania and New York. The West gets a large number of items from Greenwood that before 1820 were to be obtained only from England and even five years ago only from the factories of the East. What is more important, experts declare that these goods are better than those imported from Europe, in regard both to material and to elegance of form. I have seen teakettles and fire fenders that gave evidence of an attractive power of imagination, and the American stoves encountered in almost every cabin are, along with extreme low cost, the ne plus ultra of practicality.

I also must not forget Davis and Company, particularly since I see their firm every day across the street from our hotel. Of course, it is not the most desirable view. But the idea incorporated in it and the extent to which the business is carried on deserve mention and perhaps even imitation. It is, namely, a factory for iron coffins; upon it I can occasionally look as upon a really urgent *memento mori*. These articles—as far as I know, something quite new—in form follow a recumbent human body wrapped in folded shrouds, and the warehouse in which these mournfully elegant goods are exhibited looks as though someone had robbed a pyramid of its mummies. Consisting of two shells which are soldered together after the deceased is placed therein, and provided with a plate of thick glass at the position of the face, these cases have several advantages. First, they prevent the foul vapors when corpses have to be transported for some distance. Then, through the possibility of airtight sealing they are said to delay the progress of decay, thus affording the members of the family an opportunity to view for years the loved one in the tomb with unchanged facial features.

Since they are only a little more expensive than ordinary wooden coffins, the idea has met with approval. It is not improbable that in the course of time all Americans will be buried in this manner, protected against putrefaction—even the tanners who, as is well known, have the privilege of rotting a year later than other Christians. To be sure, the cabinetmakers would come off rather badly, and, with this procedure, Hamlet's cemetery jokes after some time would not be comprehensible without a commentary.

◊ ◊ ◊ NOVEMBER 13

Yesterday's investigations were continued today. In the morning I went to the Morgan Building on Main Street to learn something about the largest publishing business in the West. In the afternoon I inspected the yards where seagoing vessels are built seven hundred miles from the coast—another of the wonders of the Mississippi Valley that one can hardly believe until one grasps it with the hands.

Cincinnati has twelve publishing firms that, along with the required printing plants and binderies, employ nearly seven hundred people. The books and newspapers published by them represent a value of $1,250,500. If I had needed any other proof that they read more literature in this country—or, in any case, buy more—than in Germany, I should have been able to find it in the enormous printings in which individual works are sold by Morgan and a few of his colleagues. The former sold 10,000 copies of the works of Josephus during the past twelve months, 5,000 of Bunyan's *Pilgrim's Progress,* and almost 10,000 copies of Drake's *The Life of Tecumseh.* The writer Howe, who is his own publisher for his *Historical Collections of Ohio,* saw a 10,000-copy edition of this compilation disposed of completely in three years—although the book was hardly sold at all outside the state. The firm printed 14,000 copies of James von Hughes's *Expedition of General Doniphan,* and the great book business of the Methodists on Eighth Street printed 21,000 copies of the *Western Christian Advocate* and 16,500 of the *Ladies' Repository.* Understandably, school books and writings with a religious content do best. After these, geographical and local historical collections occupy the highest position in public favor, and then novels about the West (for which railroad stations and steamboat landings offer good markets). Still, a few companies have taken a chance with works of a scholarly nature and (it appears) have made a profit from it. A reprint of Macaulay's *History of England* of 1,200 copies, a very thorough work by Drake *About the Diseases of the Mississippi Valley* of 1,250 copies, and an edition of Rollins's well-known *Ancient History* of 4,000 copies were quickly exhausted. The external makeup of these publications leaves little to be desired. Paper and printing are usually excellent, and in the auctions on Main Street I have seen deluxe volumes from which our Leipzig masters could have learned much. Even in the woodcuts and lithography results are now and then attained which must be termed laudable, especially when one takes into account the difficulties with which this branch of art must struggle here.

Judgment about the products of the periodical press is less favorable. The dependence of the West upon the East is most obvious in this matter. Probably without the inspiration coming from the East, the newspapers of local development (with a few exceptions) would be scarcely more than advertising sheets with a touch of feuilleton and a few scanty political reports. It's possible that I didn't get here at the right time to see them in all their glory. It's possible that the editors have written their pens dull and their inkwells dry in the great struggle for a democratic constitution that has taken place during the past twelve months.* It's also possible that they are saving themselves for the next presidential election. But despite all this, they could apply a little more wit and wisdom to their *"day-lies."*

This would be desirable above all for the German newspaper writers, of whom about a dozen are active here. Solid knowledge is generally just about as rare among them as a respect for grammar. What they lack in the latter respect they attempt to make up for with bombast and flourishes in even the most simple things and with a skill in vituperation and prevarication that is truly prodigious, exceeding all expectations. My friends back home will be astounded when I place before them, black on white, examples of the brutality with which, for example, the editor Klauprecht customarily slashes the faces of the fat "Old Hunker" Roedter and the ex-Reichstag member Dietsch of Annaberg.[16] In fact, I know of only two or three respectable exceptions, and these earn a scanty livelihood. The public holds the publishers in its clutches. It also wants them according to its taste, and this taste—God knows with how much distress I put this down—is frightfully low. Unfortunately, it is exactly the

* The Democrats won over the Whigs by about 152,000 votes to 138,000; the Freesoilers, however, were able to lead only about 40,000 troops into the field.

same relationship as that between congregation and minister. Everywhere the more noble descends to the base, the better educated to the crude. Shame on those who have given the first impetus to this reversal of roles! Anyone wanting to measure the local Germans by their newspapers would hardly be full of enthusiasm for them or would expect anything beneficial from the preservation of this element in the American national character. Rather, he would wish, or would have to wish, in the interest of the honor of the German nation, that this race, which has maintained its bequeathed character almost exclusively in its deficiencies and vices, would as quickly as possible complete it passage through the hybrid state in which it presently finds itself.

But stop right here! Let us wait for further experiences. Let us guard against prejudices in a lump. Let the judge bear in mind that the exceptions to that which he is about to condemn may not provide a counterbalance to the rule, but they always are numerous enough. Saint Louis, hopefully, will produce more favorable impressions. For the present, let us not be blinded by the mocking devil that directs our attention to so many an awkward character among our countrymen, to so many conceited lucky fellows, to so many disgusting Gothamites, and (among the younger people) to such a distressing aversion to anything divine. Let us not be blinded to possible extenuating circumstances. Above all, let us not spoil the pleasure we take in observing how these German adoptive citizens work themselves up from need and insignificance to prosperity and importance. Cincinnati's wealth is found principally in the south, in the great businesses on the first four streets along the river. A decade ago almost all of Cincinnati's Germans lived on the other side of the canal—in those sections of the city most remote from the center of commerce. Since then, however, one German store and factory after another has crossed the canal boundary and moved southward, taking its rightful position among the Yankees; a city map upon which the buildings already occupied by these industrial storming parties were indicated in color would be most interesting.

Occupied with this thought, I walked after lunch today to the shipyards of Covington, where Swasey and Company build their seagoing ships. It has already been some time since a barque of 350 tons undertook the voyage from Marietta, a hundred miles upstream, to Liverpool in England. But it was about five years ago that yards for the construction of sailing ships of a larger type were built here. The only difficulty facing this industrial activity is found in the rapids of the Ohio at Louisville; loaded vessels can get through them only at high water. This is outweighed by the advantages found in the abundance of most excellent oak wood on both sides of the river and in the certainty that a full cargo of raw materials for the cities of the East and Europe can be obtained at all times. Thus the Queen of the West has already sent to sea, at various times, ships of considerable tonnage. The first of these, the barque *Minnesota* of 350 tons, was built in 1848 for a house in New Orleans; since then it has made several voyages to the eastern ports. Three others—a brig and two barques, the latter of 300 tons each—were completed during the year 1850; with a cargo of grain they were towed to New Orleans by steamers and then went to Boston. Since then the brig has been to Africa, and one of the barques has passed its test as a seaworthy vessel on the route around Cape Horn to San Francisco.

These are respectable and promising beginnings. Everything depends upon the elimination of the obstacle that nature has put in the way of the blossoming of this important industrial branch: the Falls of the Ohio. Since this obstacle frequently causes other sorts of trouble and since its removal is one of the conditions upon which Cincinnati's future greatness depends, the hand that removes it won't be long in coming.

◊ ◊ ◊ NOVEMBER 18

Anyone who has seen Porkopolis only before the middle of November and after the end of February should not talk about it—he hasn't seen it. He has not seen its delight and its glory, the pride of its statisticians and chroniclers, he has not seen the most precious gems in the treasury of the Queen City, the greatest wonder of the Ohio Valley—he has not seen Cincinnati's pork factories. This good fortune has been my lot for the past week. I have been looking at their magnificence and—smelling it, phew! The past week with its cold spell opened up the pork houses, caused legions of bristly sacrificial animals to swarm through the streets to Mercury's altars, piled up thousands upon thousands of barrels of pickled pork in the storehouses, saturated the atmosphere, and fumigated all rooms with the unending, unconquerable, inescapable lard vapors. From now on the watchword is: hams, pork chops, and lard oil. All energies are concentrated upon it, and

henceforth it is the endeavor that absorbs all thoughts. From
now on, for three months, it will be the topic about which ninety-
nine of a hundred conversations, newspaper presses, and cart-
wheels turn. Hams, pork chops, and lard oil: a fat, juicy trefoil!
Let it be the task of the diary page for which I now most solemnly
dip a newly cut quill into a newly filled inkwell to praise properly
your metamorphoses!

Approach, tenth muse, nameless one! Whisper, suggest to me,
accompanying demon, the words of delightful sacrificial hymns!
Or, no, Asmodi, let us forget the panegyric! Let us employ a simple
prose. Mercury requires an accounting, not rhymes and jokes,
and it is for him and his sons that this page is being written.

The lack of markets for their corn compelled the settlers of the
West to distill it to whiskey, which can be transported more
easily, and to feed it to hogs, which carry their grease to market
themselves. The 18 million bushels that were shipped to Europe in
the "Hunger Year," 1847, made up hardly more than 3 percent
of the 1846 harvest. But ordinarily only about a hundredth part
of the crop is exported and approximately a tenth consumed on the
farm. Now, since the whiskey distillers cannot pay as high a
price for the corn used by them as that brought by the grain used
in fattening hogs, the raising of these animals has undergone an
extraordinary expansion here. According to last year's census, the
United States has around 45 million swine, that is, about as
many as all of Europe. About five-eights of these are assigned to
the Mississippi Valley, where 1.7 million are packed annually.
Of this number, however, between 27 and 28 percent are slaughtered
and dispatched in Cincinnati—a tremendous number, especially
when one bears in mind that this business is limited to only
about three months.

All year the hogs run around wild in the forest, until they are
let into the cornfields at the end of September to put on fat. There are
farmers who fatten more than a thousand head for the market every
year. Those who own less than a hundred head turn them over to
dealers when the *pork season* begins; they are then penned up in a
suitable place until a herd is collected that is worth driving down to
Cincinnati or to other markets along the river. Here they are put into
pens close to the slaughterhouses, pressed together as tightly as
possible. They are killed in this position, the butcher walking across
their backs and knocking in the head of one animal after another with
a two-headed hammer. As soon as this has been done, they are dragged

by hooks to the so-called *sticking room,* where their throats are cut and the blood allowed to run into large vats, from which it is sold to the manufacturers of Prussian blue. Next to the *sticking rooms* are located steam-heated tubs for scalding. From these the hog is thrown by means of machinery upon a long bench where it is scraped and the bristles removed by as many people as can work upon it without being in each other's way. Then the back feet are held apart by means of a curved stick and it is hung from the ceiling beams. Here a worker guts it. This operation is performed so rapidly (as are all the others here) that three animals per minute, on the average, are readied for shipment.

    Cincinnati has ten of these slaughterhouses. They are located in the extreme northwest suburbs and are usually sheds built of wood, 120 to 150 feet long and between 50 and 60 feet wide. The side walls consist of movable panels that are shoved back, when it is not too cold, to permit fresh air to enter. The largest of these establishments sometimes employ over a hundred people, and the salaries paid to them amount to between $40 and $60 a month. From the slaughterhouses the hogs are transported upon mighty rack-wagons, each carrying 60 to 100 head at a time, to the pork factories for packing. Several times during the past few days I have seen a dozen or more of these wagons pass our hotel on their way to the nearest pork house, that of Davis and Company, famous far and wide for their delicious "Diamond Hams." The slaughtered animals lie piled up before and in it as high as a house. They first are weighed, are cut up with a swordlike instrument, and then are placed in salt. This occurs with such incredible speed that the hogs still grunting today are driven down to the steamboats at the landing tomorrow, well pickled and packed, by the draymen whose carts roll back and forth in the main streets by the hundreds. Last Friday, in one of the city's factories, 752 head were weighed, cut up, and salted by six men in thirteen hours. Some idea of the size of these animals can be gained from last season's statistics listing 7 head averaging 720 pounds, 5 of 640, 22 of 410, and 102 of 380. Finally, a clue to the general importance of this business is given by the calculation that the pork houses of Cincinnati during the months of November 1847 to March 1848 packed no fewer than 500,000 hogs and shipped 180,000 tons of salt pork, 25 million pounds of ham, and 16.5 million pounds of bacon. This does not take into account the lesser animals and the offal of feet, heads, and entrails that were rendered into lard in other factories or went to the thirty *lard oil factories* that last year produced some 1.5

million pounds of lard oil and stearin. It is estimated that these establishments provide employment for a total of ten thousand people, including fifteen hundred coopers, and that the value of the goods produced by them in the year 1848 ran to the enormous sum of $8 million.

The largest pork house in the Mississippi Valley—and, without a doubt, in all America—is that of Milward and Oldershaw, to which we paid a visit yesterday. It is over in Covington, close to the river, and covers an area of two acres. Its cellars hold 3,600 tons of meat, its pens—which, strangely enough, are located upon the roof of the main building—hold 4,000 head of cattle, and during the 1847–1848 season here alone 11,740 hogs and 3,000 oxen were packed for the European market. Another business of this kind, the already-mentioned firm of Davis and Company on the corner of Court Street and Broadway, ships 16,000 of the first-mentioned species and 600 of the latter in an average year. Finally, the factory of Schooley and Hugh, down on Deer Creek, annually sends between 70,000 and 100,000 hams to market.

In view of the more favorable situations of many other places in the hog-raising districts of Ohio, Indiana, Illinois, and Kentucky, it is surprising that Cincinnati has become the center of pork packing. But it is to be remembered that the raw material in this business—the hog itself—makes up 60 percent of the value of the finished product. Since the hog must always be paid for in cash, considerable capital is required for the operation of this business, capital that can be procured on short notice only in a large city with many banks. In addition the meatpacker can avoid losses in case a sudden change of weather occurs during the pickling process only if he can depend upon sufficient supplies of salt and the instant availability of enough coopers and other workers to speed up the packing operation. The matter is explained above all by the surplus value of the hogs to the trading community of Cincinnati; this results from the possibility of utilizing in various factories or as food for a large population whatever cannot be used advantageously elsewhere.

# 6

## A VISIT TO THE BACKWOODSMEN OF EAST KENTUCKY

◊ ◊ ◊ THE character of the North American people is generally conceived of as a commercial spirit: cold, sober, cleverly calculating, intelligently ambitious, perhaps a bit too hasty. Everything included under the heading of "Romanticism" has been completely eliminated from it. To be sure, a certain amount of wit must be admitted; but feeling, and everything proceeding therefrom, must be denied for the present. Therefore a person who, because of his spiritual makeup, requires a sentimental nature for the sustaining of life will not be able to live well in this atmosphere. If this view were restricted to the coast or if the judgment contained therein referred only to the real Yankees (the inhabitants of the New England states and their descendants in other parts of the Union), then such a characterization could be readily accepted. However, a glance at the religious life of these circles would compel a considerable limitation. Along with undeniable unpleasantness and rigidity, phenomena are encountered here that—you may think what you wish about their value—force you to recognize a depth and fullness of feeling such as seldom comes to light in Germany with such astonishing power. But one is generally only too inclined to extend the name, and with it the character, of the Yankee to everyone living under the flag with the stars and stripes, and to include the ill humor that seizes the observer in the cities of the coast and along the great highways. Thus an abstract judgment is made, and we get a distorted image of the subject. From the head we draw a conclusion about the whole body, forgetting that below the head also a heart beats and overlooking the fact that this heart really exists in the body of the American giant in the place where it properly belongs in every healthy organism. And it beats loudly enough to be heard by anyone who has the sense for such investigations. In short, in looking at the Yankee with his ledgers, warehouses, banks, and printing of religious tracts, we forget the chivalrous inhabitants of the South whose character differs from that of their fellow citizens of the Northeast, if not like heaven from hell, at least about like fire from water. Now it cannot occur to a corrector of the above-mentioned view to cram these two sides of the North American character into definite geographical boundaries and say, perhaps: Up to this point, the Mason-Dixon Line, Romanticism prevails, and there, at this or that river or mountain, sober Yankeeness, the great firm of Smart and Slick, has the limits of its commercial territory. On the contrary, the unprejudiced observer will willingly concede that the latter has pushed in and made its influence felt wherever there is a possibility of selling or speculating. Therefore there is hardly an important city in the Union where you do not feel the dominance of *Yankee notions*—an admission, to be sure, by which (we must confess) the above attacked view of the character of the North Americans is partially justified.

If one now asks (to stay with our image) where the writer believes that he can see the heart of which he has spoken, the answer is, first of all, not in the "deep" South, where the black two-legged domestic animals produce the material for our Age of Cotton and where their masters cultivate only the ignoble passions of chivalry. Rather, the heart—and with it the feeling, the Romanticism, and the poetry of the American people—lies under the ribs, which proceed from the vertebral column of the Alleghenies, to the left of the great aorta of the Ohio; and one chamber of the heart is called VIRGINIA, and the other, KENTUCKY. We do not mean merely that Virginia and that Kentucky which the map shows us outlined in green or red, but the heart of which we speak extends as far as specifically Virginian and Kentuckian character have spread. Thus also a good part of Tennessee, of North Carolina, and especially, however, of southern Ohio and western Pennsylvania can be included, although the two first-mentioned states must always be regarded as the center.

That this remark contains a truth that is felt, or at least suspected, by the Americans can be observed in many things. The young people throughout the West spoke of "Old Kentuck" and "Old Virginny" in a tone that sounded like deep emotion; when Pennsylvania (just as old) or Massachusetts (much older) was mentioned, not a soul expressed anything similar. The farmers in the forests of Ohio and Indiana related with glowing eyes how their fathers had emigrated from Virginia. The greater part of the "steamboat literature" of the West, selecting themes appealing most to the public taste, revolves around the adventures and heroic deeds of that race which, under Boone and Kenton, won the "Wilderness of the Dark and Bloody Ground" from the redskins and thus opened the way to the vast West for their children and grandchildren—the West on whose soil the fusion and reconciliation of the southern spirit with the eastern will take place, where a single nation will evolve from the Puritans and the Cavaliers, and where the tremendous future of the Union will develop.

Here, in fact, as nowhere else so mightily in recent times, the valiant spirit of the Anglo-Saxon peoples has unfolded to a repetition of the Heroic Age. Spirits—impatient, wild, and sinister, like the grim heroes of the *Nibelungenlied*—suffered and fought in those immeasurable forest solitudes which once covered the region in which now the paradise of Kentucky blossoms. Argonaut journeys were undertaken, more adventurous than any that could be invented by the boldest poet's imagination. The Licking and the Ohio, the Salt River and the Green (which flows past Mammoth Cave) saw battles that could inspire a Homer to a second *Iliad.* Here, on the warpaths of the Mingos and the Shawnees, roamed Ludwig Wetzel, a demon of the most horrible sort, striving (like Hugo's Han d'Islande[1]) to expiate the murder of his father in a never-stilled thirst for revenge against the Indians, until he finally breathed out his desolate soul in the darkness of some wooded valley under the scalping knife of his enemies or in the deadly embrace of a bear. Here the terrible Harpies wandered about with blood-dripping hands. Here, from their cave on the bank of the Ohio, Mason's band threatened rivermen with murder and robbery. Here lived Mike Fink, the Robin Hood of America, with his merry companions. Here the dauntless Clark gathered his bold men for a raid against the French forts of Illinois, on whose flooded prairies he made the impossible possible. Here, finally, at the beginning of this century, was lighted the fire of the Great Revival which flamed over the entire West and North, bringing forth the strangest phenomena in the area of the soul—phenomena the magic force of which not even the stoutest disbeliever was able to withstand. Here, in a word, in the brief Middle Ages of Kentucky, lies a wealth of poetic material; Sealsfield's and Gerstäcker's depictions[2] (as valuable as they may be) have not exhausted it by far—indeed, they have scarcely touched it. Nowhere in our circles is its true worth even suspected.

The poetic shimmer, however, does not merely hover over the past (as in Ohio), but the present, too, still offers an abundance of Romantic themes in even the most populous and most cultivated parts of Kentucky; to fill many a volume with the best reading material, a poet would only need to put words to the ballads and idylls shooting up from this soil in luxuriant growth everywhere. Nevertheless, circumstances have made it inevitable that the primitiveness (which is poetic despite its crudeness, or, one should say—to prevent natural misunderstanding—just because of this crudeness) has been fused with a false civilization and has, through this, vanished in large part. The chilling, sobering, leveling principle (disguised as merchants and preachers) has pushed into this region from the North on railroads and steamboats, has turned straightforwardness into hypocrisy and frankness into speculation, has clipped, restricted, and polished the wild-growing human nature, and has causes all sorts of damage. The influence of slavery (with increasing wealth, more and more gaining the upper hand) is not at all suited to resist this in a manner beneficial to custom and views.

It's different in areas where the soil is too little productive to lure the Yankee and the people too poor to have slaves. Here I have my eye mainly on the mountain districts of eastern Kentucky and western Virginia. There, in the valleys, you can still occasionally encounter the race of olden times in all its power and strength, even though the father's rifle (leaning in a corner of the cabin) no longer slays the redskin—and the bear and panther more rarely than formerly. The warlike existence has had to give way to an idyllic one in all respects. Here Romanticism still dwells in the shadow of virgin timber, on the bark of which the traveler can read the hieroglyphics of the ancient right of the tomahawk. Here among the mountaineers the custom of the ancestors still blooms plain and honest, simple and upright; the gentleman farmer of the plains, however, has exchanged it for a tone imported from New York or Washington, fashioned after Parisian or London influences. Here honor re-creates the days which are no more. Here still prevails the hospitality of a time when there were no hotels. Here the pride of true freedom still holds up its head, unspoiled by loaferdom and votebuying. Here almost every person is still a "character," whether in a good or bad sense. Here genuineness of feeling still exists. Here folksongs are still heard. Here one still lives among people of the last century. I now take the reader to this place, into these innermost recesses of the heart referred to in my introductory words, by putting before him a new section of my travel log.

Of the many interesting characters who remain in my memories of the Cincinnati hotel where I stayed for several weeks, the image of Gustav Westfeld, a German farmer from the vicinity of Florence, Kentucky, will forever be one of the most treasured and most delightful.[3] Having become acquainted on the occasion of an exchange of opinion about northwestern Ohio, we soon became closer friends, and I learned to esteem him as an experienced and enterprising farmer able to give many valuable suggestions and much information about local conditions and personalities. On a visit to his farm I found out that he intended to move farther into the interior of Kentucky along with several other Germans he had won for his plan. The idea was discussed with the neighbors at various times, its advantages set forth and the objections raised against it debated. Since I showed interest, Westfeld proposed that I accompany him on a trip to the land in question (which until now was known only from a hunter's description), to inspect it and come to a definite conclusion about it.

To be sure, the acceptance of such an invitation did not fit in with my original travel plans, but the prospect of having a newly arisen desire fulfilled by this deviation from my planned itinerary spoke in favor of the matter.

Already at home much interest had been aroused in those men who, "half-horse, half-alligator," were supposed to race around in the American West. Conversations at the table and in the reading room of friend Kopf's hotel had been well suited to make the wish for a closer acquaintance with this half-humorous, half-heroic race of centaurs grow to a strong desire, and this desire had not been fully satisfied by the trip to the Black Swamp and the backwoodsmen of Defiance. "In this region you'll still find real backwoodsmen in the sense in which the term is used in novels," a well-informed friend told me, "only across the Ohio. Otherwise, in an extended meaning of the expression, every one of us here is one." Consequently, I had often looked with longing from Mount Auburn across the brick chessboard of Cincinnati to the dark hills beyond the river and to the Licking pouring forth from them—the Licking in which so much precious blood has flowed. And now I was to travel up this Skamander[4] of Kentucky almost to its source, to see and get to know the classical sites of those battles in which the land earned its name of "chivalrous," and (still more important) to see and get to know the people who have preserved this spirit and have demonstrated in the recent wars that this name is still justified. Could I long be in doubt as to whether I should accept or decline Westfeld's invitation?

After some deliberation as to whether the trip, whose goal was some 130 English miles distant, would be better made by horse or by wagon, we decided upon the latter, since I wasn't an especially good rider—or, more honestly admitted, had had a saddle under me hardly more than a couple of times. Early on the morning of the twenty-eighth of November we got into our buggy, drawn by a spirited, strong brown horse and well supplied with all needs, and began our excursion to the backwoods of Bath and Morgan counties.

The almost knee-deep snow which had fallen three days before had melted in the warm sunshine of the previous afternoon and had made the roads almost bottomless; in truth, these roads are not much more than wagon ruts in the rich loam of the valleys and the rocky bottoms of hundreds and hundreds of creeks. So by noon we had gotten only as far as INDEPENDENCE, ten miles from Westfeld's farm, a forest village of about 150 inhabitants. Despite its small size, Independence has felt the need of a hall for the cultivation of the "royal art"—a circumstance less surprising than the fact that among the twenty-five or thirty buildings of the little nest there were no temples of the Odd Fellows, Druids, Sons of Temperance, etc. *Odd fellows* indeed, these Americans!

And on we went through the eternal forest, uphill and down, always toward the southeast, past poor log cabins surrounded by long cornfields and clearings, through brooks and marshes shaded by ancient, strangely outspread sycamores over whose white trunks endless wild vines entwined, through beech and oak leaves piled a foot deep, across crude log bridges, through quiet valleys, through damp lowlands, the trees of which, gnarled and moss-covered, had worked their way up out of the choking thickets and creeping vines, out from the shadows into the sunlight and back down again from the bright heights into the shadows. Now and then a venerable old hickory (easily recognized by its reedlike bark) or a black walnut silently expressed their praise of the soil; also the sugar maple, which has the same significance, was not lacking. Ragged Negroes showed ivory teeth in grinning salutation. Here and there we met woodcutters or hunters and even more frequently the inevitable embellishment of the American autumnal landscape: hogdealers on horseback who were driving their herds to the north to have them there transformed into salt pork and lard oil in the factories of lard-fragrant Cincinnati. Under a road sign, however, sat German music, red-cheeked and cheerful, in the form of a young organ grinder; with his peaked Tyrolean hat and his neat little sister he provided an unexpected bit of charm in this wilderness.

The sign, by the way, was more spiteful than our police would have permitted. It came close to playing upon us the not very pleasant trick of directing us—on this cold, moonless night—to a road by which our tired horse and our hungry selves would not have reached the next inn before morning—if at all. A malicious hobgoblin or an ill-bred boy had turned the arm pointing toward FALMOUTH, where we planned to spend the night, in the direction of a trail leading more toward the south. Thus we were already well on the way to playing the "knight errant" when our good fairy sent us, just in the nick of time, a rider who, apparently encouraged by an overconsumption of spirits, came springing down the hill by a side path with a loud "Hello!" and cheers. In response to our questions, he described the correct route in exemplary fashion.

"*Clear to the left, down the mainest plainest road,*" was the main part of his instruction. So—although the darkness of the forest permitted us to see no comparative among the crossing and branching trails, let alone the advised superlative—we found ourselves a few hours later at the fence and before the tall white beech in the valley that had been mentioned as the first landmarks. The barking of dogs, answered from all sides, announced the proximity of a town. After we had traveled through the half-dry bed of the south branch of the Licking, the lighted windows of a Methodist church indicated where Falmouth was situated.

Here a good supper and respectable featherbeds made us forget the discomfort we had endured, and at the table I had, for the first time, the pleasure of being waited upon by slaves.

When the sun looked down into the valley the next morning, our horse had already worked up to the top of a steep hill over which the road to Cynthiana winds. From there we descended into a deep, wooded valley and then climbed over half a dozen hills and mountains. Although here the region assumes more and more the character of a rough mountain landscape, fertile only in the valleys, the price of an acre of uncultivated land has already climbed to ten dollars, largely because of the partly completed railroad from Covington to Lexington which runs through the Licking Valley as far as Paris—it greatly facilitates the exploitation of the local timber supply. The population, however, is still very sparse. We seldom met another person. Only now and then a newly built log cabin appeared out of the underbrush which covered the land as far as the eye could reach—gray brown, sad, and cheerless. For miles the eerie silence of the forest was broken only by the monotonous screech of a woodpecker or by the fluttering up of a buzzard startled from some carrion by our approach. Occasionally could be heard the hammer of a cooper making barrels for the pork slaughterhouses of Cincinnati; now and again, too, the sound of an ax and the cracking and crashing of a falling tree. More frequently the "Cob-Cob-Cob" of horse herdsmen and the melancholy "Bu-hu-gi" with which the local farmer lures his bristly charges—the chief source of wealth of all western households —from the woods for the morning feeding of corn. The Indian corn here had a poor appearance. Also the tree growth didn't promise much, and innumerable blackberry bushes and honey locusts with their long thorns grew everywhere on the cleared land. The thorn apple, so exceedingly common in Ohio, was scarcely to be seen. Just as rarely, however, stalks of verbena were found in the meadows; in this country it is considered a sign of good grazing land. Hence it's no wonder that the lemmings' migration from east to west has avoided these regions.

Our noon meal—which we took in a lonely log shanty at the edge of a deep, rocky ravine—reminded us quite vividly that we were in the land of the "Corncrackers." Just as folk humor has given to the inhabitants of Ohio the nickname "Buckeyes" (after a kind of nut very common there), to the backwoodsmen of Indiana the title "Hoosier" (people who duck their heads), to the people of the prairie state of Illinois the strange designation "Suckers," and, finally, to the Missourians the disgusting name "Pukers" (emetic), so the Kentuckian is jokingly called a Corncracker (in German: "maize zwieback"). The meals that we received from here on at times justified this name more than we liked. Today—in addition to the inevitable coffee, which here seems to take the place of soup, and the preserved fruits seldom lacking in even the poorest household—the meal consisted of nothing but items that had originally been "corn," that is, maize. We had corncakes, which the son of Kentucky sees steaming before him on the table three times a day, 365 days a year; to these his housekeeper usually adds warm cornbread for the sake of variety. We ate pork chops—and what is a hog in this land but a certain quantity of corn ears transformed into meat and fat, bones and skin, and now running around on four feet grunting? We finally concluded this patriarchal meal with a draught from the bottle passed around the table, and behold! even the whiskey is distilled from corn!

A few miles from Cynthiana the forests and fields became better, and pretty farms announced that we were approaching the eastern end of the "paradise of Kentucky." CYNTHIANA itself is a pretty little town of nine hundred inhabitants. It is situated in a broad, fertile valley and has very good prospects of a rapid growth. We inquired about the best lodgings and were directed to a hotel where very considerable progress in civilization has been made. Here they were even familiar with the invention of the candlesnuffer, while the good people in Falmouth had still used (following the custom of their honorable fathers) a pocket knife to nip off the flames of their tallow candles. In addition our room not only boasted rugs and window blinds, but—how astonished we were!—even possessed a stove in which, unbidden, a merry fire had been lighted. Finally, our eyes, when they opened in the morning, discovered before our door two pairs of beautifully polished boots. Jim, the wooly headed houseboy, had thus given us a pleasant surprise, one such as might occur elsewhere in America only in hotels of the first class. To be sure, the convenience of a private washstand had not yet been attained, and we therefore (as at the last hotel) had to go down to the yard to the communal watering trough and use the towel common to all faces in a genuinely democratic manner. To this was added the fact—o woe! —that the joyful surprise at the sight of our polished boots upon closer inspection turned into a most unpleasant one. Little Nigger Jim, probably not accustomed to such unusual events, had mixed up the foot coverings of the various gentlemen and boys; there was such confusion that one was reminded of the resurrection of the dead, when the one-legged invalids rise from their graves and scream for their crutches with all the hundred curses of which they are capable. When the breakfast bell sounded, cursing "one-boots" could be seen limping down all corridors and steps; if the Evil One had been able to hear all the *"hell damn your bloody eyes"* that were heaped on the neck of Master Jim, the poor sinner would have become as blind as Tobias on the spot.

The inn was extraordinarily full. This reminds me of a scene characteristic for an understanding of American behavior; for this description I must go back to the preceding evening. When we entered the barroom, we found the bar and stove surrounded by a crowd of noisy people whom the just-held Circuit Court had brought to the capital of Harrison County. There were farmers who, in their joy over a lawsuit just won, behaved overgenerously; young attorneys who, in justified pride of their maiden speeches, had one glass after another; court personnel who, with no regard for their position, allowed good friends or former charges to treat them; and other "wild boys"—as the innkeeper described them to us in whispers. Along the way we had met a fellow sleeping under his nag in the two-degree temperature; later he had galloped past us uttering all sorts of discordant tones, the highway mud spattering him. Here he was, dancing to the growling of a jew's harp played with virtuosity by a redheaded, long-legged rascal sitting on the bar. The dance was a kind of roundabout or reel, similar in its position to the virtuous cancan of Parisian students. Others with throats hoarse from yelling were practicing a new Negro song. Still others manifested their happy mood in the spontaneous manner of the animal world, that is, by simple bellowing. A dance master took advantage of the good humor of the crowd that seemed to be in a mood "As 't were five hundred hogs, we feel / So cannibalic jolly!"[5] to pass around a subscription list to enroll pupils for the coming winter. An agent for Howe's *Great West* with a persuasive tongue was able to sell several copies to the men. Then suddenly a dull "Hurrah!" was heard out on the highway. It drew nearer, became louder, and in streamed a mass of humanity. In the lead was a young man in a black frock coat and white topcoat; he was escorted by a number of rough-looking fellows. From his reddened eyes, slack features, and rumpled collar I at first suspected that he had overtasked his constitution by peering too deeply into the whiskey bottle. But this was not the case. For hardly had the jubilation accompanying and receiving him subsided somewhat than he climbed upon a chair, pressed the hat (which until now he had worn defiantly low on his forehead) under his left arm, and began a speech. I remember it almost word for word, since its characteristic phrases are stamped unusually firmly upon my mind. I am fortunate in being able to convey its most edifying points as a specimen of the manner in which one must speak to the American "people." Let me remark in passing that the occasion for this curious monstrosity of bombast and crudity was the fact that recently an American vessel had been fired upon by a British warship—like other shots of historical importance, a "mere misunderstanding," but from which a great war was prophesied by the wisdom or lack of material of certain Yankee newspapers.

"*Fellow citizens and horses!*"\* the speaker began with a nasal pathos (his thoughts rushed through his head like agile rats) while

---

\* *Old horse*, an often used term of flattery among the backwoodsmen, probably derived from the centaur nature of these people; something like our "old skin" from the bearskin existence of our primitive Germanic forefathers.

he unfolded a half-worn newspaper. "Here it stands, black on white —Great Britain wants war. And I tell you, boys, hurrah! she shall have it! (Wall-shaking Hurrah!) Fellow citizens and horses! I'm of the opinion that we won't dawdle much longer, but, without wasting our time on further ceremony, we'll proclaim to the world that the dynasty of John Bull has ceased its reign on this side of the Big Water. We've got to throw the bloody British lion head over heels beyond the eternal boundaries of this western continent. Hurrah for the incorporation of Canada! (Eardrum-shattering Hurrah!) *We must have the creature head and heels*—and if we have to wade in human blood up to our knees, it must be torn down from John Bull's horns. We must—I repeat, we must, even if we have to bury the hatchet of revenge up to the handle in Johnny's befuddled brain. Where is the possum* in whose small soul these sentiments do not find an echo? (Great artistic pause.) Not anywhere, and never has been! Could not you and I, could not each one of us awaken the wolf in human nature so that it will spring up and seize the whole lot of Old England and drag it under the water so that it can no longer be seen, even at ebb tide? *Yes, Siree!* Every single citizen of this, our great land, from the owl on the pine stump up to the president in his great armchair, will vote for this resounding and freedom-promoting measure. Once these glorious ideas are stuffed nice and proper into the skull of the United States, I shouldn't be surprised if an earthquakelike shout of approval, breaking forth from 26 million rubber lungs, caused the entire world to tremble—shattering the zenith, and even knocking over the icebergs at the poles. (Effective test of this shout with a Hurrah!) I tell you, there's nothing this side of the millennium comparable to our eternal institutions; on the face of the whole terra firma only a thousandth part of a half dozen civilized people can be scraped together who know as well as we do how to extend and defend these institutions. For where is the boy who would not fight for his country up to three-quarters of his last drop of blood, and if it should cost him his life? What is England? You all know. Hardly worth talking about! Uncle Sam will again use it as a handkerchief to blow his nose when he has a cold. We must arouse the dragons of war— hesitation and feather-picking are to no avail. If we really take the matter seriously—all of Uncle Sam's boys together—I'll be a two-legged crocodile if the Yankee spear won't bore a hole as deep as eternity into the universe. And we'll sink all drops of fat on the sur-

---

* Opossum and raccoon are frequently used in folk humor as a designation for people, without any special significance attached. Coon, by the way, is a nickname for the Whig Party.

face of the world down to the bottom of the stewpot, until the last trumpet of resurrection has blown. When all that's finished, the roaring giant eagle of liberty will be seen flying over both hemispheres of the earth, *like a big rooster crowing on the top of a pork barrel.* Yes, I know, you're all loaded and primed for the attack. All that you still need is a fiery coal on your saintly heads and the gun will go off. I believe that the flashing of your eyes this evening indicates future blood and thunder; but be careful that your boldness doesn't burn you out of the pan. If you all do your duty and obligation in the approaching crisis, *you'll spit the tobacco juice of determination in fat John Bully's eyes till he has the blind staggers*—in case you don't seize him by the tail and throw him out beyond the limits of all human thought! On, on, boys of Old Kentucky! Hurrah! Let the cry for revenge penetrate every corner and every knothole of North America (cannibalistic Hurrah!), from the farthermost point of the arctic regions to the Straits of Gibraltar. Canada and the United States forever! Conceived with war cries—born in a pouring of blood—cradled in the thunder of cannon—and raised in glory and majesty!"

A storm of "Hurrahs!" greeted this backwoods crusade sermon. A stifling aroma of whiskey, pouring forth from the enthusiastic throats, hovered ominously in the room. If anyone, for example, the dance master, annoyed at this interruption of his business, had felt the desire to permit himself a syllable of doubt or contradiction in regard to the "glorious ideas" of the speaker, the hurrah boys certainly would have "burned from the pan" this evening, and to the thunder of lungs and the flashing of eyes would have been added a rain of bloody noses.

We had no desire to see and hear any more, so we went up to our room. We tied shut the unlockable door with a saddle girth, to protect ourselves from unwelcome bed companions—they force themselves (with the most naïve innocence) upon a person here as everywhere in this land of liberty and rudeness. Downstairs, however, the noise and uproar continued, while in the outbuilding the "niggers" of the establishment sang a Methodist evening song.

The next day was a "Sabbath"; the local people do not travel at all, or only to church. We paid no heed to this, and just as little to the rain and sleet that poured down upon us just as soon as we left the city; we were consoled for a few miles by a quite passable road. Everywhere here the land is well cultivated and the forest so far cleared that in many places they are beginning to build stone fences. The corn is over eight feet tall, and on pretty meadows graze herds of horses and mules—the latter are brought from Missouri as foals and later sold into the deeper South. Everywhere we met riders, their legs wrapped in colorful leggings, directing their nags with a single spur, protecting their broadbrimmed white felt hats with blue or brilliant red parasols. Also ladies on horseback were common; many of them presented an exceedingly comical appearance as they trotted past us at the usual country trot, dressed in modish costume, an infant at the breast, and behind them on the same nag a little black boy as page or bodyguard. But most numerous among those whom we encountered were representatives of the race of Ham, and it almost seemed as though more black and yellow men lived here than white. So at about ten o'clock in the morning we arrived at RUDDLES MILL, a small town that has evolved from one of those border forts around which once raged so many Indian battles. About noon we reached MILLERSBURGH, a village situated on the military road from Maysville to Lexington. A number of dressed-up darkies were loafing at the bridge, while on the street, too, not a single white face was to be seen.

Here we were in one of the most fertile regions of Kentucky; for this reason it was among the earliest settled. The farms of this district—especially the older ones, recognized by their main buildings of stone—usually have the form of an amphitheater.[6] The houses lie at the foot of the hills, the summits of which form the boundary of the property. This feature is probably explained by the fact that in early times, when there still was no thought of artificial measurement, the boundaries presented by nature were used for the determination of "mine" and "thine." In the hilly parts of Ohio, for example on the route from Dayton to Covington or in the Scioto region, this is more rarely the case; there the farm buildings stand out more picturesquely on the heights. The Kentuckian, however, prefers his location because (as a rider with whom we kept pace for a while said) with it is connected the convenience *"that everything comes to the house downhill."*

Two miles from Millersburgh stands Thormorton's Inn,[7] an elegant hotel provided with comforts not expected by us here. We stopped for lunch. As we drove into the yard, a lean, gray-haired man in a black frock coat and white neckcloth was just getting into his buggy, escorted by the innkeeper. It seemed to me that somewhere I had seen this wrinkled face with the stern features before. But we had other things to do, so I cast but a fleeting glance at the unknown man (whom I took to be a clergyman). How I regretted this when the buggy rolled on toward Maysville and the innkeeper now turned to us and, obviously greatly surprised by our indifference, hastily asked:

"Didn't you recognize him?" — "No, truly not; for we are strangers here." — "Hm! It was Henry Clay, the greatest man of our century—in my opinion," he added thoughtfully.

The revered leader of the Whig party was on the way from his country estate, Ashland, near Lexington, to the capital, Washington, where the session of Congress was about to reconvene. It was unkind of Jupiter Viatorum that he had not allowed us to arrive a few hours earlier. However, what we had lost in this manner was partly compensated for by the innkeeper who (as we found out in the first ten minutes) was a relative of George Washington, a powerful Whig, and one of the most "original" fellows I had met up to now in this homeland of the "originals." He received us completely as friends and told us stories about his famous uncle while the meal was being prepared. We sat before the flickering flames of a beautifully paved hearth surrounded by a pierced brass rail and framed in white marble. He praised in high language the good old times when there had been no preachers of slave emancipation and no railroads. Then he teased his nephew about a love affair by means of which the boy had been enticed over into the camp of the Democrats. Right after this he related to us a short biography of his favorite and bosom friend Clay, whose portrait hung on the papered wall of the parlor right next to a likeness of "Old George." Repeatedly, however, he returned to his favorite topic, slavery; scolded and complained about the North; spoke with indignation about Ohio and Cincinnati, where they encouraged Negroes to escape; and didn't even entirely approve of northern Kentucky, from whence we had come. For "the rascals there," he spouted, "are not a red cent better than the abolitionists." In short, he was an old gentleman of the most entertaining sort to whom one could listen for days without feeling uncomfortable or bored. Behind his roughness and unconventionality was concealed a pure noblesse, a noblesse such as one would like to find in many people in the Atlantic states and in the West, one which is said to be no rarity among these southern Whigs.

Unwillingly we heeded the clock that urgently reminded us that we had to leave this hospitable house if we wanted to cover the planned distance on this day. And on we went, over hill and dale, across stony brooks and along rich bottomlands, through forest and field, and forest again. We spent the night in a little inn in MOOR-FIELD; we had worked our way up to the town in pitch blackness through the creek of a mossy valley and then through the bottomless mud of one of those roads which are appropriately enough called *"dirt roads"* to distinguish them from the highways. The next morning, by way of a pretty turnpike, we reached the friendly SHARPSBURGH. After a wretched journey of nine miles the evening twilight fell, and from a high ridge the white, laughing little houses and steeples of OWINGSVILLE, our present destination, looked down upon us.

Here lived Major Sudduth,[8] the owner of the land upon which Westfeld hoped to establish his colony. Excursions were to be made from here with the Major as guide. Fortunately, we found him at home, and he immediately agreed to spend several days with us in an inspection of his property. Major Sudduth was no less an interesting character than the innkeeper in Millersburgh. Similar to the latter in many respects, he was nevertheless of nobler metal and finer stamp. Dignified without being stiff, pious without being bigoted, a nature in which mildness and sternness were combined in a pleasant manner —with all these features the Major united the education, wit, self-control, and social talents of a complete gentleman. To these were added—not usual among the Americans—a heart for the past of his homeland and an open mind for old excellence, pureness, and honesty, as well as a superb memory for the customs and deeds of the dear bygone days. In his position as an attorney (he had received the title of "Major" as the former commander of a battalion of militia) he had earned—because of the skill with which he had defended the ownership of an important piece of property in Bath and Morgan counties— a considerable portion of the disputed inheritance as his reward. He had increased it by additional purchases, so that at this time he could call his own a continuous tract of land of not less than 125,000 acres. This had been described to us as situated on the Licking: The river could be made navigable for small steamboats four to five months a year by the removal of several milldams. It had been pictured to us as very hilly but still fertile; two railroads already under construction would soon bring it several days closer to Cincinnati. Finally, it was said to contain mineral deposits, for example, iron and coal.

◊ ◊ ◊ To check on these claims, we left Owingsville on the morning of December 2. The Major had procured for us another horse on which I was to try my luck, and the riding equipment for our nag we had brought along in our buggy. A fine rain was drizzling down as we descended the steep hill beyond Owingsville. But soon the weather cleared up, and out of the fog appeared black, wooded hills and above them strangely shaped peaks resembling beehives and sugar loaves. It was an uncommonly wild region; the deep, gloomy loneliness was not interrupted for miles by human habitation. We rode through a clear stream, and then through a second, the bluish water of which came up to our stirrups. After curving around various hills, we finally came to a more traveled road that led to an ironworks. Here, on a stone foundation, stood a two-story frame house, blackened by smoke and weather; chimneys built into the entire wall towered above it on both sides. Strange thoughts were awakened when the Major told us that Louis Philippe[9] had lived here in seclusion for a time. How vividly the sight of this weird building, looking down upon us so forlornly, recalled to the observer the fate of *polytropos hos mala polla planchthe!*[10] What an Odyssey lay between this land of the Corncrackers and the coast of the whale-oil drinkers to which he had been led by his star! What a difference between 1790 and 1830! What experiences, sufferings, and adventures between the teaching position in Switzerland and the visit to Lappland, between the log cabin in the backwoods of Kentucky and the brilliant July Throne! What experiences, sufferings, and adventures—and despite this, what a Philistine soul had gone through them!

Riding out back of the house, we found ourselves after a short time again in the midst of a dense beech forest that didn't open up until we were close to OLYMPIAN SPRINGS, a popular spa of the West. It lies in a deep and rather broad valley, the rich meadowlands of which once made it the rendezvous of the buffalo herds that roamed through Kentucky sixty years ago. It consists of several white frame buildings constructed in the form of bowling alleys, with some garden plots. In the immediate vicinity are situated a number of farms through which a stream meanders. Following the latter, we came into a dark hollow enclosed on both sides by wooded mountains. Here I experienced the misfortune of having my saddle girth break, and I slowly slid down into the soft dirt of the road, to the great fright of my two companions. They were greatly relieved, however, when they saw how gently I had bedded down; I had held fast to my nag despite his rearing. The damage was temporarily repaired by Westfeld with the aid of a wooden punch, provided by a fence bolt, and a piece of rope. We trotted on in good humor until the groaning of a steam engine and the snorting of a sawmill announced that our destination for today, EAGLES MILL, was near at hand. We had already been on the Major's land for an hour, and what we had seen of it until now had not especially recommended it to us. It might please the sportsman: deer had jumped across the road several times, and wild turkeys had been heard. But the farmer could not obtain a very favorable impression of the quality of the soil from the newly established farms with their feeble stock and their sparse corn.

It might have been about noon when we dismounted outside the fence surrounding the steam sawmill and its outbuildings. This was the Major's own property, and so we were received by the occupants of the little white dwelling with friendliness and respect. Even the dogs —who at first had burst out in tumultuous barking—behaved in proper fashion when they recognized the master and his guests. Every year Sudduth sells about three thousand dollars' worth of boards and posts from here; at this time he employed four male and two female slaves in the operation of the mill and the necessary housekeeping. They lived in a building at the back and were supervised by a white foreman. The latter, a Yankee from the northeastern part of New York state, lived a rather comfortable life with his wife, a cheerful Frenchwoman from Canada. Neither a good table nor sufficient reading material were lacking, but in view of the uncommunicative, sour character of her husband and the absence of children, it must have been uncommonly monotonous for the wife—especially in the winter, when this hollow is completely snowed in and entirely inaccessible. In return for the new supply of books which our guide smilingly drew forth from the pockets of his longtailed blue coat, Mr. Colburn had a delicious meal prepared for us—the apology for the lack of butter was absolutely not necessary.

The interior of the log cabin, with its old-fashioned furniture, brilliantly white canopy beds, and, above all, its two mighty fireplaces, was a picture of cheerful comfort. It was doubly welcome to me because of my earlier difficult riding lesson. Hence when the Major, in the afternoon, went to inspect the mill and the lumber piled up around it, instead of accompanying him and Westfeld, I preferred to converse with madame; she was busy sewing vests and trousers that were to adorn the Negroes of the establishment in the new year. Mrs. Colburn was of a lively temperament and very talkative. She considered the English language ill sounding. She most painfully felt the lack of suitable society. Although raised in the Catholic faith, she had here joined the Methodists in order "to see people at least occasionally." She inquired as to whether I regarded dancing as a sin. She would have liked to see Paris sometime, the "Secrets" of which lay upon her table, along with the *Discipline* and a stack of religious tracts of the disciples of Wesley. She regretted that she had no flower garden. In short, she chattered the blue down from heaven (as we say at home), jumping from one topic to another in a most charming manner. In fact, when the conversation turned to the Canadians, she even sang a little song, which I wrote down. Later, when I showed it to a collector of western antiquities in Cincinnati, he recognized it as the beginning of one of those chansons once sung by the coureurs de bois, the nomads of the northwest inland seas. It began:

> Dans mon chemin j'ai rencontré
> Deux cavaliers bien montés,
>  Lon lon laridon daine
>  Lon lon laridon dai.
>
> Deux cavaliers bien montés
> L'un à cheval l'autre à pied.
>  Lon lon laridon daine
>  Lon lon. . . .[11]

Then we saw the Major returning from the mill with Colburn and Westfeld, and madame became silent; as a Methodist she was not permitted (at any price) to know, let alone sing, such worldly, although innocent, songs. However, the conversation had turned to songs and poems, and when we had seated ourselves around the enormous fire (the heart of a German soapmaker would have leapt at the sight of the tremendous pile of ashes), I took care that we returned to my favorite theme. My hope of discovering in this way whether the remnants of old folksongs had been preserved in Kentucky, too, was not disappointed. After Sudduth had reflected a while, he said that he remembered at least one but that I would hardly gain a good impression of the flowering of poetry in the backwoods from it. It was a war song that he had heard among the militia of Bourbon County. It had been composed (presumably by a genius of the same type as that fine boy who composed the song about "Strassburg, the Beautiful City"[12]) after the bloody battle of Point Pleasant, where the Virginians under Colonels Lewis and Field had defeated (with a loss of two hundred dead) the Mingos, Delawares, and Wyandots led by the famous Chief Cornstalk. According to reports, it is still sung occasionally in the log cabins of the valleys of western Virginia. The song goes:

> Let us remember the tenth of October
> Seventy-four, which caused woe.
> The Indian warriors they did cover
> The pleasant banks of the Ohio.
>
> The battle beginning in the morning
> Throughout the day it lashed sore,
> Till the evening shades were returning
> Down the banks of the Ohio.

> *Eleven score lay dead and wounded*
> *Of champions that did face their foe,*
> *By which the heathen got confounded*
> *On the banks of the Ohio.*
>
> *Colonel Lewis and some noble captains*
> *Did down to death like Uriah go.*
> *Alas! their heads wound up in napkins*
> *Upon the banks of the Ohio.*
>
> *King David mourned for his mighty fallen*
> *Upon the mountains of Gilboa,*
> *And now we weep for brave Hugh Allen*
> *Far from the banks of the Ohio.*
>
> *O bless our Lord, the king of Heaven,*
> *For all his wondrous deeds below,*
> *Who has to us the victory given*
> *Upon the banks of the Ohio!*[13]

This was followed by stories of heroes and heroic deeds of the early days of Kentucky, compared to which the popular *"thrilling events"* and *"hairbreadth escapes"* of American novels often seem quite tame. Also Ludwig Wetzel was recalled, and the Major was able to recite a couple of tales about the dreaded Indian hunter. I repeat them here in order to give my readers some idea of the nature of this forest demon, of his origins, and of his complete savagery.[14]

Wetzel's father was one of the earliest settlers on the Ohio, being rash enough to build a cabin at Wheeling (in northern Virginia) while the Indian Wars were still raging most furiously. He paid for this foolhardiness with his life. He had hardly finished furnishing his cabin in scanty fashion when the redskins appeared one evening while two of his fours sons were away, shot and scalped the old man, set the cabin on fire, and dragged away as prisoners Ludwig (who at that time was thirteen years old) and his younger brother Jacob. During the attack the older boy had been wounded in the chest by a bullet, but that didn't stop him from thinking about escape. An opportunity soon presented itself, since the savages didn't take the usual precaution of tying up their prisoners before going to sleep (because of the youth of the brothers). By the second night, as the party rested at Big Lick in Ohio, the two escaped. After they had gone a few hundred steps, they sat down on a fallen tree to consider the best way to proceed. "You know," said Ludwig after a short reflection, "we can't go on barefoot. I'm going back to get a pair of moccasins for each of us." No sooner said than done. They sat a while longer, then Ludwig said: "Keep quiet. I'm going back again to get one of their rifles, and then we'll go on." This daring feat was successfully executed, and now the brothers hurried on as fast as they could. Although still children, they were clever enough to find the path through the forest by which they had come. The moon, too, was helpful in leading them to the right trail. But soon the Indians, who by now had missed them, were hard on their heels. Ludwig and Jacob eluded their pursuers with great difficulty by hiding in a thicket, and by repeating this maneuver when they heard the redskins returning. The next day the boys built themselves a raft, crossed the Ohio, and arrived safely in Wheeling.

When the Wetzels grew up into men—"and our backwoods boys consider themselves men," the Major commented, "as soon as they are big enough to shoot a rifle"—they swore a solemn oath to avenge the death of their father and not make peace with the redskins until their hands were too feeble to swing a tomahawk and their eyes too dim to aim a sure shot. It isn't known what the other three did, but Ludwig Wetzel redeemed his pledge with more than a hundred scalps. Murder was the purpose of his life, and since nature had endowed him with an athletic body, for years no stronger man interrupted him in the practice of his terrible profession. He is still remembered by many people, and later on our trip I met an old man who claimed to have known him personally. He is said to have been about six feet tall, with broad shoulders and a massive chest. His face was as brown as that of an Indian. Pockmarks disfigured his features, and his hair, which he let grow like Samson, hung down to his knees like a dark buffalo mane. It is reported that when he became angry his black eyes shot forth such a fierce look that a shudder ran over even the most stouthearted. "In mixed society," my informant described him, "he was a fellow of few words, among friends a merry companion. He never boasted about his deeds, and the death of an Indian at his hand seemed to matter no more to him than the slaying of a deer or a turkey."

Of the many tales in circulation about him, let me tell one that my Major got from an acquaintance of Wetzel. About 1790 Captain MacMahon with twenty men was chasing a band of Indians that had made several raids on the Virginia shore of the Ohio. Having crossed over to the area of the Muskingum River, the scouts preceding the expedition reported that they had discovered the enemy but that the latter was far superior in numbers. A council of war was held and the decision made to withdraw. Wetzel, who had been sitting on a stump during the council, with rifle across his thighs and tomahawk in hand, not voting, didn't move when his comrades prepared to return home. When the leader asked him if he weren't coming along, his defiant reply was: he had no intention of doing so. He had come out to hunt Indians. They had now been found, and he was not at all disposed to turn back like a fool who scratches his ear. He would either get himself a scalp or let his own be taken. That's the way it was, and all arguments presented to him fell on deaf ears. Wetzel's stubborn, obstinate mind was of such a nature that he almost never accepted good advice. So they were forced to leave him alone in the wilderness, surrounded by alert enemies. However, this did not necessarily mean that he was done for; for although his thirst for blood often caused him to run into danger with the rage of a madman, he possessed, besides the grim boldness of the lion, the slyness and cleverness of the fox. When his friends had disappeared, he picked up his blanket, threw his rifle over his shoulder, and set out for another part of the country, hoping to find the opportunity that he sought. He avoided the larger streams where rather strong bands of the enemy usually camped. He slipped through the woods with the noiseless steps of a ghost and the sharp eye of an eagle. At the end of the second day he saw smoke whirling up from a bushy hollow. Softly he crept up to the fire. He found two blankets and a small copper kettle, a sure sign that this was the camp of only two Indians. He hid in the dense underbrush and, sure enough, as the sun went down, one of the two savages appeared. He stirred up the fire and made preparations for the evening meal. Soon the other joined him and they ate. After finishing their meal, they sang and told each other funny stories, breaking out into loud laughter. Little did these poor fellows dream that dark Death—in the shape of Ludwig Wetzel—was murderously lurking barely thirty steps from them. When it had become completely dark, one of the Indians wrapped his blanket about himself and left, flintlock on shoulder, taking a firebrand as protection against the mosquitoes—he probably was going to wait for game at some spring. Wetzel was somewhat annoyed by this since he had thought his trap so well set that he could already see the two scalps hanging from his belt. He waited and waited for the return of the hunter—until the sky began to grow gray. The birds were already chirping when, hoping not to lose his other victim, he crept into camp and plunged his knife (with a practiced butcher's hand) deep into the heart of the Indian who had remained behind and was still sleeping soundly. The unfortunate one shuddered, uttered a short groan, and died on the spot. Wetzel took his scalp in coldblooded fashion and continued on his

way to seek new victims. He came to the Muskingum and found
another Indian camp where four redskins had set up headquarters
for the autumn hunt. He first considered whether it was feasible to
attack such a superior force. But he finally decided to trust his luck
and to risk an attack as soon as the enemies (who feared no danger
this late in the year) had given themselves up to sleep. Around midnight he believed they were sound asleep and walked into the camp,
his rifle in one hand and his ax in the other. As he approached, the
fire was almost out, but it still gave sufficient light to allow him to
recognize the individual figures of his enemies. Wetzel stood over
them for a moment in cold deliberation. Then he leaned his rifle
against a tree, for he had decided to use only his tomahawk and his
knife—they were sure to hit their mark when wielded by a steeled
arm. "What a gruesome, horrible picture," the storyteller continued,
"to see him as he bends over the unconsciously breathing savages;
how he aims for an intant, doesn't hesitate; how the steel then
plunges down into the skull of one sleeper; how it then smashes the
skull of another; how it then, with two blows, strikes down the third,
who has jumped up in fright; and how the fourth, leaving blanket
and weapons behind, hastily escapes into the forest."

Stories and tales of this sort are transmitted by oral tradition
among the old settlers and represent, to a certain extent, our folk
tales of the horny Siegfried and the Haimon children.[15] They are told
in the same words almost everywhere—this might be explained by the
fact that ignorance of the writer's art maintains sharpness of memory. If we may believe the scholars, it was just about the same in
ancient times with the tales that form the bases of the *Iliad* and the
*Nibelungenlied*.

The conversation now turned back to more recent times, and
Sudduth related anecdotes about his favorite hero, General Taylor;
about Henry Clay, whom he, too, regarded as the greatest man of
the century; about various "characters" among the governors of Kentucky; and he concluded with elegiac laments about the present,
when the Democrats had the upper hand, and when, just a few weeks
before, two Negroes, each worth over a thousand dollars to him, had
run away to Ohio. The enormous logs that from time to time had been
placed upon the fire by a Negro had sunk down to coals during this
conversation, and our semicircle, which had moved farther and farther away from the singeing flames, again became narrower and
narrower. Mr. Colburn had begun to show unmistakable signs of
sleepiness, and so it seemed time to retire.

Thus ended the first day of my visit to the backwoodsmen of the mountains.

◊ ◊ ◊ The next morning was devoted to an inspection of the land where the colony was to be established. We passed through the valley in which the mill is located and found that its floor was covered with white, red, yellow, black, and Spanish oaks, solitary beeches, and hickory and walnut trees. Between them here and there rose, straight as arrows, foot-thick magnolias, locally called "cucumber trees"; in summer their leafy crowns are adorned with magnificent white cup-shaped flowers of five to six inches diameter. The ground was covered with various species of grasses, among them the *bluegrass* much valued as fodder. There also were rocks that had been tossed up by the stream winding through the valley—at times it becomes a raging torrent—or had rolled down from the sandstone cliffs covered with evergreens. Clematis (lady's bower) was almost completely missing from the scene; likewise, few shrubs were noted; and nowhere did I see the fever-announcing Spanish moss on the branches of trees. Much better than the valley floor were the terraces that ran, directly under these cliffs, 80 to 100 feet wide, along the edge of the valley. They exhibited the richest humus as well as gigantic tree growth, particularly in regard to the black walnut and the sugar maple. I measured a tree-colossus of the first kind and found a circumference of 18½ feet, while the pillarlike trunk from the roots up to the first branches was estimated at 50 feet. Among the bits of rock that lay around we noted numerous traces of an apparently very rich ironstone, and as we crossed over the hilltop down into another hollow, the Major pointed out to us at the foot of a cliff 100 to 150 feet high, rising as a vertical, reddish gray wall, a deposit of coal which appeared quite extensive. Here we also became acquainted with a method new to us of judging the value of the soil.[16] The test is as follows: A hole is dug into the ground as deep as one wishes, and then the material shoveled out is thrown back in. If the hole is not filled up again to the level of the surrounding land, then the soil is good and fertile. If, on the other hand, the returned dirt forms a mound where it formerly was level, then the soil is worthless. "Even our graves," said Sudduth, "are seldom entirely refilled by the removed earth and in a short time show a depression." This assertion was confirmed on the following day when we saw a number of burying grounds.

The above-mentioned advantages were not inconsiderable; at

## A VISIT TO THE BACKWOODSMEN

the same time they could scarcely move one to choose this area with its steep mountains, its sparse population, and its great distance from any markets over tracts of land in the North and West, even if the seller had offered more liberal terms than Major Sudduth. The Major, to be sure, promised to reduce the price to one dollar an acre (one-third down, the second third payable in four, and the third in five years); upon the purchase of seven thousand acres he would donate to the colony an additional three thousand acres for church and school use; and he promised to get legislation passed to make the Licking, four miles away, navigable.

Noting Westfeld's headshaking, Sudduth held out hope to us that in the next few days he would lead us to land that would surely be more to our liking. Yet both he and my friend remained in obvious ill humor for the rest of the day; only when we gathered before the fireplace in the evening did the frost which had settled over the mood of the small group thaw to some extent and give way to the earlier talkativeness and communication. In fact, the lively flickering and licking of the flames in a fireplace, especially in so primitive a one as that before which we sat, exerts an unusually favorable influence upon the soul. It warms and at the same time entices good humor; it stimulates thought by its flashing, by the sinking of the coals, and by the jumping around of the sparks among the black logs. If other matters weren't to be discusssed here, I should be inclined to philosophize a bit about the magical effect that a fire has upon the spirit—an effect which no doubt has preserved the fireplace so long in England, the home of comfort, against its modern rival, the German stove, despite the latter's more practical nature.

The love of the Major for "the good old times" corresponded to my desire to learn as much as possible about the special conditions and circumstances that stamped them here in Kentucky. Thus, by way of anecdotes about the War of 1846, merry election stories of older and more recent date, and the like, we found our way back into the previous century and its residue in the present. What Sudduth told me on this and similar occasions, together with notes about the life of the backwoodsmen, gathered on this trip from the mouths of their descendants, forms a picture of manners which, I believe, will be of interest not only to me but also to the reader. This picture contains, on the one hand, many poetic motifs; on the other hand, it as little resembles the descriptions given in many novels as the character of Wetzel resembles the kindly, Philistine trappers of Cooper.

## Moritz Busch · Travels

The first settlers of this one-time border country were a race of hunters and warriors, as the situation required and demanded up to the beginning of the present century. For them, consequently, farming, cattle raising, and the manual trades were of only secondary importance. Everyone was a soldier, and even the women knew how to handle a rifle. From the first days of spring until the depths of winter, when the *Indian summer*\* no longer threatened, everyone was under arms. Field work in particularly exposed places was taken care of by parties, each member of which carried his rifle with him; guards were posted for security so that in case of attack by roving Indians immediate resistance could be offered. Almost every settlement had its fort into which the families fled with their movable possessions whenever the enemy approached, abandoning cabins and fields. Indeed, in the most dangerous districts people lived only in such small fortresses. Here a handful of people frequently defended themselves against hundreds of savages. The forts consisted of rectangles of strong palisades, at the corners of which were erected the great blockhouses, the dwellings of the individual families. The walls were well provided with gun holes and bastions, and the fort usually contained a spring. The surrounding forest supplied the materials for these forts, and not a single hook, staple, peg, or nail was of metal.

"I remember very well from my childhood," one of my informants related, "that our family once was awakened in the middle of the night by a messenger who brought the alarming news that the redskins had been seen in the vicinity. He knocked softly on the door, and my father and mother got up at once. Father took his rifle, mother dressed the children, and everyone picked up as much clothing and food as he was able to carry in the darkness. Off went the procession, silent and treading softly, to the fort, where we remained shut in for almost a week."

Although there was no law requiring military duty, it was expected of every adult male that he would serve as soon as his turn came. Anyone who refused was unmercifully branded a coward, and even the nonpossession of satisfactory defense weapons was considered disgraceful. They had officers—captains and colonels—who

---

\* To put this into German as "Indian summer," as is usually done, is wrong. Rather, it should be called the "Indians' summer" since this return of warm weather after snow has fallen received its name from the fact that the period, which sometimes lasts for weeks, was often used by the Indians (who were compelled to stay home in winter) for attacks on the white settlements, and so this phrase once filled the whites with sad memories. It now has only a peaceful and happy meaning.

conducted the campaigns and the defense of the forts, but in almost every respect they were commanders in name only. They could advise, but not command. Anyone who had good intentions or an interest obeyed; anyone who felt no inclination did as he pleased. This often had the saddest consequences, as, for example, in the battle of Blue Licks, which was lost and the Kentucky Militia sorely defeated and almost annihilated by the Indians—all because of the impatient ambition of a subordinate who, against Boone's orders, persuaded the others to attack.

One can easily imagine that farming was not very successful with such an irregular existence, the farmer often being forced to turn his back on his work for weeks. The grain he had planted was devastated during his absence by raccoons and squirrels, and his sheep and hogs, deprived of their protector, were devoured by panthers and wolves. Hence many a family, after a spring and summer of labor and danger, faced a winter of privation and hunger.

"My grandfather," related the Major, "often spoke of such bad times, when the flour supply ran out months too early and the family had to live for long weeks without bread. The children were then taught to call the lean meat of deer and wild turkey 'bread,' while bear alone was considered 'meat'—a trick which didn't succeed particularly well. The stomach didn't care for the exclusive meat diet, and the children became sickly. They were tormented by a constant emptiness which, however, was not hunger. Thus it was a feast above all feasts when the first potatoes were ripe, and a still greater holiday when the first ears of corn were ready for the roasting."[17]

Games and recreations are—at least in most cases—nothing more than imitations or repetitions (approaching the mimic art) of the affairs of everyday life and of their purposes under these or those circumstances. Thus the *"sports"* of the old Kentuckians consisted chiefly of practice in the skills required in war and hunting, while cards and table games (or whatever else civilization employs to pass the time) were entirely unknown to them. A peculiar skill which the young people practiced was the imitation of the animal sounds of the forest. This had a doubly good purpose and therefore formed an integral part of the education. It brought the sharp-eyed and suspicious wild turkey into rifle range. It lured the young deer, through imitation of the bleating of its mother, in front of the mouth of the killing gun. It confirmed for the owner of cattle that danger for his herd was close at hand when, in the evening, he gave forth the howl of the wolf and was answered by voices in Isegrim's language. It was also a means of protection against the redskins, who during the day signaled one another with the cry of the turkey and at night with that of the owl; this skill was used as a trick to confuse them. Consequently the old folks predicted of a boy who became quite accomplished in this art at an early age that he would grow up to be an able hunter and warrior.

Another recreation of the young people was tomahawk throwing; many acquired an astonishing dexterity in this. The battleax makes a definite number of rotations in a given distance, so that, for example, at five paces it hits the target with its blade, the handle hanging down, while at double the distance it hits the target with the handle standing upright. Some practice enabled a boy to estimate the distance so well by eye that he could hit the tree chosen as the target at this or any desired place.

Pastimes of a more peaceful nature with which they filled their leisure hours were the telling of fairytales (in which Jack and the Giant played important roles) and the singing of old English ballads about Robin Hood or of love stories with horrible endings. The latter were naïvely called *"love songs about murder."* In addition they entertained themselves with horseracing, wrestling, and practice in running and jumping. Many had opportunity to make good use of these skills in skirmishes with the light-footed Indians. The famous ranger Will Kennan, still living in Flemingsburgh up until a few years ago, was pursued by Chief Meschawa after Saint Clair's Defeat and is said to have leapt over an eight-foot-high tree trunk lying directly before him and covered with grass and vines.

However, the most important of all exercises was—and still is today—that in the use of the rifle, and about this many wonderful things were told me. A boy of twelve to fourteen years received a rifle and a powder horn and then usually became a soldier in the nearest fort; there he was assigned his own gun hole. Constant hunting for squirrels, turkeys, and raccoons turned him into a real sharpshooter. The present-day rifle, which shoots a ball not much larger than a buckshot, was not known at that time. Rather, one used wider barrels —the bullets ran to about thirty to the pound. Little consideration was given to freehand aiming as a special skill. On the other hand, Boone's contemporaries prided themselves in their *"squirrel barking"* as an art which even the best shot among Swiss marksmen could scarcely equal. The procedure in this unusual hunting sport—which a few especially talented riflemen can still perform today—is explained in the following example. The narrator, a German from Louisville, **was an eyewitness.**[18]

## A VISIT TO THE BACKWOODSMEN

"When I still lived in Frankfort," he reported, "I one day visited a farmer along the Kentucky River who was famous far and wide for his skill in the handling of a rifle. He had just gone out hunting, and since in those days one didn't have to go far for that purpose, I decided to look for him. I found him along the river in a bottom covered by a dense growth of walnut trees and hickories. Already a half dozen squirrels lay around him, and he had just reloaded his long, heavy rifle. We didn't have to move from the spot, since the animals hopped in such numbers in the branches that it was unnecessary to follow them. My friend pointed to one of the animals. It saw us and ducked behind the branches of a fallen tree at a distance of fifty paces. My friend asked me to pay strict attention to where the bullet would hit. He raised his rifle slowly, until the sight was on a straight line with the target. The shot sounded like the crack of a whip. But imagine my astonishment when I observed that the bullet had struck a piece of bark directly below the squirrel, had smashed it to bits, and these in turn had killed the little animal sitting above them. The squirrel fell to the ground in an arc, like someone blown into the sky by an exploding powder magazine."

Since time immemorial the Kentuckians have been just as proficient in the use of bridle and reins, although here riding is rarely executed with the finesse that makes it an art; rather, riding is a practical matter. Here is an example that I forgot to mention earlier. On our trip through Ruddles Mill we were witnesses as a boy, at most fifteen years old, had his nag attacked by a raging sow. He therefore came racing down the street in fullest, wildest course, and then his saddle girth broke. Without decreasing the speed of his horse in the least, he freed his feet from the stirrups and managed—God only knows how!—to get the saddle behind him and finally to let it slip off over the tail. Horse and rider then flew from the village as if shot from a cannon, to return slowly when the dangerous hog had been driven away with rocks by a Negro.

The clothing of the former backwoodsmen, and especially of those who devoted themselves mainly to hunting for game and savages, was at least half that of the Indians. The *hunting shirt* was worn by all, and there still are old people who cannot be separated from it. This is a garment similar to the smocks of our traveling journeymen and to the so-called pilgrim cowls worn at our masquerades. The material is usually coarse linen or *linsey*, a mixture of wool and flax, more rarely tanned deerskin. The collar, which hangs down more than halfway on the back and chest, was formerly decorated with colorful material or multicolored fringe, and the shirt front served as a pocket for the storing of food and hunting supplies. From the belt (which was always fastened in the back) there hung, on the right, the tomahawk and the gloves, and on the left, in a leather sheath, the scalping knife. Under the *hunting shirt* the still-customary vest and shirt were worn. The legs were covered by short trousers and up to the knees by leggings; a pair of Indian moccasins seemed to be more suitable than shoes, in view of the nature of the land. The moccasins were commonly made in one piece and tied fast between calf and ankle with straps so that neither dust nor pebbles could enter. A pair could be made in a couple of hours. An awl made from the spring of an old clasp knife and a piece of deerhorn was used for the sewing. This and a roll of leather formed essential parts of the equipment of every hunter, since on a trip or campaign the moccasins had to be repaired almost every evening. In cold weather they were well stuffed with deer hair or dry leaves, and so the feet were kept warm enough. In damp weather, however, wearing moccasins meant nothing more than "walking barefoot in a respectable manner" (as the saying had it). The result was that the backwoodsmen were troubled by rheumatism almost every winter; they gave up this scanty foot covering as soon as the arrival of civilization made a more adequate one possible.

The household goods of the earliest settlers between the Alleghenies and the Ohio were just as simple (to the point of poverty) as their dwellings and their costumes. They consisted—and still consist today in the mountains, with a slight increase in the number of eating and drinking utensils—of a couple of chests of primitive form; one or two beds, wide enough so that one could lie crosswise if desired; a crude table; and a few bowls, dishes, and spoons (these were usually of tin, often of wood, horn, or gourd shell, and rarely of pewter). Iron pots, pans, and knives were introduced by the caravans that once or twice a year got salt and powder from the South in exchange for cows and calves. The use of earthenware vessels, which began here and there at the turn of the century, was regarded by many as a criminal innovation since they broke too easily and damaged knife blades. Glass was nowhere to be seen, and many a backwoodsman had no conception of a windowpane.

To these patriarchal utensils corresponded patriarchal foods. Just as today the motto of the West is *"pork and molasses,"* at that time it was *"hog and hominy"* (pork with a thick pudding of boiled, hulled corn). They lived on this—with occasional game, some green vegetables, and, at times, a hearty swallow of whiskey. Milk was scarce because of the scarcity of cows. Tea and coffee, however, now indispensable in even the most remote backwoods, were scorned as *"slops that don't stick by the ribs,"* and a real backwoodsman would have considered himself degenerate if he had shown a liking for such a brew.

"I still clearly recall the day," said one of my informants, "on which I saw a cup for the first time.[19] My father had sent me with a relative to a school in Lexington. How astonished I was when I saw my first brick house! To make my amazement complete, the interior had, instead of rough beams, artistically papered walls and, instead of loose boards, a white plaster ceiling! I had had an idea that there might be such things in the world, but what big eyes I made when the aristocratic people brought their cups and spoons to the table! I imitated them and found the taste of the brown drink they called 'coffee' excessively repulsive. Despite this, I continued to drink, although I was very close to crying. The 'little white bowls' (as I, uncivilized boy, called the cups) were filled, and filled again as often as they were emptied. I swear I didn't know what to do, since I didn't dare say that I had had enough. Finally, I noticed that a gentleman of the party turned over his cup and placed his spoon upon it, whereupon he was served no more. I followed his example, and, to my inexpressible satisfaction, the result was the same for my little bowl."

It is obvious that each family had to have its own weaver, tailor, tanner, cabinetmaker, and wagonmaker, and that, in addition, each household had to have its own mill. One should not picture the latter, however, as either a watermill or a windmill but rather as a primitive instrument such as might have been in use when the woman smashed the head of the wicked Abimelech with a millstone. I saw such equipment among the ancient household effects that had been preserved by a farm family (probably as a relic), and it appeared to have served its purpose quite well. It was constructed of two circular stones, of which the upper (I believe) was called the *runner* and the lower was called the *bedstone*. These were placed in a box which had a spout below for the removal of the flour. A rod was fixed in a hole in the *runner*, and at its upper end was fastened a two-foot crosspole, so that two persons could turn this handmill at the same time. Instead of a bolting cloth or a sieve they usually used a deerskin in which little holes had been bored with a glowing wire.

Even more common than these handmills were the *hominy blocks*, wooden mortars of the crudest form, in which the ears of corn were pounded with hickory clubs. Young ears of corn, still full of juice, were grated into a pulp that, mixed with milk, was enjoyed as a great delicacy.

We might insert here, as unusually characteristic of these conditions, an example of the rarity of money among these people of the primeval forest and, on the other hand, of the position of the few preachers who came to them in honest zeal for the affairs of God.[20]

A Presbyterian clergyman named Smith had come from beyond the mountains to the settlers at Cross Creek, not far from the Ohio. He had found them to be goodhearted, united people, but they were in no position to pay him an annual salary sufficient to support him and his family. Thus he found himself compelled—as even today most backwoods preachers are—to earn the larger part of his living by cultivating a farm. Accordingly, he bought himself a piece of land on credit, planning to subtract the cost from the salary which his congregation had promised him. Years passed, and the good pastor was still unpaid. There was plenty of wheat, but no market—and therefore no cash. The colonists had to get even their salt from beyond the mountains, and frequently they had to pay twenty bushels of grain for one bushel of salt. So finally the time arrived when the pastor either had to have the purchase price or abandon his farm, along with the labor expended on it, and, at the same time, his beloved congregation. The salary for three full years was due, but there was not a single prospect of collecting it. The critical matter was brought before a meeting in the church. Plan after plan was suggested and rejected as unfeasible. Finally it was decided to have a quantity of wheat ground and to seek a purchaser for the flour. The contributions were most generous; some gave fifty bushels, some even more. After a month they were ready to get the flour from a mill twenty-five miles away. Now another meeting was held. The big question, upon which the success of the entire plan depended, was: Who is going to take the flour to New Orleans? No one volunteered. The undertaking was extremely dangerous. The journey to that port took a half year, and perhaps longer. And at that time the Ohio and the Mississippi still ran through a complete wilderness; the crews of more than one boat had been murdered by treacherous Indians. Finally an elder in the congregation, a gray-haired man [Smiley], got up and, to the astonishment of all, made known his decision to undertake the trip rather than let the pastor leave. Despite many attempts to dissuade him, the brave man stuck to his resolution. Two young men were persuaded to share the risky venture by the promise of high reward. On the day of the departure the entire congregation marched down from the church to the Ohio to say farewell (accompanied by tears and prayers) to the boat that carried their hopes. A hymn was sung. Then the old man shouted: "Cast off, and now let's see what the Lord will do for his people!" This was done, and slowly the boat floated downstream, accompanied by thousands of good wishes.

Nine months passed, and still no news was heard of Father Smiley. Then one Sunday morning the people gathered for worship, and, lo and behold! there on his bench before the pulpit sat the long-missed, almost given up man, in excellent condition. At the conclusion of the last prayer he arose to relate the results of his mission. He had arrived in New Orleans without mishap, and there he had received the enormous sum of seventeen dollars a barrel for his flour. As proof he pulled out a heavy purse and shook out upon the table a heap of shining gold such as most of those present had never before seen in their lives. Thus their debt was erased and the pastor redeemed from his embarrassment; and not until his death did he stop presenting them with the bread and cup of the Lord. A grandson of this brave Smiley is now a preacher in Owingsville, and Major Sudduth calls him his son-in-law.

Still more interesting than the above-reported external features, many of which are still encountered in the more remote districts of southeastern Kentucky, are the facts obtained by a glance at the moral conditions among these people. Since he who asks usually also finds, I also had the opportunity to gather valuable notes about this topic.

For a long time after the establishment of the first settlements there was "neither law nor gospel" in the border regions. The first was lacking because a person hardly ever knew to which state he belonged. There was very little "gospel" because seldom could a preacher be found who, like that one at Cross Creek, was willing to expose himself to financial embarrassment for the sake of Christ. So in eastern Kentucky and western Virginia there were no courts, lawyers, sheriffs, or constables until two decades after the War of Independence. Until then, everyone behaved as he deemed right. Despite this, there was no anarchy, for everyone was (to use the Biblical expression of my informant) "a law unto himself." With a sparse population (when all members of a community know each other well) and in a warlike period (when every adult has the same value as a defender) public opinion has almost the same force as law. In addition vice has little opportunity under simple conditions of life, and where it does appear, it occurs much more openly and is much more easily discovered and punished than among us (where civilization offers it a screen, bypaths, and hiding places). Therefore, industry and justice, bravery and sacrifice, frankness and hospitality received their full measure of public recognition among the old backwoodsmen, while the antipodes of these virtues had to fear the court in which Judge Reputation passed sentence. The punishment for indolence, untruthfulness, and rudeness consisted in *"hating the offender out,"* a moral chastisement which (similar to the *Atimea* [loss of civil rights] of the Greeks) had as a consequence the voluntary banishment of the no-good. Whoever refused his neighbor the requested help in erecting a log cabin, rolling felled logs in a clearing, or in bringing in a harvest received the disgraceful title of "Lawrence"[21] and soon became aware of his reputation through the general refusal to be courteous to him. It was commonly decided at a general meeting that women with too sharp tongues could slander as much as they liked, but nobody was required to believe them. Small thefts were punished by *"tongue lashing."* Sudduth reported an example of a militiaman who, before the battle of New Orleans, stole a corncake from the ashes of the campfire from his comrades. The theft was noticed, and from then on, throughout the campaign, whenever the rascal approached a group, a voice immediately asked: "Who's there?" and another replied: "The cake from the ashes." Then a third cried: "What's the name of the cake from the ashes?" which was answered by a fourth with the full name of the sinner and confirmed by a fifth with: "That's true, and not invented."

If the object for which the Seventh Commandment was violated was of any value, then his Gracious Sir, old Judge Lynch, sat in judgment over the evildoer and sentenced him "to have the flag of the United States (with its thirteen stripes) painted on his back," or—to translate it into the humorless prose of our police style—to receive thirteen lashes. If the theft was more significant, then the "Law of Moses" was carried out on the culprit, that is, he received forty lashes minus one, after which he was ordered to get out of the district within three days. He also was directed not to let himself be seen there again; in case of violation, double the number of lashes would be administered. This punishment is still in fashion here and there for horsethieves. Even up to a few years ago the authorities in the mountain valleys of western Virginia gave the guilty one the choice of going to prison or receiving his lashes.

It's in the nature of the wilderness that it gives rise to superstition. Certainly, *"The groves were God's first temples,"*[22] but the groves and the forests were also the first dwelling of ghosts and demons. The solitude, the shadows, the magical light effects, the rustling and humming of the trees, the strange burial mounds of a prehistoric race encountered here and there in the uninhabited wilderness—all acted upon the imagination. Besides, up until the beginning of the present century the backwoodsman didn't have much of the light and consolation of religion. Everywhere you'll find it more or less borne out that where a definite faith is lacking, a stirring feeling of dependency in the human is transformed into a source of superstition—if not prevented by philosophical training. So there were witches and wizards—not to mention other things—throughout the West, and especially in Kentucky, up to the most recent times. The former (a peculiar feature of the superstition) always used their art for evil purposes; the latter, on the other hand, always employed their knowledge for good purposes. The sorceresses made children and cattle sick by shooting them with balls of their hair. They destroyed the quality of rifles with their incantations. Indeed, they even changed their enemies into horses, saddled them, and rode them to their nightly orgies. Often they milked cows that did not belong to them by sticking a new needle into a new towel for each cow to be milked, then hanging it over their door, and then, with the aid of magic formulas, drawing milk from the corners of the towel. The wizards, on the other hand, used their arts only to counteract the maliciousness of their female colleagues; in this business many of them had a more extensive practice than the most popular physicians today. The method of curing illnesses caused by magic was as follows: A picture of the woman thought to be a witch was drawn on a board and a bullet containing a little silver shot at it. It was believed that the witch herself would be struck exactly at the spot aimed at on the drawing.

Westfeld reported a comical example of this, one which had happened not long before. It had been put into a farmer's head that the malanders from which several of his horses had become ill (and a few had even died) had been caused by a witch, an old woman in the neighborhood. The old fool had also been advised to shoot a silver bullet at one of his nags while the witch was in it—she would be killed and the animal cured. The simple man did so, and in this way he killed his best broodmare. To be sure, a few days later he had the satisfaction of seeing the supposed witch die (from the consequences of the grief caused by the senseless rumors).

Another method was to burn alive the animal slowly dying under the spell. As late as 1835, a farmer in southern Ohio, believing that in this way he would burn the witch herself, was guilty of this cruelty. Still other wizards recommended that the "water" of the person ill through witchcraft be hung in a well-corked bottle in the chimney, whereupon the old woman who had "bewitched" him would suffer from strangury as long as the bottle remained there—unless she succeeded in borrowing something from her victim, it didn't matter what. The latter naturally tried to prevent this.

Probably the activities of the wandering preachers contributed more than anything else to the elimination of the just-described evils and to the gradual disappearance of coarseness and darkness. The first ones to bring the blessings of the gospel to the backwoods and to Christianize these semisavages were the Presbyterians. The Methodists followed them from Virginia and Pennsylvania. I have already mentioned several times that I am no admirer of the latter. But at the same time I cannot deny recognition of the zeal and self-denial with which their emissaries worked in this territory—like the missionaries in the Germanic forest primeval.

How the annunciation of God's word affected these souls full of primitive power, these men with muscles of steel, is shown amazingly by the phenomena—at times sublime, at times frightfully grimacing —that accompanied the Great Kentucky Revival mentioned in an earlier chapter and in the introduction to this one; it was the first consequence of the penetration of the Christian doctrine of salvation to the western forest people. This religious earthquake—which continues to shake and storm even now in the camp meetings, of which it was the origin—began in the year 1799 through the combined efforts of two brothers by the name of MacGhee. On a trip together from western Tennessee through the "Barrens" down to the Ohio, they reached a settlement on the Red River where they stopped for a day's rest. They also wanted to participate in a communion service in the congregation of the Presbyterian minister MacGrady. The brothers, one of whom was a Methodist and the other a Presbyterian, preached on this occasion. The words they spoke had a strangely awakening effect. Other speakers had already left the place, but the MacGhees still remained. William, the older brother, felt so overcome by a power from on high that he had to get up from his chair and sit down on the ground. John, the younger, trembling and, because of the nearness of God, unable to utter a sound, remained in the pulpit. In the entire congregation prevailed the deepest devotion, and loud weeping and groaning could be heard.

The favorable results of this gathering—which the MacGhees had attended unintentionally—caused the brothers to announce another "meeting" on the Muddy River, and this turned out to be the first camp meeting in America. Such a crowd gathered that no church would have been able to hold it, and they found themselves forced to move out into the forest. Here the religious exercises—preaching, praying, and singing—were continued day and night. This new kind of worship attracted widespread attention because of its peculiarity, and more so because of the unheard-of signs through which the emotions of the participants were revealed. By the year 1801 the entire West, as far as it was settled, and particularly Kentucky, was full of enthusiastic believers. Pilgrims even came from the old states in the East, and the meetings swelled to enormous size. The fear of God trembled in them like a mysterious shudder, the spirit of the Pentecost burned in them like a subterranean fire. Or was it the great Pan who was revived in this forest solitude? Or the "Manito of the Dreams" to whom Robert Sands[23] dedicated such a beautiful ode—the spirit of primeval vegetation, the shadow of the wilderness, the melancholy voice of the mountain lake? It really doesn't matter what the source of this magic was: its influence was almighty. Only a few people left without having been struck to the heart by the lightning which came from the mouths of the preachers. Those who attempted to flee from the galvanic current were often still reached by it along the way, or they were frightened back into the midst of the worshipers by some alarming sign, back to those whose fervor was expressed in a most powerful way and broke out into manifestations which, if not supernatural, were certainly unnatural enough.

These manifestations—which in the chronicles of religious fanaticism find counterparts in the convulsions of the French "Convulsionaires" and, more recently, in the ravings of the Swedish "Läsare"—bore some resemblance to epilepsy and often even to the so-called Saint Vitus's Dance; however, they were infectious, so that sometimes they were spread in the course of a few minutes from one individual to the greatest part of the congregation. Back then, when they could be explained by no known law of our mental organization, they were ascribed to the sway of divine power. Many considered them to be "the fluttering of the creatures before the return of our Lord." A religious writer of that period classified the various manifestations as "falling," "jerking," "dancing," and "barking," to which might be added "dreams and visions," full of images of heaven and hell. Falling and the visions connected therewith were the most common phenomena. The afflicted person sank into a somnambulistic state of "being outside himself," accompanied by a complete slackening of all muscular activity and the cessation of all mental and sensual relations to the outside world. The mind seemed to be occupied exclusively with ecstatic visions of a higher state of being; this impressed upon the subject's features an angelic, transfigured expression. With some people this condition lasted for only a few hours; with others, however, for days; during this period all animalistic functions, with the exception of breathing, were completely suspended. Although this phenomenon occurred chiefly in the female sex, the *jerking* appeared more frequently in men, and especially in vigorous, athletic natures. This was the most characteristic and, for the spectator, most horrible manifestation of these attacks bordering on religious insanity. The first occurrence of the terrible outbreak was reported from a congregation in the mountains of East Tennessee, where several hundred people of both sexes, gathered to celebrate communion, were attacked by the strangest muscle spasms. The person afflicted was suddenly shaken by an electric trembling and twitching; this soon spread to all tendons, nerves, and fibers. The form which this next assumed was a hurling of the arms downward from the elbows; this took place extraordinarily rapidly, with only short pauses. This was the commonest and least striking type. But the convulsive moment was not restricted to the arms—in many cases it spread to other parts of the body. If the muscles of the cervical vertebrae were attacked, then the head was thrown and hurled in the most dreadful manner, to the right and to the left, forward and backward. This occurred with such lightninglike speed that a person not moved by the same mysterious stimulus could not imitate it. The chest was elevated and the breathing turned into an anxious gasping and rattling. Forehead and cheeks dripped with perspiration, the facial features were contorted into the most abominable grimace, and the head flew through the air so that one must fear that the sufferer would break his neck or even hurl his eyes from their sockets. In the case of women with long hair, "the braids hissed and cracked like a whip," so that it "often could be heard twenty feet away" (if my source* for this remark is not exaggerating). In a few cases the back muscles were involved and the sufferer plunged to the ground, where for a while his contortions resembled the flopping of a fish that has been thrown upon dry land by the angler. In other cases, the electrical force passed through the entire body, and with similar jerkings and twistings the victim was pulled and thrown over fallen logs or, if it

\* Henry Howe's *Historical Collections of Ohio*, a very good handbook for information about the state mentioned in the title.

occurred in a church, over tables and chairs, with obvious risk of bumps and fractures. Any attempt to hold or force those so afflicted was fruitless; besides, such an attempt was seldom risked, for it was superstitiously believed that such force meant resistance to the Holy Spirit, and usually one let the paroxysm gradually wear itself out.

According to the testimony of all who have described these scenes, such phenomena were absolutely involuntary. Indeed, the fact that these jerkings continued despite all resistance on the part of the one afflicted, that, to be sure, every attempt to suppress them only resulted in increased violence—these testify sufficiently as to their involuntary nature. But this becomes even clearer through the observation that those who had come to make fun of the falling, jerking, grimacing, dancing, and barking were attacked by the mysterious force as much as the others; indeed, they frequently were thrown about even more swiftly and madly, although they accompanied each of these convulsive attacks with blasphemies and curses.

The Baptists and, in a few places, the Catholic priests have worked almost as successfully—even if less strikingly and powerfully—in those regions I have designated above as the "heart" of the Anglo-American land. On the other hand, of all the denominations that bustle about here on behalf of those dispersed of the House of Israel, the Episcopal Church (to which most of these settlers have belonged since childhood) has done the least. It is the church of the aristocrats and has behaved that way, too; but it has also reaped the reward for such neglect and snobbery by having to watch while the West turned away from it more and more. For this it may console itself with the "almighty dollar" with which its wealthy members fill its treasury, with the buckram liturgy of its Common Prayer Book, and with the silken priestly vestments with which its bishops, rectors, and pastors have an advantage over the clergymen of those sects which have far outstripped it!*

Despite all their crudeness and wildness, the contemporaries of Boone and Kenton were hospitable in the broadest sense of the word. This beautiful virtue has been handed down to their descendants in Kentucky, especially here in the mountains; but stories of the hospitality of western farmers are (according to my certainly

* The Catholic Church in the United States is divided into 59 dioceses and at the beginning of 1851 had 1,595 clergy and 89,359 adult communicants. Fifty new churches and chapels were consecrated in the year 1850, and the contributions of the parishes amounted to $342,936. However, there are about 3 million Baptists—if one counts the 4 different branches of the sect together.

unauthoritative experience) applicable only to the homes of Dunkards and Mennonites, and perhaps to the cabins of the interior of Indiana and Illinois, that is, those somewhat remote from the highways. Furthermore, the *mountaineers* are loyal neighbors who live peacefully next to one another in their lonely wooded valleys. There is not, to be sure, a complete absence of conflict; for Kentucky blood is hot knight's blood mixed with an uncommonly fine feeling for honor, something which, as a rule, is totally foreign to the German farmer in America and, in good part, to the Yankee farmer. While their more aristocratic brothers around Lexington and Frankfort duel at thirty paces with pistols, the mountain people of the East usually end any exchange of words with a fist fight; this sometimes takes place on the spot, but it often is set for a future date and then carried out in proper fashion, with seconds and referees—as in the tournaments of old. The barbaric custom of so-called *gouging,* in which the opponents in a fight tried to press out each other's eyes with their thumbs, now exists only as a memory—at least hereabouts.

Instances of seduction are a great rarity in these valleys (as among the country people of the West in general), although the parents almost never place any hindrance in the way of the association of their daughters with the young men of the neighborhood, and *sparking* (the local term for *lovemaking*) often continues boldly and unrestricted far into the night. Despite all this, however, there are practically no illegitimate births; the reason for this is to be sought less in the prudence and virtue of the youth of Kentucky than in the early marriages customary throughout all America and in the fear of summary punishment from the family.

At these weddings rather strange things happened (and still do where the Methodists have not forbidden whiskey and dancing), so the description of a backwoods wedding will be the last scene unrolled before the reader in this picture gallery of customs.[24]

From the earliest times the bride's parents had the obligation of arranging at their home the party which accompanied the ceremony, but in return for this they also had the right to select the minister who would unite the couple. Such an affair claimed—and still claims today—the attention of the entire neighborhood, far and wide, and old and young looked forward in anticipation to the day when Jack would marry Polly or Bill would marry Peggy. On the morning of the great day all the invited guests gathered at the home of the groom; they left in time (naturally by horse) to reach the home of the bride before noon, at which hour the nuptials customarily were performed.

## A VISIT TO THE BACKWOODSMEN

Their journey (on which they rode by twos) was frequently interrupted by the narrowness of the trail winding through the dense forest, between fallen trees and rocky walls, through murmuring creeks without bridges. These difficulties were at times augmented by annoyed neighbors or relatives who had been offended because they had not been invited; during the night they had tied vines across the trail or lay hiding in the background, suddenly to fire a salvo of blank shot at the procession. Imagine the scene that followed such a crude joke: picture the rearing of the horses, the screaming of the ladies, and the cavalier efforts of their gallant escorts to save them from falling—something which could not always be prevented, despite all exertions! When they were about one English mile from their destination, a halt was made, and two young men rode ahead to arrange a "race for the bottle." The worse the trail, the more swamps and logs, roots and vines, bushes, stones, and holes that obstructed it, the better; for these obstructions gave the gay fellows a chance to exhibit their fearlessness and firm seat. Truly, the English fox hunt is scarcely half as dangerous for horse and rider as such a "ride for the bottle." The starting signal was given by the company with the shrill scalping cry of the Indians, and off the rivals flew—through thick and thin, over sticks and stones. The bottle was held ready at the door of the wedding house, and the one who reached the goal first received the bottle as prize, returning to the company with triumphant shouts. He first passed it to the groom for a drink, and then to the other couples in turn. He then put it away in the front of his hunting shirt for later refreshment of his own spirit. The meal which was brought forth after completion of the marriage ceremony consisted of mighty portions of roast and boiled pork and poultry, to which were frequently added bear paws and other delicacies of the forest. In addition there was an abundance of sweet potatoes, corn prepared in various ways, and an enormous supply of greens, cabbage, and turnips. The most abandoned gaiety prevailed at the table, although the table itself seldom was more than a rough board smoothed with an adze. It stood upon four plump legs, and upon it were found (instead of an elegant service) troughlike wooden bowls, tin dishes resembling washbasins, spoons of horn or hickory (often of pewter), and some knives. In many cases there were not enough utensils for all the guests; those who couldn't get any cheerfully used the scalping knives hanging from their belts. Of forks, only the five-pronged sort were known that are described in the dictionary under the article "hand."

After the meal the company arranged itself for the dance in the wide hall that here divides the larger cabins into two halves. This usually continued without pause until the next morning, and it always began with a sort of quadrille (square dance) and later resolved into reels and jigs. No one was permitted to become tired; whenever a feeble soul crept away to take a little nap in some hiding place, he was soon hunted down, brought back to the dance floor, and the fiddler ordered to play the tune *"Hang out until Tomorrow Morning"* to cheer up and deride the sleepy one.

About ten o'clock in the evening a deputation of young ladies spirited away the bride and put her to bed; it frequently happened that instead of using a staircase she had to climb a mere ladder from the dining room to the garret where the marriage was to be consummated. After the abduction of the bride had been discovered, a procession of young men also took the groom up and placed him nice and neatly beside his new wife. The dancing continued without interruption during these maneuvers. If it happened that there weren't enough chairs and stools—a situation that occurred only too frequently—the gentlemen who weren't dancing were obliged to offer their laps to the girls and ladies as seats, and this invitation never was declined. The bridal couple was never entirely forgotten in the midst of all this celebration, and around midnight one of the party would remind the guests that "the little people up there" might need refreshment. *Black Betty* was called for (this was the name of the bottle) and it was sent upstairs to the newlyweds, often accompanied by such a quantity of meat, bread, and vegetables that a half dozen hungry threshers could have satisfied their appetites.

During the course of these festivities (which among the well-to-do often lasted several days), if a guest wanted to help himself to a drink and toast the newlyweds, he got up and shouted in a loud voice: "Where is Black Betty? I'd like to kiss her charming lips!" After he had gotten what he wanted, he said (holding the bottle in his right hand): "To the health of the groom—not forgetting my health; and to the happiness of the bride—big-fisted happiness and sturdy boys!" Whereupon he took a hearty swallow and passed the bottle on to his neighbor, who did the same and passed it on. Old and young shared the beautiful wish; for in those days, when the Indian Wars were raging throughout the West, sturdy boys were a very real marriage blessing.

◊ ◊ ◊ During the next few days, favored by excellent weather, we made various excursions on foot and, introduced by the Major, got to know many other more or less peculiar "characters." On one of these walks through the wooded mountains, taken in the company of a young man of the neighborhood who was employed in the felling and rolling of trees for the mill, we were forced to stay out all night, while Sudduth and Westfeld, who had turned their steps toward another district, had returned to the headquarters in time.

My companion was a silent man, and our path took us in the direction of the boundary of the adjoining Montgomery County through an almost uninterrupted wilderness, absolutely impenetrable for wagons and riders. Only in the valleys and hollows were there any signs of cultivation, and even these were very recent. After we had traveled for several miles and had descended into a hollow next to one of those above-mentioned sugarloaflike peaks, I noticed a number of cabins in a clearing. I at first took them to be a little village, but this was an error that my guide corrected by explaining that it was a Methodist camp where the people of the area held their camp meetings in summer. These gatherings are held elsewhere in tents; but since tents are difficult to transport to this region (and besides cost money), the *mountaineers* have considered it better to replace them with cabins that remain standing year in and year out. I persuaded my companion to make a detour to this lonely place of God in the primeval forest, now as quiet as the grave. Not a soul was to be seen. The camp comprised a rectangle formed of eighteen log shanties; the area enclosed by them, where the ashes of several large cooking fires could be seen, measured about 150 paces long and a bit more than half that wide. The cabins were not much more spacious than the booths at our yearly fairs, and their roofs sloped toward the rear. Only a few possessed windows, but without panes. On one of the short sides of the parallelogram stood a roofed canopy, supported by four posts and shaded by a giant oak; it was about forty feet wide and twenty-four deep. Under it stood a crude pulpit, and in front of this lay a log, peeled on the top, that served as a *"seat of repentance."* Some distance away lay several more such logs, partly grown over with blackberry vines; they probably are used as church benches. Despite the crudeness of form, all of this made a solemn impression. The stumps rotting here and there in the dark forest are a silent but impressive *memento mori*. The falling leaves swept everywhere by the wind give a picture of human existence without consolation from above. The deep melancholy of the scene provides an excellent background for the bright, heavenly bright Christ figure that the preacher calls down from the right hand of the Father with the promise: "Wherever two or three are gathered in my name, there I am amongst them." Certainly genuine piety prevails here, and I have no doubt that they pray more sincerely here than in the white marble Grace Church of New York's Broadway, in that temple of the aristocratic Pharisees *"above Bleeker"* from which one is cast out if he doesn't place a schilling in the silver plate passed around by the head warden for the privilege of worshiping our dear Lord in good society.

    The few settlers here—and even more so those in the wilder valleys extending farther to the southeast—can sell only whatever (as they put it) runs to market by itself, that is, cattle, hogs, and sheep. These forest meadows are excellently suited for the latter, and it might be profitable to carry on large-scale sheepraising for the production of the coarser kinds of wool—provided that something is first done for the construction of passable roads. Because of the transportation difficulty, farming is now carried on only to supply one's own needs. The fields show practically nothing but corn, with now and then a few plots of wheat and buckwheat on higher situated places.

    About noon we came to a road that took us to a log shanty in a valley. For some years this had been the home of my guide, and it was evident that he was using this opportunity to pay a visit to his parents. The fence around the house and its outbuildings had no gate, so we had to climb over it. A gray hound barked out the residents, and we were given a hearty welcome by the mother of the house, a small, thin woman. It was a poor cabin, but in the four years since they had moved from the Big Sandy in Virginia the people had not only cleared ten acres, but they had also fixed up the interior quite comfortably—their little room showed how much a feeling for cleanliness and order can accomplish even under unfavorable circumstances. It was a really charming genre picture into which we stepped. The few furnishings were tastefully placed and carefully kept free of dust and dirt. In the two corners opposite the fireplace stood high, wide canopy beds with snow-white curtains and colorfully decorated covers (called *"quilts"* in the West). These are made of a white cotton material filled with wadding and embroidered with multicolored designs in the form of flowers and arabesques. In one corner next to the fireplace stood a cupboard with cups, dishes, and other utensils. In the fourth corner sat a venerable old man, leaning against the oak family table, his moccasin-clad feet stretched toward the flames. He was of athletic build and peered into the world with such expressive and majestic features that he could have served as model for a statue of Jupiter—if he hadn't chewed tobacco and spit the ugly brown juice incessantly in an arc toward the burning logs. He was the grandfather of the family. His daughter, the mother of the house, after placing chairs for us, crouched down before the fire to prepare the meal, meanwhile eagerly asking her son about the news from beyond the mountains. A long rifle leaned against the wall near the old man, and between his knees he held a sturdy staff, curved at the top and made of a peeled hickory branch. After the customary greeting he said nothing. Following a pause, however, during which he had regarded me intently, he reached into his pocket and asked: *"Chaw, stranger?"* This is a question with which they frequently begin a conversation in the backwoods; it takes the place of the *"Fine weather, Sir!"* usual in the city. I declined the proffered chewing tobacco with the excuse that we were not accustomed to it in my homeland, and from this developed a discussion of all sorts of topics. We were finally interrupted by the woman's blowing one of those tin trumpets that I had heard earlier in the Black Swamp; it signaled the absent members of the family that the meal was ready. Shortly thereafter they arrived: the master of the house, a tall, vigorous forty-year-old, and a son and two daughters, all healthy and strong, although more or less disfigured by pockmarks. After friendly greetings and mighty handshaking, we all sat down at the table. The food—which the grandfather dedicated with a prayer after I had declined the honor—was tasty, and the coffee, mixed with precious cream and sweetened with maple sugar, left little to be desired.

After lunch I inspected the vicinity of the house, accompanied by the old man. I now observed that he limped. To my question as to the cause of this infirmity, he replied that it was an old injury produced by a bullet shot into his hip by Tecumseh's Indians while he was participating in Harrison's campaign against Proctor, a bullet he had not been able to find. A second bullet had also been in his flesh for a long time, but a few years ago, after a strenuous ride, he had discovered it and without hesitation had cut it out with his razor. Next to the dwelling and connected to it by a roof was a little log cabin in which the womenfolk wove the cloth which was used to dress the entire family. A short distance away neighed the farmer's horse, a coarse-haired pony, in one of those stables which might be called a "plank cage of convenience." Still a bit farther, between a recently set out peach orchard and a cornfield, we came upon the barn, that is, a rectangle of logs placed one upon the other, notched at the corners, and without door or roof. The people now husking corn in the field were throwing masses of the light yellow ears into its interior area, which measured about twelve square feet. When such a simple shed is filled, it is covered with straw or boards, and the grain in it keeps pretty well, since the constant draft through the cracks dispels any dampness. The work of picking and husking was being done quite rapidly by the people. I tried to help and earned praise, although I couldn't do it one-third as fast as they could and soon had to give up completely since the sharp leaves cut my hands.

A few hundred paces from here a new settlement had been established. The log cabin which had just been completed was soon to take up one of the two daughters of the family as a young housewife. The erection of such a dwelling proceeds with unbelievable speed; seldom are more than three or four days required. The procedure is as follows: First of all a suitable site is chosen (above all, it must not be damp), and then a day is fixed upon which, with the help of the neighbors, the building material is collected. With the exception of a few nails, this is furnished by the locality itself in the form of trees which the practically constructed American ax fells and properly smooths in about as many hours as the German ax would require days. A man with a team of horses or oxen drags them to the building site and places them ready at hand at the ends and sides of the rectangle upon which the structure is to be erected. The following morning the building men gather for the setting and raising. For this purpose four "corner men" are selected who notch and join together the logs while other men place them one upon the other. As soon as the first course is fixed, the carrying beams and floor planks are fit in. When the walls have reached the intended height, a three-foot-wide entrance is chopped or sawed, and on one short side of the rectangle an opening where the fireplace is to be attached. The latter is constructed below of fieldstones and mortar and above usually of pieces of wood cemented with clay; sometimes it appears quite slanting and unfirm. The roof, which generally slopes only very little, projects in the front on some of these cabins, forming a small porch; on others it projects toward the rear. With this the backwoodsman's home is finished, and the third day is used only for the laying of a ceiling over the room, for the caulking of cracks and joints (using lime), and for the finishing of the door (which seldom has a lock, but commonly only a wooden handle). Windows are considered superfluous. Where the people are not wealthy enough to provide themselves with the colorfully painted chairs and the polished posts and sides of a regular bed that the Cincinnati factories now deliver to even the most remote districts at low prices, ax and knife must produce for the new household a table and several three-legged stools, a rocking chair (an indispensable requirement), and a bedstead. The latter is a complete triumph of simplicity. A forked branch is stuck into the earthen floor and a pole laid in the fork. Its other end is pushed into a crack in the opposite wall, and this forms the foot of the bed. Over this pole a second is placed which runs to the wall at the head; this forms the upper end of the bed. Over these are fastened the boards that form the bottom, and the bed of the house occupant is completed. To satisfy him, only a mattress filled with cornsilk and a few covers and sheets are needed. Before the occupant moves into his new shell, however, the product of his skill and neighborly assistance must be dedicated; just as our carpenters and masons have their "lifting celebration," so the workmen in the backwoods have their *housewarming*, at which there is much dancing and an abundant consumption of whiskey. This ceremony was to take place in a few days, and I regretted very much that I was unable to accept the invitation to participate.

The remaining hours of the afternoon I spent in the company of "old Jupiter"; I had to describe to him the ocean and New York, and especially Cincinnati. He remembered the latter quite well as a fort with about fifty log cabins—now it has about twice that many churches. He had heard people talk about railroads and steamships, but he had never seen such marvels. When I told him about the telegraph lines by which a person could send his thoughts from the Ohio up to the Lakes in a minute, he looked at me in disbelief and the word "humbug" seemed to want to form on his lips. But in matters which were closer to his sphere he exhibited a surprising amount of sound human understanding, and more than once I was astonished at the sharpness of his judgment and his striking comparisons.

The hours after supper were filled with hunting tales and similar stories by the old man and his son. The latter showed me the skin of an enormous bear that he had killed a few weeks before in a grove of hickory and walnut trees that could be seen from the door. The hole made by the bullet proved that the shot had struck the bear right in the heart. When it was time to go to bed, the young man accompanied me to the previously mentioned weaving cabin. Here we found a neat bed ready for the two of us and had a nice opportunity during the night to make astronomical observations through the chinks in the wall.

The graying morning saw us on our feet, and after I had taken my departure from the good people, we set out on the return journey, the master of the house accompanying us for a short distance. "You were welcome, stranger,"* he said in response to my thanks for the friendly reception. "I hope you'll call again if your way brings you here."

Eagles Mill was no more than nine English miles by the shortest route, so I arrived there in good time and did not delay the departure for the inspection of the better areas of Sudduth's property, which had been set for today. Around ten o'clock we (namely Westfeld, the Major, and I) left the mill, again on horseback, and rode back through the bottoms to the Bath. Here, however, we turned off to the right from the highway which leads to Owingsville, for our destination was the Licking and Morgan County. First we rode through a narrow, dark beech valley called *Murder Branch* because here, in the bloody days of yore, the Indians had killed several women captured from a settlement; this had been done so that the Indians would no longer be hindered by them on their flight from pursuing men led by the Major's father.[25] From here our nags climbed over a steep mountain and down into another valley; here babbled one of the thousands of American "Beaver Creeks." This valley soon spread out into a broad, well-cultivated basin; from here we again turned into a hollow of this unendingly uneven land and soon had to ride up the side of a steep mountain. The trail was narrow and dangerous, especially for a rider such as I, just having his second riding lesson today. The trail, a mere footpath, was bordered on the left by a ravine in which, at a depth of twenty fathoms, the creek flowed dark blue over a white limestone bed. A false step of my horse could have led to a fateful plunge—a prospect at which I should rather have had my feet on the ground than in the stirrups.

Another rider had joined us at a farm. Hung over his shoulders he wore a leather bullet pouch and a powder horn, and he carried a long rifle. He accompanied us over the ridge and down into a second basin where, behind a large blockhouse, we found several other riflemen gathered. We dismounted with him and tied our horses to a fence. The Major wanted to pay a short visit to the families living here, and we wanted to watch for a little while the shooting match which was about to begin. The group consisted of ten young and old men, all of them tall and well built. They had set up a four-cornered target on a half-charred stump that stood in the cleared field. In the center of it a three-inch nail had been hammered in up to about two-thirds of its

---

* The poetic expression *stranger* is customary everywhere among the backwoodsmen of the mountains; one is almost never addressed as *sir*.

length, and the skill which was being tested here was to hit the nail so that it would be driven into the board up to its head, as by a well-placed hammer blow. A shot that bends the nail counts for less; a shot that doesn't touch it at all is greeted with great laughter. The distance from the fence upon which the rifle was rested to the target might have amounted to sixty paces. Surprising was the small amount of powder used in loading—I saw no one take more than just enough to cover the small ball placed in the left hand, and I was told that even at a distance of a hundred yards no greater quantity was required. The results proved the correctnesss of this assertion, for already at the second shot the nail was driven into the board. This seemed to be regarded as nothing extraordinary, for a dozen more nails were ready, and Westfeld remarked later that on the average one out of three shots would hit in this manner. When all had fired, those who had been successful fired a second round among themselves, and as soon as the winner had been determined, the amount of the entry fee was handed over to him (usually a small amount), and he treated the group to whiskey or brandy.

After riding out of this basin again into a hollow, and from here to the left over a ridge crowned with lone cedars, we found ourselves facing the deep, dark, winding Licking Valley and upon the land which Sudduth had praised as excellent. Westfeld declared himself satisfied with it. The terraces on the heights exhibited a very good wheat soil. In the valley between the river and the foothills we were sure to find the richest black soil. The slopes, finally, could be used very well for sheep grazing. Besides, the protected hollows and hillsides were well suited for growing peaches. The Major pointed out in the midst of the wilderness an old orchard which had been planted years ago by a fellow who had retired here to devote himself to a contemplative hermit's life and (on the side) to hog stealing—an occupation which eventually had been ended for the "Robber Knight" by a "Crusade" of his neighbors.

Another natural curiosity of this forest wilderness is a large cave; it extends possibly very deep into the mountains, but until now it has been explored for only about four hundred paces. The rock in which it is located is a type of limestone. The height of its arch may be seven feet, its width twelve to fourteen feet, and a clear stream pours forth from it. Only a few half-charred logs remained of a log cabin which Sudduth had had constructed near the entrance. How the fire had started couldn't be guessed.

From this point, which we had reached by way of a rocky, mossy ravine, we rode through a thicket that many a German rider would have declared absolutely impenetrable. Reins wrapped around the pommel, pushing aside the branches and vines with both hands, now and then whipped or pricked by a twig springing back, we rode down into a gloomy oak bottom. In climbing out from a depression, my horse again lost saddle and rider. Finally we stood on the bank of the Licking, which here is a beautiful clear river thirty to thirty-five feet wide and seven feet deep on the average. Soon we also saw a clearing and a log cabin. A bit farther downstream stood a second cabin which a certain Mr. Trombo had rented from Sudduth, along with the surrounding fields. It was not possible to spend the night here. The cabin contained no more than one room, and this was already too small for the master of the house, his brother, his tall, thin, hollow-eyed wife, and his six children—along with just as many chickens that happened to be visiting. Besides, the people appeared to be as poor as Job. So, after a short stay in the gloomy, inhospitable dwelling, we left again to wander through a ford in the Licking to Morgan County on the opposite shore. In approaching darkness we worked our way over a hilltop covered with mighty boulders and down into a broad valley with handsome farms, watered by the North Fork of the Licking. In this stream I took an involuntary bath—either because of the maliciousness of my horse, or because of the unscrupulousness of Westfeld (who had not buckled my saddle properly), or because of some water spirit who could not stand the sight of such a poor rider —I swear, it was not due to my own clumsiness! Despite the coldness of the season, and thanks to a good constitution and a half hour's ride at a brisk trot, the bath had no disastrous consequences.

Anyway, this plunge was the last installment of the tuition I had to pay. The following day, leaving our night's lodging at the cabin of a certain Mr. Pierce or Pears, we rode to Owingsville, a distance of twenty-four English miles, in a little over 4½ hours—and nothing like this happened again. That evening—although I was somewhat shaken and lame, but with a whole skin and unbroken bones—I was able to attend a performance of the Bloomers. A company of traveling male and female performers (the latter in the well-known, strange uniform of feminine young America) caused, through their abominable singing and still more abominable acting, the art-loving public of good Owingsville to produce a hecatomb of resounding "Bravos!"

Thus we had happily carried out our excursion to the wooded mountains of the Licking, and the purpose for which it was under-

## A VISIT TO THE BACKWOODSMEN

taken had been achieved. Westfeld entered into further discussions with the Major, and on the following morning the agreement was signed. Now all that remained was the opinion of the participants in the colonization plan and the recruiting of additional settlers. This is not the place to tell how the matter progressed. It is sufficient to report that when I left Cincinnati it was said that buyers had already been found for two thousand acres of the land in question.[26]

Our leavetaking from the old Major was heartfelt. His image will always be preserved in my memory with those that caused me to forget, among the country people of the West, the prejudices about the Americans which I had brought along from Germany and which had been reinforced by my experiences in the East (even though they may have been unjustified). I apologize to the nation in silence.

◊ ◊ ◊ We returned by way of POPLAR PLAINS, FLEMINGSBURGH, and MAYSVILLE through one of the most fertile regions in Kentucky. The land, which at first is rather hilly and wooded, drops off toward the north to a gently rolling plain upon which one rich cornfield is followed by another and where wheat, hemp, tobacco, and (if I heard correctly) hops are raised. To judge by the age of the trees in the numerous orchards, the farms here must belong to those established earliest. Cattle of good breed, beautiful roads, brick houses, and (unfortunately) a large number of Negro slaves from the darkest black to the lightest brown—all told of the prosperity of this district, in the canebrakes of which the scout Kenton in the days of old built the first log cabin in northern Kentucky.

In Poplar Plains we were unexpectedly present at a spectacle. On trees along the way we had already read advertisements that on Tuesday, December 9, an auction of Negroes would take place at Mac Intire's livery stable. Our horse was nice enough to bring us to the inn, next door to which the operation was underway, just at the right time.

We encountered a very mixed gathering before the door of the building in question: hats of all shapes and colors, and faces under them representing all possible characters. Most of those present appeared to be ordinary farmers, yet there were among them a few physiognomies that I might have taken to be slave traders. They talked in groups and spiced their lively conversations with curses and oaths—among ordinary Americans these seem to take the place of capital letters and punctuation marks. They joked and laughed, smoked and chewed. They spat artistically into the distance and blew their noses with praiseworthy frugality through their fingers, finishing off with their handkerchiefs. Meanwhile the black flesh to be disposed of waited patiently, squatting on boxes in a corner behind the door, for the auctioneer who would determine its fate. There were (to speak in a businesslike manner) five, or really six, pieces: an old female mulatto with shaking hands and almost toothless, two young males of vigorous build and almost ebony black, and finally a man of about thirty and a woman with an infant. Judging by their expressions and gestures, the old woman and the two young men seemed to have no concern for their futures. The former was of no use to the cotton plantations of the South—which the blacks of Kentucky fear like hell, with good reason—and so had hope of remaining here, where the Negroes are treated humanely—if not as humans. The two boys either did not yet know the terrible significance of the phrase "to be sold *down river*," or they were dully submitting to the inevitable. But it was different with the two other adults who (as we learned) formed "a sort of married couple," and for whom the fateful hammer of the auctioneer could strike the hour of eternal separation. They sat next to each other and embraced as if, in defiance of fate, they would never be parted. The poor woman—who like the Sulamith of the *Song of Songs* was "black, but very lovely" and therefore not only had to fear being torn from husband and child but easily might be sold to New Orleans into a house of sin—poured forth a flood of tears. A fat fellow in a light blue coat, his red bloated face protruding like a beet from the fence of a white and yellow striped high collar, pushed past us to look over the wares. He went up to the boys first. They had to stand up, show their arms, let their mouths be inspected like horses, bend down, jump up, and run a piece. The man, the woman, and the child were subjected to a similar investigation. When the unfortunate woman, to whom this was perhaps happening for the first time, resisted the hand that felt her, the stout faun made some indecent remarks to a companion. For these he should have received a few strong boxes on the ear, but his friend rewarded him with a horselaugh.

"Oh, if only somebody buys us together!" I heard the woman sob. The man shook his head with a sad look. She pulled on our coats, and her big, dark eyes looked so despairingly, so pleadingly, so indescribably painfully, now at me, now at Westfeld, that her face follows me even today like a ghost.

"Well, I want that young woman there," rattled the voice of the beet-face behind me. "First-class goods—*fact, by Jove!*—neat girl—

y'understand?" And with this he winked with his left eye and shot a stream of tobacco juice six feet out into the road.

"But she'll raise hell when it's time to leave the fellow—and then there's the child?" — "Of course she will. They all do. But she'll calm down in time. My niggers have it good. I train them with gentleness. Besides, as far as the little one is concerned, I'll get it for a small additional amount. — And I'll get rid of it in a hurry, too," he added thoughtfully, and again he shot off a salvo of tobacco juice.

I had already heard and seen too much to be able to attend the actual auction, which was about to begin. Also friend Westfeld had thought he had stronger nerves, and when we went into the barroom to wait at a distance for the outcome of the disgusting business, we confessed to each other that the air tasted like heavenly ether (despite the whiskey fumes) when compared to the oppressive atmosphere of the auction locale. A painful quarter hour passed during which we clearly heard the bawled repeating of the bids by the auctioneer and still more clearly the falling of the hammer that struck the death hour for the happiness of two human souls. Finally, after a long pause, the last blow fell. Soon Mr. Beet-face came in with the two young male Negroes in order to have leg irons placed upon them and (as he growled in a bad humor) to console himself with a good drink about the vexation that the woman had been fished away from him.

The barkeeper inquired about who had gotten her.

"Oh, one of those *big bugs* from over there in Mason County has the yellow girl along with her brat! *By gum*, I'd like to know how he's going to raise the twelve hundred dollars that she cost him. Probably a plaything for his wife, or. . . ."

We heard no more, but while getting into our buggy we learned that the purchaser of the woman who had fortunately escaped the clutches of the dealer had the reputation of being a mild master and that her husband had been taken as a servant in a not too distant tavern.

I must leave reflections about this to the reader. For the present, changes in the conditions which produce such scenes are not likely, since the talking and writing of the abolitionists—partly well intended but ill advised in greater part and dictated by entirely different interests from those of humanity—have brought the South to a point where it fears even the slightest relaxation of its strict slave laws and views with suspicion and threatens with punishment anyone who questions them.

The trip from Maysville (whose streets we found perfumed by

the most abominable bacon grease odor) to Cincinnati was made by us and our horse by steamboat. It presented nothing remarkable, for the thick fog which enveloped our boat throughout the night would have permitted us to see nothing but shadows even if our weariness had not kept us in our staterooms in bed until the breakfast bell.

# 7

## A RIVER TRIP
## THROUGH THE MISSISSIPPI VALLEY

◊ ◊ ◊ IT WAS now closer to the middle of December than to the beginning. The citizens of Cincinnati could be surprised any morning by the unwelcome news that Indian summer—which during the past week had brought back over the land on the Ohio, as if by magic, something of the blue sky and the warm air of September—had suddenly departed during the preceding night and conveyed its rights to winter. Temperature changes of the most rapid and extreme sort are as common in the West as in the Atlantic states, and nothing guaranteed that within twenty-four hours rapidly falling cold would not cover the river with ice floes and bring steamboat travel to a standstill, perhaps for months. It was high time, if the river trip down to the "Father of Waters" and up to the "Mound City," Saint Louis, were still to be undertaken.[1] But at the same time it was the most favorable period. While this journey sometimes required a week (and frequently even longer) in the summer, with a low river level, it now took three or four days; and while the passage for one fare with stateroom had amounted to fourteen dollars four weeks ago, I now paid no more than half that sum on one of the most beautiful and fastest boats. A ridiculously small amount—when one considers that for this one could travel almost five hundred English miles and that this price included ten to twelve meals, meals which on our steamer were in no way inferior to those in the better American hotels.*

---

* This at first glance inexplicably low rate finds its basis, in part, in the low cost of the wood provided to the boilers by the enormous forests and in the low

*Moritz Busch · Travels*

Our departure was delayed a full twenty-four hours by the constant arrival of additional freight, by means of which the boat gradually assumed the shape of a mighty mountain of goods—flour barrels, chairs, tables, etc. This was all the more unpleasant since at first I could not find out how long I could remain off board without being left behind. Still, the matter also had its good side. When the captain finally announced that he would not depart before the following afternoon, I went back to the city. That evening I saw a performance of Schiller's *Robbers* in the National Theater[2]—who would have imagined them brought this far from the Bohemian woods? The translation was rather good; but the acting, especially the Karl Moor done by a Mr. Murdoch,[3] was a ranting bordering upon the bestial, the costumes were ridiculous, and the audience (particularly in the parterre) no more and no less unmannerly than had been exhibited on earlier occasions.

If all this is hardly gratifying, the performances on the stage (where both the High and the Low Germans let themselves be entertained and moved) are far more unedifying. Plays such as "The Country House on the Military Road"[4] were here applauded for an execution that affected any halfway educated person like an emetic. Red Republican, miserably clumsy pieces, such as Hassaurek's *Wenzel Messenhauser*,[5] whose platitudes, crudeness, and highly affected swaggering would have caused the muse of drama (if she attended at all) to jump down her own throat for shame, were repeated as though they were the most elevated outpourings of human genius. Costumes and scenery, music and ballet—these could not hold a candle to the accomplishments of the troupes which we see at home performing in the rathskellers of provincial towns and in the barns of village mayors. And yet Cincinnati has around forty thousand German inhabitants, and among these certainly quite a few who would consider it a rude insult if it were denied that they were educated people!

As I was returning to the boat from the theater, I suddenly heard a shot up on Sycamore Street. I didn't pay any attention to it, since this is nothing unusual here, and mixing in somebody else's business

---

cost of the necessities of life on the markets of the West. The principal cause, however, is to be sought in the lively competition that ensues when several boats are ready to depart at the same time. During my stay in Cincinnati this once resulted in the owners of a Louisville-bound steamer advertising in the papers that they'd take along passengers "at any price." The consequence of this was that the cabin was filled with people who had paid 5 cents (i.e. 22 Prussian pfennige) for the 120-mile trip (two good meals included). What was gained thereby remains the secret of those speculating in such a colossal fashion.

is far less advisable here than elsewhere. A few days later I read in the papers that a robbery had occurred. Three rowdies had attempted to attack a gentleman from Covington who likewise was coming from the National Theater. He, however, had seen them in time and was waiting for their assault. They began to throw rocks at him. He answered with a shot from his revolver, and this had the favorable effect of causing the rascals to retreat. Similar disturbances of public security occur in Cincinnati just about as frequently as the fire alarms heard day after day. During the same night a German worker was knocked down by a slungshot and robbed of his cash. The following morning, at daybreak, a Mr. Ammond was laid low by the same gang weapon while on his way to market and likewise was relieved of his money. If the press for lack of material has not now and then invented and exaggerated a little, then (according to my conscientious calculation) in the course of the six weeks that I spent in the "Queen of the West" fourteen such robberies were carried out and eleven more attempted in the streets of the city. If one reflects that almost half these villainous acts were perpetrated while the sun was watching, and that scarcely a third of them could be punished, then one has a picture better suited for almost anything but a badge of honor for the local police. To be sure, Alfred Allen, presently captain of the same, once was leader of the notorious *Flymarket Boys;* and also the city council president, Cassily, might occasionally recall that years before, as head of the *Fourth Street Rangers*, he would have been glad if the guardians of order and property had been deaf and blind to his deeds.

The next morning friends took me to a court scene typical of local conditions. It was a riot and lynch case being heard before Justice of the Peace Röwecamp. About a dozen ladies—almost the entire world of beauty of the village of Lockland—had been summoned to answer charges of having threatened the local innkeeper, Fisher, with tar and feathers and finally with drowning. Fisher, a fellow with common features, had recently mistreated a girl in his service so cruelly that upon complaint of his neighbors he had been fined fifty dollars and costs. The ladies of Lockland had found this sentence too mild, and in their coffee circle they had decided to assist public justice by lynching the too gently treated sinner with their own delicate hands and throwing him into the deepest part of the canal. Fisher hadn't waited for the execution of this nice idea but had fled to Cincinnati and under the wings of the court. The squire found the indignation of the members of the coffee circle quite in order but their threats not as dangerous as the complainant and his attorney did. He rejected the damage claims of the latter and ordered Fisher to pay the costs—which were not inconsiderable, since almost all Lockland, with the mayor in the lead, had appeared as witnesses.

About eleven o'clock I was again on board my steamship, and a half hour later the bell announcing the approaching departure was rung for the first time. The swarm of book salesmen, who provide the passengers with easy and frivolous reading material; of candy boys; of the "Irish," who hawk apples and nuts; of Jews, who extol their cotton handkerchiefs as silk to goodhearted simpletons and exhibit similar treasures on the boxes and crates—all now reduced their prices and sold off cheaply, then packed up their bundles, and finally left, tripping and hobbling down the only gangplank still connecting us with the land. Both chimneys began to puff and expel short clouds of smoke. The vessel rolled and rocked and slowly pushed out into the middle of the river, accompanied by the good wishes of a Hibernian who called a hearty *"go to hell and be damned"* after the stoker. Cincinnati gradually faded into a few straggling houses, and when we went up to the top deck for a promenade after lunch, the steamer was floating in a very lonely, late autumnal, gray forest valley that in no way reminded us of the nearness of a great city.

The day was pleasant, so I remained on deck until evening. In this stretch the river really deserves the name *"la belle rivière"* given it by its discoverers, the French. If someday the forest primeval which now crowds and shades it is cleared a bit more, if its hills are crowned with country homes, if its bush-covered islands are adorned by little white cabins, and if its side valleys are cleared for views into the distance—then from the series of beautiful and unique landscapes presented to the eye by its often very sudden bends and windings a total impression will be formed in the mind of the observer that will be inferior to that of our Rhine only because it lacks memories of historical significance.

About sixteen miles below Cincinnati, on the spot where fifty years ago NORTH BEND was established to vie with the former for the crown of the "Queen of the West," stand the former home and grave of President Harrison. The dwelling, which is still occupied by the widow and several of the children, is a simple whitewashed frame farmhouse; the tomb, situated directly below on a charming hill, is a simple rectangular brick wall, with no ornamentation or decoration other than that bestowed by nature with grass, shrubs, and wild flowers.

Four miles farther the BIG MIAMI, which in its lower course forms the boundary between the Buckeye State and Indiana, pours forth into the Ohio, and soon after, the steamer slips past the friendly LAWRENCEBURGH. Then, in rapid succession, appear from behind projecting hills PETERSBURGH and BELLEVIEW on the left and AURORA and RISING SUN on the right. These are all small towns of which nothing particular is to be noted except the striking difference between the first two, situated in slaveholding Kentucky, and the latter two, belonging to Indiana. While Petersburgh has scarcely more than three hundred inhabitants and Belleview only about sixty, Aurora counts a population of at least three thousand and Rising Sun approximately two thousand. Yet the location of all is equally favorable, and the quality of the soil can't differ very much. What is the reason, then, that the former—which, by the way, are older—have lagged behind, while the latter, conforming to their names, have risen joyously? Since this relationship continued to Louisville and beyond to the mouth of the river, the answer can hardly point to anything else than the consequences of slavery.

About three o'clock we were opposite the village of HAMILTON, Kentucky, near which the salt-impregnated Big Bone Lick Creek flows into the Ohio. Here a tremendous number of bones have been found which natural scientists have attributed to the antediluvian mammoth and to the arctic elephant. The ribs are said to have been over five feet long and were used by the first discoverers of the site as tent poles. Two teeth which were dug out measured eleven feet from root to tip and were seven inches in diameter at the thick end. The redskins' imagination based a nice story upon this curiosity of natural history. The "Salt Lick of the Big Bones" was one of the favorite gathering places of the buffalo and deer of the country and, accordingly, one of the most productive hunting grounds of the Delawares. But the frequent appearance of herds of mammoths, causing great devastation among the game, disturbed the hunting and threatened the red man with starvation. So the Great Spirit took pity on him. One day he came down from the sky, with the bow of lightning in his hand, stepped upon a rock above the spring (where his footstep is still to be seen today), and shot his fiery arrows at the giant animals until all were slain—with the exception of the lead bull, who caught the projectiles with his forehead and shook them off. Finally, however, the god struck him in the side, and then he turned around and jumped across the Ohio, the Wabash, the Illinois, and finally over the Northern Lakes—beyond which he is still living. A very nice fable; only too bad that the mammoth—like his more recent cousin, the elephant—was not a meat-eating animal!

Evening approached. We had quickly sped past WARSAW in Kentucky, VEVAY, where the Swiss in 1804 planted the first grapes in North America, and CARROLTON, where the Kentucky River (two hundred miles long and navigable for steamboats for about sixty miles) empties. I was about to go down into the cabin when a number of passengers came storming like mad up the steps and hurried to the pilothouse, where the captain just happened to be standing at the wheel. A lively conversation ensued, and I saw that they were pointing to a dark point ahead of us. I finally gathered that it was a matter of overtaking another boat that was following the same course that we were. In other words, it was to be one of those insane races in which the Yankee risks his life and limbs, in which pitch is thrown into the flames when the wood gives out, in which the genius of American *goaheadiness* is transformed into a demon dancing upon a volcano that at the next moment can hurl him into the air as *disjecta membra poetae,* turn him into a piece of coal, or first boil and then drown him. Sensible men will not take it as a lack of courage if I admit that this discovery didn't make me feel very comfortable. At first the captain didn't seem inclined to give in to the urgings of the gentlemen (the most eager of whom later turned out to be professional gamblers). It can only be guessed as to what finally persuaded him, after some hesitation, to give the order to fire up. But no sooner had the command been given than a part of the men who had pleaded with (and, perhaps, bribed) him rushed down to the main cabin. In a few minutes a sort of betting office was set up; a not inconsiderable sum of banknotes piled up quickly as soon as the name and character of the boat to be overhauled became known. Meanwhile, they must have been firing quite vigorously down below, for when I again stepped out on deck I noted that the shores were flying past us much more rapidly. After a half hour the distance between us and the vessel ahead began to decrease quite noticeably. After sixty more minutes we were within hailing distance of them. And when we went around the next island, our rival, which had put in to take on fresh fuel, was left behind. However, the cry of triumph which rang in chorus from the winners and the partly intoxicated crew was a premature one. The losers refused to acknowledge the validity of the wager since a closer inspection showed that the overtaken steamer was not the one bet upon. This objection could not be disputed. Besides, the fellows who had arranged the whole troublesome affair did not seem to be

that bad sort who enforce their supposed rights with fists and even
with bowie knives and revolvers—as is said to occur frequently on
the Mississippi boats. After some argument they came to an agreement, and the matter was settled for the time being.

The fact that the bell rang for supper during the dispute may
have contributed to the happy and speedy adjustment of differences.
Such a supper, dinner, or breakfast on the steamboats of the Mississippi Valley is a unique experience. As soon as the large folding tables
are set up, laid, and covered with various vegetables, fruits, jelly
molds, meats, cakes, biscuits, and slices of bread, everyone rushes for
the chairs at both sides of the table in order to be at the first serving
if possible (although this is not a bit better than the second). Soon
thereafter the main courses of the meal, a mighty roast of beef or
beefsteak, are placed before the captain's chair; he presides as host
to the passengers. Then a bell sounds, and each steps behind the back
of his chair to wait until the ladies—for whom the place of honor,
closest to their cabin, is reserved—take their places. If the ladies
tarry too long, then the captain is accustomed to calling attention to
their delay and enticing them forth from behind their red silk curtains
by whetting the carving knife. As long as they linger, the entire Round
Table stands at attention without moving a feature, like soldiers on
parade. In fact, it was a strange Round Table. Anyone who can afford
it certainly does not travel as a deck passenger. Hence upon the
magnificent carpets of the cabin, along with the most refined aristocrats, walk a mass of people who absolutely are not suited for the
saloon. Hence at times the most beautiful and the noblest physiognomies are reflected in the pier glasses, and a moment later the
roughest and most repulsive. Hence the most charming girl of the
aristocracy of New Orleans now dines with the same fork that was
used six hours before by the dirtiest and most uncivilized horsedealer
of Kentucky to dispatch his lunch between his ribs—after removing
his chewing tobacco from his cheek with his fingers and placing it
carefully beside his plate.

Without a doubt it was a strange Round Table to a European
eye, this dinner company on our *North River!*[6] A curious selection
from the most varied strata of the population! A gallery of contrasts
in which the inequality of the individuals constantly seemed about to
rebel against the equality of all. Here a national blue coarse wool coat,
and in it a half-savage Hoosier from Indiana. Beside him, in a long
black cloth *talar* [gown], pale and pious, a scholar of the Jesuit college in Saint Louis. Farther on, with a red silk Spanish sash about

his body, a returning gold miner from California (incidentally, my neighbor in the stateroom). From the bar rushed a crowd of professional gamblers. Behind them waddled a pleasantly smiling, fat Dunkard—in the afternoon I had engaged in an instructive conversation with him about the sacrament of baptism, the advantages of hog breeding, the necessity of celebrating communion at night, the profitableness of tobacco growing in Ohio, and other homogeneous topics. My vis-à-vis was an old, smooth-shaven major, as stiff and cold as if he had breakfasted on a thirty-inch icicle and had not digested it yet. As neighbors to his right and left he had two loafer-visages with whom he certainly would not have fraternized—if only because of their dirty collars. Similar and worse physiognomies, upon which drunkenness disputed precedence with roguishness, alternated with the Saint John countenances of Methodist preachers peering gently forth from chalk-white neckcloths, with fine and active "smart" New Englanders in high collars so brilliant that they appeared to have been washed in snow and rinsed in milk, and with tree-tall, rawboned, coarse fellows from the forests of western Kentucky. At the head of the table, however, sat "the ladies in a circle of beauty," escorted by husband, fiancé, or brother.

As soon as the ladies were seated, the entire company sat down. The waiters poured coffee or tea into the cups standing on the table, and now the loading and clearing off of the plates was undertaken with such eagerness, skill, and speed that a habitué of transatlantic tables d'hôte would have been absolutely unhappy. In ten or, at most, twelve minutes the pushing back of chairs could be heard, and after a quarter hour the waiters were already clearing the table to set it for the second sitting—on our boat this was followed by a third for the kitchen and service personnel.

With the single exception of the roast beef, I found the food excellent on the various boats on which I traveled. The poultry was particularly good, and the great variety of sweets, especially the fruit pastries (*pies*), are superior in their kind. It is not the custom to drink wine at the table. Anyone who needs it goes to the bar after dinner; there, however, I did not see anything other than distilled spirits consumed. The meal is spiced with conversation just as little; it almost seems as though dining is not regarded as a pleasure but as an unpleasant business upon which one tries to turn one's back as quickly as possible.

◊ ◊ ◊ The boat was standing still when I awoke in the morning in my berth. We had been lying since midnight at the landing of Louis-

VILLE, before the Falls of the Ohio. An expedition through a few streets convinced me that the city differed in no particulars from its sisters that I had already seen. Besides, since no one was able to say when the boat would be finished with the unloading and loading of its freight, I soon returned on board. The history of Louisville resembles that of other western cities almost to the point of confusion: here as there, the rapid growth of an insignificant seed to magnificent bloom and fruit. The city was laid out in 1773 by Captain Bulitt, but not until five years later did a few colonists settle down on one of the many islands situated here in the rapids. Since the region was considered unhealthful and moreover was made unsafe by Indians, the population of the place had increased to only about five hundred by 1800. This changed after the last war with England. By 1820 Louisville had four thousand inhabitants, twenty years later about twenty thousand, and presently the population is estimated at more than forty thousand souls. It is now the largest commercial city in Kentucky and its factories are second only to those of Cincinnati, Pittsburgh, and Saint Louis in importance for the West. Religious needs are taken care of by thirty-one churches, newspaper readers by eighteen periodicals (including two German), and the education of youth by twenty-eight schools, two orphan asylums, and one university.

The rapids of the Ohio, located about a mile below the city, stop all navigation at low river level. To get around them, a canal has been dug that empties at the village of SHIPPINGSPORT, two miles away. The greater part of the canal has been excavated through rock, in some places forty feet deep; this is an enormous construction, the costs of which, however, are amply covered by the lively river traffic that brings through all kinds of vessels during the entire summer and autumn.

On September 24, 1816, the first steamboat left Louisville for New Orleans. It required forty-one days for the round trip. Upon returning, the captain was given a public dinner at which he prophesied that the day was not far distant when the upriver trip, for which he had required twenty-one days, would take only ten, and behold! since then the distance has been covered in not quite five days. The number of steamers supporting commerce on the waters of the Mississippi Valley and the lakes of the Northwest was estimated to be twelve hundred in 1848. The value of the vessels was (in round numbers) $16 million; the total value of the goods transported by them and by innumerable keel- and flatboats was about $260 million—a sum amounting to about double that of the total foreign trade of the United States.

*Moritz Busch · Travels*

Our boat slipped through the canal without steam and therefore so slowly that most passengers sprang to shore and hurried ahead to the great lock. Here they climbed on board again, and, once back on the river, the puffing and snorting Leviathan gaily shot between NEW ALBANY and PORTLAND and an hour later past the mouth of the Salt River. The shores from here on consist mostly of low bottom lands from which a melancholy, quiet, and (in the long run) monotonous forest rises like a brush that is miles long. The small towns that from time to time interrupt the loneliness of the region offer nothing to the eye and imagination other than what has already been seen a hundred times. So I gradually found my stay on deck putting me into the mood that had occasionally overcome me during the ocean trip; to prevent it from developing into downright bad humor, I gave up my observation of the river pictures and fled to the cabin to study people a bit.

In general the making of acquaintances here is not as easy as at home, and one can speak of good fortune when one succeeds in bringing about a rather long conversation. Some were playing poker before the bar, some were watching, and others were reading or writing. Meanwhile, during the course of the afternoon, a sort of club had formed around one of the two stoves; when a couple of sharp boys from Kentucky climbed on board toward evening and joined the circle, the conversation became quite lively, and I heard for the first time that the Americans could tell stories as well as the Germans.

Many a good old tale and many a bad new one was related, we were favored with much humbug, and many an atrocious lie was served up. Perhaps nowhere else in our century do the *Münchhausiaden* turn out so well and the hyperboles grow as luxuriantly as in the hotbeds of Brother Jonathan's humor—especially where the same are properly "watered" with whiskey. Among the loudest and most unpolished tongues that could be heard at this evening reunion about the stove were those of the two sturdy, suntanned men who (I believe) had boarded the boat at Owensburgh. Their talk at times aroused bellyshaking laughter among the listeners and at times disapproval through glances and expressions. They were burlesque fellows with the naïvest opinions of manners, propriety, and education. The question as to whether they had really been trappers (as they maintained) and were now on their way back to the upper Missouri and Indian country, I shall leave open, as not germane to the matter. Likewise the probability of the following story—which I recount less for the subject matter than for the style—may be rather doubtful, particularly since I heard the same anecdote claimed as a personal experience by another person a week later, and in a somewhat more believable transformation.

We had just been talking about the approaching winter, and several of the farmers present had unanimously prophesied that we could expect severe cold in a few days, when one of the two fellows (who had meanwhile been cutting off a fresh chew from a plug of tobacco resembling a chocolate bar) interrupted the conversation with the doubt that the winter would be as hard as the one he had once experienced. He was urged to tell us about it, and, after he had preluded with a couple of well-aimed saliva shots at the glowing stove, he showed an inclination to do so.

"Next February," he began his marvelous tale (which I reproduce as well as I could put it down in my diary the next morning), "next February first it will be three years since we had the grayish freeze that put icicles on the moonbeams and froze the sun so solid that it couldn't rise until noon. I'll be a nigger if it isn't true that I"—here he fired a sizzling shot between his knees at the stove door—"couldn't spit without the tobacco juice freezing on the way to the ground and rattling down like pebbles."

"Good heavens, you don't really mean that it was that way!" cried an astonished voice.

"So? — Not?" the storyteller replied drily. "Do you think I'd lie to you, stranger? Hey, Jake, tell me: do you remember that time when seeing-power froze in the eyeballs of the animals so that you could go right up to the turkeys and deer and comfortably stroke their skins?"

Jake seemed about to confirm the miracle with an "Of course," but the crowd shut his mouth with a *"Never mind, go on!"* and the narrator, pleased to have such willing listeners, continued—after planting his chaw of tobacco on another molar with a clever stroke of the tongue.

"Well then, boys, it was about this time that I had completed my catch of beaver pelts up on the Platte River and meant to come down to Brown's Cave to crawl in there for the rest of the winter. Suddenly, as I'm trotting along the river, I see—I'll be damned if it's not true—a half dozen of those devilish rascals, the Pawnees, galloping up to me. I was all alone with three pack mules, for the others had gone by a safer route. I looked around and thought: this is the end of old beaver Matthew. But I had a real good horse under my behind, and in spite of the generally poor prospects I had absolutely no desire to let my hair be lifted by such miserably ragged scoundrels as these

Indians. So I throw another glance at them, then I look myself over and find that my rifle is hanging on my saddle horn and that its offspring—my pistols—are stuck in my belt and that bowie knife and tomahawk are likewise in their right places. Then I swore that Old Nick should take me if I didn't believe that I'd come through. Meanwhile the red rascals were vigorously tickling the ribs of their nags; each had a bow in his hand, and in each bow stuck a long arrow. I knew that my mules were lost and also my furs and traps. But just that made me mad as hell, and I thought that if I could cause a couple of the rascals to bite the dust, a few cuts wouldn't bother me too much.

"Well then—hipp, hopp, up they galloped, thundering like a newly discovered earthquake, and my stomach felt like a beaver in the trap. When they were so close that their winged arrows could reach me and they noticed that I didn't try to run, the rogues had the audacity to halt and glare at me with eyes like six pairs of freshly peeled onions. By jingo! I think; I'll show you fellows with whom you're dealing. And I put the rifle up to my cheek—puff!—and one of them tumbles so that it was a real delight. Well, that stirred up the others, and wiff, waff, a dozen of their little things whistled through my jacket into my flesh, so that I felt like the back of a whipped nigger. The fellows howled and roared like Satan's firemen and were already sure that they had me in the bag. However, I pulled out my rifle's offspring and let them bark so that two more of the redskins fell out of the saddle and found out how the snow tasted. I now knew that there was no more time for tomfoolery and informed my mare with my heels that she'd have to be pretty fast if she wanted to save her master's scalp.

"When the shameless Pawnees saw me running away, they tried to run me down, but I slipped very nicely between them—for which I got another arrow in my back. And confound it, boys, now I found out what a good nag can do. Hui, she shot forth so fast that her hoofs left a trail of fire on the frozen snow like a mile-long streak of lightning. I'll be eaten by grasshoppers if that's not literally true. But it was of no use. The rascals were behind me like the devils themselves, and I realized that their mares, too, were of the real stuff. So we raced and raced on, until the nags steamed and foamed as though they were just that many steamboats. I figured that the scoundrels would finally tire of the chase, but I was wrong; their patience was just as long as a midsummer day. Then the heart in my chest began to paddle like a duck in a muddy pond, and my sins began to burn in my conscience like the Pawnees' arrows in my belly and back. I tried to pray, but I hadn't learned any prayers when I was young, and I had bummed around too long to learn any new tricks. To make it short, boys (the storyteller called everyone *boy* or *stranger*), I had lost my courage—and I knew it. May the tree toads sing me to my grave if I could keep my hair from standing on end! At the same time I became so North Pole cold that the thoughts stuck in my brain as if they were nailed down with icicles, and my blood rolled lumps of ice as large as hickory nuts down through my veins. May I hang in the chimney like a bear shoulder if I didn't feel and hear the rolling!

"Well, I finally tell myself, if you've got to depart this life, old coon, you can at least take along a bit of game, and with this I ram a charge into the belly of my rifle so that it growls and snarls. Then I lay on, aim, and fire. Now I know quite well, boys, that you will have your strange thoughts about this, but I'll be tarred and feathered if the shot didn't stay stuck for a minute until the fire had melted the ice from the powder and could drive out the bullet. It's a fact, by God! I'll call myself a skinned polecat if it's not the naked, pure, shining truth!

"Well then, finally the rifle went off with a piff, shish, crash, and waff, and again one of the Indian fellows somersaulted from the saddle into the snow. Well, I think, that's finished; the last fellow will take the example and turn around. But the one who guessed wrong was me. Hussa, hopfa, he came galloping up behind me, as if he had been taken in tow by a lightning bolt. Thunderation, I say, you're going to get a hole in your jacket from me, as sure as it's noon at twelve o'clock! I once again fill my rifle with powder and lead, aim—a nice pointblank shot—paff! Will anyone believe it? That shot had no more effect upon that rascal of a Pawnee than if I had loaded with butter.

"I was completely dumfounded, knocked over by astonishment. Never since I had started shooting flies with popguns had it happened to me that I had missed my target. I had a feeling like a chewed-out plug of tobacco: extremely disgusted and comparable only to the mood I was in when I recently asked Peg Malone if she'd have me and she simply answered 'No!'

"Well, boys, now the situation was critical. Trapp, trapp, he came toward me, that damned cutthroat. There he was (as surely as my nose is above my mouth), his rope in his hand, ready to throw. Faster than half a wink I had again loaded my rifle. Quaff, another pointblank shot struck him right in the wrist of the arm that was swinging the lasso. But does anyone think that I even bent his accursed paw? Not by even the shadow of a quarter inch! There he sat stiff and silent, there he came pattering up, as if the earth had been created only for him. Now I was really frightened. I thought: what if the devil has gotten into this bestial redskin to fetch you? And then I had the idea of seeking my salvation with a silver bullet, but as luck would have it, I as usual had none with me.

"Finally he had caught up with me. I escaped through a gully—or rather, I merely attempted to escape, for my pony was finished. She stumbled, caught herself, plunged, and suddenly I flew over her head and rolled on the ground like a castaway whiskey bottle. Now it's all over, I tell myself, as I see the Pawnee shoot past me and quickly turn about. Still I drew my old bowie knife and tried to load one of my pistols, but I couldn't do it, because my fingers were too numb.

"Well then, now he stops before me, Mister Pawnee, now he stares at me with a face like a polished penny and a couple eyes like burning coals. And now—what do you think, boys, what did he do to me? Did he shoot me dead? — No. — Did he choke me with the lasso? — Not at all. — Did he try it? — I'll be a nigger if he even thought of it!"

"Well, what was he going to do?" — "Yes, indeed, out with it—what did he do, the redskinned heathen?" — "Jesus Christ, if he knows, why does he make us wait?" various curious voices screamed all at once. The storyteller, however, smiled and remained silent, most pleased, it appeared, at the general eagerness for the outcome of his adventure. Finally he rolled his wad from the right to the left side, spat once, and then remarked to his comrade: "How comfortable it is sitting next to such a stove."

"But the end of your story? The Indian—what did he do to you?" I asked, smelling a surprise. "What did he do, stranger? Well, now, just what I said: he turned around and stopped before me, nothing else." — "Of course! He was finished. You had shot him twice." — "Not in the least." — "Well, by the head of the Sphinx, what?"

"Well, if you really want to know, stranger—in the cold he had *frozen to death on his horse*, the Pawnee, and only his nag had chased after me."

◊ ◊ ◊  When I stepped out the next morning, the region had changed again. We were steaming along between rocky banks of considerable height. On the Illinois side they stretched without interruption for almost two miles; in the middle is situated the cave where the robber Mason and his band once lived. By chance we put in here to take on

fresh wood for the fires, and thus there was an opportunity to visit
the notorious hiding place. The surroundings are very picturesque.
Civilization, which has spread out or at least made itself noticeable
above and below "Cave-in-Rock," has avoided this bit of Romanticism.
All about stare rugged, strangely shaped bluffs, crowned with dark
cedars and half covered with yellow, green, and red shrubs and trees.
The entrance to the cave is close to the water, and when the river rises,
it flows in. A passage which may be about twenty feet high leads into
a spacious, almost rectangular chamber, over which is situated
another room, supplied with strange limestone formations now and
then resembling Gothic scrolls. An opening at the rear end of the dome
affords a glance into an abyss which drops deep into the heart of the
rock; it is said that the evildoers pushed their victims into it. Judging
by the sound, stones thrown by us fell into the water covering the
bottom only after several seconds.

A number of stories are in circulation about the cave, one more
bloody than the other. The historical fact is only that at this place,
around the year 1800, a bold pirate by the name of Mason gathered a
number of like-minded men. With them he plundered the flatboats
traveling downriver loaded with flour and meat, and merchants
returning north from New Orleans with the proceeds from the sale of
their goods were waylaid, robbed, and murdered. They plied this trade
undisturbed for several years, until their insolence increased to the
point that the governor of Mississippi set a price of five hundred
dollars on Mason's head. Thereupon this Rinaldini[7] of the Ohio was
shot by a member of his own gang and the band scattered.

The towns situated between here and the emptying of the Ohio
into the Mississippi are not worth mentioning, with the exception of
the last, CAIRO. On the other hand, I must not forget the two great
rivers that empty into the Ohio in this stretch, so that from here on it
barely increases in width, but much in depth. The first is the
Cumberland River, which is about six hundred English miles long
and navigable for steamboats for a third of the distance. The second,
sighted about an hour later, is the Tennessee River, the most important
tributary of the Ohio—in fact, the question has been raised as to
whether it might pour more water into the latter than the Ohio itself
carries up to this point. Twelve hundred miles long, it is navigable for
large steamboats for about six hundred miles and for smaller vessels
for over a thousand. Traffic upon it is uncommonly lively as far as
Florence in the state of Alabama.

Between three and four o'clock in the afternoon we passed from

the Ohio into the Mississippi. On the Illinois shore can be seen a
group of little white houses, in the center of which a taller building
rises. Upon inquiry I learned that this shabby place was the much-
mentioned Cairo—much mentioned because of the repeated attempts
to establish a large city here. Situated right at the juncture of two of
the most important traffic arteries of America, the site undoubtedly
presents one of the most favorable points for the attaining of that goal.
The entire commerce of the Mississippi Valley—from Pittsburgh to
the western boundary of Missouri, from southern Wisconsin to New
Orleans—would have to flow past here. But the shorelands around
Cairo are so low that the establishment of a metropolis such as that
envisioned would require construction of the most gigantic sort, and
for this, enormous capital. No one disputes the fact that well-
constructed dikes would protect the triangle upon which the city
stands from floods and that skillful, systematic draining would dry
out the adjoining swamplands, thus removing the miasmas that make
the region unhealthful. It is even less doubtful that in time all
investments would yield a 1,000-percent interest. The failure of all
previous attempts does not seem to prove the opposite. The location of
New Orleans is still more unfavorable (if possible), and yet the hand
of man has there conquered the forces of nature. Rather, the failure
of the Cairo plans has been due less to the site than to the ignorance of
the English company that began to carry out these plans a few years
ago. This company, namely, undertook to monopolize the land for
itself—not only that where the city was to stand but for miles into the
interior. A dike was thrown up, a foundry and other buildings were
erected, and they then believed that they could keep the remaining
ground and soil as their property by merely leasing it to interested
settlers for a number of years. At first a goodly number of them came,
but when the fever time arrived and illnesses of all kinds prevailed,
most of them left the district to which they were attached by no
permanent interest, and the town dwindled to a dozen occupied
houses. In 1849 another company took over the scheme and the rights
connected therewith, and since this one is pursuing its interests more
wisely (that is, is allowing others to acquire property under certain
conditions), it may still happen in the course of time that Cairo will,
to a certain extent, begin to correspond to the idea of its founders.

  The suddenness of the transition from the gentle flow of the Ohio
to the muddy current of the Mississippi, racing on in angry haste, is
extremely surprising. If I had been sleeping during our entrance into
the latter and had not observed the river until an hour later, it still

would not have escaped me that another body of water was carrying us. Not that the formation of the shores shows any striking difference, nor is the main stream significantly broader than its mighty tributary. But the character of the former is entirely different. It is no longer the gentle, peaceful flow of an amber clear water in which charming groups of hills and nicely rounded islands are reflected. Rather, it is the wild, downstream raging of a sinister, proud demon of the wilderness. It rushes furiously between sandbanks which, in its pleasure of destruction, it throws up to the right today and to the left tomorrow; between wildly mangled islands upon which a confusion of uprooted trees has been piled; between roughly caved-in stretches of shoreline, mad eddies, dangerous shoals, projecting jagged stumps, washed-out pieces of rock, and mud-filled forests over which the late autumn had drawn a reddish brown mourning cloak trimmed only here and there by the dark green of cedars. If it is also recalled that from here to the vicinity of Saint Louis human habitations are much more infrequent and far more wretched than on the Ohio, then the picture of the "Father of Waters" preserved in memory will indeed remain one of grandeur but certainly will not be counted among the friendly ones. In short, viewing of the Mississippi is something much more depressing than inspiring (as long as intellect doesn't intervene and divert the glance to the glorious future of the river and its giant valley), and the mood which is awakened by this may be compared to that produced by a contemplation of the migration of peoples from the mountains of their Hunnic homeland to the Catalonian Fields.[8]

No one who travels for the first time on this, the mightiest of the primitive rivers of North America, receives a clear and adequate concept of its vastness and the amount of water it rolls toward the sea. Between Cairo and Saint Louis it is broader than an English mile only where an island dams it up, but often narrower where bluffs hem it in. However, if one considers that from the Falls of Saint Anthony to New Orleans it swallows up river after river with mouths as wide as itself, without widening its bed at all, and if one sees on the map that it takes up the mighty Missouri, the broad Ohio, the Arkansas, and the Red rivers (all of them larger than the Rhine)—then one begins to suspect the measure of its depth and to be astounded at the quantity of the liquid element that, forced into its bed, flows toward the destination of rivers. And just as immense as the river itself will someday be the development of its valley and the power of the states along its banks. When we read about the myriads of people who inhabited the banks of the Nile in ancient times and compare with this the broad surfaces to the right and left of the Mississippi, then we catch a glimpse of a world before which the thoughts of even the sober-minded become hazy.

Opposite the mouth of the Ohio on the Missouri shore lies OHIO CITY, a small, rather miserable village. Then for almost thirty miles there is not another town and hardly a single log cabin in the desolate forest region with its groups of rust-colored trees, all of which are almost the same height, appearing to have been cut out with scissors. Finally the upstream traveler is greeted by the stately CAPE GIRARDEAU with its tidy streets and its Jesuit church built in medieval style.

Between here and BAINBRIDGE we encountered the small steamer *Robert Fulton* which had run into a *snag* and had gone down a few hours before. Its passengers had fortunately escaped to shore and there were camped around a large fire. A few of them let themselves be taken aboard the *North River*. The others probably camped on the spot until the following morning, for soon thereafter the sun went down and the evening quickly became night. This time I preferred to remain outside the cabin for awhile, waiting to see whether anything of the romantic regions we were now approaching could be observed by the light of the stars. Between the mouth of the Ohio and Saint Louis the bluffs seldom recede from the river for any great distance. At least this is true of the western side. As vertical masses of limestone, they frequently draw quite close to the water, occasionally rising to form towers and pinnacles—resembling, at a distance, the walls and bastions of a city. In places where the current has washed away their foundations they overhang the river in strange shapes.

The most interesting of these rock formations are the "Grand Tower" and the "Devil's Bake-Oven," not far from one another and situated eighteen miles upstream from Bainbridge. We passed quite close to the first. It is a rock about fifty feet high and of the same diameter, standing in the middle of the waves which break upon it with a murmur, and it is almost as round as a pillar. The top is flat and covered with bushes and low trees. The origin of this strange play of nature is undoubtedly to be found in the fact that the current from the opposite shore has cut through the promontory of which the "Grand Tower" formed the front, has isolated it, and then gradually has rounded it to its present shape.

The place also has a sad significance. Here above the raging, mysterious current dwells the Lorelei of the Mississippi. Here in earlier times many a raft and many a boat were seized by the swirling water and hurled against the rocks, and here many a daring boatman—

## A RIVER TRIP

who before the invention of the steamboat had to land at this place to pull his vessel upstream with ropes—was a victim of the Indians, who liked to set up their ambushes especially at such places.

These boatmen are such a characteristic feature of the American past that I believe I might commemorate them with a rather long description. Shortly before the beginning of the present century—at a time when the settlements on the Monongahela and the Ohio had become somewhat more populous and their inhabitants were striving to establish and support a connection with the South, particularly New Orleans—an entirely new, unique class of fearless rivermen originated. On the waters of the wilderness they were the rough forerunners of civilization—like the backwoodsmen on land. They rowed through the longest rivers in their pirogues, barges, and keelboats, penetrated on their Argonaut voyages to the most remote points of the interior, and took care of trade and communication between the most distant settlements. Accustomed to hunger and thirst, wind and weather, they scorned comfort and luxury. Dressed in the costume and armed in the style of the westerners, they were always ready to exchange oar for rifle and to let the war cry of the Indians be heard instead of their wild boatmen's songs. Exposed to the double effect of the sun's rays (which they caught directly from the sky and reflected from the surface of the water), the color of their skin to the waistline was only slightly whiter than that of their foes, the copper-colored Iroquois and Delaware. With the strong current of many of the western rivers it was no easy task to bring the vessel upstream. Naked to the hips, the crew toiled all day to drive the boat against the current, pacing from bow to stern with long poles braced against their shoulders or, harnessed to a rope, dragging the barge toward its destination, bending to the ground at each step. After a hard day's work, they'd tie their vessel to a tree or rock, swallow their *fillee* (that is, their ration of whiskey), hastily devour a meal of half-raw fish and half-burned bread, and then stretch out for a short slumber—with the sky as their cover, their cargo as pillows, their rifles as sleeping companions—until the mate's ox horn awakened them to new labor. It frequently happened that a band of redskins would waylay the unsuspecting ones from a thicket or that a gang of white robbers would break forth from the bluffs to murder the boatmen and drag the cargo to their hideout. It often occurred, too, that the weather demons would suddenly send forth one of their grim tornadoes to smash the little keelboat against a reef; and not infrequently one of those *snags* would unexpectedly run into the belly of the vessel floating slowly on the quiet water—snags which, pulled into its bed by the changeable primeval river, project from the malicious depths like the fangs and horns of antediluvian animals.

And yet how enviable was their lot, these boats, as they slipped along in the morning under a deep blue sky through the green, fragrant, dew-covered forest! Here a rich bottomland could be seen. There rose mighty bluffs in strange shapes, covered with colored moss and crowned with cedars. There jumped sparkling fish. There in the distance a sail, like a gray swan, cheerfully traveled the same route upon the broad, island-adorned, softly murmuring water. At such times no danger was to be feared, or at least not to be seen, and since nothing urged work, pleasure was given free rein. The boat followed its path by itself, and little did the witness dream toward what destiny, what entirely different scene the merry boys on board were perhaps traveling. One of the crew scratched on an old fiddle and his comrades danced.[9] Greetings and propositions to the girls, abusive remarks and challenges to the boys rang out toward the inhabitants of the shorelands. The whiskey bottle circulated busily, and the keel- or flatboat glided on quietly, until it disappeared behind a wooded point or an island. Perhaps the tones of the horn with which all these vessels were provided rang out at this moment. These scenes had a magical effect upon even the crudest spirits, and these melancholy, lovely sounds, reverberating ever more softly from the hills of the beautiful Ohio, had a deep-reaching attraction for the ears of even sober, commonplace individuals, so that in many a breast they awakened a desire to join the merry, wild, free rivermen on the boats of the West.

Without doubt the life of these boatmen had its dark side, and it required strong spirits and bodies. But very seldom did one hear of one of them being inclined to exchange it for a more comfortable and peaceful occupation. For these unruly natures there was magic even in the danger of their situation and in the difficulties and deprivations to which they were exposed. The mad pleasure waiting for them at the end of their trip was sufficient compensation for all their troubles. Anyone would only have reaped scorn if he had complained about weariness when he got up from his hard bed at the earliest hour and, after the morning drink, the order was given: *"Stand to your poles, boys, and set off!"*

Their athletic labors endowed their muscles with unbelievable strength, and they gladly demonstrated it. Fist fights were their favorite pastime. Whoever boasted of never having been defeated had to fight with anyone doubting his superiority. The men of the keelboats and barges formed an aristocracy that looked down with scorn upon the raftsmen and flatboat people, so that a meeting always was an occasion for a magnificent brawl. In this they strictly observed the rule that everyone had to fight out his own affair, and it never happened that several attacked one. Their arrival at a port was the signal for a celebration of the entire set, and it frequently happened that hundreds of these wild boys gathered for carousing and dancing, their exuberance often turning into open disregard for law and authority. If their number had grown to the same degree as the population of the West, the peace of the land would have been seriously endangered by their inconsiderate impudence and mad highhandedness. But the bell of the first steamboat that traveled down the Ohio struck the death knell for this race of giants. The rivermen of the West have gone down in the current of civilization, never to rise again, and only in the Far West, in the backlands of the Arkansas and Red rivers, can a remnant of their times and customs be found.

*Mike Fink,* in popular speech termed "the last of the rivermen," was an example of these prodigious heroes, and even today a goodly number of marvelous tales about his adventurous life and deeds still circulate among the riverside inhabitants of the Ohio and the Mississippi. I shall relate some of the few that can properly be retold as illustrations.[10]

Mike (that is, Michael) was born in Pittsburgh. In early youth his passionate desire to become a riverman had already found fulfillment. As a boy he served on the Ohio and its tributaries and later in the keelboat fleet of the Mississippi, until the use of steamers took the bread out of his mouth. When the Ohio was too low in summer for the continuance of navigation, he occupied his time by going around to shooting matches in the vicinity of his hometown. Here he gradually acquired the reputation of being the best shot in the entire country. Because of his sure hand he received the nickname *Bang-all,* and for this reason it often happened that he was excluded from the competition when they shot for beef—a treatment that he permitted only under the condition that he be given as tribute and compensation *"the fifth quarter,"* that is, the hide and tallow. It was his customary practice then to take his "fifth quarter" to the tavern, sell it for whiskey, and treat all those present—naturally not omitting himself. In this way he became accustomed to hard drinking, and it is said that he could consume a full gallon in twenty-four hours without showing the least effect. Mike was about six shoes tall, broad-shouldered and muscular, and possessed a Herculean strength combined with unusual agility. A rough, weatherbeaten face carried the stamp of kindness, although he demonstrated on various occasions that this was not exactly his dominant feature. His manner of expression was the "half-horse, half-alligator" dialect of the back-woodsmen of that time. He considered himself a witty fellow, and in this respect he won the admiration and inspired the fear of the whole fraternity. He generally accompanied his jokes with a vigorous dig in the ribs whenever anyone dared to show displeasure with his humor by refusing the required laugh-tribute. A put-out eye, a slit nose, a half-torn-off ear and similar marks of distinction of the mania for fighting of those days were certain to win the favor of this bear-nature. He even proclaimed himself "a real howling devil from the Salt River, full up to the neck with pugnacity and in love with pretty women up to his ears." He was right in all points, especially the latter; for a sweetheart waited for him in every port. In addition to many admirers he also had a goodly number of friends. Among his friends —who would have run "through blood and fire" for him, as they expressed it—the most famous were Carpenter and Talbot. Both were distinguished by strength and shrewdness, by boxing skill and marksmanship, and they were in every respect a credit to their teacher, Mike.

Mike once had with him for some time a woman who passed as his wife, although she would have found it difficult to produce a marriage certificate. Whatever the case may be, the following anecdote is a nice example of conjugal discipline.

Shortly after the end of the late war with England several keelboats, among them Mike's barge, landed one day in late autumn in the vicinity of the Muskingum. After all had been made fast, it was observed that Mike went to shore and gathered together under the overhanging bank a pile of dry leaves blown down by the wind from the treetops. He maintained a dark silence to all questions concerning the purpose of this activity. After he had assembled a pile about as tall as himself, he pushed apart the leaves and formed an oblong ring in which he lay down as if he wanted to convince himself whether or not it was a good bed. Then he got up, strolled on board, reached for his rifle, loaded the weapon, and finally in a commanding tone called Peg, his wife, and ordered her to follow him. Both headed toward the leafy bed—poor Peg tortured by a deadly fear, since she had noticed that her Mike was by no means in a good humor.

# A RIVER TRIP

"March, crawl in, and lie down," commanded Mike with one of his choicest curses.

"Well, but Mr. Fink," said Peg, who always called her pseudo-husband "Mister" when he was in a rage, "what have I done, I really don't know, how—"

"Crawl in and lie down, or I'll shoot you down!" screamed Mike with a still stronger oath, while he aimed.

Poor Peg obeyed instantly and crept into the pile of foliage, whereupon Mike covered her up to the neck with leaves. He then took a flour barrel, split the staves into fine shavings, and lit the same by the fire on the boat. During this entire time he watched the leaf pile and swore that he'd shoot Peg as soon as she moved. When the shavings were burning, he took them in his hand and set the leaves in which his wife was buried on fire in four different places. In a moment the whole mass was in bright flames, and a sharp wind blew it up even more, while Mike watched the "joke" in a most peaceful state of mind. Peg held out as long as she could for fear of her Gracious Husband's rifle. But finally it got too hot for her, and she sprang up and ran to the river as fast as her legs could carry her. Hair and clothing were all ablaze. In a few minutes she reached the water and plunged in, thanking God that she had gotten off so well.

"There you have your due," said Mike, grinning. "That will teach you not to make eyes at the fellows in the other boats."

As regards the handling of the rifle, Mike Fink was a perfect Robin Hood, and the tales told about him in this respect are innumerable. Two of the most incredible (which I have from the best source) fall in the year 1816, when Mike navigated the Mississippi for the first time.

Between the mouth of the Ohio and Saint Louis, while the boat was slowly traveling upriver, he saw a sow with a half dozen young feeding on the bank about a hundred feet away. The sight aroused his appetite for roast suckling pig, and he reached for his rifle to shoot one of the animals. His companions begged him not to do it. However, he paid no heed to their remonstrances and, while passing by, very calmly shot off the curly short tail of one little pig after another, close behind the rear, without doing any other damage to them.

Later on, when he came to Saint Louis and surveyed the landing from the boat, he noticed a Negro lounging on the shore watching the activities of the rivermen. In addition to other ugly features, the blacks have (as is well known) heels that project unpleasantly toward the rear. Mike found this unevenness not entirely in order, and to look at

Sambo, reach for his rifle, and shoot away the poor devil's heels was the work of only a half minute. The Negro, severely wounded, fell to the ground and screamed bloody murder. A riot commenced, and the rifleman was taken from his boat by the police. Questioned by the court about this "damage to another's property," he readily admitted all but excused himself by claiming to have meant well. The heels of the nigger had projected much too far beyond the laws of nature, and since this circumstance had prevented him from wearing an elegant boot, he had felt compelled to cure him of this defect.

As mentioned, Mike's bosom friend Carpenter also was an uncommonly good marksman, and this gave rise to unusual shooting tests. Namely, Carpenter and Mike were accustomed to filling a tin cup with whiskey and placing it on each others' heads in turn, shooting at it from a distance of eighty paces. It was always drilled through without harming a hair of the one carrying it on his head. The feat is too well founded for there to be any doubt about its truth. It was executed often, and the two friends liked it all the more because it was a test of the mutual confidence that they had in each other. Now, in the year 1822, Mike and his two comrades Carpenter and Talbot joined the trappers Henry and Ashley to travel up the Missouri to do business in their threefold capacity as rivermen, trappers, and hunters. In the first year a company of about sixty men journeyed up to the mouth of the Yellowstone, where they erected a fort for their security and for the carrying on of hunting and trading. From there smaller parties of ten to twelve men were sent out to trap and hunt on the various tributaries of the Missouri. When winter came, Mike and his group returned to the mouth of the Yellowstone, and since they preferred to live outside the fort, they dug a deep cave in the bluffs on the bank. Here, protected from wind and snow, they lived comfortably until the return of the warmer season.

Here it was that a violent argument arose between Mike and Carpenter since (as the story goes) they had run into each other as rivals for the love of an Indian beauty. The quarrel had almost ended in violence before their companions settled it temporarily by persuasion. Upon the arrival of spring Mike's party returned to the fort, and here he and his opponent recalled, over a glass of whiskey, the quarrel they had had, but once more they made peace and agreed to seal the treaty by again shooting the cup from each other's head. To decide who should have the first shot, Mike proposed that they toss a copper coin and let the heads or tails decide the issue. This was done, and the result favored Mike. Carpenter seemed to suspect the vengeful, treacherous intention of his companion. However, he disdained saving his life by breaking their agreement and calmly prepared for death, bequeathing to Talbot his rifle, pistols, powder horn, and his share of the hunting bag. Then he filled the whiskey cup to the brim without changing his expression.

Mike loaded, whetted the flint, and took aim. He cocked the hammer, but then he took the butt from his cheek and said, smiling:

"Carpenter, hold your poodle-head quite steady! Don't spill the whiskey—I'll need it right away."

Then he raised the rifle once more, fired, and at the same moment Carpenter fell, never to rise again. Mike's bullet had struck him square in the forehead and he died without breathing a sigh. His murderer put down his rifle coldbloodedly and without uttering a word pressed his lips against the mouth of the barrel and blew the smoke from the touchhole. Then he turned his glance to the corpse of the murdered one. Finally he said scornfully:

"Well, Carpenter, you spilled my whiskey after all."

He was reminded that he had shot him dead.

"Nothing but an unfortunate accident!" he replied indifferently. "I aimed as sharply at the black dot on the cup as ever at a squirrel's eye. How could it have happened?" Then he began to curse most horribly the rifle, the powder, the bullet, and, finally, his hands and eyes.

For the time being, in a distant wilderness to which the strong arm of the law did not reach, this catastrophe was allowed to pass as an unfortunate accident. But revenge was not asleep. Talbot decided to punish the murderer of his friend. Several months passed before the opportunity presented itself. One day, finally, Mike Fink was led astray by an attack of boastfulness to declare in the presence of several others that he had killed Carpenter intentionally and was glad of it. Instantly Talbot pulled one of the inherited pistols from his belt and shot Mike through the heart. He fell down and died with a half-spoken curse between his teeth. Talbot also got off unpunished since nobody had the authority or the inclination to call him to account. In fact, he was as fierce as the grizzly bear of the Rocky Mountains and just as strong and clever as this dreaded beast. But he, too, met his match: a short time later he drowned while attempting to swim through the eddies of the Missouri.

◊ ◊ ◊  At supper I noticed a new face among the ladies at the upper end of the table. She was a most lovely blonde with dark eyes; she sat beside a young man who with great civility served her from the various delicacies present and later escorted her back to the ladies' cabin. Neither of them could have been much more than twenty. I could not at all account for the reason for the interest I took in the couple. It could not have been the striking beauty of the girl alone but rather, perhaps, the unconscious notice paid to her and her escort by the others. Especially my talkative old friend, the fat Dunkard, had instantly taken an interest in them; he, who in his good-natured curiosity (which only occasionally was a bit annoying) struck up acquaintances everywhere, had quickly made inquiries about the two young people, and the energy he had expended thereupon had been crowned with appropriate success by his finding out the names and destination of the couple.

"Thou (he always spoke Pennsylvania Dutch to me and addressed me with 'thou')—thou hast seen the fine lady with the yellow hair who at supper sat just across from the pumpkin pie?" he asked me as we were about to go to bed.

"Certainly. What do you know about the young lady?"

In reply he drew me to a chair and told the following jolly story:

About four weeks before, a young man had brought a girl to a boardinghouse in EVANSVILLE on the Ohio. Here, on the very next day, she was fortunately delivered. The man, who had traveled on, had occasionally paid her a visit and generously paid for all that she needed, but he refused to fulfill his promise to make the youthful, lately confined girl his wife. Finally she told her troubles to the landlady. The latter, a goodhearted soul, took an active interest in the fate of the beautiful unfortunate one and was able to enlist several of her boarders and guests in a plan, the purpose of which was to save the honor of the young lady either through kindness or force. When the sinner again came to visit his sweetheart, the resolute landlady hurried after him, locked him in with the girl, and summoned her coconspirators. They fetched a preacher as quickly as possible and demanded (after the door was unlocked) an instant wedding. The young gentleman resisted at first, but he finally gave in to the eloquence of the landlady and the representations of the others—who muttered about "lynching" and the like. He pronounced his "Yes!" and the unexpected bride happily added hers. The clergyman performed his office, and the unbidden best men and bridesmaids wished the newlyweds luck and happiness, whereupon the couple left by the next steamer. The story is silent as to what became of the child. However, the good wishes couldn't have been very powerful, for the couple had been among the passengers of the unfortunate *Robert Fulton* that we had encountered near Bainbridge submerged up to the first deck.

When, in the morning, I went to the room where the two hundred cabin passengers washed—it, by the way, was rather dirty—the boat was steaming past the ruins of the old French FORT CHARTRES. After breakfast we were at HERCULANEUM, one of the chief ports of the lead-mining district. Two hours later the JEFFERSON BARRACKS, where two companies of the regular army of the United States are stationed, could be seen and, a little later, CARONDALET—called *"Vide Poche"* by the French, who form a majority of its population. It is a relatively old town but, like all the French settlements in Missouri and Illinois, very backward compared to the cities where the vigorous speculation drive of the Yankees has the upper hand.

Finally, directly before us, upon the high prairie behind DUNCAN'S ISLAND, appeared the brick-red mass of buildings of the farflung SAINT LOUIS, with the midday sun shining down upon it. Down at the edge of the river its mighty fleet of steamboats was giving off smoke, and rafts, ferries, and keelboats lay at the wharf. Up at the landing square could be seen the new city hall with its splendid façade, farther inland sparkled the crosses of a dozen large churches, and at the north end of the town stood out the tall, dark gray shot tower.

My first walk after our *North River* had forced its way into the immense line of boats was to the Friedrich House. This hotel had been recommended to me as the best among the local German inns, and the price of four dollars a week was not high in comparison to this praise. But the nasty smoked walls of the bar and reading room, the horribly filthy cloths on the tables, and the society of bragging Magyars and Poles who, instead of going to Uihazy's colony[11] and working, were lounging around here—all this soon gave me cause to regret that I had followed this recommendation.

In fact, the German traveler in America is in embarrassment in almost every city as to how he should find respectable accommodations that are not too expensive and that correspond in some degree to his habits. Hotels such as the Astor House and the Irwing House in New York, the Clifton House on the Niagara, the Burnett House in Cincinnati, and the Planters Hotel in Saint Louis are too grand for the man of average means; in the long run they are too expensive for a purse that is not set up for a daily bill of three to four dollars. Besides, despite their splendor they are without any real comfort. On the other hand, the German hotels are inexpensive (costing as much here for an entire week as there for one day), but they are (from my experience) unpleasant dens full of uncleanliness, bad odors, and common people—with a few exceptions. The Shakespeare Hotel in New York is larger but little better than the abominable emigrant houses on Greenwich Street and Washington Street. Of the German hotels in Cincinnati, Kopf's *Farmers and Traders Tavern* is recommended above all. Their table combines in a pleasant manner the merits of American cooking with those of German. The handsome beds are provided with mosquito nets. Boarders (who pay three dollars a week) receive their personal washing apparatus—a convenience which is lacking in most American hotels of the second class. If a person requires a room by himself, he adds one dollar weekly. In addition the host is a jovial young man who is very well informed about many conditions in the West, and the location of his house (not a hundred steps from Main Street) is also no small advantage.

For the person who does not find it convenient to scout around for suitable accommodations directly upon arrival, it is suggested that he look around for an American hotel of the middle class. Here the price is $1 to $1.50 per day, the selection of food is unusually abundant (although planned for rather strong digestive organs), the service is prompt, and the utensils and equipment are respectable. If one plans to spend some time in a city, one should rent a room with an American family; in New York such a room, including breakfast, costs around $5 per week (with lunch and supper, $7 to $8), and one also has the advantage of perfecting one's English free of charge. In Saint Louis I should recommend Brüggerhoff's Boardinghouse on Walnut Street to people who don't require a single room. To be sure, this house—which during my stay was occupied entirely by respectable boarders; its table, supplied with the most delicious fish and excellent wild game, being capable of satisfying even a gourmet—may now perhaps offer just the opposite of all this (in this land in which conditions change with such extraordinary rapidity).

◊ ◊ ◊ In the afternoon I looked up an old acquaintance, Theodor Dietsch[12] of Annaberg, once a representative of the Frankfurt Left, now a subordinate editor of the *Saint Louis Tribune*, in his shabby, smoke-filled "office"; it contrasts unpleasantly with the magnificent palaces and elegant "sancta" of the editors of the *Republican* and the *Intelligencer*. He is still the jolly companion of old, and if, with his morning ration of hops decoction in the "Traube," he polishes off a few dozen potentates as a snack, this is a rather harmless cannibalism fifteen hundred German miles from the objects of this cruelty. In the "Traube"—where an excellent beer is served, as in most German taverns of the city—I was introduced to other refugees and emigrants with famous names. Thus to the former chief justice and chamber member Hennig from Wilsdruff,[13] who in association with Schneider from the Palatinate has established a law firm; to Dr. Hiller from the Saxon Erzgebirge who had just returned from California and was later to become my roommate at Brüggerhoff's; to the bookdealer Schuster, an upright, goodhearted, active nature for whom a bit more success in business might be wished; and to the honest Dr. Alfred Behr[14] from Koethen, who after living some years in Texas had moved here and purchased a drugstore. All seemed to be getting along fairly well in the New World; yet I now and then felt that behind the praise of American liberty lay a bit of the lamenting mood of the exiles "by the waters of Babylon." If in any one of the large cities of America there is reason for Germans to console themselves about the distance from home, it is in Saint Louis—where our countrymen are comparatively as numerous as in Cincinnati and, it appears, generally much more highly regarded. But it will be possible even here for a well-adjusted soul to forget the fatherland only at times with the tongue and never with the heart.

A visit to the Mormon apostle Wrigley,[15] to whom I had a letter of recommendation, concluded the day. He was a short, fat man with a red, plump, smooth-shaven face, and he spoke a very nice cockney English. He received me like a candidate for confirmation, even offered me a room in his house, and when I declined this friendly offer, he promised to recommend me to one of the elders of the "Church" who had just returned from the "Valley," was about to leave on a missionary trip to Germany, and would preach for him next Sunday. His household furnishings were extremely simple, and the sole adornment of his large, empty room was provided by two pretty steel engravings in gold frames, one representing the expulsion of the sect from Nauvoo, the other the murder of their prophet; a slender, black-eyed wife; and two very nice children. To my questions about the more recent history of the sect beyond the Rocky Mountains he was able to tell me nothing that I did not already know. Saint Louis is only one of the transit points for the Saints of the Latter Day, but the most important one. If Wrigley was not exaggerating, over two thousand members of the sect were located here at this time, fifteen hundred of them planning to leave next spring in a great caravan led by him through the desert to the new Jerusalem on the Salt Lake.

Wrigley himself had been in America for only eighteen months, so little weight could be placed upon his strong denial to my inquiry as to the basis of rumors concerning polygamous arrangements in Deseret (for he himself could have been deceived). On the other hand, his comments about the distribution of the Mormons in England and Wales were worthy of my acknowledgment, and with him I found the opportunity to complete my collection of literature about the disciples of Joseph Smith.

◇ ◇ ◇ The weather during the week had certainly not been winterlike. How astonished I was, therefore, upon awakening in the morning, to see the roofs covered with snow and, when I went out, to encounter a cold of at least four degrees below the freezing point. However, this did not prevent me from devoting the entire morning to a walk, this way and that, through the city. A brief retrospective glance at the history of Saint Louis and a consideration of the same as the commercial center of the "Far West" might precede the picture resulting from this and later excursions.

Saint Louis owes its origin to the fur trade. It was founded in the year 1763 by the Frenchman Laclede who, as director of an association of merchants, had acquired a monopoly on this business from the government. Soon, through additions from Fort Chartres, it began to grow. However, in the following year this immigration was interrupted by the cession of this territory to Spain—although that power didn't take real possession of the city until 1770. In the year 1771 Saint Louis consisted of 120 houses containing a population of about 800 souls. In 1780 the town, which had a garrison of only 50 soldiers, was attacked by Indians numbering 1,000 to 1,500 warriors. Unable to storm the earthworks and palisades behind which the garrison defended itself with the courage born of desperation, the savages threw themselves upon those inhabitants who, occupied with the cultivation of their gardens and fields, had not been able to flee to the city. The Indians killed such a number of them that the unlucky year in which this attack took place was given the name *"l'Année du Grand Coup"* by the French. Thereupon Saint Louis acquired a strong fort with stone towers armed with heavy weapons, and from then on the redskins left it in peace. Despite this, the town remained small and unimportant as long as the shores of the Mississippi were in the possession of the Spanish. Not until the Americans (with their laws and activities) awakened the growth power inherent in the town, that is, not until after 1814, did it begin to blossom. In 1810 the population amounted to about 1,400; twenty years later to almost 7,000; a decade after this to 16,000; and at the census of 1850 to 82,744 souls (it should be noted that the French now make up only about a quarter of the total).

This surprisingly rapid growth, particularly in recent years, is easily explained by the following considerations. Saint Louis is situated about midway between the sources and mouth of the Mississippi and the Missouri, and a few miles from the joining of the two. Here the trade route which supplies the South with lead from northern Illinois and Wisconsin, cattle and hogs from the prairies on the upper Missouri, planks and timbers from Iowa, and grain and flour from the entire Northwest meets the route which brings up from New Orleans rice, sugar, cotton, and the products of eastern factories as exchange goods for those raw materials. To this must be added the fact that the city is the center of the North American fur trade, the point of assemblage of emigrants who take the overland trail to California and Oregon, and the market for the caravans that several times a year transport the manufactured goods of Yankeeland across the prairies down to New Mexico. Finally, to all these advantages will be shortly added the great Central Railroad, upon which one will be able to travel to Cincinnati in twenty-four hours and to Baltimore in three days. Today the chief artery of the city is the Mississippi; in 1850 no fewer than 267 steamers used it, making 3,305 trips and transporting goods to a value of nearly $60 million.

The site of Saint Louis is beautiful. It stands upon a plain up to which one has to climb about a hundred paces from the river. In the immediate vicinity of the city the land is covered here and there with groves of leafy trees, mainly oaks. Beyond this stretches a broad, rolling prairie encircled on the horizon by a dark forest. The city plan resembles that of most North American cities: it is like a chessboard or, if you will, like a drawer with infinitely many compartments. Broad streets, running straight as an arrow landward from the banks of the river, are intersected at right angles by cross streets which are narrow and crooked below and straight and broad above. Of the former the busiest are Walnut and Market streets, which divide Saint Louis into a northern and a southern half; of the latter (the streets parallel to the river) Fourth Street is considered the principal one. The landing square is regarded as the center of the city. The farther one goes from it to the right or left or to the west, the more frame houses and the fewer people and wagons meet the eye, and the more vacant the blocks become. Little is to be seen of public squares, for the markets—in which I found, incidentally, a greater abundance of wild game of all kinds, bear, deer, birds, etc., than anywhere else—are nothing more than wide places in the streets. One looks in vain for beautiful public buildings. On the other hand, one notes various quite elegant private dwellings, and among the summer residences of the local aristocracy (mostly situated on the outskirts of the city) can be found many a pretty gem. But the basic feature in the character of Saint Louis, especially in those sections extending beyond Fourth Street, is one of growth, struggle, and joy in development. The most glaring contrasts spring up exuberantly side by side. Everywhere there is building, demolishing, and remodeling. Not a single street can be regarded as mature, complete, and finished. There may be ever so many colossal warehouses, magnificent stores, and stately dwellings, but suddenly the line is interrupted by a smoke-stained, slanting frame hovel, the ruins of a fire, or a vacant building site enclosed by planks or boards. Everywhere, even on the more distinguished streets, stand half-completed buildings, and trash piles and brick piles are scattered about; nowhere is the eye gladdened by the cleanliness and regularity manifest in the streets of the large cities of Germany. Here we still have the childhood of these centers of population, but what a manhood this suggests!

It is understandable that the composition of the mass of inhabitants is a rather mixed one. In Saint Louis almost as many languages and dialects can be heard as at the Leipzig fairs. The nasally lisping New Englander, the rough-voiced trapper of the Rocky Mountains, the immigrant from "Old Hingland," the Irish day laborer, the Spanish merchant from Santa Fe, the High German and the Low German, the Magyar, and the Frenchman—how different each is from the others, and how different all of them are from the redskinned son of the wilderness who even now still visits the markets of Saint Louis—although much more rarely than before (I saw only four of them, rather shabby fellows).

The French are more and more disappearing from sight. Only a few of them possess the enterprising spirit of the Anglo-Saxon race, which here tramples everything underfoot. For this reason only a very few have become wealthy. The majority have withdrawn to small houses and have restricted themselves to association with their likes. They support themselves mostly as laborers and gardeners, many also as hunters and trappers on the upper Missouri, the Platte, and the Kansas. On the other hand, the Germans (of whom a considerable number moved here more than twenty years ago) seem to have preserved their national character here with more luck and tenacity than in Cincinnati. Several of them are among the most well-to-do merchants of the city, and the relationship between them and the Anglo-Americans is a much more friendly one than in the East—where the German population is granted complete equality of rights only at election time.

Here, too, the administration of the police leaves much to be desired. Loaferdom is thriving in such a terrible way in Saint Louis that no one is advised to enter the more remote streets after dark unarmed. Faces are encountered in the taverns that look like wickedness incarnate. The number of gambling hells and disorderly houses is exceedingly large, and everywhere force and deception lie in wait for the unsuspecting. Frequently Judge Lynch improves upon the sentences of the legal authorities; often he also anticipates them. A short time before my arrival the sovereign people had found the pardon granted by the governor to a Negro sentenced to the gallows for rape not to its taste and had hanged the poor sinner on its own responsibility. One evening a few weeks later thirty or forty soldiers, led by an NCO on horseback, had left their quarters in the Jefferson Barracks, had marched into the city, and had stopped before the house of Lize Hollis, a temple of *Venus vulgivaga* in which one of their comrades had died in a mysterious manner a few days before. Upon command of the NCO, the band had first broken the windows, then pushed into the house (the police who happened to be there were driven away), had smashed and burned much of the furnishings and clothing of the owner of the house, and had finally robbed the girls of their money (about four hundred dollars) and their valuables. After they had spent about a quarter hour in wrecking the place in this manner, the rioters had returned to their barracks unmolested. I could not learn whether they had been punished, but I doubt it, for the "mobbing" of houses like that of Lize Hollis—which, incidentally, also occurs frequently in Cincinnati—is customarily regarded by the citizenry as an easily pardonable excess.

Otherwise military discipline is administered with barbaric strictness, and since the army consists of the dregs of society (except for the officers and a few unfortunate immigrants whom necessity puts under the blue shako), there probably is good reason for this. An example of how the military authorities got into a serious conflict with civil authority threw the press into a violent uproar during my stay in Saint Louis. A dragoon had deserted from the Jefferson Barracks, but he had returned after about thirty-six hours. Nevertheless, directly upon his return he was placed under arrest and handed over to a court martial for trial. His mother, who lived in Alton, came to Saint Louis when she learned of this, and she was able to obtain a writ of habeas corpus from Commissioner Colvin on the grounds that her son was a minor and was therefore being held in the barracks contrary to the laws of the United States. The writ was issued on Friday, to be presented to the major on Saturday, demanding the immediate release of the young man. The senior officers had gotten wind of this and, not to lose their right to the deserter, had held an immediate trial and sentenced him (after he had admitted his guilt) to the loss of all pay and privileges due him, to branding with the letter D on his shoulder, and to fifty lashes, whereupon his head was to be shaved and he was to be drummed out of the service in disgrace. This sentence was signed in the name of General Clarke and executed on the same day. The civilian authorities thereupon instituted proceedings against the commandant, but I cannot say whether they succeeded.[16]

Religious needs are abundantly provided for in Saint Louis, as everywhere in North America. The largest and most beautiful of the city's thirty-eight churches belong to the Catholics. After them the Methodists are probably the strongest denomination. Many of the Germans belong to the Old Lutherans,[17] who in the late thirties evolved from the Stephanists who had immigrated from Saxony; recently they have been organized throughout the Union into a sort of church by Pastor Walther, a man as zealous and quarrelsome as he is talented. The Catholics are said to make many converts among the Yankees and here exert a not inconsiderable influence upon state and city elections. They have a university conducted by the Jesuits; with it is connected a church with a colorfully decorated image of the Virgin Mary. The altar, dedicated to the latter, carries an inscription stating that during the terrible cholera epidemic of 1849 the professors and students of this institution had promised the Holy Virgin a silver wreath if they should be spared. This veneration of His Mother *placuit Deo filio*, and see! while nine thousand persons were taken away in the city, there was not a single sick person in the Jesuit college.

Although we might wonder at such a curious view of heavenly and earthly matters, the absolute lack of belief that has taken root extensively among the local Germans of the middle class and that puffs itself up in the press with truly knavish insolence has a far more disgusting and distressing effect. However, a sense for anything higher is generally rare in these circles, and the common man (inflated by the knowledge that he is in "a free land") tries in this way to make the educated person aware that he considers himself, if not better, at least just as good. In this he is strengthened by his newspaper writers and other meddling intruders. These, under the pretext of wanting to lead the lower classes from superstition and slavery to true humanity, mislead him to the most insane views of religion, custom, and state. In contemplating this, it sometimes appears as a consolation that the Anglo-Americans—among whom such madness finds no echo, or only a very weak one—hold the power in their hands in all important matters. I shall come back to these conditions later. For the present, only one question: What would happen if the impossible became possible and a completely German state were formed in America, and if (which then might be possible) the Messrs. Börnstein and Franz Schmidt and the Honorable Heinzen[18] had to shape the course in the same—as the first two now do in the League of "Free Men"?[19]

◊ ◊ ◊ The next day was a Sabbath (as one expresses it here) and I utilized the morning to visit the Mormons, who held their service in the Concert Hall. In this beautiful, spacious hall about five hundred people were gathered, most of them belonging to the prosperous middle class, judging by their appearance. Various songs, almost all with lively melodies, were sung quite well. Then a priest (who looked rather strange in his great red wool shawl over a black frock coat) gave a long, somewhat jumbled sermon, the purpose of which was to extol the new Jerusalem and to encourage emigration to it. Then a prayer was spoken, kneeling, to which the entire congregation said a loud "Amen!" In conclusion the latest numbers of the *Frontier Guardian*,[20] a Mormon periodical published in Kanesville in the Far West, were sold down from the pulpit.

# 8

## A VISIT TO BELLEVILLE AND A WORD ABOUT THE GERMANS IN AMERICA

◊ ◊ ◊ THE Sunday with which the last chapter ended was concluded with a trip to the beer hall of a former German representative, the Silesian Mandrella, located in an extreme suburb of Saint Louis. On the way home we stopped for a quarter hour to listen to the concert of several Tyroleans who have settled here—after wearing out their voices at the Leipzig fairs, they had hit upon the clever idea of utilizing the remainder in America. This notion had turned out to be very practical, for in the course of a few years they had yodeled for themselves a rather spacious inn. That evening, despite twelve-degree weather and almost knee-deep snow, the place was packed with guests and listeners.

Having returned to the "Traube," the headquarters of the gentlemen from the *Tribune*, we were surprised by the news that Kinkel had arrived from Chicago, and a deputation left to fetch him from the steamboat. Opinions concerning the expediency of his plans were more divided here, and so his reception was less brilliant than in Cincinnati. A strong party led by Börnstein[1] was working directly against him. To silence this opposition and to allow time for preparation for a successful mass meeting, Kinkel departed for Belleville (situated in Illinois) after visiting the various German societies in this city.

Not to see gay BELLEVILLE is a serious sin of omission for the traveler who passes through Saint Louis. The arrival of the preacher of the Revolution Loan would bring out en masse the busy people of the village and cause the Rhine wine, which appears to make up three-quarters of the blood of its citizens, to sparkle doubly merrily. Thus Schuster's invitation to accompany him (he intended to use the opportunity to settle some book business) was doubly welcome.

At the start this excursion was most unpleasant. It was only with difficulty that we got across the half-frozen river with its floating ice. The trip by stagecoach in sixteen-degree weather was just as fatiguing as the four-hour journey over endless snow-covered prairies and through leafless gray groves was monotonous. When the first houses of West Belleville finally appeared, we heard gun salutes and music and soon saw Kinkel, who had preceded us with the tailor Fleischmann. He was just making his triumphal entrance into the flag-bedecked town, surrounded by a jubilant crowd and escorted by a company of green-uniformed riflemen and several riders.[2] All Belleville seemed to be there, and all the dignitaries of the place (at least half the population is German) were there to pay their respects to the guest of honor. In the barroom of Winter's Hotel, where we stopped, there prevailed such a cannibalistic drinking and screaming on behalf of the German Republic that one could suppose himself (with only a slight expenditure of imagination) carried back to the Baden Revolution of 1849—an impression heightened by the predominance of the Upper Rhineland dialect among these noise-makers.

Little edified by this spectacle, I withdrew to the back of the room. Here a man in a gray cap and green jacket sat down with me, apparently impelled by the same annoyance. His features seemed familiar to me—"of pipe bowls and cups" ran through my head. A second quick glance at the face wreathed in a blond beard and the ensuing conversation confirmed my suspicion. The taciturn guest was Friedrich Hecker,[3] once a lawyer, later standard bearer and field captain of the Revolution in the Black Forest, now one of the most active and most respected farmers on the great Looking Glass Prairie[4] eight miles southeast of Belleville. Unlike many of his associates —who wash the dirty laundry of the parties in the newspapers, preach war against religion and state, and in barroom tones curse conditions in their old fatherland which they are in no position to judge—he has at least demonstrated a better understanding of the present (if not *more* understanding). I must confess that I was somewhat surprised to meet him here and to hear him later as he wasted his oratorical talents (which certainly are effective upon some people) on such a stillborn child as the Revolution Loan of the firm Kinkel and Company.

That this was being done by others, even by Anglo-Americans, was easily understandable. To be seen and to be heard here was as effective as a dozen newspaper announcements, and far cheaper. The speakers had to show off their good democratic thinking and eloquence to the fine people of Belleville, had to make sure that they would be remembered at the next election, and also probably had no clear view of the matter being discussed. But none of this could be the case with Hecker. He appears to be a thoroughly honorable and chivalrous character and could scarcely be deceived about the state of affairs in Europe. Since he nevertheless took part in the farce, it must be assumed either that he believed he had to fulfill a friendly obligation or that, for a moment, he was lost in the burning enthusiasm of bygone days and by means of the fantastically adorned present was able to forget the disappointments of the past.

All this was clear at the mass meeting held on the following day, December 18, in the courthouse. With the exception of Kinkel and Hecker, the speakers were Anglo-American lawyers who were about as well qualified to talk about our conditions as a blind man is about color. Nevertheless they won great applause with their humbug about *intervention for nonintervention*.\* The meeting was chaired by Judge Körner,[5] a refugee from the thirties, at that time an attorney and newspaper editor and six months later lieutenant governor of Illinois. The English-speaking inhabitants of the town were present only in very small numbers. The final result here will be relatively more favorable than anywhere else but hardly will have completely fulfilled the hopes held out for the undertaking.[6]

◊ ◊ ◊ Belleville is a pretty, medium-sized town of about five thousand inhabitants. The people do some winegrowing and, as already mentioned, about half of them come from Germany. Among the latter, several have attained considerable prosperity, as, for example, the Tittmann brothers from Dresden who had to flee in 1834 because of fraternity activities and now are among the wealthiest merchants in Illinois.[7] As far as I could discover, the Low German element is relatively unimportant here in comparison to the Middle and Southwest German elements. Among the acquaintances I made were particularly many Rhinelanders, and one afternoon, to my considerable surprise, I was welcomed by no fewer than four friends

---

\* This expression, heard frequently during Kossuth's visit to the United States, refers to the alleged duty of the American Republic to interpose itself, either through intervention or—as the hotheads desire—with weapons, wherever one monarchy comes to the assistance of another against a republican uprising of the people.

from different parts of Saxony. At present the tone seems to be set by people from the Palatinate and from Baden; in recent years a large contingent has come over from there, among them several wealthy and well-educated people. Although I spent many a happy hour with them over a glass filled with the juice of the native grape, I must not forget the pleasure and instruction I found in the company of Dr. Jörg and his Anglo-American friend Judge Niles.[8] The former participates in politics merely as an observer, but he follows the progress of his science with an attentiveness not common among the physicians of the West. Although I cannot agree with all his views concerning America and the Americans, I am still indebted to him for many valuable suggestions and explanations. It must be difficult indeed for someone who lived for nine years in the Pearl of the Antilles not to judge more harshly an existence upon the monotonous prairies of Illinois, among prosaic Yankees, than someone who is not familiar with the contrast. I should already have felt attached to Niles because of the circumstance that he had known our friend Alexander Conze, one of the noblest representatives of German life in America; he had loved him as I had, and he had seen him fall under Mexican cavalry lances in the battle of Buena Vista alongside Clay's son.[9] But he is also an amiable man, his newspaper is one of the best written in Illinois, and his abilities as an orator and jurist will pave his way to an important position.

The same cannot be said of a majority of the local attorneys. According to the report of an expert in these matters, most of them in their knowledge of the law are quacks, similar to that Fürster-Kohl of Chapter 1 in regard to medicine, and to those leather merchants, schoolteachers, and physicians that we saw applying for the preaching position in Cincinnati in matters of religion.

Here the legal profession is the nearest door to a political career. Most of the governors and presidents and the most influential senators and representatives of the Union began with a law office. To be sure, these positions usually pay very little, but because of all sorts of side income they sometimes become as profitable as the best ministerial posts in Europe.* Since a scholarly education generally is not necessary to acquire the title and privileges of an attorney, everyone pushes toward this door to honor and profit. The route is then the following: It suddenly occurs to a farm boy or to a trade apprentice who feels that he knows what it's all about that he has a calling for

---

* The squire of Hamilton County, Ohio, earns up to $10,000 annually through court fees. The county treasurer has just as much and can, if he knows the ropes, increase it to $20,000 without having to fear accusations of roguery.

the law. He goes to an attorney, explains his desire, and receives permission (for a small fee) to study the latter's books. After he has done so for a few months, he announces himself to the county judge as a candidate. The judge calls together a kind of examining committee from the jurists of the area, this subjects the colleague *in spe* [hopefully] to questioning (under favorable circumstances this to some extent reminds one of a German examination), and the new attorney is ready. An example of this rule shone for a time in the vicinity of Belleville. A driver whose business was not doing very well sold his stagecoach and horses to go, as he claimed, to California. But before he left he applied for the title of attorney and his request was gladly granted—under the assumption that he was serious about his trip, and probably in the opinion that anyone could be a legal expert in the farthest West. How astonished and annoyed the good examiners now were when the newly made attorney cooly announced to them that he had decided to remain since he now was a lawyer. The sly fellow really did stay and appeared before the court on various occasions until he finally found a good opportunity to change himself into a merchant and millowner; he is presently well on the way to becoming a rich man.

That is "Yankee smartness," which, however, only a Yankee can get away with. A German could hardly succeed at this, even if he were a complete master of the English language. It is well known that almost all German lawyers in this country have an Anglo-American partner who takes care of the pleading; and I was assured by various sources that a judge and jury had frequently pronounced a defendant guilty simply because the defense attorney had been of German origin.

If the question about the reason for this and similar unpleasant manifestations is to be properly answered, a detailed examination of the position of the Germans in the United States is necessary. Several times in the course of the preceding pages this subject has been mentioned, not, to be sure, in a tone of praise and admiration. If the same tone is continued in the following section, I beg the favorably disposed reader to believe that I am writing neither to praise nor to offend anyone and that I should have wished with my whole soul to be able to honor truth in a different way. Also I hope that he might—since the heading of this chapter promises "a word about the Germans in America"—regard this as an abbreviation since the writer is far from presuming to pass judgment on a total of almost three million humans on the basis of experiences and notes gathered as an eye-witness or from credible witnesses in a few districts of Ohio, Missouri, and New York state.

## A VISIT TO BELLEVILLE

I thank my countrymen in the New World for many a courtesy, and I have met many a noble heart that has preserved the treasures of German life, honesty, comfort, and the striving for ideals. I by no means fail to recognize that the Germans have the destiny—in this "conglomerate of nations" of North America—to make the best of those treasures and that it now and then seems that this destiny is being fulfilled already, even though only very indirectly. However, those good people are, in my experience, exceptions; those enriching influences are weak beginnings scarcely perceptible to the naked eye; and the rule (obvious to anyone free of the illusions of sentimentality) is—I utter it with pain and shame—that the Germans play a miserable role in the just-mentioned states of America (mostly through their own fault). In many respects they deserve the contempt in which they are held by the great mass of Anglo-Americans. And they will never attain the majority and independence aspired to by a few of them unless an inspiring genius suddenly arises among them or some other extraordinary event pushes them forcefully onto another track.

It doesn't mean very much to point to the Pennsylvanians: their jabbering language still contains a few thousand words recalling Germany, but their thickheaded peasant's conceit everywhere resists, in a most disgusting manner, any education beyond reading and writing, Bible and catechism.* The immigration of capable heads brought by the years 1848 and 1849 has changed the state of affairs in only a few points. Since, in general, the best members of this immigration (like the better people among the earlier immigrants) soon withdrew and the babblers and bawlers remained as practically the only teachers and directors of public opinion, exerting a depressing rather than an elevating and improving effect, one ought to regard as a real gain the few dozen newspaper articles written in a good style, several witty attacks upon imperfections in the character of the Anglo-Americans, and a few new terms of abuse for the believers and property owners, or it ought to be considered as progress that here and there a society has been established whose members seek to gain fame by passing as atheists—without being able to give any account of this.

Yet enough by way of introduction—let's get to the facts. As the principal and basic faults of the American Germans must be

---

* One example of many should suffice. The state of New York has 8,070 school libraries with 1,338,858 volumes for its approximately 3 million inhabitants, while Pennsylvania with its 2,314,897 souls can show only 29 such institutions with 8,134 volumes.

emphasized their factionalism, their submissiveness to unjustified claims of the Yankee paired with a disregard of their native character, and their crass indolence and apathy when it's a matter of something other than materialism.

The factionalism shows itself, first of all, in the thoughtlessness (mentioned earlier in another connection) of hundreds and hundreds of little groups persecuting, goading, and stigmatizing each other, and then, above all, in the great cleft between the old immigrants, or the "Grays," and the newcomers, or the "Greens." The former, mostly of the uneducated class, moved to this country solely to improve their material situation (with the exception of a few impelled by religious motives). They did this at a time when nearly all conditions were more favorable for this ambition than today, and thus it was easy for them to attain their goal. To be without education and to become rich in a hurry results in most cases, that is, to the average brain, in a product generally termed "a lucky fellow." The distinguishing marks of this product are mainly contempt of everything that does not contribute directly to the acquisition of money, conceit toward those whose capital consists only of intelligence and knowledge, and boundless self-esteem in all other matters, based upon the sight of chests and boxes filled without effort. If these earmarks are summed up and to them are added the feeling of being at home with conditions that must be incomprehensible and uncomfortable to the newcomer, and the knowledge (acquired from newspaper reading) of living in a free land and therefore—as the stupidly proud one concludes—of being allowed to play the bully toward everyone who does not yet have a certificate of American citizenship in his pocket, especially toward those who are his intellectual superiors—then you have an exact likeness of the "Gray."

Compared to him, the "Green" (on his estimable side) appears to be an enthusiastic advocate of a striving for the heights, a worker for the evolution of already existing institutions, a bearer of new ideas, and an admonisher of the vices and ugliness that have developed in the New World along with much excellence. If he does not feel himself called to this activity and if he is one of the peaceful and simple ones, he at least brings along a heart full of illusions that he has long cherished and cultivated, illusions from which he has built charming castles in the air on his way to the promised land. Now how does the Gray behave toward the newly arrived countrymen? With decided hostility toward the ambitious ones, with heartlessness toward those full of hope, and frequently as a betrayer and cheater toward the trusting ones. He does not want to hear that he has weaknesses, least of all from people who have no money. He does not want to know anything of new ideas that have nothing in common with the almighty dollar. What can these greenhorns, who must first have eaten a bushel of salt in this land of liberty before they are permitted to join in the discussion, have to say—to him who has become a made man without such rubbish? Those men of illusions, however, appear to him not only as deceived but as men to be deceived, as good prey that he may exploit with his knowledge of affairs, as fools who must experience the same things that he did after he landed here without a dollar in his pocket. Above all, he regards them as a sort of public nuisance against which he must defend himself, for they have come to compete with him. The result of the Grays' opposition is that the disagreeable Greens gradually dry up, the ambitious ones grow weary, and the hopeful ones despair of their ideals. If ever a dam should be built to the stream of immigration, or if it should take another direction, in a few decades the American Germans would present a Gray in Gray cheerless beyond all conception.

Without doubt it is praiseworthy to adapt one's self to the customs of the country, at least to the extent required by necessity. But it provokes smiles, and, in a few cases, even disgust, to see how eagerly the newly immigrated Germans exchange custom and manner of the homeland for the fashion of the Yankee—even when this is not expected, and when the old is not only handier but more beautiful and nobler by far than the aped new. Of course, there could be no objection if the virtues of the Anglo-Americans were taken as a model. But generally it is just the opposite that is imitated. Instead of allowing the great features from which a unique art of living has developed here to serve as model, one fancies that he has to cast off honor and integrity as European rubbish. Instead of adopting the restless activity of the dominant race, he prefers to learn the art of tobacco chewing. Instead of taking up the genial drive of this race with which it in a way springs past minor obstacles to greater things, one clings to the motto of the American Philistines, *"to save appearances,"* and anxiously observes rules that in the best case are mere externals, often are simply ridiculous, and occasionally are even quite crude manners.

This can be observed above all in the attitude toward language. If there were no other German language than the nonsensical mishmash of which a few samples were given in Chapter 2,[10] we could find no fault with anyone who laid aside, with clear conscience, this jargon for a good English—just like an old, ten times mended smock

for a new dress. But what should one say when not only the common
man but even the man who considers himself cultured gives up the
language in which his mother raised him and his father blessed him,
and gives it up as quickly, perhaps, as the mustache or goatee he
enjoyed at home? Certainly the learning of English is one of the first
obligations of the person living in America. But to describe it as the
more distinguished language, to have it prevail in the family circle,
and to have the children educated in it alone (as do many respected
Germans in Cincinnati and, according to all accounts, also in
Philadelphia and New York)—this is not only ridiculous but almost
disgraceful. America is the land of extremes and contrasts, and upon
these many a fool turns his somersaults—none, however, as a more
woeful figure than the German who in this way is ashamed of his
mother. The argument that political unity requires linguistic unity is
too silly to need refutation. The excuse that English is the language
of business and therefore to be preferred is a self-accusation surprising
for its naïveté since it puts business above personality and the
businessman above the man.

    This commercial spirit of the American German, who is more
concerned with *business* and moneymaking than anything else, is
further expressed as a boundless apathy when it is a question of
promoting intellectual interests or of one's own education. The
Anglo-American, as soon as he has worked himself out above the first
necessities (usually very soon), thinks of buying books and reading.
Although he almost always does so with his eye on the material gain to
be attained thereby and frequently makes the wrong selection, he
enjoys, on the whole, an average education. The German, on the other
hand, even when he is not lacking in means, usually limits himself
to the Bible, a few other religious writings, and the almanac. Worldly
minded ones sometimes add *Eulenspiegel*[11] and a newspaper. Finally,
those studying medicine, law, and theology provide themselves with
the *pons asinorum* covering their field and procure for the family
Meyer's *Universum*[12] or another illustrated work. Anything else
purchased is taken to get rid of the annoying salesman, or as room
decoration, or for other reasons having no connection with the desire
for information or intellectual pleasure. If anyone should argue that
some German-American bookdealers do a good business and a few
have even become wealthy, this is to be rejected by the fact that these
exceptions to the rule also deal in English literature and paper and
stationery and that it is principally school, prayer, sermon, and
popular books to which they owe their profit. Furthermore, it must be

## A VISIT TO BELLEVILLE

taken into consideration that they also have Anglo-Americans as customers, especially in New York and Boston.

The interest in literature may be a very weak one, but there is complete indifference to any other branch of art—with the exception of music, the German heritage, which is cultivated with love by the singing societies established some years ago. The theater in New York, where eighty thousand Germans live, can hardly be compared to the smallest town theater at home, and that in Cincinnati far less so. Even if German names such as Leutze and Frankenstein[13] can be found among American painters, the bearers of these names have long since been alienated (according to language and manner) from the nation of their origin. If one of the transatlantic Germans should have distinguished himself in another area of art, certainly his countrymen have not inspired him to this.

The German-American gives what he must for elementary schools. For institutions of higher learning he doesn't stir a finger. As yet Ohio has no university in which the mother tongue of 800,000 citizens of this state is the basis of instruction. There is the same deficiency in Pennsylvania, for the theological seminary in Mercersburgh and a couple of similar institutions are of too private a nature to be cited as contrary evidence. As far as I know, a scholar of German tongue and nation has not yet been born and raised in America, although three generations have already passed since the first members of this nation landed in Philadelphia.

In this consideration the peak of wretchedness is finally reached when one observes the inertia of the American Germans in political matters and sees how they (excepting the newspaper editors and a few lawyers) regard so lightly the rights given them by the "free land" (mouthed so excessively by them).* Even where they form the majority, the helm is in the hands of the Yankees. The facts that the Democrats of Illinois made "Judge" Körner the lieutenant governor and that the Whigs of Ohio almost succeeded in electing "Editor" Klauprecht[14] to the legislative assembly of the state were exceptions to the miserable rule—to be regarded not as attainments but as concessions. If it were conceivable that a vigorous spirit could shake the German citizens of the Union out of their bearskin existence and unite them to a compact whole, then quite different results would be

* In New York as well as in Cincinnati I became acquainted with people who had not yet taken out citizenship although they had been in America for ten to fifteen years and had no thought of returning. And these people belonged to the better classes.

seen. Pennsylvania and Ohio would then have German governors from time to time and always have a distribution of officers and representatives proportionate to the origins of their population; the representation in Washington would consist of up to one-eighth Germans, and it would not even be entirely impossible that (with clever utilization of the circumstances) the United States would sometime get a German as president for four years. If someone should ask what would be gained by this, I should answer: nothing directly but the honor, but through this the great advantage that the contempt that the Yankee has for the *"dutch people"* (and conceals only at elections) would have to cease and make way for an honest recognition of equal rights. To be sure, this would not bring in money, and since the thoughts of the great majority of the local Germans aim past honor toward the dollar, everything would remain the same, that is, our countrymen would continue to vegetate as those tolerated and exploited by the parties as handymen, while the Yankees (not bothering about the caterpillars who do not look beyond their leaf) would represent the real life in the powerful body politic. That is lamentable, but not unfair. Whoever does not take what he may and can take is not to be pitied if he has nothing, and it is only fair to regard as no voice the voice that remains silent when it could turn the scale. The old Athenians punished such laziness or cowardice in political matters more severely than with mere scorn.

If it were not too unreasonable a demand, I should advise those who doubt the generality of these miserable conditions to find confirmation in the first available issue of any German-American newspaper (it's understood that here and in the following only political papers are meant). Not always, to be sure, but as a rule the periodical literature of a nation is its characterization. This is undoubtedly true where unlimited freedom of the press has prevailed for a long time. If I apply this to the collection lying before me of about sixty German-language periodicals from the most diverse sections of the Union, then from almost every one the most impertinent physiognomy of that wretchedness looks out at me in daguerreotype; it hardly seems believable that I have been assured that German journalism before the year 1848 was far more deplorable.

If it occasionally happens in Germany that a writer is overpraised to the point of self-worship, among our countrymen in America just the opposite is usually the case. The arrogance of the mob rests like an alp upon anyone of intellectual distinction. Just as the teacher upon the platform, so also the educator in the newspaper is pulled down from the start into the position of a lackey. The latter must join a party first of all—in case he doesn't want to write into the wind. This would not be objectionable if by this joining were not meant an absolute slavery, that is, if it did not include the obligation to go along with the leaders of the party even when they were obviously striving for the wrong, to praise black as white, and not only to permit five to be an even number, but expressly to declare it as such. In addition the "patrons"—and especially those of the Democratic party, to which at least seven-eighths of the German-Americans belong—usually demand that their newspaper fodder-choppers be very skilled in the lexicon of invective and work hard at digging up personal scandal. A noble tone, a reasonable refutation would not penetrate through the thick skin produced by such usage. Coarseness of expression passes for resoluteness of mind, and boorishness of writing for zeal of conviction. Anyone who cannot pay his respects to this will do better to wield a spade rather than a pen. The first issue of the paper he'd send into the world would bring him the reputation of being an aristocrat, even though every fiber in him were democratic. There can be no talk of a middle way when a gross mass sees truth and justice only in the extremes.

These same claims are made whenever the journal occasionally concerns itself with church affairs. Anyone wishing to preserve some independence—rejecting, on the one hand, the customary yelping against unbelievers and children of Satan and omitting, on the other, the just as common mocking of religion and the weekly tearing down of the "priests"—would do better if he sat down upon a shoemaker's stool rather than upon an editorial chair. "Toward one's own party slavish, toward the opponent's knavish!" would be in not a few of these speculations about the baseness of man a far better motto than the distinguished slogan that they carry between the title and contents.

Anyone bringing himself to taking on this yoke has to solicit his first subscriptions himself (in case he doesn't get a position with an already existing newspaper business), just as preachers out in the country are accustomed to talk up a congregation by personal visits to Farmers A to Z. If the candidate for journalistic office succeeds in finding favor in the eyes of Mr. Tailor or Mr. Cobbler, then they sign for the paper and in addition place advertisements in the same and persuade their friends to do so. These advertisements are well paid for and form the chief source of income of all American newspapers, particularly since they are usually given for repeated insertions. It is well understood that the editor now and then will mention the advertised business in glowing terms in the editorial section of the paper, that he will under all circumstances conduct himself as a good Whig or Democrat, and that, finally, he will at all times place before his readers the usual fodder in church matters. If he succeeds in this and possesses in addition an open ear for bribes for these or those purposes and a strong persuasive power for electoral assemblies at which he campaigns for votes for candidate X or Y in return for clinking coins, then with favorable conditions he can make not merely "a living, but money" and in a few years get to the point where his friends call him "very well off." But if he ever makes a mistake and somehow falls awkwardly into the error of honesty, then at once there comes a protest from the readers who have hired him for themselves. If he cannot make up his mind to repent and retract, then subscriptions to the paper which has become objectionable are abruptly cancelled, and the editor may see where he can get other subscriptions and advertisements.

This, however, can only happen to a "Green" who has not yet completely cast away our concepts of honor and respect—never to a "Gray" (as far as I learned to know them). Besides, the Green is naïve enough to find the tyranny practiced here in this country by the common man toward the educated man more unbearable than that from which he fled. The Gray either no longer feels the pressure or he adapts himself to it, since for him the money earned is a sufficient counterweight. But, as said, the difference between the two colors levels out very quickly almost everywhere. First the newcomer's air castles collapse, then his principles. The process of becoming assimilated and becoming absorbed is more and more evident in his views and actions, and inch by inch he sinks down into the same state of commonness that he initially criticized.

I repeat that I have met many an exception to this rule, exceptions that appear all the more admirable since they have had to keep their characters pure through constant battle. I believe and hope that in places that I was not able to visit a larger number of such exceptions exist—and, to be sure, among the Grays as well as among the Greens. I believe and hope so all the more because otherwise it would be unaccountable that at least a few better and more decently written papers stay alive.

As I have suggested on the occasion of a glance at the church conditions of the American Germans, one part of the Greens does not deserve the praise paid to this color in the preceding section in contrasting them to the indolence of the Grays. That the fellows described there are not lacking in arrogance and coarseness is shown (among other things) by the final words with which Karl Heinzen took leave of the readers of one of the three newspapers which died, one after the other, under his hand. This delightful document ends with the following magnificent, stinging comment:

"Socrates was decidedly in the minority when he drank the cup of poison, Christ was decidedly in the minority when he was nailed to the cross, and I and my fellow combatants: were we not supposed to be able to forget about our minority? Surrounded by grunting swine to whom I had to cast my pearls daily, I have nevertheless seen them picked up by many a knowing hand that will not let them be lost for the intellectual adornment of the better Germanism of this country."

In fact, a peculiar geometric progression: Socrates, Christ, and Heinzen, and a strange farewell to the readers, comparing the majority of them to grunting swine! And yet—can one believe it?—this half-mad self-worshiper has a not insignificant following, especially among the younger people of the working class, who with their lack of education are generally inclined to swear *in verba magistri*, even if the same is hardly three steps from the summit of madness.

In order to anticipate the argument that there is too much of the shadow in this characterization of the German-American periodical press and to show at the same time how this is judged by the Anglo-Americans, I add in extract the remarks of a widely read English paper published in New York. The *Christian Inquirer*—incidentally, no organ of hyperorthodoxy—says the following in its issue of May 31, 1851:

"We have procured copies of eight different German papers published in New York and have gathered sufficient information about three others, making eleven newspapers in all that are published here in that language.* Four of these eleven appear daily and the others are weeklies, with the exception of that published monthly by the Christian Union.

"We surveyed these papers and were astonished at the spirit and the opinions expressed in the individual articles. With the exception of the just-mentioned monthly which is more an organ of American orthodoxy than of German thinking, of another paper which defends a petrified Lutheranism, and of the Roman Catholic paper which is

---

* The number of German-American journals varies constantly in view of the ease with which such a paper can be established and the difficulty of keeping it going. When I left New York in February 1852, four of the papers mentioned in the above report had gone under, but five new ones had appeared—probably to disappear again just as quickly as the ephemera that had preceded them.

ultramontane through and through, they all are completely irreligious and disorganizing in tone and belief. The most respectable among them, the *Abendzeitung*, does not have the worst failings of its associates and probably could join the ranks of worthy political journals if it did not promote destructive principles and their application by its advertisements and occasionally by its articles. The daily morning paper, the *Staatszeitung*, is impetuous in its policy but is not inclined to the attack in religious matters. Of the six others, the four that we saw are completely oriented to destruction and are irreligious in every sense of the word. They extend from Red Socialism to the crassest atheism, and the remaining papers, as we learned, are unfortunately just as bad, if not worse. If we understand the language correctly, the *Schnellpost*, a daily edited with great literary skill, denies the personality of God and sets up self-esteem as the highest religious virtue, while its views about morality can be judged by its selection of the "Memoirs of Lola Montez" for its literary supplement. From this ably edited journal there is a rapid descent to the low shallowness of the *Lucifer*, a Sunday paper presenting the extreme abasement of the character whose name it bears with no trace of his former glory. This paper belongs completely to the earth, and its true nature seems very well characterized by the woodcut over its advertising columns: a jumping goat and a beer stein. It is anti-Christian, sensually lewd, blasphemous, and coarse in opinion and language. It reprints the dirtiest slop of irreligion, holds the satisfaction of sensual desire to be the highest goal, and carries communism so far as to calculate the amount that every individual in our cities would receive through a division of all property—thereby employing, in anticipation of its future triumph, the words applied in the Scriptures to the divinity: Ours is the kingdom and the power and the glory forever!

"While we lament the tone of the German daily press here and in the entire land and note that within the Union over sixty different newspapers are published in this language,\* we must take into account a few circumstances. Above all we must consider that our country has been flooded by political refugees who have brought along a quantity of passions but no industrious habits, and they find it easier to be insignificant journalists than to undertake useful labor.

\* This figure is exceeded by the political papers alone, and if one adds to these the papers devoted to belletristic, religious, and other matters, the estimate of about 150 German-American newspapers cannot be too high. At the end of 1851 Pennsylvania alone had 47, Ohio 28, the state of New York 23, Missouri 12, and Illinois 5.

Further, we must take into account the fact that the German immigrants have a prejudice against religion, quite regardless of the nature of the religion itself. In their fatherland they turned away from a faith whose advocates usually made common cause with despotism. Thus to them liberty seems almost equivalent to irreligion, and certainly hostility toward Christianity is a part of the Republican code of almost every one of these refugees.

"We feel compelled to say about the entire German press in this country that it finds itself in grievous uncertainty about the spirit of our institutions and about the right way to elevate the German population. It is regrettable, in fact, that a people already numbering three million in this country has so many foolish advisers and so few wise advocates. They frequently seem to deplore our spirit directed merely to the useful and our lack of generosity, while we have far more reason to lament their lack of energy and their self-indulgence. Nevertheless, we are glad to note a few signs of beginning moderation among them, seeing that they are intent upon acquiring their own land and houses, and we believe that such good endeavors would become far easier for them if they would renounce their beer halls and dancing on the Sabbath. The sooner such excesses cease, the more quickly will the German race rise from its obscurity and impotence, and the sooner America will have cause to congratulate itself that the countrymen of Luther and Schiller have found a home within its boundaries."

How much of the last part of this judgment can be true, the reader will be able to say for himself. I, on my part, am able to see in Sunday dancing no cause for and in the discontinuance of it no cure for the corruptness and weakness of the German element in the United States, although it cannot be denied that the churchly minded almost always make a better impression than their opponents.

The causes of these lamentable conditions lie entirely elsewhere. They are partly internal, partly external, but mainly accidental. First of all it is the inherent cosmopolitanism of the German people, that predominance of mental centrifugal force, that drives our nation to all the winds as seed for the future; at home it has permitted no real unity until now, and in foreign lands it leads them farther apart and in this isolation subordinates them to others. A second explanation is to be found in the effect of the right of the majority, this highest shaping principle of all relationships in North America; from it a minority can wring stipulations and concessions only when it pushes itself wedgelike as a compact phalanx between the factions of the majority and, through joining the one most favorable to it, pushes the others down to a minority. However, for such operations our countrymen in America cannot be brought together, just because of that centrifugal force; besides, they are mostly too uneducated. The latter is the third cause for their pitiable position. Until recently the great majority of German immigrants consisted of farmers and handworkers, to which were joined now and then a few members of the higher classes. The latter, however, almost everywhere avoided any contact with their lower-class countrymen. These did not know how to appreciate the treasures they had in their language and custom. In their awkwardness and ignorance they contrasted very much with the quick and clever nature of the Yankees, particularly in the cities. If they ever thought about it, looking up from their moneymaking, they had to perceive that themselves, and thus they gradually accustomed themselves to the thought that they were the lower caste. No one will be surprised that the sort of intelligence that the most recent times have assigned to them has not been able to elevate them when he learns that the frequently mentioned Heinzen is considered (even by many of his opponents) as the most talented among the bearers of such intelligence active in the illumination and education of German America.

To specify remedies for the cure of these shortcomings is a difficult matter, since their roots—the cosmopolitanism of the Germans and the majority right of the Yankee Republic—absolutely cannot be eliminated, to judge by human foresight. It's a different matter with the third point. Here much can be done, and even though twenty experiments aimed at this in current literature may have failed, the task is too beautiful and the goal too noble not to urge the twenty-first. Beginnings of an awakening of the indolent and a joining together of the ambitious can be observed in the recently founded singing and gymnastic societies that are spreading mightily over all sections of the Union where Germans have settled. In a later generation, perhaps, they will form the nucleus of a German party that, if properly led, would certainly have prospects of some success in the impending reform of the old parties. Only fools and dreamers will demand any more than an organically incorporated independence of the Germans in the customs and political life of the North American Union. However, it is an indisputable fact that they need more independence and self-reliance than they exhibit now; may a good genius assist them in this improvement before it is too late.

## A VISIT TO BELLEVILLE

◊ ◊ ◊ It has been said of Hecker that he keeps slaves. This could be believed only by such as did not know that he lives in Illinois and that Illinois lies north of "Dixon's and Mason's Line." The statement is just as little true in a metaphorical sense, that is, in the meaning that he is supposed to treat his people *like* slaves. Anyone at all familiar with the position of servants in America knows very well that almost everywhere is observed a reversal of the relationship in which they stand to their masters in the Old World. In nine cases out of ten the master is rather the slave to the whims of his hired hands and maids. We encountered an interesting example of this on our return trip.

Probably as a consequence of the temperature, which had dropped to eighteen degrees, our coach's off horse collapsed about six miles from Belleville, dying instantly. Fortunately, a tavern was not far away, and here the loss could be replaced quickly. In the meanwhile a good fire thawed our half-frozen spirits. The only other guest was a farmer from the vicinity, a recently emigrated Englishman (judging from his dialect). He complained first to the innkeeper and then to us of his troubles with the servants: within a period of three months no fewer than seven had left him. For a week he had been hunting for a nursemaid; he had been unable to discover a suitable person, although he was willing to pay four dollars a month. I could not advise him to try his luck in Belleville, since similar complaints were heard there on all sides. Therefore I suggested to him that he ride along to Saint Louis with us, where a shipment of emigrants was expected any day on the *Grand Turk* and several other steamboats that were frozen in a few miles downstream. He agreed to this, and when I met him again a few days later on the Mississippi ferry he introduced me to the fulfillment of his desire in the shape of a strapping Swabian girl with whom he was able to communicate quite satisfactorily by means of a mixture of pantomine and a couple dozen German words.

Now it might be that our Englishman felt himself the master more than the customs of this country permit and regarded his people as an English establishment of servants, thus giving rise himself to the difficulties about which he complained. But the main fault lies in that custom of this country which is the product, on the one hand, of a theory of equality carried to extremes and, on the other hand, of the high value placed upon hand labor. I leave it to the judgment of others to decide whether such conditions, of which I had already encountered curious examples in Ohio, are in conformity with nature—and the same for the question as to whether they have much of the poetic. But I don't want to hide the fact that they were extraordinarily uncomfortable to me and even to many a eulogist of all other American institutions.

It is well known that in the West only the slaves are designated as *servants* and that free persons do not "serve," but "help," and consequently are *helps* or, according to the more common expression, *hands*. With this is connected the fact that only a slaveholder can be a *master*. For this reason they were embarrassed as to how to term the person who avails himself of the assistance of other citizens in a trade, commerce, or housework, and so for this purpose the expression *Baas* was borrowed from the Dutch language, which originally was the prevailing one in New York.

To this subtlety of concepts corresponds the actual position of the servants or workers in respect to the master of the house or the employer. The former, as a rule, display the greatest independence, or rather, impudence of behavior; the latter, as a rule, must show the greatest possible consideration, especially toward the young ladies who do him the honor of devoting a part of their time to him for his good money. Many examples of this practice belong in the picture books that are sold at our yearly fairs as illustrations of the topsy-turvy world. In a house in New York I found four maids who, according to the assurance of the friend who was plagued by them, all together cost about six times as much and did approximately half as much as two individuals of their class in Germany. In Dayton the market porter of a merchant drove his friends about the city streets every morning, wherever he wished, in his master's own carriage, without the least objection being raised. And that man would be denounced as the cruelest tyrant who would expect any assistance from his servants after the evening meal.

These abuses are felt most unpleasantly "in the bush," that is, on isolated farms where young girls take service most unwillingly, since there is a lack of gossip, dancing, and opportunity for marriage. Here the master and mistress of the house have to observe extreme patience with all deficiencies of their female servants. A request refused, a word of reproach, and Miss Susy or Betsy sulkily turns her back on the threshold of such barbarians as soon as her month is up. It would be as great a crime to forbid such a tenderly strung heart to receive a lover's visit every evening (often lasting until midnight) as it would be to work her in the field, to refuse her the buggy or riding horse for attending a ball, or even to scold her if the dear little one should not turn up until the next morning, sleepy-eyed and ready for breakfast. Sunday belongs completely to the servants, as do the weekday evenings. The younger ladies are reimbursed for the remaining six-times-twelve hours with $3 to $4.50 a month, while the older ones are paid $5 to $6.

The same holds true for the male help. The opinion that the worker on an American farm must exert himself very much is false, at least in the West. The average German farmer works much harder. The clearing of trees is, to be sure, quite laborious for the newcomer, and the splitting of rails with which the cleared fields are fenced is even more exhausting for the person not accustomed to it. But the work period is all the shorter, and not a soul stirs a hand before the rising and after the setting of the sun—except during the period of the wheat harvest. However, the pay is very high; a good "farm hand" could not be had in Ohio during the summer months for under twelve dollars monthly, and new immigrants not yet familiar with the customary procedures were given at least ten dollars. Finally, the food is more abundant and better than it usually is in Germany. Everywhere in the country the entire household eats at one table, and at none of the three daily meals are meat and coffee lacking—unless one should prefer tea in the morning or evening. In addition I found sugar and honey everywhere, various sorts of baked goods, and, among the more prosperous farmers, fruit pies and preserves; to all these the hands helped themselves in the same manner as the master and his family.

That still isn't all of it. During the wheat harvest the day laborer in Ohio receives $1.50 a day, and if he shows industry and skill, even $2 (in addition to five meals and as much whiskey as he is able to polish off). In dispensing the firewater a kind of point of honor is observed, and to deny the traditional treat (even when the denial is accompanied by an offer of reimbursement) is considered sacrilege. A farmer near Springfield in the mentioned state, a Methodist and Son of Temperance, had dared this experiment and had offered his reapers the equivalent in clinking coins for the gallon of whiskey that he had to give them every morning and afternoon. What happened? Without saying a word and refusing the offer with looks of deepest indignation, five of the gentlemen put down their scythes and departed. It was a bit of luck that on the same day two vigorous Germans came along the road looking for work; they were persuaded by the sole remaining reaper, likewise a countryman, to help the enemy of alcohol and his sons mow and bring in the grain.

◊ ◊ ◊ We had left Belleville about eight o'clock in the morning and could hope to be back in Saint Louis around noon. The accident with the fallen horse had held us up scarcely half an hour. The Mississippi, however, half-frozen and covered with floating ice, seemed to want to compel us to remain in Illinoistown, which was overfilled with carts and coaches. We had waited almost three hours upon the sandbanks south of Bloody Island[15] that were covered with thin, mirror-smooth ice, and still the steam ferry was unable to clear a path through the ice floes to the landing. Several times it had returned to the opposite shore, and soon the depressing rumor was spread among the masses of those waiting—who were camped upon the ice with market goods of all kinds, especially with an abundance of the handsomest deer, turkeys, and prairie hens—that the ferrymen would give up trying to get across today. But this was not so. Once again the brave little steamer risked combat with the current and after a half hour of tacking landed a half mile downstream.

The ensuing scene was a very amusing one. Every one of the hundreds who had been waiting tried to be among the first to reach the boat since the last could not count with certainty upon finding room. The consequence of this was a higgledy-piggledy race across the mirror ice and then a hopping and a clattering over a wide island of ice floes thrown together in confusion. At the point of this, projecting far out into the river, the ferry had taken its position. As participants in this game, which was not without danger, we had only a half pleasure in it. But from the shore it must have appeared extraordinarily comical, this wild chase in which even ladies in hats and veils took part, dragging along bundles and sacks, panting under suitcases and loads of wild game, tripping, slipping, somersaulting, pulling themselves up again from the tumble with speed, falling again, and again getting up, plunging toward their goal.

In Saint Louis we found just the opposite of this mad mood. The levee was as if dead. Not a single one of the forty to fifty great steamboats gave off any smoke. The lower streets were empty. There were no customers in the stores and warehouses, and it was as though even the shops were making sullen faces. Everywhere in the commercial district down to the general stores morose headshaking and the shrugging of shoulders, everywhere complaints about the lack of business, particularly now when Christmas and the New Year were so close with their presents and their claims on the purse. The cause was the freezing weather which, with its ice, prevented river travel—indeed, the freezing weather alone. I should scarcely have believed that a single week of cold could have so transformed the physiognomy of the cheerful city, and never was I more aware than on this Saturday that the greatness of Saint Louis is a river-borne one and that its life artery is the Mississippi.

# 9

## A WINTER JOURNEY FROM THE MISSISSIPPI TO THE NIAGARA AND BACK TO THE HUDSON

◊ ◊ ◊ MONDAY was spent in taking leave and in making preparations for the return trip, which had to be undertaken by post coach since a freeing of the river from ice was not expected for at least a week.[1] There was nothing attractive about this journey by coach in the intense cold, and I should have liked very much to have celebrated Christmas in native fashion with my German friends. But necessity compelled, and so I went to the office in the Planters House and made a reservation for the stage to Cincinnati, got myself a double wool blanket and a pair of buffalo shoes, said farewell to my acquaintances, and on Tuesday, the twenty-third of December, began the first stage of the trip to the distant homeland that I had not been able to find again here. Whoever looks for roses will find them everywhere along the road, and the careful person will seldom scratch himself on the thorns. But

> Alas, in no place is the thorn as tiny,
> Alas, in no place blooms as red a rose,
> As where we little children found repose.[2]

◊ ◊ ◊ It was bitter cold in the morning when I went down to the Centre Ferry to cross over to the Illinois shore where the post coaches were waiting for us. A dense fog lay over the river, so that one was able to see barely twenty paces ahead, and one became aware of the presence of the giant river only by the dull roaring of the ice floes that it was carrying to the South. The cabin was full of travelers and hunters in furs, overcoats, and light green and bright blue blankets thrown over in poncho fashion, and it was full of heat, noise, and coal smoke, from which one fled from time to time out into the biting air, only to be driven back in the very next minute. Finally, after a delay of an hour and a half, the ferry shoved off with its load of pedestrians, riders, and oxcarts, and about nine o'clock we sprang to land on the eastern bank of the Mississippi.

The fog had lifted and a magnificent winter landscape unfolded before us. On the other side the pale red brick houses of Saint Louis, their roofs covered with snow, the steeples sparkling in the rays of the morning sun; above them, the retreating mist mixed with the black fumes of the chimneys; to the right and left and far above, a clear blue sky. In front of us, the dark river with gray floating ice in the middle and broad, white, confusedly piled-up ice fields on both sides. On this side, a barricade of carriages of those waiting in the midst of the forest through which busy axes had hewn a path from the regular highway to this unexpectedly chosen landing place. Finally, in the distance, above the forest, river, and prairie, immense, cloudlike flocks of birds. Indeed, it was an interesting picture under whose impression I said farewell to the Father of Waters and his Daughter!

The post coach was soon found. Even though the drivers wear no uniform, throughout the Union the coaches are the same uncomfortable, clumsy machines, equally accessible to cold and dust; from them one descends in dry weather as a gray man, in muddy weather speckled with spots of dirt, in cold weather half-frozen, and in all circumstances—since nine persons must find room in their confined space—half-squashed, with swollen necks and stiff knees. On the other hand they have one good feature, the cardinal virtue in America: they travel with astounding speed (taking into account the roads, which at times are terribly bad)—this increases to absolute madness when the passengers give the coachman *"a quarter to grease his throat with."* Then the ponderous carriage flies over log bridges and corduroy roads, over swamps and mudholes, uphill and down, as if the Evil One had gotten into it. The travelers, however, are hurled together and piled up so that their teeth rattle. At times they have to lean to the left, at times to the right, so that the coach does not overturn. They are in almost constant danger of breaking neck and limbs—but, as said, they fly, and for this pleasure the Yankee risks his life.

It is quite understandable that under such circumstances one loses his desire to make observations. Anyway, there would not have been much to observe in my case. The part of the "Prairie State" through which we drove during the day offers nothing remarkable. Unending grasslands, with the high, yellowed grass resembling gigantic fields of grain, now and then a rolling hill sparsely covered with trees, occasionally a small valley through which a brook meandered, then again, and always again, the oceanlike prairie—this was all that nature permitted us to see through the cracks of the wagon canvas. Generally speaking, man had only just started cultivation here, although the main highway from east to west passes through. The towns at which we stopped were—with the exception of the handsome HIGHLAND, inhabited mainly by Germans, and the stately VANDALIA —unpleasant nests of log cabins, full of coarse, dirty people. Finally, the inns were the poorest and most uncomfortable holes that I had seen in the entire United States.

It was likewise understandable that under such conditions and with the horrible cold coming through a large hole in the bottom of the coach that was poorly stopped up with a bundle of straw (cold that almost chewed off our toes despite the buffalo shoes), no especially cheerful mood prevailed in the traveling company. One limited himself in conversation to only the most necessary, crawled down into his fur or blanket, and tried to forget the bad situation in a sort of half-slumber.

Beyond Vandalia the cold began to let up and—perhaps as a result of this—first the curiosity and then, gradually, the communicativeness of the passengers began to thaw out. Except for a furrier from Cincinnati and myself, they were all salesmen from the New England states. We spoke first (as is proper) of business matters, then about county and state elections, and finally of national politics, slave emancipation, and the enthusiasm for Kossuth—until a stout clockdealer from Bristol, Connecticut, returning from New Orleans, opened up his treasure store of anecdotes and began to regale the company with them. The abundance of serious and humorous stories to which the cheerful man treated us was, after the vexatious mood that had prevailed for so long, too pleasant not to be enjoyed gratefully by all. They also were in themselves so original that I can't refrain from inserting here a retelling of the last story.

It came quite warm from the mouth of the thirteenth cousin of our storyteller and described the manner in which the former had swindled himself out of imprisonment in Cuba and naturally was "a little bit truer than the truest of true stories."[3]

"You know from the papers, gentlemen," our traveling companion began, "that Captain Korry of the Lopez Expedition was pardoned last fall and sent back to New Orleans. But you probably do not know that he is the thirteenth son of my grandfather, and I believe that you also do not know how he pulled his neck out of the noose. I tell you, gentlemen, he is the tallest, handsomest, and smartest boy in New England, and if a year were to consist of nothing but Sundays, no more clever fellow could be born in it. His only stupid trick was to go along to Cuba. He defended himself like a lion, but what could he do when there were a dozen Spaniards to one Yankee? He was therefore taken prisoner. As you know, gentlemen, most of his comrades were shot in the back, and others sent in chains to the Spanish quicksilver mines. How did he manage it, now, that he alone was freed?

"On the way to Havana a brilliant idea came into his mind. 'I have it,' he thought. 'I'll put on that the bigwigs in the government in Washington are my most intimate friends.' And straightway upon arriving in prison he demanded ink, pen, paper, and envelope, and wrote a letter to His Excellency Daniel Webster, Secretary of State of the United States in Washington, that read about as follows:

" 'Dan, old hoss! You will probably open your eyes wide when you get a letter from here from my pen. But as the old maid said when she broke her teapot: What has happened, has happened, and what good does it do to let out a damned wailing about it? To be sure, six months ago today, when we ate onion salad and roast pork at your home in Marshfield and polished off a dozen bottles of that choice old Madeira well known to you, I little dreamed that I would now be in this fix. But who can say what will happen to him tomorrow? If I had followed your suggestion when you advised me to accept the consulate in the Barbary States, at least I would not have been treated so barbarously as in this citadel, where they have shaved the hair from my head. Concha, I believe, is a good fellow, and if you'd put in a good word for me with the Spanish ambassador in Washington, I certainly would get off all right. Greet our mutual friend, the Secretary of War—when I got him appointed, I always called him Charley. Etc.'

"He wrote a similar letter to Henry Clay, gentlemen, and a third —to what other leader of the Whigs I do not know. These three letters came (naturally unsealed) to the prison commander, who sent them on to the captain general. The latter had hardly read them when he sent for my cousin, who appeared before him in a rather strange costume. Namely, in place of his clothing he had been given the uniform of a Spanish soldier compared to whom he was a giant. The cuffs were at his elbows, and the pantaloons on his legs played the role of knee pants. Picture also, gentlemen, the shaved-off head and beard, and you will not doubt that Concha could not help laughing in the face of this intimate friend of Webster and Clay. He looked like an enormous street urchin who had been put in a hothouse and there had outgrown his clothes in a single day. Cousin Korry noticed that his bait with the letters had worked, and he utilized the merry mood into which the general had been put by his appearance to apologize nicely and smartly. He had had to leave Bahia Honda too quickly to be able to take along his clothing, so an unknown benefactor, to whom he owed repeated thanks, had provided these. Concha told him he was free, got a respectable suit for him, asked him to convey his compliments to the gentlemen in Washington, and bought him a ticket for the steamer to New Orleans. There the captain is presently dealing in our Yankee clocks, and there you can hear the story repeated by him himself." (Here the captain's address was inserted.)

◇ ◇ ◇ On Wednesday evening we met, not far from a small town, the post coach coming toward us from Terre Haute. It lay overturned at the edge of a small forest running over a hill. The coachman, encouraged by the passengers, had raced down the hill at full gallop. In this wild chase the coach, running against a root, had been hurled up so violently that the jerk had broken the iron bolt that fastens the coach body to the wheel frame and had thrown the poor devil of a driver from the box. He had fallen so unfortunately that a hemorrhage had occurred and he was carried away as dead. Miraculously, only one of the occupants of the coach had suffered injury, having bitten away a piece of his tongue. If it had been the tongue that had incited that preceding wild chase, then this lesson could only have been salutary to it; and if I were the Jupiter of travelers, then I should regularly put an end to such a lack of common sense by shortening the organ with which it is expressed.

Early Thursday morning we crossed the Wabash into the state of Indiana. From TERRE HAUTE, a pretty, medium-sized city, a brand-new locomotive, which had been hitched before a crudely constructed wood shack set on wheels, transported us over a just-completed stretch of track to a post station twenty-five miles away. It was located in the midst of a primeval forest which here and later displayed magnificent trees and was interrupted only at great intervals by isolated clearings and settlements. Here the stagecoach was waiting for us again to take us through gloomy wild forests to another stop on the partially completed railroad. From here we rode in elegant cars to

## A WINTER JOURNEY

the capital of the state, INDIANAPOLIS. After a two-hour stop, which I utilized to inspect the beautiful capitol, we were again packed into a post coach which, after a night and a day, deposited us in HAMILTON on the Little Miami Railroad. By this means four of the nine of us—the others had remained in Eaton and Hamilton because of exhaustion—reached CINCINNATI at nine o'clock Friday evening after seventy hours without sleep.

Also here there was no time for lingering. Letters from New York advised me to speed up my trip, since the weather, which now was almost as warm as summer, could change very soon into such cold that the journey from Cleveland along the southeastern shore of Lake Erie would become impossible. Therefore farewells were quickly taken and a railroad ticket to the last-named city purchased. Sunday saw me in Columbus by noon and in the "Forest City" by evening. From here a section of track leads to the small town of PAINESVILLE. Using this, I arrived late Monday morning at the stagecoach station of the just-mentioned little place, and from now on, for three days and two nights, the torture I had experienced on the prairies of Illinois was repeated. Slowly the coach crept along the lakeshore, the beautiful green of which had been transformed by winter into an ugly dull gray, across the valleys of the emptying rivers and streams. The passengers walked through knee-deep snow for miles to make it easier for the horses on the slopes. Twice we had to right our coach, and three times the one following us, and although none of our traveling companions froze to death—which had happened to a group four days before—this fate could easily have befallen our driver when we were between ERIE and BUFFALO. It had suddenly become bitter cold again between midnight and morning. The coachman had fallen asleep unnoticed—perhaps because he had partaken too freely of the punch glass at the last station—and probably would not have waked up again if the all-too-long standing of the coach before an insignificant hill had not made us aware, just in time, how things were with the fellow. He was awakened only with effort, and when this had been accomplished, he was able neither to move nor to speak. Two of us now walked ahead through the snowdrifts as scouts, to warn of slopes and ravines. Two others who knew how to drive took the place of the driver, and the others pushed and pulled him into the coach. Thus we went at a snail's pace to the next tavern, three miles away, which we reached in about as many hours. There, with the help of several cups of hot coffee, we gave our invalid back to himself and his nags, and he now drove us cheerfully into the New Year.

No one will ever again experience the discomforts and terrors of such a land journey along Lake Erie, for the railroad from Dunkirk to Cleveland has been completed, and in a few years the National Road, which runs across the grass plains of Illinois, also will no longer see a post coach. Rapidly the West is drawing the East to it, and before twenty years have passed, all states of the quadrangle between the Ohio, the Mississippi, the Northern Lakes, and the eastern boundary of northern Pennsylvania will enjoy the same blessings of civilization as New England and New York.

◊ ◊ ◊ BUFFALO, where we arrived on New Year's Day at eleven in the morning, is a city like all other western metropolises, the plan and character of which we attempted to indicate in Saint Louis; they represent on a small scale what the mighty Yankee Republic is as a whole. As the latter was born from the sea, so those great centers of commerce were born from the rivers and lakes—a statement which can be applied to only a few of the metropolises of the European inland regions. As the latter, the North American Union, exhibits almost everywhere in all circumstances of life—with a regularity passing over into monotony—unconquered chaotic remnants, so the former, its cities, still show in their uniform straight streets hundreds of memories of the wilderness from which they have developed. As the Union, the Republic with its star-spangled banner, gives the impression more of the prodigious than of the solid and more of the provisional than of the completed, so does the memory of Saint Louis, Cincinnati, and even New York, with their miles-long streets and their colossal hotels—and, at the same time, their brick walls concealed behind marble fronts, their ugly backyards and dirty alleys, their wooden suburbs, and their ruins of innumerable fires.

Buffalo is the most important port on Lake Erie. Founded in 1801 and burned to the ground in 1812 by the English, it since has grown to a city of almost fifty thousand inhabitants. Because of the railroad from New York and various canals, it was, until the completion of the Erie Railroad, the main transit point of the emigration to the West. At present it has a rapidly growing rival in Dunkirk. The German population seems to be rather strong since firms with German names can be seen in all streets, and three German newspapers were published here during the year 1851. Also in Buffalo the winter exerted its influence upon commerce and traffic. Throughout the summer around 130 steamboats and a large number of sailing vessels travel between here and the other ports of the inland lakes. Now they were all frozen in, and with them a good part of the life of the city;

however, there still was some activity, especially on Main Street, where I stopped at Huff's Hotel.

I had chosen the route by Buffalo instead of the shorter way by Dunkirk since I did not want to leave America without having seen Niagara Falls. A twenty-two-mile railroad leads to the Falls; I took it to the natural wonder on January 2, in the company of a Scottish merchant I had met in the post coach from Painesville. In the small town which has sprung up around the Falls I unexpectedly met an old university friend, the former Reichstag member Thieme;[4] he had operated a small business in New York and was now supporting himself here as a schoolteacher. He became our Cicerone to the cataracts.

It is superfluous to describe the latter here in view of the tremendous number of detailed descriptions and illustrations that exist. The remark might suffice that the plunging mass of water of the mighty river makes a terrific impression at first sight, especially when viewed from below, and that the winter heightens this impression by freezing the mist rising from the foaming basin to form gigantic icicles on the rocky walls and to form all sorts of grotesque shapes upon the dwarf cedars that crown the Falls on the American side. However, upon further contemplation this impression is moderated, and finally little remains of the ruggedness, wildness, and frightfulness of its initial effect upon the spirit of the observer; rather, something gentle is felt in the phenomenon. It might further be mentioned that the frequently expressed opinion that Niagara requires some alpine scenery in the vicinity to attain perfection is asking too much. In what proportion would the mountains have to be created to correspond to the magnitude of the waterfall? The Alps, the Himalayas, and the Andes could not satisfy this requirement. By the way, it might be reported that the stone tower at the edge of Goat Island from which one looks down into Horseshoe Falls has not collapsed, as the newspapers claim, but it is still standing there as solidly as on the day of its completion. Finally it might be permitted to relegate the thunder of the cataracts, said to be audible miles away, to the area of poetic license. For as overwhelming as the rumbling and roaring are directly above the three falls, yet I strained my hearing organs in vain to hear their voice at the railroad station of the town, that is, about four hundred paces from the river. Since the same thing happened to my companions (although the day was absolutely windless), I must be permitted, at least in this regard, to be of the same opinion as my Scot when he remarked upon the return journey that the wonders of Niagara were *"not quite all they are cracked up for."*

## Moritz Busch · Travels

Ten miles from here is an Indian village inhabited by the remnants of the Tuscaroras. To the best of my knowledge they are the only redskins who live this side of the Mississippi, with the exception of the tribes in northern Michigan. They have a sort of queen whose civil list consists of the produce of a piece of land of three thousand acres, and they presently support themselves by farming. A few possess quite well-ordered properties; most of them, however (if our informant spoke the truth), live in filth and debauchery, and seldom does a market day pass that several of them do not wander through the streets of the village staggering drunk, a laughingstock to the white people—who even impute such offences to her dignity to Her Majesty the Queen. Their women prepare beadwork on velvet, purses and watchholders, knitting bags, shoes, etc., with which they and the inhabitants of Niagara Falls carry on a prosperous business since almost every visitor to the place takes away something as a souvenir. Also people who are not salesmen take part in this, and the workbag I brought home with me comes from the shop of a doctor of medicine who had one of the largest stocks of such articles.

◊ ◊ ◊ Led astray by a newspaper announcement that proclaimed that the way via CANANDAIGUA to the Erie Railroad was the cheapest and shortest route to New York, I struck out in this direction from Buffalo. If I made a mistake here, reaching my destination in forty-eight hours instead of the promised eighteen, I may perhaps console myself with the fact that this route possessed the advantage of being the more beautiful. In the matter of scenery, the region through which it passes is very much entitled to praise for its charm, variety, and—within certain limitations—for its magnificence.

Friends of the picturesque, in both Europe and America, have suffered many a severe loss through the construction of the railroads. With few exceptions every country turns its best sides toward its great highways. Everything connected with art does this quite naturally. Man likes to show himself and his achievements in the provinces as well as in the capitol. Now everything that has been created in this respect in the past has suffered considerable disturbance through the rise of the railroads, for one was often forced to avoid the beautiful for the sake of level land or to avoid expensive property. The attractively winding curves of the old roads, their rising and falling, the alternation of forest, meadow, and grainfield, have in large part been lost. One no longer travels through the best parts of cities and villages, but the traveler usually sees rows of sheds, warehouses, chimneys, and similar ugly features that spoil his viewing pleasure. Occasionally, however, an exception is encountered, and among these are not a few places along the Erie Railroad, especially where it borders Lake Seneca.

Here is the opportunity to reflect in a few words about the American landscape in general and about how it differs from ours. In this regard it must be generally noted that Europe displays to the senses far more varied scenes and far more elevated and mightier pictures than are found within the limits of North America, excluding the Rocky Mountains and the mountain ranges of New Mexico; that it exhibits a greater number of works of art; and that it bears the character of the polished and completed to a far greater degree than even the most populous states in the East of the Union. However, with this last statement no subordination of the New World to the Old World is intended. The lesser limitation on natural freedom manifest in all American landscapes and the abundance of small forests in them make individual sections extremely attractive. This applies particularly to the East, where many areas come close to being parklike, while the West as a rule still possesses too much forest and—with its unending rail fences and cornfields, its girdled and charred trees—presents almost anything but beautiful views. With that impression of the unfinished is connected—in another direction, to be sure—a feeling that something is lacking. While, in the course of time, a special character has developed in almost every European city (even the smallest), causing it to appear to us as an individual, almost all localities between the Hudson and the Mississippi, especially the smaller ones, look as though they were taken from one mold. When one has seen one beehive or one anthill, one has seen all; so when one has seen one of these groups of little white houses with green shutters, one has seen all the rest. Since the spirit is revealed in variety, one might feel inclined to deny it in this phenomenon—if one did not have to consider that the drive for the useful must first be fully satisfied before stirrings toward that lying beyond can awaken, even if one did not encounter such stirrings already here and there.

The question has been raised by admirers of natural beauty as to whether the presence or absence of isolated houses and farms is an important factor in the effect of landscapes, and since in this is expressed one of the differences between European and American scenery, I must devote somewhat more attention to the matter. If the cities and villages in a region are sufficiently numerous to catch the eye and if occasional groups of trees are located within the same, then the viewer does not deplore the deficiency so much because of the impression of comfort and lively beauty that such a distribution of human habitations produces to such an eminent degree. But a great deal depends upon the type of construction, and even more upon the color. Only in very special places and with very dim light—as in the forest regions of Pennsylvania or Ohio—is the contrast of white and green of pleasant effect. We are never dissatisfied with the natural tones of rock, for the mind willingly accepts the natural arrangements of nature; and although one color may be preferred to another now and then, they are all pleasing in their appropriate place. Thus one expects a marble building to be white, and the same can be said of other colors not laid on artificially. But I believe that most of us, if we consult our taste seriously, will prefer gray and other soft tones to all the more brilliant ones that art is able to produce. In this respect the European landscape has the advantage over the American, where the majority of houses are built of wood and painted with the whitest white, from which the green shutters stand out. Only in a very favorable situation does this have a pleasing effect; in most cases it is offensive. A variously colored work of architecture is, under most circumstances, almost as peculiar as a painted column. The bright green often chosen for this purpose is particularly repulsive. If one should place a house, that in this manner cries out to the world its master's lack of taste, next to another, the shutters of which are of a darker shade, and if one should compare them to a third displaying only one color on its entire exterior, then anyone endowed with some feeling for beauty would declare that the builder of the last was the most civilized and that the builder of the first was the most uncultured of the three.

If we now return to the great distinguishing characteristics of America and Europe in the matter of landscape, then the first (as well as I am able to judge from my own observations, from the reports of others, and from illustrations) is inferior to the latter in regard to its mountain regions and superior in regard to its rivers. The mountain landscapes of the United States cannot possess that defiantly wild character and those gigantic shapes that are peculiar to granite formations. Instead the American praises—rightly—his many beautiful bodies of water. Since they have in large part remained unsung and unpictured up until now, art in general has been able to do very little with them. But where this has occurred—for example, on the Hudson and the Ohio, as well as on a few of the smaller lakes in the state of New York—there they and their innumerable islands and delightful wooded shores exert an extremely effective influence upon the charms of the region.

It has been asserted by scientific writers that the western continent shows many signs of an earlier origin than does the surface of Europe, and with great acumen they have collected a mass of evidence for this—which recently, however, has been attacked several times and in part refuted. I am too little of a geologist and, besides, too little traveled to intervene in this controversy. But here even the eye of the layman is struck by a certain freshness, youthfulness, not to say crudeness in the natural formations, just as in the creations of the human hand. It's possible that I deceived myself now and then by taking the youthful culture for a more youthful nature. Generally, however, the thought returned too often, even with the soberest consideration, for me to dismiss it from my mind. One knows of no mountain peaks this side of the Mississippi that have the rugged, eroded appearance, washed away to nakedness, that hundreds possess in Europe. Almost everywhere in America that the eye rests upon mountain features it encounters rounded outlines that are covered with a fresh green—if they show any definite color at all. I say this without regard for the more recently settled regions; rather, I am talking mainly about the old states. The banks of the Hudson, for example, with their hills and windings, their mountains and coves, reveal in no place the effect of time as clearly as does the valley of the Rhine or any other German river, and it frequently seemed to me that this feature differentiating between "over there" and "here" could also be observed in other phenomena.

In conclusion, still another difference in the scenery of Europe and America should be mentioned, but it stands out sharply only if the Catholic regions of the former are drawn into the comparison. Over there the city with its gray exterior lines and medieval walls is grouped almost without exception about the high roof and tower of the church. How different it is here! A half dozen ugly shaped and yet presumptuously projecting little towers and cupolas, painted in screaming colors, look out over the town, while the main building obviously is the tavern. That can be easily explained and satisfactorily excused. But it doesn't do the friend of the picturesque much good. It jars his feelings and often even repels him. No relatively unbiased person will want to coerce consciences to attain pretty landscapes; but this is one of the hundreds of cases in which the thoughtful mind finds cause to regret that the church in America has not retained more of the character of the Catholic Church.

CONCLUSION

◇ ◇ ◇ WHEN fragments of the observations and studies put down in the preceding chapters were shown to a friend, the question was raised as to whether a unity could be found in the diversity of the phenomena in the life and literature of the North Americans, or, in other words, whether or not the citizens of the United States already bear the character of a nation. At that time, when the view was still too much engaged by the variability of the subject, the answer had to be postponed for further collection and reflection. If, however, there was present at that time an inclination to answer the question in the negative, now, after further inspection of the facts, it must be answered affirmatively—in the sense that the character formation does not yet appear to be completed, but a clearly recognizable trait runs through the nation in which is stamped the growth and development of a character different from that of all other nations.

As with individuals, so it is also with nations. Both have definite goals and features by which they are distinguished from others. In regard to the former (the goals), nations are less aware of them than individuals are; yet they control both the life of the individual and the history of the nation. Often the striving of a nation is directed toward a strengthening of the central power. France is an example of this. Often it is directed toward the development of an aristocracy, as in old Venice. Often it appears as military ambition, as, say, in old Rome, or as the craving for power of the church, as in the new Rome. This object of the struggles of a nation can be a constant one and prevail during its entire history. It can also be a merely temporary one; for it cannot be expected that a human or group of humans will

CONCLUSION

pursue a single objective without deviating occasionally from the main path. America, now, is a young country populated by diverse elements; in addition these elements have different interests in the West than in the East, different interests in the North than in the South. With the irresolution resulting from this, it is not easy to say what is the chief aspiration of the nation. However, if we look at its annals, we recognize at once that its basic impulse is the love of individual freedom. It is pushing its way—in part consciously, in part merely instinctively—toward democracy, the government of all, by all, for all. This fact is particularly manifest in New England, and New England once was (and to a certain extent still is) the soul of America. Nevertheless, there are for individuals as for nations also temporary secondary goals, and these are pursued so actively at times that the observer can be deceived about the constant basic impulse. Wealth is such a secondary goal in America at present. Currently the dollar is the dominant goal in the consciousness of the people. The passion for it has increased astoundingly since the beginning of the century, and the two roads that lead to it—business and politics— are almost the only ones upon which the so-called better class is to be encountered.

To the goals correspond certain traits in the life of the individuals as well as of the nations. Just as every nation has its destiny, so every nation has its character. If we look over the history of every single nation, we encounter a pattern that advances toward us continually—sometimes clear, sometimes more blurred—from the language, the laws, the religion, the customs, the art, and the literature. Thus the Hebrews appear to us as the religious people and the Greeks as the beautiful people. Thus we find in the Romans the idea of justice, the genius of legislation. Thus we find among the Anglo-Saxons from Hengist and Horsa to Sir Robert Peel[1] the same practical and egoistical, bold and active race that acts more as a servant of intellect than as a child of reason, relies more upon experience and facts than upon the inner light of ideas, is militarily efficient more through strength and courage than through the love of fame, avoids no obstacles that nature or man puts in its way, seeks constantly to colonize and incorporate distant lands in its sphere, puts business above all poetizing and philosophizing, loves liberty and law, and—not to omit the lesser traits—is fond of handsome horses and dogs and is devoted to strong drink.

Just as the basic impulse of a nation occasionally disappears for a time behind its secondary endeavors, so also its basic pattern is not without the relief and shadows of subordinate characteristics. These vary with the circumstances and frequently change the physiognomy of the nationality so much that it becomes difficult to recognize the character concealed beneath them. They are either offshoots of the main type or results of external factors, such as climate, soil, natural events, etc. Thus modifications of the national character take place constantly, but through all the change perseveres a calm spirit, the character nucleus. Once the Israelites were a nation of shepherds, today they are merchants; but upon closer inspection the same nature is found in them as in the days when David and Solomon were kings. If we apply this to the Americans, then the *idea of liberty* stands out incontrovertibly as the character nucleus of the nation, and its unfolding to the earth-shading tree is the destiny of America in the organism of history.[2]

It is not to be denied that when this yardstick is applied, much in the life of the Americans appears to be an exception. It is true that they sell the freedom of three million humans—who without a doubt are inferior to them mentally as well as physically, but who nevertheless are humans—for an annual income of less than three million bales of cotton. And it is likewise true that they have knowingly trodden under foot sacred rights in other connections. Nonetheless, however, and despite all exceptions, in the history as well as in the present of the nation nothing appears with such clearness as that love for individual liberty and that striving to realize it.

I have attempted to substantiate this in preceding chapters. Here we are more concerned with those subordinate characteristics of the youthful nation that, branching off from its character or having come to it from the outside, modify that basic pattern and in part impair that basic impulse. They are signs of the times, and it is important to examine carefully the most prominent of them if one wishes to get a correct picture of the nation.

The first of these characteristics is hostility toward all authority. Every single thing must state its reason and say why it exists and what justifies it to be so and not otherwise. From this results an absolute lack of respect, which not infrequently becomes impiety. Nowhere does the past count as little as here. "Our fathers did it this way," someone says. "Well, what does that mean?" answers the American. "Well, now, our fathers were giants compared to us," replies the friend of the past. "Oh, not in the least," responds the

## CONCLUSION

other. "They were nothing but big boys, and we are not only a great deal taller, but, standing upon their shoulders, we can see a great deal farther. We are the old ones, not they, and so we very gladly accept their wisdom and thank God for it, but keep off our necks with their authority." Furthermore, the example of ancient nations neither frightens the American nor does it teach him. Slavery was a curse for Athens and Rome. "It makes no difference to us," says Jonathan. "We aren't Greeks or Romans, but republicans and good Christians of the New World. We live in the nineteenth century, and although slavery may have caused all sorts of trouble there and at that time, it is an advantage for us—for we make money with it." Contemporary nations are just as little an example. No ordinary American wants to listen when the institutions of other nations, for example, in school or military matters, are praised. He understands all that much better, and even if he didn't understand it better, it would still be unpatriotic to admit a superiority of foreign states. To him the Mexican War is a miracle of modern military leadership that has covered him with eternal fame.

But while he stubbornly refuses to admit and emulate the good points of other nations, he imitates their follies and weaknesses without hesitation—especially in the higher classes of society. Like all upstarts he makes a point of aristocratic customs, hoping that strangers will admire him if he adopts a coat of arms with lions and leopards instead of with the hand tools that enabled him to earn the money to have it painted.

From this hatred of all authority—which, however, does not prevent him from urgently inquiring what they think of him in Europe—comes an aversion toward everything old. This is one of the explanations for the continual change in all affairs of the American. His house, his books, even his churches must always be new. The frame house that the eye encounters so frequently here, freshly painted every year if possible, is a suitable emblem for this incessant striving for renewal. But this love of change is also expressed in more important matters. It is asked: What right to existence does this or that law have? Upon what is the existence of the government based? Who gives the majority the right to dictate its will to the minority, to limit commerce, levy taxes, and the like? If the entire nation forms a committee to make decisions about an important matter, then certainly a shoemaker or a brushmaker will form a committee all by himself and take the opposite position. The state of South Carolina is a nice little sample of this kind of self-reliance and this disregard of all authority. This tiny little speck of land, with scarcely half as many free white inhabitants as the city of New York, believes, nonetheless, that it represents the best part of the patriotism and the political wisdom of the nation. This "chivalrous" little state crows with swollen comb: If the Union does not pass such laws as suit us, if it doesn't permit us the expansion of our institutions and doesn't grant us the tariff that we desire, then we'll say "No," we'll secede from the federation, and we'll leave the other twenty-nine states to their fate.

It's the same in church matters. America is the land of heresies and sects, partly because it is hostile to any authority. If a congregation of believers excommunicates a small pastor in some obscure corner because of deviating views, he immediately strikes an attitude and hurls an anathema at it. To be sure, there are also people in America who are interested in antiquity, but they appear in the crowd like individual stragglers of a bygone race. The present permits them a place and listens to them when they speak enthusiastically of old armor that has been discovered in an old ruin or hollow tree, of an Indian Bible dug up from the ground, or of fossilized mammoth bones. But they permit these and other remnants of the past to exert absolutely no influence upon the matters closest to their hearts, such as commerce, factories, and politics.

A second characteristic of the American is a certain philosophical trait, manifest in a questioning and searching after ultimate causes and general ideas. To be sure, one first looks for the facts, but then he looks immediately for the law of the fact and finally for the reason for the law. A sign of this is to be found in the titles of books and in the public lectures of traveling scholars. One is less concerned with treatises about the eye, the ear, and sleep; rather, one discusses the "philosophy" of seeing, hearing, and sleeping. Theological sects are not always the first to feel such a movement among the people. Still, almost all of them here, from the Episcopalians down to the Quakers, have a philosophical faction that has prospects of overcoming the conservative faction. This inclination has its representatives even in the pulpits, and it frequently happens that the "philosophy" of religion is preached to a devout circle.

This holds true particularly in the East. There the young ladies have seriously taken up Fourier's ideas, the best and deepest thoughts of Germany are accepted and considered even more readily than in England, and shopkeepers and tailors lend an attentive ear when Agassiz and Emerson, men who certainly do not speak in a very

CONCLUSION

popular vein, announce a series of lectures.* There is no doubt that thereby many an error slips in and that many a person participates simply for the sake of fashion, but even the circumstance that it has become the fashion indicates that such a philosophical trait runs through the nation. No doubt, too, that these opposing tendencies exist principally in the area of the church and that the old shouting about irreligion and freethinking often sounds louder than the word of the innovators. But despite all this it is evident that the future belongs to the latter, even though they will never be able to control the atheism that here and there makes a great show.

Despite this deep-running impulse, however, a closer examination shows a lamentable lack of principles. The validity of the traditional has been disavowed, but the authority of truth and justice has not yet been duly accepted. One does not want to be regarded as a boy but is not yet old enough to step forth as a man who is aware of his intentions. So nothing is established as yet, and America presents the picture of a continual ebb and flow of opposing principles. In politics no party has yet completely decided whether commerce should be restricted by laws or whether it might not be better to leave it to the people to buy where they can get the goods most cheaply and to sell where the most is paid. A similar indecision of opinion was revealed when the slavery question seemed to get into conflict with the stability of the Union, and it's no different with the internal improvements that the Democrats will finally have to leave to the central power to a certain degree. It's the same in matters of faith. Some declare that for them the Bible no longer is valid as the Supreme Court, but they dare not replace it with reason and conscience. Others act as though the Holy Scriptures were the highest authority for them, but if they should be asked their opinion about the miraculous birth and resurrection of Christ, they'd avoid answering with a "Yes" or "No."

A third characteristic of the American people is the unusual intensity of their living and striving, shown in their actions and talk, in their speculations, and in the "revivals" of the more serious sects. Everything that is done appears an exaggeration—and in most

* Also Theodore Parker, the reformatory Congregational preacher in Boston, is to be kept in mind; we adopted part of the above from his intelligent judgment about American conditions. His solid lectures, based upon a unique philosophy and an extensive education, attracted so many listeners that no church was able to hold them. He is considered one of the most influential leaders of the Progress Party of Massachusetts. As we hear, a translation of the most interesting of his sermons and essays will soon leave the press in Leipzig.

cases it is. Perhaps the Americans among all peoples have the most self-confidence, and so they behave like heaven-stormers—which often appears titanic, sometimes ridiculous. The soul of the Yankee leaves its work as soon as it's finished. His forefathers considered the Revolution a great deed. But he is already thinking about quite different revolutions. In his high spirits, which spring from his superabundance of vigor, he would like to join up with the entire world, with nature as well as with men. He considers a railroad from the Mississippi to the Pacific as a trifle. He talked about the incorporation of northern Mexico, and he effected it. He is now reaching for Cuba, for Central America, for the whole western continent—and he will take it. His deeds are not to be underestimated, but his hopes and designs go far beyond them.

If this intensity of living and hoping has its good side, it also has its bad. It produces haste, superficiality, and vanity. Seldom does it accomplish a completed work. English and German goods usually bear the mark of solidity, and French that of good taste—American goods usually lack both. One strives for the big, the many, and the spacious—not for strength and quality. One forgets that a thoughtful procedure is the shortest route to any goal and that a person who is certain about the end of his journey before he departs travels better than one who only thinks a little about it along the way. In America speed is the chief requirement of all thoughts and desires. A Yankee vessel is recognized from a distance by the enormous number of sails that it carries. A Yankee state revises its constitution in such a rapid manner that a European would be almost frightened by it. In education the goal is not to learn as much as possible but to snatch up rapidly as much as is absolutely necessary. From school the boy plunges quickly into business life, and here his efforts are directed toward becoming rich rapidly—in this it frequently happens that he falls to the ground two or three times in the course of his life. His entire existence is a journey on a steamboat or railroad. He can't even remain quiet in sitting, so he puts his chairs upon rockers. Everything is activity, running and rushing. One is so bent upon creating and working that one has no time for enjoying and hence enjoys very little of the poetry of life. America has only two annual festivals,* and even at these there is more noise than pleasure. Everything is done "in less than no time," from the tanning of a cowhide to the training of a soul for the work and earning of life;

* Christmas and the Fourth of July, the day of the Declaration of Independence.

## CONCLUSION

and if flying is ever invented, it certainly will be done in the United States.

A fourth characteristic of the American way is its exaggerated love for material things. This is not limited to preferring the useful to the beautiful but consists in putting the external in place of the higher and more valuable internal and in putting money above the value of man. The American does not comprehend that a great man may be poor, and so the great man sells himself, and the crowd calls it a good piece of business. An otherwise quite intelligent and cultivated gentleman didn't know how to honor a painter except by pointing out that he had earned $20,000 with his paintings. It was typical that in Boston a man believed that he was praising a distinguished writer by remarking that his books had earned him more money than anyone else in the field.

One can object that other nations suffer from the same deficiency. True, but then one overlooks the difference. Elsewhere a man's possessions—his rank and wealth—are placed above the man himself, and this sort of materialism is not inconsistent with public opinion. In America it is an insult to the same and a challenge to the basic principle of the country. Moreover, in most civilized nations there is a hereditary propertied class who devote their lives to the sciences and arts and thus rise above the sphere of merely material elegance surrounding them. This class is rarely found in America. Young, rich people infrequently turn themselves to higher and nobler endeavors, but usually they strive either to transform their talents into gold or their gold into splendid houses, furnishings, coaches, and horses. If Socrates came to Boston, the Athens of the western continent, and set about to outwit the stockbrokers of the exchange (as he once did the Sophists), he would reap praise. On the other hand, if he followed his old method, the crowd would soon have forgotten him.

It is a feature of this disgusting materialism that one is proud of the wealth, which is but accumulated labor, and ashamed of the labor, which merely represents the striving for wealth. With all the talk about democracy, labor is honored less in the eyes of many Americans than in Berlin or Leipzig. Almost everyone whose exertions have been crowned by success is ashamed of the ladder by which he rose. The aristocrat who arrived in New York thirty years ago by the travel method of the apostles,[3] carrying all his worldly goods wrapped up in a cotton kerchief, becomes red when he recalls that his father was a drayman or cobbler and that out in the country live a couple dozen cousins with his name who are distinguished only for their large hands and excellent memories.

It is not surprising that superficial souls traveling here laugh at such absurdities. The person looking more deeply smiles no less about it, but he sees the causes and predicts the future end to this foolishness. Every nation has its aristocracy. In one country it is permanent, based upon the noble blood which, flowing in the veins of ancestors, has performed valiant deeds; in another country it is based upon wealth, which comes and goes. This is the case with the American aristocracy. However, peace is better than war, labor is nobler than the use of the sword, the aristocracy of money is in itself undoubtedly more valuable than that of blood. It is an absurdity only in the manner in which it is expressed in America: not wanting to look back to where its value and justification lie, looking down with the insolence of the parvenu upon those who are climbing up along the same route. But this pleasure in material possession still performs certain services for the nation, goading it to incessant activity and—as low as the motivation might be—leading to progress. It is a praiseworthy ambition when a people aspires to acquire as much useful property as possible. It becomes an evil only when money is sought as God and an excess of material goods as the final goal and not as a means. Never yet was a nation too rich, although many a nation has lost its soul in the striving for material possessions.

There are many contradictions in these secondary characteristics of the American way; they must be considered as signs of the times. Quality struggles with quantity; not a single one [of these characteristics] strives for harmonious relationships [with the others], and so they appear as national weaknesses. Whether these will improve, and soon, is a question that the future will answer. The present can only hope. For these deficiencies are merely incidental, as unpleasantly as they may affect us. They come from external circumstances and especially from the situation of the nation that has been fused together from heterogeneous elements and dwells upon a new, still-untamed soil. They do not belong to the basic idea of America and in their present form are even hostile to it. But some day that aversion to all authority and that philosophical impulse will lead the nation to the unique internal regulation of its life, and then the time of the reconciliation of those contradictions will dawn. The ebb and flow will become a mighty stream, its fullness of life driven to its destination by definite moral principles, restrained from

## CONCLUSION

flooding, and kept from twisting paths. America has already achieved the unlimited in the area of the material. Never was a country so full of grain and cattle and all food and necessities. The struggle for these things occupies an important position in the metamorphosis of mankind. Nowhere is its favorable effect more visible than in America, where in less than two generations the Irish semisavage becomes a respected, industrious, moderate, and cultured citizen. Once this is completed, the nation will proceed to the realization of its great national idea and begin, first at home, then over the entire earth (we hope), the sublime work that lies as a germ in the nucleus of its character.

From new perceptions and previously unheard-of ideas new forms of social life will originate, compared to which the present day will appear like the barbarism of the Middle Ages. An American art will blossom—no tasteless imitation of the creations of the Old World but a fresh, independent weaving and working. An American literature will develop that satisfies the country and its character, that no longer requires alms from beyond the sea, and that does something other than import and cite. Finally, also, an American church will be formed upon the ruins of the present-day sectarianism —a marriage of the faith content with its present-day enemy, reason, and a re-creation and renewal of aging Christianity by the spirit of liberty. No genius has appeared as yet to draw the plans for the construction of this holy temple; not even the foundation stone has been laid as yet. But in many of the hundreds of little churches and chapels in which Americans now worship, the presentiment is nourished in the belief in the millennium that its construction is no longer as far off as many of the so-called signs of the times would indicate. For this transformation of our race in and through the genius of the New World, this transfigured revival of the Old World in the New, *is* the Millennium!

# EDITOR'S NOTES

## Chapter 1

1. Robert Livingston Stevens (1787–1856), the noted American marine architect, decided that a ship's speed could be increased by reducing the skin friction. In 1849 he built a ship, the *John Neilson*, in which bubbles were forced under the steamer's bottom (the planks were not filled with air as Busch reports). This increased its speed considerably, but not enough to pay for the installation and pumping. S. C. Gilfillan, *Inventing the Ship* (Chicago: Follett, 1935), pp. 240–41.

2. Fröbel (1805–1893) was a nephew of the famous educator Friedrich Fröbel. A professor of mineralogy at the Technische Hochschule in Zürich, he was elected to the Frankfurt Parliament. After taking part in the October (1848) Revolution in Vienna, he was arrested, condemned to death, and pardoned; he fled in 1849 to the U.S., where he edited the *Deutsche Tribüne* in New York. In 1850 he went to Nicaragua to establish a colony of German refugees, but the plan was a failure. He later engaged in commercial ventures in Mexico and in 1855 became editor of a San Francisco paper. Fröbel's career and those of many of the refugees encountered by Busch in America are described in Adolf E. Zucker, ed., *The Forty-eighters* (New York: Columbia University Press, 1950).

3. As German immigrants poured into the United States in unheard-of numbers, various travel agencies were established, largely for the purpose of profiting from the mass movement. One such office was that opened in New York in 1850 by three Forty-eighters: Franz Zitz, Friedrich Kapp, and Fröbel. However, it was not very successful: Fröbel soon departed for Central America, Kapp apparently was too honest to put his heart into the business, and the competition was very strong (many of the competitors had already become American citizens and thus had an advantage).

4. An organization founded in 1784 by a number of prominent German-Americans in New York. By the mid-nineteenth century, when it had about 500 members, the Society's main function was to protect and assist newly arrived German immigrants, warning them against pitfalls and providing medical and financial help. A full account of the Society's activities can be found in Anton Eickhoff, *In der neuen Heimath* (New York: E. Steiger, 1884), published as part of the organization's centennial observance.

5. *Phelps's Travellers' guide through the United States; containing up-*

## Editor's Notes

*wards of seven hundred rail-road, canal, and stage and steam-boat routes, accompanied with a new map of the United States* (New York: Ensigns & Thayer, 1849), supposedly compiled by one Humphrey Phelps.

6. Philippe Ricord (1800–1889) was born in Baltimore but went to France in 1820, received his medical degree, and had a distinguished career as a surgeon. He was chief surgeon at l'Hôpital des Vénériens du Midi from 1831 until 1860, investigating the nature of and developing treatments for venereal diseases.

7. The publishing firm of Gottfried Basse in Quedlinburg (Central Germany), later transferred to Leipzig. In the early nineteenth century it was well known for publishing trash.

8. Theobald M. Mathew was an Irish temperance reformer who, after succeeding in partially drying up Great Britain and Ireland in the 1840s, made a very successful tour of the United States in 1849–1851.

9. The more recent, post-1848 emigrants from Germany.

10. The founder (in 1845) of the religious sect known as the Millerites or Adventists. He had prophesied that the second coming of Christ would take place in 1843.

11. An expedition undertaken in 1851 by American volunteers to free Cuba from the Spanish yoke. See also n. 3, chap. 9.

12. An allusion to the lines by Goethe, *Faust* I, "Walpurgis-Night's Dream" (or "Intermezzo"): "The Blocksberg has a summit broad, / Like Germany's Parnassus." Bayard Taylor translation (New York: Modern Library, 1950), p. 165. The Brocken (*Blocksberg*) is the highest peak of the Harz Mountains in Central Germany and the source of much poetic inspiration.

13. The careers of these three charlatans, or "pill-pushers," are described in detail in chap. 2.

14. Louis (Lajos) Kossuth (1802–1894) was the leader of the Revolution of 1848 in Hungary. After the failure of the uprising he was forced to flee to Turkey, where he was imprisoned. Through the efforts of Great Britain and the United States he was released in 1851. Soon after, he toured America to raise funds for another attempt to set Hungary free. The Germans and their press responded most eagerly to the "Kossuth craze": as he journeyed from city to city, Kossuth was met by wild enthusiasm. Carl F. Wittke, *Refugees of Revolution* (Philadelphia: University of Pennsylvania Press, 1952), pp. 96–99.

15. A phrase from the German poet's "Ode to Joy."

16. Mephistopheles describes himself in Goethe's *Faust* I, "The Study," as "Part of that Power, not understood, / Which always wills the Bad, and always works the Good." Bayard Taylor translation, p. 46.

17. A phrase in the famous Grimm fairytale "The Table, the Ass, and the Stick."

18. A famous (and competent) physician of the seventeenth century who because of his commercial tendencies became a model of the medical quack and the hero of a popular German folksong, "Ich bin der Doctor Eisenbart."

19. Founded in Vienna in 1776 by Emperor Joseph II (renamed the *Burgtheater* after the dissolution of the Empire in 1918), this theater, specializing in productions of the classics, has long had the reputation of being probably the best German-language theater.

20. Karl Peter Heinzen (1809–1880) was one of the most radical of the Forty-eighters. After an early career characterized by much storm and stress (he was expelled from the University of Bonn for a revolutionary speech), in January 1848 he came to New York, where he edited the *Deutsche Schnellpost*. As soon as the Revolution broke out, he hastened back to Germany and took an active part in the Baden uprising (antagonizing most of the other leaders). Upon the failure of the movement he fled to Switzerland, from which

## EDITOR'S NOTES

country he was subsequently deported, arriving back in the U.S. in 1850. During the remainder of his life in America he edited various German-language newspapers, all of them dominated by his absolutely radical spirit, reflected in a brutal use of invective and a narrow, dogmatic intolerance. "A born satirist, he spared neither friend nor foe; opposition he could not tolerate; the value of tact and cooperation he never learned." *Dictionary of American Biography*, s.v. "Heinzen, Karl Peter." The best account of his career is to be found in Carl F. Wittke, *Against the Current: The Life of Karl Heinzen* (Chicago: University of Chicago Press, 1945).

21. Ferdinand Fenner von Fenneberg (d. 1858) was a refugee from the Vienna Revolution, where he had been first adjutant to Wenzel Messenhauser. Editor of a number of well-known German-language newspapers in Ohio and Kentucky, he was a capable journalist but changed jobs so frequently that many accused him of being "a mere opportunist." Carl F. Wittke, *The German-Language Press in America* (Lexington: University of Kentucky Press, 1957), p. 88. By the time of Busch's arrival in Ohio he had transferred from the Cleveland *Germania* to the Cincinnati *Republikaner*.

22. Much of the material concerning Columbus can be found in Henry Howe, *Historical Collections of Ohio* (Cincinnati, Ohio: Bradley & Anthony, 1850), pp. 172–76.

## Chapter 2

1. The first nineteen pages of this chapter have been omitted. They relate the early history of Cincinnati and describe political and economic features—information Busch gained from various secondary sources.

2. General Arthur von Görgey was commander of the Hungarian National Army and succeeded Kossuth as leader of the Hungarian Revolution. When Russia intervened in 1849, Görgey surrendered to the Russians, for which he was branded a "traitor" by the nationalists.

3. See n. 14, chap. 1.

4. Not the more famous Erie Canal in New York state, but the Miami and Erie Canal from Cincinnati to Dayton.

5. It has not been possible to identify Cousin Theodore or any of the Cincinnatians mentioned later in the text by initial only.

6. A collection of devotional poems and hymns, *Morgen- und Abendopfer in Gesängen*, published by Johann H. W. Witschel in 1803. Although of but slight poetic value, the volume was probably the most popular such work in German throughout the nineteenth century.

7. Probably *Cincinnati in 1810*, found in Howe, *Ohio*, p. 217.

8. An additional page of such testimonials has been omitted in the translation.

9. The book of the Apocrypha called Ecclesiasticus is known in German as *Das Buch Jesus Sirach*. The quotation is from 3:24.

10. Quite possibly Busch was thinking of August Moor, a German who came to Cincinnati in 1833. After serving in the Mexican War, Moor was made major general of the First Division of the Ohio Militia. *History of Cincinnati and Hamilton County, Ohio* (Cincinnati, Ohio: S. B. Nelson, 1894), pp. 273–74.

11. Term applied by the conservatives to the democratic, unified German government demanded by the radical revolutionaries of 1848–1849.

12. A type of confidence game. Busch's detailed, eight-page description of this particular fraud (in which a "greenhorn" buys a brass watch, believing it to be solid gold) has been omitted.

13. The career of Nicholas Longworth, Sr., one of the most influential of the early Cincinnati citizens, is described in detail in chap. 5.

14. A small town in Indiana, seat of Switzerland County, on the Ohio

## Editor's Notes

River downstream from Cincinnati; founded in 1801 by Swiss emigrants who here planted the first grapes imported from Europe.

15. Most of the following material concerning grape culture is taken from Charles Cist, *Cincinnati in 1851* (Cincinnati, Ohio: Wm. H. Moore, 1851), pp. 266–67.

16. Noted German architect (d. 1318), builder of the Strassburg cathedral; immortalized by Goethe in his essay "Von deutscher Baukunst" (1772).

17. Two pages of statistics concerning the Catholic Church in America have been omitted.

18. The Hungarian refugee and freethinker Samuel Ludvigh published various editions of *Die Fackel* (*The Torch*) and several other newspapers.

19. Radical organizations established in Germany and later imported to the U.S., where a few were started in the larger cities in the 1840s. However, the greatest stimulus and support for these *Freie Gemeinde* came from the refugees of 1848. They represented "a rationalist revolt against supernaturalism, clericalism, and dogmatism." Wittke, *Refugees*, pp. 122–46.

20. See n. 20, chap. 1.

21. Goethe's *Faust* I, "Walpurgis-Night's Dream," Bayard Taylor translation, p. 168.

22. A German weekly published in Cincinnati in 1851 by a Mrs. Stahl and edited by the Revs. Suhr, Kroell (probably the "pastor Kr." of p. 51 of the text), Goebel, and Grassow, pastors of United Evangelical churches. Cist adds: "These are all Rationalist Churches." *Cincinnati*, p. 82.

23. It should be kept in mind that in Luther's Bible translation, which Busch undoubtedly used, the Sixth Commandment is the injunction against adultery.

24. A second outbreak of the Revolution occurred in Baden in 1849. The grand duke and his government fled to France, leaving power in the hands of a provisional revolutionary government. The president of the Assembly was Lorenz Brentano; in 1851 he was living in Kalamazoo, Michigan, making it unlikely that he was a candidate for the pastorate in Cincinnati. However, the candidate's reported background seems to point to Gustav Wilhelm Eisenlohr, a Cincinnatian who had served as a pastor in the Black Forest, had fought in the Revolutionary Army, and had escaped sentence for treason by promising to leave the country. It is reported that he subsequently held a pastorate in Cincinnati and edited the *Protestantische Zeitblätter* for twenty years. Zucker, *Forty-eighters*, pp. 291–92.

## Chapter 3

1. German Lutheran theologians of the seventeenth century. Abraham Calov (Calovius) was the chief representative of Lutheran orthodoxy. Johannes Andreas Quenstedt was more moderate and showed an inclination to reform.

2. Justinius Kerner, German poet (b. 1786, d. Weinsburg 1862). A physician by profession, he practiced in several towns in Germany. He was a champion of occultism on a rational basis and wrote poetry that is fanciful and full of strange, fantastic humor.

3. A religious movement started in Pennsylvania by the followers of Jacob Albright (Albrecht); a forerunner of the present-day Evangelical United Brethren Church.

4. The Shaker community of Watervliet (also called Beulah), Ohio, was organized in 1806, comprised two "families," and had a maximum membership of about 100 at any one time and a total membership of about 127 during the period of the settlement's existence. It was sold in 1910, the surviving members moving to Union Village, Ohio. Edward D. Andrews, *The People Called Shakers* (New York: Oxford University Press, 1953), p. 291.

## EDITOR'S NOTES

5. From the description it appears that Busch observed a flock of the now extinct passenger pigeons.

6. Busch's use of the term "communists" (*Kommunisten*) is of more than ordinary interest, for in 1851 it was still relatively unknown both in Germany and in America—at least as a description of the members of various socialistic communities or common-property associations. In Germany Berthold Auerbach spoke of the word as "brandnew" in 1846.

7. Elder Richard Pelham (b. 1797 in Indiana near Louisville, d. 1873 at Union Village, Ohio) was one of the pioneer Shakers; he helped organize the community at North Union, near Cleveland, in 1822. Later, in 1847, he was sent to become an assistant in the elders' order at Watervliet, becoming First Elder in 1850. He "was considered by the Shakers to have been an extraordinary man, and intellectually had no superior among them." John P. MacLean, *Shakers of Ohio* (Columbus, Ohio, Heer Printing Co., 1907), p. 170.

8. From Molière's comedy *George Dandin* (1668), act 1, sc. 9. George brings trouble upon his own head by marrying above his station. The original uses the *vous* form ("Vous l'avez voulu"), but in Germany the French phrase is commonly altered to the *tu* form.

9. It has not been possible to identify David. The scanty records of the Watervliet community, published by MacLean in *Shakers of Ohio*, mention no deacon by name until 1854. Since David apparently was a trustee or office deacon, handling the business affairs of the community, he may have been the David Price listed in the records in 1832 as having been "sent from Union Village to act as gardener and peddlar." Or he may have been the David Eastwood who in 1859 "removed to the Office at South Family."

10. Here, as throughout the text, Busch gives the temperature in Réaumur degrees, the system commonly used in Germany for household thermometers. Fifteen degrees Réaumur would be about 66 degrees Fahrenheit.

11. Karl August Hase, professor of church history at Jena from 1830 until his death in 1890, first published his popular *Kirchengeschichte* in 1834.

12. It has not been possible to discover the original English texts of any of the Shaker hymns translated into German by Busch. Although Shaker songs—particularly those composed during the Great Revival of 1837 and in the following decade—appeared in such great numbers, "that, for purposes of use and preservation, the ministry directed that all be recorded in written hymnals," this was usually done in handwritten notebooks, most of which have been lost. Edward D. Andrews, *The Gift to Be Simple* (New York: J. J. Augustin, 1940), p. 21. It is likely that Brother Harmon's and David's songbooks, mentioned by Busch as his sources, experienced this fate. Nevertheless, the themes and many of the phrases of the songs translated by Busch show up in various forms in the collections of Andrews and others.

13. Busch's description of the tall deacon dancing alongside the short, fat brother with the "Falstaff belly" recalls two of the figures in a lithograph made by A. Imbert, New York, about 1830, and later copied by Currier, Kellogg, and other lithographers. It is reproduced in Howe, *Ohio*, p. 502, and as the frontispiece in *The Gift to Be Simple*.

14. Many of the poems of the nineteenth-century German Romantic writer Heinrich Heine end with the poet's destroying the illusion that he has built up carefully during the entire poem, a technique known as Romantic Irony.

15. Five pages of Busch's text have been omitted here; they present a standard account of the history and principles of the Dunkards.

16. The general uprising of the German peasantry in Swabia and Franconia (1524–1525) as a result of the increasing exactions laid upon the peasants by their masters in a declining feudal system.

*Editor's Notes*

17. A collection of hymns compiled by Gerhard Tersteegen, first published in 1721. The *Gott-geheiligtes Harfenspiel der Kinder Zion* was popular with Lutherans as well as with members of the Reformed Church, for whom it was written.

18. Influenced by the Pietist movement in Germany, Alexander Mack (1679–1735), a well-to-do miller living near Heidelberg, organized a church with the distinctive feature of trine immersion—hence called the "Dunkards." In 1719, due to persecution in Europe, a first group of emigrants settled in Germantown, Pennsylvania. They were followed by others under Mack until the church existed only in America.

19. A party or wing of Lutheran reformers in sixteenth-century Germany held that certain customs and ceremonies, the adiaphora, practiced by the Roman Catholic Church were unessential and therefore might be accepted by Protestants.

20. Elhanan Winchester (d. 1794) was a Baptist minister and writer who settled in 1780 in Philadelphia, where he became well acquainted with the Brethren (Dunkards) in Germantown. He preached for them quite frequently but never joined their church. He was a prolific writer, the author of more than forty volumes, two of which, *Universal Restoration* and *Lectures on the Prophecies*, gained a wide circulation among the Brethren and were the main factors in establishing the "Doctrine of Final Restoration." John H. Moore, *Some Brethren Pathfinders* (Elgin, Ill.: Brethren Publishing House, 1929), pp. 140–43. Born in Maryland in 1796, Peter Nead was successively a Lutheran and a Methodist until he joined the Brethren in 1824. Called to the ministry in 1827, he continued to practice his trade as a tanner. In 1848 "he moved to Ohio, and finally settled on a farm, partly donated to him, nine miles northwest of Dayton, where he spent the remaining years of his long, useful and active life." Moore, *Pathfinders*, p. 186. Nead, who knew German as well as English, was the author of the first widely read and genuinely accepted doctrinal book of the Brethren, *Nead's Theological Works*.

21. On the eve of May Day, or Walpurgis Night, the Brocken (see n. 12, chap. 1) was popularly supposed to be the scene of a witches' sabbath.

*Chapter 4*

1. Busch was off course, for Beaver Island, on which James J. Strang established an offshoot Mormon colony in 1849, is located in northern Lake Michigan near the Straits of Mackinac, approximately 270 miles from Detroit.

2. A slightly inaccurate quotation from *A Midsummer Night's Dream*, act 2, sc. 1, l. 2.

3. The following stories are to be found (as Busch suggests) in Howe's *Ohio:* that of the Gnadenhütten Massacre on p. 485, the report of Crawford's campaign on pp. 543–45, and Dr. Knight's account of the burning of Colonel Crawford on pp. 547–48. Howe repeats the same stories in another of his works, *Historical Collections of the Great West*, 2 vols. (Cincinnati, Ohio: Henry Howe, 1854), pp. 109–15.

4. Busch took the following explanation of the origin of this name from Howe, *Ohio*, pp. 237–38.

5. Busch's anecdotes, as well as a description of Johnny's person, can be found in ibid., pp. 431–32.

6. The father of homeopathy, Samuel C. F. Hahnemann, published the fundamentals of his method of healing in *Organon der Rationellen Heilkunde* (1810). The basis of the system is summed up in his phrase *Similia similibus curantur*—"Like cures like."

7. A description of this area in northwestern Ohio can be found in Howe, *Ohio*, pp. 245–46.

EDITOR'S NOTES

8. No other mention of a village of this name could be discovered. From the information supplied by Busch, however, it must have been situated about where Leipsic is now located in Putnam County, Ohio, and the ridge running northwest from this town probably was the elevation termed the "German Ridge" by Busch.

9. "Alex Craig, generally known as Judge Craig, kept one of the more pretentious houses of the town. He was a tailor by trade, but he was elected sheriff of the county for a couple of terms, and served as associate judge, from which service he received his title." Nevin O. Winter, *A History of Northwest Ohio*, 3 vols. (Chicago, Lewis Publishing Co., 1917), 1: 468.

10. The following information concerning Girty can be found in Howe, *Ohio*, pp. 246–48.

11. The hero of a very popular, three-volume "robbers-novel" entitled *Rinaldo Rinaldini, der Räuberhauptmann* (1798) by Christian August Vulpius, Goethe's brother-in-law; dramatized in 1799 by Karl Friedrich Hensler.

12. Two pages of Busch's description of a dream have been omitted.

13. Much of the remainder of this chapter is based upon material found in Howe's *Ohio* (which is arranged according to counties). The reservoir is described on pp. 354–55, illustrated by a woodcut of the "view from the east shore." The history of the Negro colony and the Emlen Institute is told on pp. 355–56 in an "annexed extract of a letter" from Augustus Wattles himself. The two other black colonies are described on pp. 71–72 and 465–66. Finally, the "myth of Piqua" is recounted on p. 362 but is much elaborated upon by Busch.

## Chapter 5

1. A small town in Central Germany, north of the Harz Mountains, in the vicinity of Braunschweig. The linguistic boundary between the Low German and High German dialect areas passed just south of Schöppenstedt in the mid-nineteenth century.

2. In his writings, particularly the *Discourses on Religion*, the German philosopher and theologian Friedrich Schleiermacher (1768–1834) emphasized the emotional relationship of oneness between the individual person and the All—the finite self feeling its absolute dependence upon the infinite.

3. The account of the excavation of the Indian mound (and an illustration of the mound) are found in Howe, *Ohio*, pp. 375–76.

4. Five pages of Busch's text have been omitted here. They describe the construction of the Cincinnati Observatory, most of the information coming from Cist, *Cincinnati*, pp. 341–45.

5. Gottfried Kinkel (1815–1882) was a poet and professor at the University of Bonn when he became involved in the Revolution of 1848. Serving as a private, he was wounded, captured, and sentenced to life imprisonment. He escaped from Spandau Prison with the aid of Carl Schurz and fled to London, where he joined the colony of refugees. When he was sent to America in 1851, Kinkel was at first greeted with great enthusiasm and welcomed by scores of German organizations; his American tour is well described in Wittke, *Refugees*, pp. 99–103. But the enthusiasm soon waned, and the trip turned out largely a failure.

6. As noted above, Kinkel was sent to dramatize the appeal for a second German revolution and to raise funds for an armed revolt. It was hoped that $2 million could be raised through this "loan" (also known as the "German National Loan"). The matter was complicated by the fact that the German revolutionaries were divided into two competing groups. One, for which Kinkel was spokesman, stressed the sale of bonds for another try at revolution. The other, representing the extremely radical "Red Republicans" of London,

## Editor's Notes

hoped to establish a worldwide Revolutionary League and use any money collected for revolutionary propaganda and education. The battle between the two groups became quite bitter and was reflected in the German-American newspapers by an increased division between the "Greens" and the "Grays." Wittke, *German-Language Press*, pp. 70–72.

7. The refugee colony in London at the mid-nineteenth century was made up of radicals of every shade and nationality, including Marx, Engels, Ruge, and Kinkel. Enjoying British freedom of speech and of the press, they plotted and quarreled as they planned a new world order.

8. It is estimated that the tour netted less than $10,000 in actual cash donations after expenses for travel and printing had been deducted. Wittke, *Refugees*, p. 106.

9. A composition by one of the original twelve apostles of the Church, William W. Phelps.

10. Arnold Ruge (1802–1880) was a noted advocate of radical doctrines and an associate of Karl Marx in Paris in the 1840s. Accused of complicity in the Revolution of 1848, he fled to England, where he was a member of the extreme Left. Hans Blum, *Die deutsche Revolution 1848/49* (Florenz/Leipzig: Eugen Diederichs, 1898), describes Ruge's philosophy as similar to that of the Jacobins of the French Revolution.

11. A refugee of the Vienna Revolution, Friedrich Hassaurek (1831–1885) arrived in America in 1849. He founded the Cincinnati *Hochwächter*, described as "one of the most violent anticlerical sheets in the country in the 1850's" in Wittke, *German-Language Press*, p. 109, and as "socialist and infidel of the deepest dye" in Cist, *Cincinnati*, p. 75. But apparently outgrowing his adolescence, he "in due time became a rational American Republican." Gustave P. Koerner, *Memoirs of Gustave Koerner: 1809–1896*, 2 vols. (Cedar Rapids, Iowa: Torch Press, 1909), 1: 548. He was elected to the Cincinnati City Council (1851–1855) and was named ambassador to Ecuador by President Lincoln.

12. Most of the material concerning educational institutions in Cincinnati is based upon information found in Cist, *Cincinnati*, pp. 52–70.

13. Busch's report is based upon a short biographical sketch (with portrait) in ibid., pp. 333–38.

14. "Ogelism" is not defined elsewhere, in either German or English dictionaries.

15. Much of the following information concerning various Cincinnati manufacturing establishments can be found in Cist, *Cincinnati*. It seems probable, however, that Busch actually visited most of the firms, guidebook in hand, and later elaborated upon Cist's sketches with material gained from firsthand observation.

16. Emil Klauprecht (b. 1815 in Mainz) first practiced lithography in Cincinnati and then turned to journalism. In 1843 he published the *Fliegende Blätter*, the first German illustrated paper in the United States. Later he became editor of *Der Republikaner*, a rival of the Cincinnati *Volksblatt*. Klauprecht apparently had a rather violent temper, for in the course of his editorship he shot and wounded a Dr. Wilhelm Albers, but he was pardoned by the governor. Heinrich Roedter (d. 1857) was one of the *Dreissiger* (those who came in the 1830s) and the first editor of the *Volksblatt*, established in 1836. He also published the *Congress-Halle*, a monthly report in German of the proceedings in Congress, and later was editor and publisher of the Cincinnati *Demokratisches Tageblatt*. "Old Hunker" was a term used in the 1850s to designate a member of the conservative wing of the Democratic party. Theodor Dietsch (d. 1857), a former member of the city government of Arneberg, was a political refugee from Saxony. In 1851 he was on the editorial staffs of the St. Louis *Anzeiger* and *Tribune* and later worked on German-language newspapers in Cincinnati, Louisville, and Evansville.

# EDITOR'S NOTES

## Chapter 6

1. The hero of Victor Hugo's first novel (of the same name), published in 1823.
2. Charles Sealsfield (pseudonym for Karl Anton Postl) and Friedrich Gerstäcker were German writers of the early nineteenth century who visited America and wrote many novels and sketches about the "exotic" life they found there.
3. It has not been possible to identify Westfeld.
4. A river near the ancient city of Troy, figuring largely in accounts of the Trojan War.
5. Lines from Goethe's *Faust* I, "Auerbach's Cellar," describing students drinking wine; Bayard Taylor translation, p. 81.
6. Many of the features attributed to the farms of this district, as well as the quotation concluding the paragraph, are found in Howe, *Great West,* p. 197, where, however, they apply to farms in western Pennsylvania and Virginia.
7. The correct name was Throckmorton's Inn. It was built on the Maysville Pike about 1810 by John Throckmorton.
8. Although not further identified in the text, the Major must have been James Sudduth, born in 1800 as one of nine sons and two daughters of William Sudduth, who settled in Kentucky at Hood's Station in 1785. Major Sudduth was prominent in politics throughout his life, serving as county clerk of Bath County, Kentucky, and in the Kentucky State Legislature as representative and senator (1855–1859). He was killed near Owingsville in 1862 "while defending himself from capture by a band of 'rebels.'" Lewis and Richard H. Collins, *History of Kentucky,* 2 vols. (1874; reprint ed., Frankfort: Kentucky Historical Society, 1966), 1: 114.
9. The "Citizen King" of France (1830–1848). Born in 1773, the oldest son of the Duke of Orleans, he joined the revolutionary army, shared in its defeat in 1793, and fled to Switzerland, where he became a teacher of mathematics and astronomy under an assumed name. In 1795 he traveled through Scandinavia and in 1796 went to America. Eventually, with the downfall of Napoleon, he returned to Paris. It was the overthrow of Louis Philippe in February 1848 that led to the German Revolution. Not much is known concerning his stay in the United States; hence many stories have sprung up and his name has been identified with many localities. One such tale, repeated most recently by John A. Richards, *History of Bath County, Kentucky* (Yuma, Ariz.: Southwest Printers, 1961), pp. 79–80, reports that "in 1814 Louis Philippe came to Owingsville as the guest of Colonel Owings. While here he occupied a suite of rooms in the Owings house . . . and spent considerable time at the old Bourbon Furnace in the company of Col. Owings and hunting and fishing with the hands at the furnace who called him King Philippe. . . . When in 1815 Napoleon was finally overthrown . . . King Philippe was called to return to his native land, but twice he refused, preferring the backwoods life he found here among his congenial friends." According to Richards, he finally took his departure from Owingsville on January 14, 1815. Some, however, deny that Louis Philippe ever visited Owingsville. Young E. Allison, in *The Curious Legend of Louis Philippe in Kentucky* (Louisville, Ky.: privately printed, 1924), expresses the belief that someone did indeed visit Colonel Owings but that the man was an impostor who deceived the colonel. Busch, of course, quotes Major Sudduth, who, born in 1800 and living in Owingsville all his life, should be considered a reliable witness. The Major, too, may have been fooled by an impostor.
10. "The storm-tossed man who wandered long," the first line of the *Odyssey.*

## Editor's Notes

11. Found in Howe, *Great West*, p. 87, where, however, it is a song about "trois cavaliers." Busch's version makes better sense in view of the line "L'un à cheval l'autre à pied."
12. A German folksong of the late eighteenth century, the oldest recorded version being found in the *Sesenheimer Liederbuch* of ca. 1771. The author, of course, is unknown.
13. Found in Howe, *Great West*, p. 83, but with enough variations in wording to indicate that Busch may actually have heard it sung.
14. Most of the following material concerning Wetzel can be found in ibid., "Lewis Whetzel, the Indian Hunter," pp. 144–49.
15. The four sons of the legendary Count Haimon who made war upon Charlemagne. Many versions of the legend have been written in Germany, including a very popular *Volksbuch* first published in 1604.
16. See Howe, *Great West*, p. 198.
17. See ibid., p. 197.
18. The following anecdote is related in ibid., "Kentucky Sports," p. 248, and is ascribed to James Audubon, who saw the feat performed by Daniel Boone.
19. The following anecdote is related in ibid., p. 199, but in the original the boy is sent to a school in Maryland.
20. The following anecdote, about a Presbyterian minister named Joseph Smith, pastor of the Cross Creek and Upper Buffalo congregations in Washington County, Pennsylvania, is related in ibid., pp. 188–89, and is ascribed by Howe to Charles Cist, *The Cincinnati Miscellany* (Cincinnati, Ohio: C. Clark, 1845.)
21. Probably an allusion to the proverbial expression "lazy as Lawrence." According to legend, while the third-century saint Lawrence was being broiled to death on a gridiron, he asked to be turned, saying: "For that side is quite done."
22. A line from William Cullen Bryant's "A Forest Hymn," often quoted in the early nineteenth century.
23. American poet, essayist, and editor (1799–1832), founder of the *Atlantic Magazine*, later the New York *Review*.
24. The following description of a frontier wedding is in Howe, *Great West*, pp. 202–4.
25. A somewhat different story is told by Thomas U. Fann in "An Economic History of Bath County, Kentucky" (Master's thesis, University of Kentucky, 1937). In an appended report an old settler, Luther Hess of Owingsville, relates that "in 1793 the men were away clearing land and the Indians came and captured the women and children. Except one woman and she got to this cave and they did not find her but smothered the child to death. They took these people south, got up in what is now Menifee County on Beaver Creek. The whites followed the Indians there and killed nineteen. They were buried on a branch running south from Beaver which carries the name Murders Branch until this day."
26. No other record of this colonization plan has been found. Two factors contribute to the lack of information: (1) the Bath County courthouse, along with county records, was accidentally burned to the ground by troops during the Civil War; (2) the southeastern section of Bath County, where Sudduth's property was located, was split off in 1869 and organized as Menifee County. Apparently the Sudduth family still owned property in the area in 1867, for Collins and Collins, *History of Kentucky*, 1: 177, record that on February 10 of that year "Butterfield, Stacy & Co., of Cincinnati, purchase of William L. Sudduth 11,000 acres of land on the Licking River, in Bath County—valuable for coal, iron and timber." In any case it seems likely that the "125,000 acres" mentioned earlier was something of an exaggeration.

EDITOR'S NOTES

*Chapter 7*

1. Busch was given good advice, for Collins and Collins, *History of Kentucky*, 1: 63, 64 record for December 22, 1851: "Ohio River closed with ice for six days. Deep snow"; and for January 19, 1852: "During the night (Monday), Ohio River closes with ice for the second time—the only winter, within the memory of old inhabitants, when this has occurred."

2. A so-called English theater, built in 1837, located on Sycamore between Third and Fourth streets.

3. Undoubtedly the distinguished American actor James Edward Murdoch (1811–1893), who in his later years was professor of elocution at the Cincinnati College of Music.

4. A one-act Shrovetide play, *Das Landhaus an der Heerstrasse* (1809), by August von Kotzebue, the most popular German dramatist in the early 1800s. Many of von Kotzebue's plays were adapted in English and were frequently performed in the U.S.

5. No record of this play can be found. Kosch's *Deutsches Theaterlexikon* lists a number of plays about Kaspar Wenzel Messenhauser, the military leader of the Vienna uprising who was executed in 1848, but none by Hassaurek. It is reported that Hassaurek (see n. 11, chap. 5) and a few friends organized a German theater in Cincinnati in 1851; possibly the twenty-year-old Hassaurek contributed such a play to the repertoire, but if so, it never saw print.

6. Neither this nor any of the other riverboats mentioned by Busch is listed in the standard reference work: James T. Lloyd, *Lloyd's Steamboat Directory* (Cincinnati, Ohio: J. T. Lloyd, 1856). This is not surprising since most of the boats had short lives, either exploding or running aground. However, E. W. Gould, *Fifty Years on the Mississippi* (St. Louis, Mo.: Nixon-Jones, 1889), describes a *North River* contracted for and built (ca. 1847) by Captain William Dean for the Cincinnati-Louisville run.

7. See n. 11, chap. 4.

8. The wide plain in northeast France where Aëtius, the Roman general, and Theodoric I, king of the Visigoths, gained a complete victory over Attila and the Huns in A.D. 451.

9. The scene depicted by Busch is extraordinarily reminiscent of some of the genre paintings by George Caleb Bingham, particularly *The Jolly Flatboatmen* (1846). This painting had been sold into private ownership in New York in 1847 by the American Art Union, but not before an engraving on steel (in an edition of about 8,000) and a mezzotint (in an edition of about 10,000) had been printed and distributed widely. John F. McDermott, *George Caleb Bingham: River Portraitist* (Norman: University of Oklahoma Press, 1959). It is quite likely that Busch saw one of these copies, probably on a barroom wall.

10. The following stories about Mike Fink are to be found in Howe, *Great West*, "The Western Boatmen," pp. 250–55.

11. After the unsuccessful Hungarian Revolution many Hungarians fled to America. In 1850 a number of these exiles, under Count Ladislaus Uihazy, selected a tract of virgin prairie land in Decatur County, Iowa, near the Missouri border, which they named New Buda. Finding the climate unsuitable for raising grapes, Uihazy and some of the settlers moved to Texas in 1853. Others remained in Iowa, but the colony soon disappeared. Lillian May Wilson, "Some Hungarian Patriots in Iowa," *The Iowa Journal of History and Politics* 11, no. 4 (October 1913): 479–516.

12. See n. 16, chap. 4.

13. Many of the famous men to whom Busch was introduced in St. Louis —Chief Justice Hennig, Schneider from the Palatinate, Dr. Hiller, Schuster

## Editor's Notes

the bookdealer—seem to have been content with modest anonymity in the New World, for nothing concerning their later careers could be established.

14. A member of the Prussian Constituent Assembly, Behr was forced to flee when the Revolution was suppressed. He arrived in America in 1849, practicing medicine first in Texas and then in St. Louis until his death in 1863. Zucker, *Forty-eighters*, p. 277.

15. An "apostle" of this name is not recorded in the official history of the Church.

16. Gustave Koerner in his *Memoirs*, 1: 572–73, relates a very similar incident. In 1851 Koerner was hired to procure the release from the army of an underage boy from Illinois who was accused of a minor crime. Koerner, too, visited the Jefferson Barracks on a Sunday, but in his account the mission was successful.

17. An orthodox Lutheran group of about 600 Saxons who had come to Missouri in 1839 seeking religious freedom; they had feared that the rising influence of liberal Lutheran and Catholic groups in Germany would make it difficult to practice their orthodox faith there. Under the leadership of "Bishop" Martin Stephan, former pastor of St. John's Church in Dresden, they established the towns of Wittenberg and Altenburg. At the latter, one of their pastors, Carl F. W. Walther, founded a theological school which was moved to St. Louis in 1850 and named the Concordia Seminary. In 1847 he organized the German Evangelical Lutheran Synod of Missouri, Ohio, and Other States, known as the "Missouri Synod."

18. Franz Schmidt was a veteran of the Frankfurt Parliament and a pioneer freethinker who lectured throughout America. Heinrich Börnstein was a colorful figure in German-American life. A journalist, actor, manager, playwright, and medical student, he had traveled widely in Europe and considered himself one of the Forty-eighters. He acquired the St. Louis *Anzeiger des Westens* in 1851 and also ran a hotel, a brewery, a theater, and several saloons. Although a radical anticlerical in his youth, as an editor he was more moderate than might have been expected, supporting the Republicans and taking a strong antislavery, free-soil position. He regarded Kinkel's plans as impracticable and argued the matter with Kinkel at great length in public debate. Wittke, *Refugees*, p. 95. Heinzen's career is summarized in n. 20, chap. 1. Busch obviously selected these men as examples of the worst sort of German radical immigrant.

19. The *Bund freier Männer* was a nationwide association of German radicals with local chapters in many cities. It was formed not as a political party but to defend German immigrants against Nativism and to protect their rights.

20. A Mormon periodical published between February 1849 and July 1852 in Kanesville, Iowa, a stop on the migration route from Nauvoo, Illinois, to Utah.

## Chapter 8

1. See n. 18, chap. 7.
2. Koerner, *Memoirs*, 1: 576, describes Kinkel's arrival in Belleville as follows: "Late in the evening of the 17th of December, Kinkel arrived in Belleville. In West Belleville a committee of reception awaited him, as did also Captain Eimer's Rifle Company and a band of music. He declined entering the carriage ready for him, but marched at the head of the soldiers to the Belleville House. He was serenaded late in the evening and made a speech from the balcony." The next day, according to Koerner, Kinkel called at his home and then spoke at a mass meeting at the courthouse.
3. Friedrich Hecker (1811–1881) has been described as "perhaps the most

distinguished and certainly the most romantic of the Forty-eighter refugees." Wittke, *Refugees*, p. 67. A lawyer from Mannheim, Hecker became the leader of the Revolutionary Army. A Hecker cult developed, reaching most fantastic extremes. The "Hero of 1848" was honored by workers, peasants, students, and Turners wearing "Hecker hats" and singing the "Hecker song" in taverns. After the failure of the Revolution Hecker fled to America, arriving in October 1848. He was received with a triumphal tour across the country.

4. A typical midwestern prairie, situated in St. Clair County, Illinois, east of Lebanon. Charles Dickens visited it in 1842 and described it rather scornfully in *American Notes*.

5. Gustave Körner, or Koerner (1809–1896), was one of the leading intellectuals of the earlier emigration from Germany. A young practicing attorney with a law degree from Heidelberg, he took part in the unsuccessful Frankfurt revolt of 1833. Forced to flee, he came to America, settling first in St. Louis, but because of his dislike for slavery he soon moved across the Mississippi to Illinois. After taking a refresher course in law at Transylvania University in Lexington, Kentucky, he returned to Belleville, which from then on was his permanent residence. Editor of the *Belleviller Zeitung* and lawyer, he became a justice of the Illinois Supreme Court (1849–1850) and lieutenant governor of Illinois (1852–1856.)

6. Koerner, *Memoirs*, 1: 580, reports that about $600 was raised in Belleville for the National Loan and was sent on to the German Revolutionary Commitee in London.

7. Charles and Edward T. Tittmann, natives of Dresden, had been fellow students of Gustave Koerner in Leipzig in 1833 and, like Koerner, had fled after the unsuccessful student uprising of that year. Koerner, who had preceded them to America, reports their arrival "in 1837 or 1838" in Belleville, where they soon became leaders in German society and "successful in the mercantile business."

8. Jörg could not be further identified, but presumably he was the Eduard Jörg who published the two-volume *Briefe aus den Vereinigten Staaten von Nord Amerika* (Leipzig: Weber, 1853), a series of letters from Highland, Illinois, throwing light on American agricultural operations and the conditions of the Germans in America. Apparently Nathaniel Niles spent most of his life in Belleville as a newspaper editor and lawyer. Koerner, *Memoirs*, 1: 495, reports that in 1846 Niles was elected second lieutenant of the company of volunteers that fought in the Mexican War. Koerner also indicates that Judge Niles was one of the English speakers at the 1859 Schiller centenary celebration in Belleville. The records also show that Niles was clerk of the Illinois House during the legislative session of 1849.

9. George C. Furber, *The Twelve Months Volunteer* (Cincinnati, Ohio: J. A. & U. P. James, 1848), lists a Private Conze, member of Company H, Second Regiment of Illinois Volunteers, as killed in the final Mexican charge at the battle of Buena Vista. The Illinois Second Regiment and the Kentucky Militia, with Lieutenant Colonel Henry Clay, Jr., fought side by side.

10. The examples in chap. 2 of German corrupted by English were omitted as untranslatable.

11. An illustrated humorous biweekly published in Louisville, containing much satirical humor in prose and verse. Leonard Koester, "German Newspapers Published in Louisville," *The American-German Review* 20 (1954): 24–27.

12. One of the best-known German encyclopedias, profusely illustrated. First published (1839–1852) by the firm of Joseph Meyer in Hildburghausen, later transferred to Leipzig.

13. German-born painters who emigrated to America. Emanuel Leutze (1816–1868) is best known for his paintings *Washington Crossing the Dela-*

## Editor's Notes

*ware* and *Westward the Course of Empire* (in the national Capitol). There were two Frankenstein brothers, Johann Peter and Gottfried, both of whom enjoyed popularity for a short time and both of whom were living in Springfield, Ohio, in 1851. Cist, *Cincinnati,* pp. 123–25.

14. See n. 16, chap. 5.

15. An island in the Mississippi across from St. Louis, made infamous the country over by a long series of duels fought there; ultimately joined to the Illinois shore.

## Chapter 9

1. The first three pages in this chapter have been omitted. They describe the suicide in St. Louis of a young man named Rostros who had accompanied Kinkel from Chicago.

2. Lines from "Ode to My Country" by the Danish poet Jens Baggesen (1764–1826). Busch quotes them in the original Danish.

3. The following anecdote concerning Captain Korry and his adventures refers to a series of expeditions undertaken under the leadership of the Venezuelan revolutionary Narciso Lopez to throw off the Spanish yoke in Cuba. Lopez landed near Havana in August 1851 with several hundred men of various nationalities recruited in the United States. This third attempt at invasion, also called the Bahia Honda Expedition, ended in failure with the capture and execution of Lopez. The Spanish captain general at the time was José Gutierrez de la Concha. A good account of the expedition is to be found in A. C. Quisenberry, *Lopez's Expeditions to Cuba, 1850 and 1851,* Filson Club Publications no. 21 (Louisville, Ky.: Filson Club, 1906). No Captain Korry is to be found in the list of participants. Possibly Busch was thinking of the Captain Kelly of New Orleans whom Quisenberry mentions as being pardoned by the captain General. It is more likely, however, that the anecdote, whether based upon fact or not, was current throughout the United States at the time of Busch's travels. Quisenberry, "Rousseau's Serio-Comic Letter," pp. 135–37 quotes a version that is almost identical.

4. August Thieme (1822–1879) had a Ph.D. in theology and philology from Leipzig, as did Busch. In 1848 he was elected a member of the Frankfurt Parliament, where he represented the extreme Left. Fleeing to America in 1849, he supported himself by various occupations, working his way west. Arriving in Cleveland in 1852, he established a German-language newspaper, the *Wächter am Erie,* which he published until his death.

## Conclusion

1. Busch probably had the British statesman in mind because of Peel's accidental death by a fall from a horse the year before (1850).

2. During the period of the American and French revolutions trees were often planted as symbols of "growing freedom." One of the most popular American ballads of the time was Thomas Paine's "Liberty Tree" (1775).

3. On foot, as expressed in the proverbial Latin phrase *per pedes apostolorum.*

www.ingramcontent.com/pod-product-compliance
Lightning Source LLC
Chambersburg PA
CBHW020638230426

43665CB00008B/226